330.9

SOCIAL C
LACE AN'
NOTTIN'

D1492431

ECONOMIC AND SOCIAL CHANGE
IN A MIDLAND TOWN

F. C. Tighe, Nottingham Public Library

NOTTINGHAM AND THE MEADOWS, SOUTH ASPECT, 1846

ECONOMIC

AND

SOCIAL CHANGE

IN A

MIDLAND TOWN

VICTORIAN NOTTINGHAM
1815–1900

ROY A. CHURCH

FRANK CASS & CO. LTD.
1966

First published in 1966 by
Frank Cass & Co. Ltd.
10 Woburn Walk, London, W.C.1

Copyright © 1966 R. A. Church

Printed in Northern Ireland by
W. & G. Baird Ltd. London and Belfast

TO
MY MOTHER
AND FATHER

CONTENTS

Tables in the text

LIST OF ILLUSTRATIONS

Figures in the Text

INTRODUCTION

THE city of Nottingham grew from the nucleus of a smaller and older town to become one of the nation's leading industrial centres, and although it was not a product of the industrial revolution Nottingham was completely transformed by it. For most of the nineteenth century the major activities were the production of hosiery by an industry whose methods, organization, and outlook remained traditional for many decades, and the manufacture of machine-made lace, a progressive and mechanized industry which from its early years featured factory production. In some respects the machine-made lace industry typified the industrial revolution insofar as the cost reductions brought about by technological change put the purchase of lace within the reach of a larger market where demand was responsive to changes in price.

Although its introduction post-dated the important changes in other textile trades, even in the manufacture of lace, steam power was in limited use until the 1840's. In the hosiery industry, where for a variety of reasons a comparable transformation was delayed until the third quarter of the century, frames were manually operated unassisted by power. The history of these two industries, therefore, while in itself an interesting comparative study in resource allocation, also underlines Clapham's observation that before 1830 no single British industry had passed through a complete technical revolution. Even after these changes had taken place, in both industries the optimum size of firms continued to be small. Both industries produced articles of fashion and were subject to sudden and frequent changes in consumers' tastes, while the relatively high proportion of total output made for export rendered both industries, especially lace, highly sensitive to variations in demand overseas.

Because of this double susceptibility to fluctuations in trade, until the last quarter of the century, when the region's economic base widened, the livelihood of the community was precarious. But the social and political implications of the town's economic structure went beyond the problems that arose in a community where employment opportunities were highly unstable. The structure and organization of the two industries produced contrasting industrial relations. Until the second half of the century there existed a wide gulf between framework knitters and the hosiers who employed them, whereas the bridge from lace maker or mechanic to lace manufacturer was heavily trodden. These factors influenced the local social structure which also reflected the difference in performance of the two industries. Among the working classes the dissimilarity in the conditions of hosiery workers and lace operatives affords a salient contrast between people in an industry which experienced a technical revolution through attempts to adjust to the market, and those in an industry in which an increase in output was obtained as much by increasing the number of frames as by building larger frames. In comparison with the progress of mechanization in the lace industry, technical change was slow in its introduction until steam power was applied to hosiery frames during the middle decades of the century.

Corresponding roughly to the economic and social differentiation between lace and hosiery workers, political activities differed. This was demonstrated by the strength of the Chartist movement in the town which derived its main support from framework knitters. The election of Feargus O'Connor in 1847 earned for Nottingham the distinction of becoming the only constituency to return a self-styled Chartist to Parliament, although his success can only be explained by reference to the longstanding radical tradition in Nottingham and to trade conditions, as well as to the social and economic framework.

For two main reasons the middle decades constitute a watershed in the region's history. Until the Enclosure Act of 1845 the old town was surrounded on three sides by unenclosed land. The appearance of this land on the market, which coincided with important technological changes affecting local industries, precipitated rapid economic expansion which so impressed contemporaries that they spoke with astonishment of the "New Nottingham". Commercial and industrial buildings and private dwelling houses were erected on the newly enclosed land, and the constellation of industrial villages which surrounded Nottingham began the transformation from satellites to suburbs.

The expanding regional economy was fortified by a growth in population which, in contrast to that of the previous decades, occurred chiefly within the town. In earlier years a chronic shortage of land for building aggravated problems of overcrowding and disease and led to an expansion of the industrial villages. For though in terms of steam power Nottingham was much less industrialized than the larger manufacturing towns in the north, social conditions were comparable, owing to the postponement of enclosure. Problems of urban growth were also similar, and, as in other towns where government was the responsibility of a close oligarchic municipal corporation, the few attempts that were made to improve the quality of town life were the work of individuals and private institutions. Not until many years after the municipal body was reformed did the Town Council show initiative, often only after national legislation had pointed the way.

The efforts of leading citizens of goodwill, public spirit, and social conscience—many of whom were Evangelicals—exerted an important leavening influence upon society. This enlightenment appeared in the works of voluntary institutions and charitable bodies, and in municipal achievements, while the arbitration machinery inaugurated in 1860 by one of the town's leading Evangelical manufacturers became the model for other Industries. Although individual effort continued to be a beneficial influence upon the community after the middle decades, national legislation and municipal action assumed increasing responsibility for shaping the urban environment, and this later period brought about the civic transformation which earned for Nottingham the title of city.

One general and undoubted conclusion—albeit banal—to emerge from this history of Nottingham in the nineteenth century is the complexity of the processes which were involved in the transformation of a provincial market town into a populous industrial city. Furthermore, owing to the localization of industry in the town specialized firms grew up enabling the small manufacturing units to obtain economies which otherwise would have been limited to large firms producing for very wide markets. Added to these external economies the geographical concentration of many small competing firms in Nottingham generated a climate conducive to technical progress—an 'industrial atmosphere', to borrow a phrase from Alfred Marshall—which, during the first half of the century, was midwife to the machine-made lace industry. Through the presence of these external economies of urbanization Nottingham became a source of innovation and enterprise.

PREFACE

IN writing this book I have experienced one major disappointment for in 1957 appeals made through the Sub-Department of Economic History of Nottingham University, and personal visits to a number of firms, failed to unearth business records which are such valuable local sources for regional studies. However, records were located in the offices of the Nottingham Chamber of Commerce, the Nottingham and District Trades Council, and the Amalgamated Society of Lace Operatives, and I wish to acknowledge the co-operation of the officers of these organizations in placing them at my disposal. There are many people to whom I am indebted for assistance, but especially to Miss V. W. Walker and Mr. G. L. Roberts of the Nottingham Public Library Archives and Local Collection Departments, and to the staffs of the Nottingham Public Library and of the Nottingham University Library. I must also acknowledge the kind permission of the *Yorkshire Bulletin of Economic and Social Research* and the *Transactions of the Thoroton Society* to reprint part of the articles which I contributed to those journals. It remains for me to thank those who have read and criticized all or parts of the manuscript—Professor T. C. Barker, Mr. S. D. Chapman, Professor W. H. B. Court, Mr. J. Purkiss, Mr. D. E. Varley, and Professor F. A. Wells. To Professor J. D. Chambers I am especially grateful not only for the benefit of his intimate knowledge of Nottinghamshire history but for inspiration and encouragement; Professor A. W. Coats has been a most generous and valuable source of advice and criticism. I wish to express my thanks to Miss Vicky Hands who, at short notice, kindly undertook to type the manuscript and to Mrs. B. M. D. Smith for compiling the index. Finally, it is impossible for me to express how great is the debt which I owe to my wife, both for her assistance in preparing the original thesis and the manuscript and for her patience throughout the project.

ROY CHURCH.

University of Birmingham.
May, 1965.

SELECT BIBLIOGRAPHY OF MANUSCRIPT AND UNPUBLISHED MATERIALS, OFFICIAL DOCUMENTS, AND CONTEMPORARY PUBLISHED SOURCES

1. MANUSCRIPT AND UNPUBLISHED MATERIAL

a) Mss.

In the Nottingham Public Library:
Corporation Hall Books, 1815-1835.
The Enfield Collection, Trade partnership agreements.
Census of lace machinery taken in 1828.
The diary of Ichabod Wright.
The diary of Samuel Collinson.
John Marshall, "The Nottingham Suburban Railway", 1963 (typescript).
Agreement for the Execution of a Restriction of Hours Deed, 1830 (incomplete).

In the muniment room of Nottingham University Library:
The James Fisher Papers.
The Hadden Papers.
Minute books:
Papers of the Amalgamated Society of Lace Operatives, 1869–1900.
Minutes of the Lace Trade Board of Arbitration, 1876–80, 1883–85.
Minutes of Nottingham Association of Organized Trades, 1882–1890.
Minutes of Nottingham Trades Council, 1890–1900.
Minutes of Nottingham Hosiery Trimmers' Association, 1874–1900.

At the Nottingham County Records Office:
Newcastle Mss.
At the Offices of the Nottingham Chamber of Commerce:
Minutes of Nottingham Chamber of Commerce, 1860–1873, 1886–1900.
At the Factory of John Player & Son Ltd.:
History of John Player (anonymous typescript).

At the Factory of Messrs. Manlove and Alliott:
John Lancaster, works manager, "Some Recollections of Bloomsgrove Works" (typescript, 1916).

At the Public Record Office:
Records of the Board of Trade; In-letters (B.T.I.), Miscellanea (B.T.6).
Records of the Home Office (Disturbances) Papers, 40/47-59, 52.

At the British Museum:
The Francis Place Collection, Add. Mss. 2, 7800–7, 127, 798.

At the British Library of Political and Economic Science:
Webb. Trade Union Mss., Section A, Vol. 39, The hosiery and lace trades, Vol. 21.

At the British Transport Commission Historical Records department:
Accounts and boat cargo tables of the Trent Navigation Company, 1817–1887.
Minutes of the Nottingham Canal Co., 1811–1855.
Minutes of the Midland Counties Railway.

Loaned by Mr. S. D. Chapman:
"The Story of William Felkin III" (typescript autobiography).

Loaned by Mr. D. E. Varley:
Lace Makers' Union Branch Contributions Minute Book, 1853–59 (typescript).

b) Theses.

E. M. Becket, *The Development of Education in Nottingham during the Nineteenth and Early Twentieth Centuries,* (M.A., London) 1922.

G. E. Bell, *The Railway as a Factor in the Location of Manufacturing Industry in the East Midlands,* (Ph.D., Nottingham) 1958.

S. D. Chapman, *The Life of William Felkin, 1795–1874,* (M.A., Nottingham) 1960.

R. A. Church, *The Social and Economic Development of Nottingham in the Nineteenth Century,* (Ph.D., Nottingham) 1960.

J. M. Golby, *The Political and Electioneering Influence of the Fourth Duke of Newcastle,* (M.A., Nottingham) 1961.

C. Holmes, *Chartism in Nottingham, 1837–1861,* (B.A., Nottingham) 1960.

J. C. Weller, *The Evangelical Revival in Nottingham,* (M.A., Nottingham) 1957.

2. OFFICIAL DOCUMENTS:
Census of Population.
Chief Factory Inspector. Annual Reports.

Select Committee on Framework Knitters' Petitions, First and Second Reports, 1812.

Select Committee on Framework Knitters' Petition, 1819.

Select Committee on Artizans and Machinery, Fourth Report, 1824.

Annual Reports of the Board of Poor Law Commissioners, from 1837.

Select Committee on the Administration of Relief under the Poor Law Amendment Act, Twenty-second Report, 1837.

Commission of Enquiry into the State of the Poor Law. Report and Evidence, 1834.

Childrens' Employment Commission. Reports and Evidence, 1833, 1843, and 1863.

Municipal Corporations Commission. Report and Evidence, 1835.

Select Committee on Import Duties. Report and Evidence, 1840.

Select Committee on the Exportation of Machinery. Second Report and Evidence, 1841.

Royal Commission on the State of Large Towns and Populous Districts, First and Second Reports, 1844.

Royal Commission on the Condition of Framework Knitters. Report and Evidence, 1845.

Select Committee on the Stoppage of Wages in the Hosiery Manufacture. Report and Evidence, 1854.

Select Committee on Postage. Second Report, 1837–8, with Minutes of Evidence.

Report to the Home Secretary on the Expediency of subjecting the Lace Manufacture to the Factory Acts, 1861.

Select Committee on Equitable Tribunals. Report and Evidence, 1856.

Royal Commission on Trade Unions. Report and Evidence, 1867–8.

Royal Commission on the Truck System. Report and Evidence, 1871.

Commissioners' Enquiry into the Factory and Workshops Act. Report and Evidence, 1876.

Royal Commission on the Housing of the Working Classes. Report and Evidence, 1884–5.

Royal Commission on the Depression of Trade and Industry. First Report and Evidence, 1886.

Select Committee on Artizans' and Labourers' Dwellings. Report and Evidence, 1889.

Select Committee on the Merchandize Marks Act. Report and Evidence, 1890.

Royal Commission on Labour. First Report and Evidence, 1892.

Royal Commission on Market Rights and Tolls. Report and Evidence, 1890–1.

Board of Trade. Report on the Cost of Living of the Working Classes. 1905, 1908.

Royal Commission on Poor Law and the Relief of Distress. Report and Evidence, 1909.

3. CONTEMPORARY PUBLISHED SOURCES:

a) Periodicals.
The Nottingham Journal,
The Nottingham Review,
The Nottingham and Newark Mercury,
The Nottingham Daily Express,
Hosiers' and Glovers' Gazette,
Knitters' Circular,
The Hosiery and Lace Trades Review,
The Textile Recorder,
The Stocking Makers' Monitor, 1817–1818,
Nottingham Town Council. *Minutes of Council and Committee,* 1836–1900,
Nottingham Medical Officer of Health. *Annual Reports,* 1873–1900,
Nottingham Finance Committee. *Annual Accounts,* 1858–1900,
William White, *Directory of Nottingham,*
J. Wright, *Directory of Nottingham,*
The Nottingham Social Guild, *Annual Reports,* 1879–1891 (the Library of the Mechanics' Institute, Nottingham),

b) Other contemporary printed sources.
Account of the trial of Jeremiah Brandreth . . .' 1817 (Nottingham Public Library).

Address of the Nottingham Working Mens' Association to the People of England on the New Poor Laws (Nottingham and London, 1838).

Address to the Working Classes on the System of Exclusive Dealing and the Formation of Joint Stock Companies. By a member of Nottingham Co-operative Store, 1840 (London University Library).

A Report of the proceedings of the conviction of Benjamin Taylor etc., part of the Framework Knitters' Committee, 1821 (Nottingham Public Library).

A Report of the proceedings at a public meeting at Nottingham Forest . . . in regard to sentence of transportation passed on six members of the Trades Union at Dorchester, 1834 (Nottingham Public Library).

A. Workman (Anon.), "A Reply to 'A Manufacturer's Remarks' on the Hosiery Bill", 1847. (Library of the Mechanics' Institute, Nottingham).

Anon., Facts submitted to the consideration of Ratepayers of Nottingham in justification of the erection of a Workhouse, 1840 (Nottingham Public Library).

Allen, R., Illustrated Handbook and Guide to Nottingham and its Environs (1866).

Airey, Railway Map of Derbyshire and Nottinghamshire Districts (1877), History of Derbyshire.

Anon., Walks Round Nottinghamshire (Nottingham, 1835).

Bailey, T., Annals of Nottinghamshire (Nottingham, 1853).

Becher, J. T., Anti Pauper System (Nottingham, 1835).

Beebe, G. D., Lace, Ancient and Modern (1880).

Blackner, John, History of Nottingham (Nottingham, 1816).

Briscoe, J. P., Nottinghamshire and Derbyshire at the opening of the Twentieth Century (Brighton, 1901).

Brown, C., Lives of Nottinghamshire Worthies (1882).

Brown, W., The Spirit of the Times, or leading political questions temperately discussed in a series of dualogues between two workmen (Nottingham, 1822).

Butler, Rev. W. J., A Friendly Letter addressed to Richard Oastler Esq., on his speech upon the New Poor Law delivered at Huddersfield (Nottingham, 1838).

Channer, C. C., and M. E. Roberts, Lace-making in the Midlands, Past and Present (1900).

Clark, S. F., Derby Road Baptist Chuch 1847–1897 (Nottingham, 1897), Collinson, S., High Pavement Centenary.

Cooke, G. A., Topographical and Statistical Description of Nottinghamshire (1810).

Curtis, J., Topographical History of Nottinghamshire (1844).

Dearen, W., Historical and Topographical Directory of Nottingham (Nottingham, 1834).

Felkin, William, Facts and Calculations Illustrative of the Present State of the Bobbin Net Trade (Nottingham, 1831), Remarks upon the Importance of an Enquiry into the Amount and Appropriation of Wages by the Working Classes (Nottingham, 1837), 'Statistics of the Labouring Classes and Paupers of Nottingham', Journal of the Statistical Society, II, 1839, pp. 457–9.

Observations in Favour of a Property Tax (1842).

An Account of the Machine Wrought Hosiery Trade (1845).

The Exhibition in 1851 of the Products and Industry of all Nations (1851).

"The History and Present State of the Machine Wrought Lace Trade".

Journal of the Society of Arts, IV (1855–6), pp. 475–485.

"The Lace and Hosiery Trades of Nottingham", Journal of the Statistical Society, XXIX (1866), pp. 536–541.

A History of the Machine Wrought Hosiery and Lace Manufactures (1867).

"The Lace and Hosiery Trades" in G. P. Bevan, ed. British Manufacturing Industry (1876).

Field, H., The Nottingham Date Book, 1800–1884.

Fyffe, W. W., Rambles Round Nottingham (Nottingham, 1856).

Gardiner, W., Music and Friends, 3 vols. (Leicester, 1838).

Glover, S., Nottingham Directory for 1825 (Nottingham, 1825).

The History and Directory of the Town and County of Nottingham (Nottingham, 1844).

Gilbert, A., Recollections of Old Nottingham (Nottingham, 1901).

Godfrey, J. T., The History of the Parish and Priory of Lenton (1884).

Godfrey, J. T., and J. Ward, The History of Friar Lane Baptist Church, Nottingham (Nottingham, 1903).

Gordon, W. J., Midland Sketches (1898).

Granger, B. B., The Tourist's Picturesque Guide to Nottingham (Nottingham, 1871).

Grainger, J., Old Nottingham, Its Streets and People (Nottingham, 1902).

Green, J. H., The History of Nottingham Mechanics Institution, 1837–1887 (Nottingham, 1887).

Harwood, G. H., The History of Wesleyan Methodism in Nottingham (Nottingham, 1872).

Henson, Gravener, and George White, A Few Remarks on the State of the Laws at present in Existence for Regulating Masters and Workpeople (1823).

The Civil, Political and Mechanical History of the Framework Knitters in Europe and America, Vol. I (Nottingham, 1831).

Hill, G. A., History of Dress from Saxon Times to the Present Day (London, 1893).

Hodder, E., The Life of Samuel Morley (1887).

Howitt, M., Autobiography (1889).

Howitt, W., The Rural Life of England, II (1838).

Lascelles and Hagar, Commercial Directory of the Town and County of Nottingham (Nottingham, 1848).

Lowell, A. L., The Government of England, II (1908).

Napier, Sir Charles, Life and Opinions of General Sir Charles Napier, II, 1857.

Nicholls, G., A History of the English Poor Law (1854).

Nottingham and Nottinghamshire Illustrated (1892).

Orange, James, History and Antiquities of Nottingham, Vols. I and II (1840).

A Plea for the Poor (Nottingham, 1841).

Palliser, F. B., Revised ed. M. Jourdain and A. Dryden, History of Lace (1902).

Paterson, D., General View of Roads of England and Wales, 1811.

Pinnock, W., History of Nottingham (1820).

Porter, G. R., and F. W. Hirst, the Progress of the Nation (1902).

Priestley, J., Historical Account of the Navigable Rivers, Canals, and Railways throughout Great Britain (1831).

Richards, W., Quarter of a Century Revolution of Sanitary Science in Nottingham (Nottingham, 1875).

Rowlett, W. T. (trans.), Technology of Framework Knitting (1885).

Roworth, W., Observations on the Administration of the New Poor Law in Nottingham (Nottingham, 1840).

Smith, T. H., Hints to the Churchwardens, Overseers and Ratepayers of St. Mary's Parish Nottingham partly designed to assist them in forming an opinion of the effects likely to result to their parish from the intended alteration of the Poor Laws (Nottingham, 1834).

Stretton, C. E., History of the Midland Railway (1901).

Sutton, J. F., Nottingham Cricket Matches, 1771–1853 (Nottingham, 1853).

The Stranger's Guide through Nottingham (Nottingham, 1827).

Datebook of Remarkable Events Connected with Nottingham and Neighbourhood, 1750–1850.

Ure, Andrew, The Cotton Manufacture of Great Britain (1861).

White, William, History, Gazetteer and Directory of Nottinghamshire (Nottingham, 1832).

Whitehead, W., Old and New Nottingham (Nottingham, 1874).

Williams, F. S., The Midland Railway; Its Rise and Progress (1876), Nottingham, Past and Present (Nottingham, 1877).

Wright, Ichabod, The Evils of the Currency (Nottingham, 1847).

Evidence as to the Distress in Nottingham and the Neighbourhood (Nottingham, 1848).

Wright, John, Letters to Country Bankers (Nottingham, 1828).

Wylie, W. H., Old and New Nottingham (1853).

Wright-Wylie, C. N. Nottingham Handbook (Nottingham, 1858).

Wylie, W. H., and J. P. Briscoe, History of Nottingham (Nottingham, 1893).

CHAPTER I

NOTTINGHAM IN 1815

THE ancient town of Nottingham stands on a sandstone bluff which rises steeply from the river flats of the Trent. In 1815 the town was bounded on the north by a plateau; formerly covered by the forest trees of Sherwood, this had become the site of the town's thirty windmills, impressive landmarks for the traveller approaching from that direction. The plateau, known as the Forest, terminated at the river in a ridge and the old town was built on the steepest crag of the escarpment. Below, the area between the foot of the cliff and the river was meadow land and running through it was the little River Leen. In his *History of Nottingham* which was published in 1816, John Blackner, the self-educated framework knitter, described these meadows which each spring were covered by a mass of brilliant crocuses. Situated within the borough boundaries, they were a source of beauty and enjoyment for the town dweller who would hear, if he paused there a moment, on one side

a confused sound arising from the voices of conversing thousands and the motion of their feet; and on the other . . . a hollow murmur, occasioned by the rolling of the Trent.[1]

The conversing thousands to whom Blackner referred were the townspeople busying themselves in and around the town's Market Place whose size and splendour were almost unrivalled throughout the whole of England.[2] Standing on nearby Parliament Street, facing the Derby Road, it was possible in the appropriate season to watch harvesters as they toiled in the fields or to gaze at grazing cattle, while birdsong competed with the thump and running click of stocking frames.

Blackner continued: 'So much is this town dependent upon the . . . stocking frame and its appendant machines that if it stood still, all other business must stand still also.'[3] Indeed, with well over one half of the occupied population working frames to produce hosiery or lace net, Blackner's claim was hardly an exaggeration.[4] For closely allied to these activities were the dyers, bleachers, finishers, and merchants who handled hosiery and net produced in the town and in the villages scattered within a circle of an approximate ten mile radius, while Nottingham was renowned also for its

1

framesmiths, needlemakers, and setters up of hosiery and lace frames.[5]

Shortly after the beginning of the nineteenth century, competition from the cotton mills of Lancashire caused a decline in cotton spinning in the Nottingham district,[6] but in 1815 the town possessed, at the most, six small mills. There were also two foundries, two glass-making firms, a tannery, a wire and pin-making concern, a brickworks at Mapperley, and a colliery at nearby Wollaton.[7] The town was also served by no fewer than five banks, two of which were of very long standing while the other three had been established since 1801.[8] Banking, however, employed few people and that part of the population which was not occupied in the town's minor industries or in the textile and allied industries found employment in the crafts or in the distributive and service trades common to most towns at this time. Because of this economic base, which remained characteristic of the town until the second half of the century, we shall be concerned mainly with the changes that occurred in the hosiery and lace industries and with their repercussions upon the people and the town of Nottingham. It is not denied that in aggregate the customary urban trades such as tailoring and shoemaking, building and carpentry, baking and butchering accounted for an important part of the whole of economic activity, but individually they normally employed a relatively small proportion of the total population, while in comparison with the town's textile manufacturing industries the amount of capital involved and the value of their output must have been small. Only when these minor trades move to the forefront of events, therefore, do they figure in the narrative.

Until the second half of the century hosiery was produced on frames which were identical in principle and similar in construction to those designed in the sixteenth century by William Lee of Calverton, the Nottinghamshire parson.[9] On his frames the stocking was made flat and seamed by hand and for each loop or stitch he used separate needles, the number of needles determining the width of the fabric produced. The operation of a stocking frame required the use of both hands and feet. The knitted fabric consisted of a series of loops, each of which was called a course, and each loop was formed by the operation of needle leads, or 'jack wires', which were controlled by two treadles worked by foot. When the jacks were drawn the movement of the slur-cock along their tails would cause the sinkers (thin plates of iron made to pass between the needles) to fall, and it was the sinkers which effected the looping process. A wooden presser bar was also required to depress the needle points into the grooves of the needle stems so as to allow the loops last formed to pass over those in the process of formation, while the shape of the article was controlled by the hand. An observer describing the framework knitter at work drew attention to the strain of coordination involved:

> While the hands are thus busy and the feet moving at the rate of four feet per second, the eye must keep watch on the needles as to their soundness and position, and upon the work, that it be perfect and without blemish.[10]

This operation was performed mainly by males, women and children being employed in performing the simpler auxiliary tasks of seaming and stitching.

Together with Leicester, Hinckley, and Derby, Nottingham had grown in importance as a framework knitting centre during the early eighteenth century, when the demand for plain (and therefore cheaper) worsted and cotton stockings had begun to increase. This regional expansion also followed the failure of the Framework Knitters' Company in London to regulate the trade of the east midlands where hosiers, in taking advantage of the abundant supply of cheap labour, had refused to restrict the number of apprentices admitted to the trade, thereby contravening the rules of the Company. The establishment of the early silk and cotton mills in Derbyshire and Nottinghamshire had encouraged the trend towards localization in the hosiery trade; furthermore, as the century progressed intra-regional specialization developed, and while many Nottingham hosiers continued to manufacture silk hosiery, cotton hosiery soon became identified as the county's major product.[11]

For more than two centuries the technology of hosiery manufacture had remained virtually unaltered; the mode of industrial organization was of similar longstanding. The high cost of frames and the use of expensive raw materials had led to the establishment of the trade on a capitalist basis from the beginning.[12] The frames were rented to framework knitters who fetched yarn from the hosiers' warehouses; the stockings, made on the frames in the workmens' homes, were then returned to the warehouse, after which the knitters received payment by the piece. By the end of the eighteenth century the middleman, who distributed and collected the work for the hosier, had become an important link between the outworkers scattered in their homes and the hosiers' warehouses in the town. But because some middlemen let workshop floor space to other framework knitters, or could distribute as they wished yarn and orders for stockings, many middlemen became employers of a kind. It was, however, the 'respectable gentlemen hosiers', some of whom employed several hundred frames worth many thousand pounds, who dominated the trade, and this situation gives rise to the question: to what extent were the hosiers responsible for the poor performance of the industry during the first half of the nineteenth century?[13]

The previous century had witnessed two long periods of growth with one intervening depression of a quarter of a century ending in 1783, at the close of the war with America. Between 1727 and 1782 the number of frames in the industry had risen from eight thousand to about twenty thousand, and by 1812 the figure had reached 29,588.[14] The expansion that occurred in the last quarter of the eighteenth century was largely the outcome of the inventiveness of Nottingham framework knitters who, during the depressed years, had devoted much effort to the adaptation of the stocking frame so as to increase its versatility. The result had been the appearance of a wide range of fancy hosiery and simple lace nets which quickly became fashionable and which, with some exceptions, retained their hold on the market until after 1800.[15] Many of these fabrics were sold at prices which placed them within the reach of popular demand and 'spider net', according to John Blackner, was worn

> by women whose reputation was little better than its own: and they used it for no other purpose than that of giving a bewitching appearance to the bosom, while they falsely assumed its concealment.[16]

One of the most successful of the numerous mechanical experiments was that which resulted in the construction of the warp frame which, by employing needles as on a stocking frame for stitching and warp as on a loom, could make either hose or lace. The point net frame was the other most successful invention which grew out of the same ferment of ideas. The favourable response of the market to warp and point net laces and the subsequent efforts of local mechanics to devise machinery capable of manufacturing lace nets of higher quality at lower cost led to the foundation of the machine-made lace industry in Nottingham. This dates from 1809 when John Heathcoat's invention of the bobbin net machine revolutionized the manufacture of lace.[17]

Technically an offshoot of the hosiery trade, the early lace trade was established with capital and labour from the parent source. Lace manufacturers, several of whom combined the production of point net with their principal function as hosiers, were able to take advantage of the services offered by finishers and the various merchants who already existed to serve the needs of hosiery manufacturers. The local newspapers abounded with advertisements offering loans on land mortgages, and through the same medium travelling merchants with London connections in the haberdashery trade invited commissions from manufacturers of lace nets. Thus, very similar technology, the use of common raw materials, and the exist-ence of similar problems connected with finance and marketing were factors which explain why the pre-bobbin net lace trade was organized in a similar fashion to the capitalist domestic system. Likewise in the new bobbin net industry frame renting was a con-spicuous feature of its organization in its early years, but outwork, on the pattern that existed in the hosiery trade where workmen paid frame rent to employers, was not. Appropriately for one of the first industries to be formed when the factory system was no longer new to the textile industry, some machines were driven by power and housed in factories from the beginning, but small independent machine operators also existed in large numbers and not until after 1850 could lace be described accurately as the product of a factory industry.

The expansion of Nottingham in the eighteenth century had been invigorated by the impressive economic growth which had taken place in the Vale of Trent.[18] The location of Nottingham on the River Trent, and the proximity of the southern part of the coal-field of the Erewash Valley north west of the town were of crucial importance in determining the position of Nottingham in the country's transport system.[19] By the completion of the Soar Navi-gation, the Erewash, the Trent and Mersey, and the Cromford Canals between 1777 and 189, this coalfield was opened up for extensive development. In 1792 the Act authorizing the cutting of the Nottingham Canal expressly mentioned shipment of coal from colleries belonging to the Duke of Newcastle at Brinsley, and the next two years saw the construction of the Derby, Nut-brook, and Beeston Canals. The importance of coal in stimulat-ing improvements in transport was thus evident in Nottingham-shire and Derbyshire, as it was in the Black Country and Lan-cashire; and by the close of the century the completion of a network of canals had secured for the coalmasters access to the Nottingham market as well as to those of towns further to the east. Referring to the beneficial influence of the Nottingham Canal upon local trade, Blackner noted that the canal passed through Eastwood, New-thorpe, Cossal, Trowell, and Wollaton, whence pit coal was trans-ported to midland towns and to eastern England. In 1816 nearly one and a half million tons of coal were carried from the Notting-hamshire and Derbyshire coalfields, via the Trent Navigation, to Gainsborough and Hull on the east coast. Hull was also the port through which hosiery and laces were shipped to continental Europe, and twice weekly the Nottingham Steam Packet travelled between Nottingham and Gainsborough.[20] The link from Notting-ham to Liverpool was the Grand Trunk Canal connecting the Trent with the Mersey, while the completion of the Grand Union Canal in 1814 made it possible, by using the Soar Navigation and the Grand Junction Canal, to reach London.

In 1815 Blackner described the banks of Nottingham Canal 'where coals, timber, corn, iron, slate, stone, plaster and tile wharfs abound with their contiguous warehouses.'[21] Five large wharfs advertised regular transport services; from the wharfs of Acton & Company goods were conveyed nightly at nine by fly-boat to London, and twice weekly boats left Nottingham for Manchester and Liverpool.[22] Water-borne traffic was limited mainly to coal, corn, and building materials, though the town's supplies of cod and haddock from the east coast probably travelled by boat,[23] as did London groceries; otherwise goods which were of low bulk but high in value—like local textiles—travelled by road.[24] The danger of spoilage by water carriage, the importance of speedy deliveries in trades affected by fashion, and the proximity of the town to relatively good turnpikes were factors which ensured the continued use of road transport, despite the excellent waterways connecting Nottingham with London, Liverpool, Hull, Bristol, Birmingham and the Black Country, South Yorkshire and the West Riding, Lancashire and Cheshire.[25] As in other areas where economic expansion had taken place during the latter half of the eighteenth century, the road system of Nottinghamshire was extended and improved. This development took place in response to the needs of a growing trade between the mainly extractive industries of the region to the west of Nottingham and the predominantly agricultural areas to the east and south. The Derby Road development in 1758–9, and later Mansfield Road, London Road, and the connection with Newark via the Fosse Way were important improvements to the town's external communications, and by the end of the century the existence of adequate trunk roads reaching to the town's medieval boundaries was largely the achievement of the turnpike trusts.[26] In 1815, however, Blackner contrasted the satisfactory state of the roads that left Nottingham with the town's own narrow streets. 'Deep roads and heavy mud,' wrote one traveller, 'proclaim the approach to the town of Nottingham',[27] a condition which was explained by their frequent use by coach and carriage.

The expansion of the framework knitting industry and the increase in population which accompanied it had enlarged the urban market for food as well as for coal and building materials, and in turn this had affected the growth of the town's retail trade. Responding, no doubt, to the pressure of competition for space in the central market place, the Corporation passed a resolution which forbade all sales, excepting food, in the market place on days when a market was not normally held,[28] while shopkeepers were ordered not to display their wares upon the public streets. The market place was the principal focus for trading. It was surrounded by tall houses whose fronts projected over the ground storeys to form a continuous colonnade, and located beneath were the town's most elegant retail stores. It was into Long Row that in 1804 John Townsend moved from London to open a shop for the sale of haberdashery and millinery; many years later Zebedee Jessop was to become the proprietor of this establishment.[29] By 1815 the scale of distribution had assumed such proportions that the market place had already become a centre of almost uninterrupted commerce.[30] Each year it was the scene of two minor fairs in March and May, while October was the month of the great Goose Fair.

The fairs existed primarily for the sale of livestock, but all kinds of wares were customarily offered for sale by merchants, dealers, and producers. Until 1808 the main cattle market was held regularly in Market Place each Wednesday, a horse market being situated on the southern side, and a beast and swine market on the west, but the sheep and cattle market was subsequently moved to Beastmarket Hill. The shambles, which sheltered the town and country butchers, were located at the eastern end alongside the market place; the shoe booths were behind the Exchange between Smithy Row and the Poultry. Each Saturday the Hen Cross was the scene of a poultry market and on Wednesdays and Fridays Week Day Cross attracted buyers and sellers of poultry, fish, fruit, and butter. On Saturdays Market Place was filled with stalls for the sale of articles of every description and in addition to these special markets and fairs, in Blackner's day stalls for the sale of food were out every week-day until midnight. Although geared to this well-established market organization, the town's food supply was occasionally disrupted. For example, in 1800 high bread prices had caused fierce riots. In September magistrates had circularized the Nottinghamshire gentry urging them to persuade farmers and tenants to dispatch their corn to market, suggesting that millers and bakers, rather than corn factors, should receive preference as buyers. At a meeting of landowners and farmers a resolution regretted that due to the demands of harvesting little corn had hitherto been sent to market; those present at the meeting agreed to act upon the magistrates' suggestion to send supplies quickly, and henceforward regularly, while undertaking also to register the name of the purchasers with the town clerk.[31] Improvements in the transport and distributive systems later reduced the threat of emergencies of this character.

The most important factor which contributed to the expansion of

the urban market was the rapid growth of population, a phenomenon common to other areas where economic development was
taking place. Due to an extremely high birth rate and to heavy immigration, the population grew by 11,000 between 1779 and 1801,
a rise of more than 60 per cent. Professor Chambers has argued
that owing to improved living standards and the charitable gesture
of a local surgeon who inaugurated a free vaccination service, 'the
town had broken through the demographic barrier.'[32] Yet while
continued population growth represented progress it intensified the
problems of urban life, and although the power of epidemic disease, hitherto the most serious check to population expansion, had
been reduced by the beginning of the century, the child death rate
had actually risen as overcrowding increased and health standards
deteriorated. The appearance in the town of unpaved lanes, mean
courts, and alleys, which early in the century provoked complaints,[33]
while symptomatic of general problems associated with urbanization, derived, nevertheless, from a problem which was peculiar to
Nottingham and which shaped the regional pattern of population
distribution.

Forming a garland about the busy town the meadows, waste, and
fields were at once the source of pleasure and beauty, misery,
disease, and filth. For apart from the lands owned by the Duke of
Newcastle, Lord Middleton, and Mr. Musters, the open land on
three sides of the town—the Forest in the north to West Bridgeford,
the Meadows in the south, and Mapperley Plains in the north east—
were subject to common rights and were controlled by the Municipal Corporation. Only on the east was there a break in the garland
which, as the population expanded, threatened to choke the growing town.[34] (See Figure I.) Signs of congestion had already appeared
in the closing decades of the eighteenth century when concentra-
tions of modest houses for the labouring poor existed to the north
of Market Square between Long Row and Back Side (now Parliament Street), while others were beginning to appear in Narrow
Marsh and Broad Marsh.[35] In 1796 Benjamin Darker, a needle
maker, took advantage of the land released for building by the
Lenton Enclosure Act of the same year and erected a row of back-
to-back houses at Radford, where it bordered the Nottingham open
fields. This earliest venture in overspill housing foreshadowed the
development of the village satellites located on the periphery of
Nottingham's green belt. In the 1820's New Radford, New Lenton,
New Sneinton, New Basford, Carrington, and Hyson Green were
transformed from semi-agricultural settlements into thriving industrial village suburbs, all of which were later to become part of
Nottingham.[36]

For those who lived and worked in the town in 1815 accommodation was for the most part reasonably sound in construction and design had been compared with that which had been built fifty years before.[37] Land scarcity, however, encouraged the construction of compact houses of two and often three storeys. Blackner described the housing of the working classes in Nottingham:

> (they) generally consist of a cellar, a room to dwell in called the house place, a chamber, a shop over it to work in, a roof called a cockloft and a small pantry, though in the manner of building there are many exceptions, some for better some for worse; and they are generally composed of plaster floors for the upper rooms, lightly timbered with deal; brick walls some $4\frac{1}{2}$ and some 9 inches thick; and cast iron grates for the fire-places, frequently with ovens and boilers of the same material.[38]

In order to economize land, by 1815 more than three hundred such dwellings had been built back-to-back around courts; moreover, growing numbers of these were built in the lower part of the town between the foot of the cliff on which the old town was built and the river. This increased the danger of flooding from the Trent, and indeed in 1809 water had entered houses in Narrow Marsh.[39] Given the local topography and the state of the science of sanitation, the population density of these areas, rather than the construction of the houses, was the source of increasing squalor and disease in later years.[40] Population pressure also appears to have affected the lives of members of higher income groups, for between 1810 and 1815 two of the town's largest mansions, Nottingham 'Castle' and Plumptre House, were divided into apartments for such people.[41] However, the erection of back-to-backs and the further subdivision of large residences offered only a temporary solution to the problem of accommodating the town's natural increase and the many hundreds of workmen who, together with their families, flocked to the town in the twenties in response to the opportunities opened up by the industrial and commercial expansion associated with the great lace boom.[42] Despite the striking economic growth which occurred during these years the rate at which the population of Nottingham grew was only slightly higher than the national average, and fell below it in the decade 1831–1841. When the Nottingham Enclosure Act was passed in 1845, growth of the old town's population had almost stopped. (See Table I.)

If the urban environment was worse in Nottingham than in towns of similar size the local governing body was likewise no better than its counterparts, concerned as its members were not with town improvement and the provision of social amenities, but rather with the management of properties and the regulation of privileges. The

c

Corporation was charged with keeping the peace and administering justice in the Town Court and Quarter Sessions, but the prevention of crime received scant attention, for it depended upon subscriptions raised among householders—the Associations for the Prosecution of Felons—which appointed watchmen to guard prescribed districts. The Corporation had adopted the provisions of the Watch and Ward Act in 1816 when local gangs were destroying private property, but after the disappearance of Luddism the Watch soon deteriorated. In 1820, 'twelve drowsy and for the most part superannuated watchmen' comprised the entire police force in a town

TABLE I: *Comparative Population Figures 1801–1841.*

Year	Actual Nottm. Population	Population of England & Wales		Nottingham Population at same rate of increase	
		Decade	% Increase	Population	+ or −
1801	28801				
1811	34253	1801–11	14	32833	+1420
1821	42415	1811–21	18·1	41253	+1162
1831	50680	1821–31	15·8	50050	+ 630
1841	53091	1831–41	14·3	57827	−4736

Source: *Enumeration Abstract* 1841 (412) pp. 229–230. Following the table by E. Sigsworth 'Modern York' *The Victoria County History of Yorkshire*, P. M. Tillot (1961).

with more than 40,000 inhabitants.[43] The only public service which the Corporation provided was the scavenging and cleansing of the Market Place and its immediate vicinity, an undertaking which was carried out under the supervision of the Churchwardens and Overseers of St. Mary's Parish who received in return an annual sum of £60.[44] As for the rest of the town the disposal of refuse was taken care of by the 'muck majors', to whom the court and alley dwellers sold the accumulated putrid mess of filth and sewage; it was then carted through the streets to be loaded into barges and sold to farmers along the canal and Trent banks.[45]

In addition to the parochial Highway Boards, which confined their attention to the highroads and refused to carry out any operations in overcrowded districts, the only institutional machinery existing for social purposes consisted of a Court Leet—the Mickleton Jury—the sole body claiming any special authority in matters of public health. The Jury made an annual perambulation in order to draw up a list of offenders and fine them small sums, chiefly for encroachments on waste land, but it was a lax and leisured body which took its duties lightly and refreshed itself liberally with food and wine at the Corporation's expense.[46] Street lighting was the responsibility of an *ad hoc* authority from 1762 until 1819, when a private company was formed to illuminate the town centre with coal gas.[47] The people of Nottingham depended for their water either upon the long-established Waterworks Company and the purchase of drinking water in pails from the carriers, or upon the Corporation's pumps, nine of which had been erected in the last quarter of the eighteenth century. The water from these pumps was unfit for drinking and hard for washing purposes, and according to Blackner many people continued to use water for culinary purposes from the River Leen, even though this was the town's main sewer.[48]

As population grew, so public health and transport within the town boundaries deteriorated. The course of this decline and the response of the Corporation to the needs of the community in the early years of the century suggest the operations of a self-elected clique, imprisoned by the ideas and practices of earlier generations and faced by problems whose principal novelty was their magnitude. Even had the Corporation possessed the will to tackle the problems, it lacked the means both in terms of power and money;[49] but fortunately for the community an important minority was prepared to devote its energies towards the improvement of town life.

Some sought to combat ignorance, others cared for the sick and helped the destitute, the inspiration for much of this voluntary effort originating in the Evangelical revival which achieved notable successes in Nottingham in the early decades of the century.[50] By 1802 the Evangelicals had succeeded in attracting to the Sunday schools about 26 per cent. of the age group from five to fifteen, and the drive to expand day school places began in earnest in 1810 when, with the financial support of a number of Whig Evangelicals and the assistance of the similarly constituted Corporation, the Lancasterian Boys' School opened in a disused cotton mill.[51]

Like the assault upon mass ignorance the relief of sickness and poverty was the work of charitable institutions and enlightened individuals. The General Hospital, which after voluntary subscription had been opened in 1782, claimed by 1814 to have treated nearly eleven thousand in-patients and almost three times as many out-patients; by 1815 free vaccination financed by public subscription was available to the poor.[52] The Lunatic Asylum opened in 1812, and the dispensary at St. Mary's Workhouse, which was supported from town rates, was established in 1813, although a fever ward built in the workhouse yard was paid for in part by public subscription.[53] The charitable trusts, which were the responsibility of the Corporation, were devoted mainly to the relief of widows. In Plumptre Square the Plumptre Hospital offered accommodation to thirteen poor widows, and income from the foundation's property was distributed to thirty out-pensioners who thereby received £10 annually. Collins' and Willoughby's Hospitals also afforded accommodation and a small allowance with coal to a number of widows and widowers; Lambley Hospital consisted of twenty-two tenements for the benefit of burgesses and their widows; Sir Thomas White's Loans consisted of money to be lent to young burgesses embarking upon a business career, while numerous other benefactors had bequeathed sums of money to be distributed in the form of cash, loaves of bread, or coal, to the town's poor.[54]

Such charities, however, were not designed to cater for the casualties of an urban industrial society which, by 1815, had already begun to take shape. Already in 1783, and again in 1795, the Mayor of Nottingham had felt it necessary to open a public subscription from which to supplement the charity already offered by the trusts; bread tickets allowing one-third reduction in prices were distributed among the poor, the bakers being reimbursed by the public committee, and in 1800 soup kitchens were opened during the winter months.[55] These emergencies, which were due largely to local unemployment and high food prices, became more frequent and more urgent as the proportion of the population dependent entirely upon industry and trade increased; the result was that existing *ad hoc* arrangements for the relief of poverty became increasingly inadequate, while the Poor Law authorities also found themselves in difficulties during these periods when they were pressed to give out-relief.[56]

According to the report of David Love, a humble tract vendor and poet who spent the winter of 1814 inside St. Mary's Workhouse, it was the refuge of the 'lame, lazy, aged, and crazy.' The rooms were cleaned daily and the inmates were allowed one day's leave weekly, affording a respite from tailoring, shoemaking, or framework knitting, the trades in which they received instruction. The diet was wholesome and the inmates were well fed. Adults drank beer, and milk was served to children; breakfast daily consisted of milk porridge, and Love looked forward eagerly to the broad and cheese which was served twice a week. The dinners were almost lavish, with large helpings of potatoes, greens or turnips, and plenty of meat followed by pudding. In writing his memoirs Love expressed considerable satisfaction with his treatment during his stay.[57] It would appear from this account that prior to 1810 life in the town's largest workhouse was not a strong deterrent to prospective inmates. The year 1819, however, one of acute depression, saw the appointment of a new Overseer, Absolem Barnett, under whose administration reforms were carried out on principles which anticipated the nationwide reforms that occurred under the Poor Law Amendment Act fifteen years later; thereafter, workhouse life became less congenial.[58]

As the town's population increased, greater demands were made upon the Poor Law authorities, especially during the years of unemployment and distress. It was estimated that during the depression of 1808 more than sixteen thousand persons in Nottingham were dependent on poor relief; in 1812 twenty-two thousand received aid, and in 1816 relief was granted to between seven and eight thousand.[59] The reasons which explain the growing frequency and severity of distress in Nottingham are to be found in the local economic structure and the character of the town's staple industries, as well as in the general increase in economic interdependence which was due to industrialization. The extremely heavy dependence of local employment and prosperity upon the framework knitting and lace making industries has already been noted. Furthermore, between 40 and 50 per cent. of Nottingham's hosiery output and at least a comparable proportion of manufactured lace were shipped to overseas markets.[60] The significance of fluctuations in British overseas trade for a community whose livelihood depended heavily upon the prosperity of these two export-oriented industries needs no elaboration; neither does the connection between fluctuations in trade, the level of employment, and the recurrence of *ad hoc* public relief committees which became a feature of urban history in this period.[61] The instability of employment was increased further by the seasonal character of demand. This arose from the existence of two major markets for Nottingham goods, one in Europe, the other in America. Hosiery and lace found their way to various parts of the Continent through the great spring fairs at Leipzig, Frankfort, Novgorod, and Beaucaire, and to America through commission houses which made their large purchases mainly in the autumn; thus it was common in the trade to speak of the German and American seasons, the prelude to each being weeks of enormous activity and high levels of employment.

The tempo of economic life and the large scale unemployment which accompanied each slump are features which shaped the town's history; they helped to produce Luddism in the first two decades of the century and Chartism in later years. But although cyclical and seasonal fluctuations were common to both trades, changes occurred during the two decades centreing upon 1800 which led eventually to changes in the town's social structure. A differentiation developed between framework knitters, most of whom were semi-skilled men working in a largely stagnant industry, and highly skilled lace makers, who belonged to a progressive and rapidly expanding trade. This division influenced the character of local working class movements, for whereas cyclical and seasonal fluctuations in employment typically affected the lace trade, from the second decade onwards workmen in the hosiery industry suffered from underemployment as well as from fluctuations.[62] By 1815 this division had already begun, for the war years, according to Blackner, had seen a drastic decline in the demand for most classes of silk and cotton hosiery, while the invention which formed the basis for the machine-made lace industry did not appear until 1809.

Growth in its economic importance had been accompanied by a change in the social significance of Nottingham which, to an observer in 1814, seemed to be 'rising . . . daily . . . in useful refinement and high respectability.'[63] The truth of this observation is open to question, for already many of the town-dwelling gentry had quit their mansions for the country, while the frequent and regular gatherings of the 'polite society' at the Nottingham 'assemblies' had been discontinued.[64] Nevertheless, the town possessed a social élite consisting of its prosperous bankers, merchant hosiers, lace manufacturers, men from the professions, and members of Nottingham's old trading families, and important social occasions continued to attract some of the aristocracy and gentry to the town. The occasional balls held at the Exchange building for people of 'rank and fashion' would attract a handful of peers and knights, a number of military officers, several professional men, and members of the local business élite.

The October race meetings, held annually on the Forest, were such occasions when these congregations took place, and while the grandstand would shelter the noble patrons of the turf, large crowds watched the races from the incline to the south of the course, a vantage point which offered spectators a splendid view of the oval track one mile and a quarter in length. The prizes of amounts up to £500 attracted entries of calibre and encouraged good sport.[65] It was customary to terminate the races with cock fights which took place at one of the local inns, and the White Lion on Long Row established a reputation as one of the great cocking centres of the midlands; for example in 1815 the Gentlemen of Nottinghamshire challenged their counterparts from Staffordshire, the stakes being five guineas a battle and £200 the main. After the day's racing and cockfighting had ended, a ball at the Assembly Rooms was the climactic social event.[66]

The town's two cricket teams likewise often played for a purse or to settle a wager and in 1817, two years after a portion of the Forest had been levelled to form a cricket ground, twenty-two members of the Nottingham Cricket Club, on behalf of J. Brewster Esq. of Radcliffe, Nottinghamshire, played against eleven of the All

England side who represented W. Lambert Esq. The purse was worth one thousand guineas, and although the odds quoted were one hundred to five against the Nottingham men their numerical superiority proved sufficient to bring a local victory.[67] Cricket matches and race meetings held on the Forest were both occasions for general public entertainment, when booths and marquees were erected to cater for the needs of thirsty spectators who picnicked on the southern slopes. Sporting events which caused misgivings among some sections of the public, such as bull baiting, had long since lost their popularity in Nottingham, for when the Act banning cruel sports was passed in 1835 neither of the bull rings near Angel Row in Market Place and at Burton Leys had been used for such contests for many decades.[68] Pugilism, however, could still muster considerable popular support, even though the authorities were obliged to prevent the sort of unregulated contest which took place in Nottingham in 1836. On that occasion two youths stood toe to toe, the blood flowing freely, raining blows upon each other for more than an hour until neither was able to stand. A correspondent writing in the *Nottingham Journal* complained that for half that time the Mayor had been present, holding the watch and calling time for rounds, and even gave 2s. 6d. to the victor. When a constable who was standing nearby was asked to intervene to stop the fight, the Mayor's presence had inhibited him from performing his duty. No doubt the informer reserved his approval for such harmless yet enjoyable activities as bowling, a sport which was gaining in popularity. The ancient green at the White Hart in Lenton had long given pleasure, but during the latter part of the eighteenth century several more had been opened, and in 1807 the Park Bowling Green was formed close to the Castle.[69]

Social life in Nottingham derived its character from the town's position as a local capital which had long attracted persons of rank. As a commercial and financial centre where professional men and 'gentlemen merchant hosiers and lace manufacturers' resided, it possessed a sufficiently large portion of the community with education and an interest in the arts to be able to support a modest but lively programme of cultural activities. In 1816 John Wright Esq., the banker, who lived at Rempston Hall at Lenton, was one of the gentlemen who established the Nottingham Subscription Library at Bromley House which soon became the cultural centre for the town luminaries.[70] The Exchange on Market Place and the Assembly Rooms in Low Pavement were the scenes of balls and feasts for the aristocracy and gentry, while the tradesmen held their social functions in Thurland Hall. This reflected the distinction between 'polite and middle life' to which Laird referred in 1810. According to one contemporary, assemblies in Nottingham for dancing and card parties were very popular; they were, 'as in all other places, the resort of the young and gay, who go to see and be seen.'[71] Numerous people in the town derived pleasure from play-acting or making music. Sacred music at the church and chapels, concert music sung by the Harmonic Society, and songs, airs, and glees performed by the Nottingham Musical Society offered opportunities for enjoyment and exercise to those in voice, and entertainment for those who preferred to listen. In his youth William Felkin, later to become Mayor of Nottingham, although a Baptist, attended St. Mary's Church to hear amateur instrumentalists perform some of Handel's works. He listened also to music played by the military bands which were attached to the regiment quartered in the barracks in the Park, another popular source of entertainment, and band concerts were sometimes given at the Theatre Royal in St. Mary's Gate.[72]

The Nottingham theatre, which had been in existence since 1760, was described by Dearden in 1834 as 'a very dull looking building'; he remarked that its appearance bore more resemblance to a prison than a place of entertainment. Like most theatres at this time it was run by two actor-managers who toured with their company. James Robertson specialized in comic characterization, while his partner, Thomas Manley, portrayed tragic figures. The programmes presented by this 'genteel company' varied to extremes. In 1815, for example, its repertoire included a grand spectacular presentation entitled 'Timour the Tartar', together with supporting features consisting of 'Blue Beard', a melodrama, and a 'scene representing Nottingham Market Place, with a local comic song, dancing, etc.'[73] According to Dearden, writing a few years later, the theatre lacked support, a situation which he attributed to the hostility shown towards theatrical entertainment by a large proportion of the town's numerous and wealthy middle class dissenters. In addition to the plays performed at the theatre, band concerts, recitals, and public lectures were also held on its small stage. The town possessed amateur groups too, and for the Nottingham Thespian Society the year 1815 was one of enthusiasm and activity. Its members presented a farce called 'Raising the Wind' in aid of the Waterloo Fund and the production proved so successful that within a week rehearsals began for 'Richard III', to be presented in aid of the Lunatic Asylum.[74] Some of the town's youth also showed an interest in drama, and a room in Bottle Lane was fitted up as a theatre for amateur performances. This project came to grief in 1817 when the Mayor appeared in the audience just at a point in the play when, with youthful abandon, the actors were portraying a passionate love scene.[75]

From time to time the opportunity arose to witness spectacular entertainments like the equestrian and other exhibitions held at the Riding School in Castle Gate. But the 'equestrian extravaganzas', menageries, and circuses which occasionally visited the town were rarely able to match some of the spectacles presented at Radford Folly and in 1839 the newspapers carried advertisements for an 'unequalled Novelty and Attraction to be held in Radford Grove Gardens.' It was to consist of

> a grand representation of Mount Vesuvius and the city and the Bay of Naples . . . forming a splendid combination of panoramic and pyrotechnic display . . .

Weather permitting, the public was informed that Mount Vesuvius was to erupt in realistic fashion. Another unusual experience was that offered in 1826 by Mr. Green who invited spectators assembled in Market Place to join him as passengers in his balloon. He persuaded nearly one hundred ladies and gentlemen to pay 10s. 6d. each for this privilege and, according to one observer, these joy riders were then gratified with ascents to a considerable height and after enjoying the prospects from their giddy elevation' returned safely to earth.[76]

Gardening was a form of recreation that absorbed many of the leisure hours of the town's menfolk and the Ancient Society of Flowerists, established in Nottingham in 1761, held annual shows like that which took place at the Blue Bell in 1815. Local anglers fished in the Trent for pike, barbel, trout, and even salmon, a healthy pastime which, Blackner assured his readers, 'keeps animal juices in due order and circulation.'[77] More invigorating, no doubt, was the walk which it was possible to take along the entire ten miles of footpath which encircled the town, passing through coppice and meadow. The less energetic might follow one of the many walks leading to delightful rural haunts such as the nearby village of Wilford, which was situated on the south bank of the Trent and was famous for its cherry eatings, or Clifton Grove, Radford Folly, or St. Ann's Well. On some of the popular trails, like that which led to Sneinton, tea houses catered for the holiday customers.[78]

Occasionally a curious public congregated to observe a public whipping, the last of which occurred in 1830, or to witness a public execution—that which took place in 1831 attracted several thousand spectators.[79] But even if the taste for brutality continued to exist, opportunities to gratify sadistic appetites were generally on the decline. Nevertheless, reports published in the local press of the proceedings at the Assizes with detailed descriptions of this diabolical murder or that brutal rape, this unusual hanging or another horrible incest, continued to pander to the taste for sensation. At the same time, such reports revealed not only a degree of violence that was a part of urban life but, equally important, problems of petty crime, prostitution, and drunkenness.

Some people argued that one of the chief sources of these problems was the excellence of Nottingham ale, the depth and coolness of the town's cellars contributing to its unrivalled taste and strength. Treating the celebrated libation with appropriate ceremony, landlords both at the Punch Bowl in Peck Lane and the Peacock in St. Peter's Gate served the ale in silver cups, doubtless to a discriminating clientele. This was a practice which must have added to the general atmosphere which so impressed a visitor who referred to 'the volumes of smoke and politics in which . . . lovers of malt and hops are nightly encircled.'[80] Indeed politics in Nottingham, with its considerable artisan electorate, was an inexhaustable subject for conversation. Election campaigns were accompanied, almost invariably, by a rowdy hurly-burly at the hustings, street fights, drunkenness and general disorder.[81] Election results were always the occasion for celebration; processions and bands of music would march through the streets, tea parties, dinners, and balls were held at the Exchange, and the populace would eat sheep roasted in the streets at the victor's expense.

The personalities and policies at each national and local election were the subject of public debate through the columns of Nottingham's newspapers, the *Nottingham Journal, Nottingham Review,* and the *Nottingham Gazette.*[82] The latter, whose editorial column frequently bordered on libel in its expression of fanatical Tory views, discontinued publication in 1815. The *Nottingham Gazette* had first appeared in 1807 as a reaction to the moderate Tory position which Stretton, the editor of the *Nottingham Journal,* presented in his newspaper. Although the *Journal* tended to expound Tory views it remained independent of official party influence until Stretton sold the newspaper to John Hicklin and Job Bradshaw in 1832. Henceforward Hicklin, who edited the newspaper, sought to 'check the spread of . . . democratical and irreligious doctrines.' The *Journal's* chief adversary was the *Nottingham Review,* which was established in 1808 by the Methodist printer Charles Sutton. The *Review* was an organ of radicalism and nonconformity and the need for a newspaper of this character became apparent almost immediately. By 1812 the *Review* had a circulation of between fifteen and sixteen hundred, approximately one-half of the total copies going to Nottingham readers, the remainder to other towns and villages in the east midlands. In 1833 the *Review's* circulation reached thirteen hundred and fifty, while that of the *Journal* fell short of this figure by more than five hundred. Neither Charles nor his son Richard, who succeeded as owner-editor in 1828, became councillors, but through their editorials the *Review* waged a relentless campaign against the government's handling of the war against Napoleon and inspired three petitions which demanded the abolition of the Corn Laws. After many years of advocating parliamentary reform, in 1830 Richard Sutton declared his support for universal suffrage, annual parliaments, and vote by ballot.[83] Both newspapers appealed mainly to the middle classes but although, like the *Sheffield Independent,* the *Nottingham Review* drew its chief support from middle class dissenting Radicals, it also made a serious attempt to attract working class readers.[84] In 1816, after publishing a letter signed by 'Ned Ludd' criticizing government policy, Charles Sutton was prosecuted for libel and served one year in prison. This was but one of more than two hundred press prosecutions instigated by the Tory government at this time against their Radical critics. A stranger from Manchester who visited the town in 1830, referring to the *Review,* commented 'whatever might be the case in other towns, in Nottingham the working classes have their advocate.[85] The price of the newspapers, sevenpence until the reduction of the stamp duty in 1836, meant that for many people a private subscription was too expensive, but the News Room in Pelham Street and another at Bromley House stocked both provincial and London newspapers,[86] while newspapers were also often to be found at inns and public houses.

Probably the largest and certainly the most celebrated of Nottingham Inns was the Blackamoore's Head in the High Street; it was owned by the Duke of Newcastle and catered chiefly for the aristocracy. The White Lion was another reputable inn which, together with the Ram on Long Row, the King's Head in Narrow Marsh, and the Flying Horse was one of the principal stops for travellers.[87] With more than one inn or public house for every two hundred persons (including children), the importance of these centres of social intercourse in the life of the community cannot be ignored.[88] Undoubtedly some were, as their critics insisted, centres of gambling, vice, and drunkenness. As the only major focal point of the mass of people who did not belong to the various clubs and societies which were chiefly the preserve of the aristocracy, gentry, and the upper middle classes, it was inevitable that criminals, mischiefmakers, pimps, and prostitutes should meet over tankards of ale to discuss their business, just as it was the practice of the eminently respectable Nottingham Ancient Imperial Order of Oddfellows, founded in 1810, to meet regularly at the Three Salmons or the

Eight Bells. Indeed many of the town's numerous friendly societies which aimed to help their members to provide for future medical bills or funeral expenses found the pub to be a cheap, convenient, and congenial rendezvous.[89]

Not all public houses, therefore, were dens of iniquity, but neither did insurance, conviviality, and thirst provide the only motives for men to congregate within their walls, for the pub was also at the hub of working class movements. Some of the trades met regularly at one particular pub. The Sir Isaac Newton, for example, was a favourite with Gravener Henson and other leaders of the framework knitters. John Blackner, another of the most popular and influential men in local working class movements, a former framework knitter who shortly before his death edited the *Nottingham Review*, kept the Rancliffe Arms in Sussex Street. According to one contemporary 'this became the principal place of resort, in Nottingham, for all the leading members—among the humbler classes in particular—of Radical reformers.'[90] In 1817 the Three Salmons was the haunt of Jeremiah Brandreth, the 'Nottingham Captain', leader of the abortive Pentridge Revolution, whose depleted band of followers were arrested that year between Kimberley and Langley Mill before they could reach Nottingham.[91] As centres of protest, trade union activity, and political argument, as places were the exchange took place of information concerning employment opportunities and sometimes co-operative enterprise, and where shop talk led naturally to discussions of the merits of new ideas and technology, the institution of the pub served as a social axis in importance second only to the family, and the lives of a large number of craftsmen, mechanics, labourers, and others, revolved around it.

For the most part illiterate, by 1815 the framework knitters had become also economically depressed. The struggle to earn enough on which to live, henceforward became a pressing problem for a growing number of families.[92] Long hours of work left little time for leisure, and although Monday continued to be a day of rest, times when the frames stopped working eliminated any margin above a bare subsistence income. In such circumstances as these the meetings at the pubs assumed greater urgency. From these centres originated strike plans and petitions, while the dejected workman might find solace in reminiscences with a friend over a pint of ale. In 1822 a framework knitter in such a mood reflected:

> Times are very different now from what they were when you and I were shopmates Ben. We used to club together then and get a comfortable tit-bit two or three nights a week and Saturday night never passed over our heads without a general meet-

ing of all the shopmates somewhere or other when the foaming
tankard cheered our spirits . . . Now we are all half starved.[93]
While framework knitters were conscious of the changes that were
taking place in industry, they were equally aware of the changes
occurring in the character of the town in which they lived. Within
the memory of the framework knitter who recalled better times,
Nottingham could be referred to as 'a pleasant garden town'; in 1857
a journalist from Leicester described it as 'the Manchester of the
Midlands'; shortly after 1900 Nottingham became one of the few
English cities containing within its boundaries nearly a quarter of a
million people. It is to the course of this transformation that we now
turn.

References

[1] John Blackner, *History of Nottingham* (Nottingham, 1816), p. 29.

[2] *Ibid.*, p. 54.

[3] *Ibid.*, p. 213.

[4] This rough and very conservative estimate has been calculated by assuming that about one-quarter of the population, which numbered some 37,000 in 1815, were males upwards of 20 years of age. There were in that year according to Blackner and Felkin 2,600 stocking frames, 400 warp frames, and more than 1,500 point net frames. These would employ directly approximately 50% of the adult males but this makes no allowance for employment arising from the allied industries. Felkin estimated that each point net frame employed altogether at least 10 men, women, and children. John Blackner, *op. cit.*, p. 235; William Felkin writing in *British Manufacturing Industries*, ed. G. P. Bevan (1875), pp. 49–50.

[5] John Blackner, *op. cit.*, pp. 245–47. A setter-up was a workman who, after the smith had made the ironwork of the machine, adjusted the various parts in preparation for the operative. G. Henson, *The Civil, Political, and Mechanical History of Framework Knitters*, (Nottingham, 1831), p. 321.

[6] J. D. Chambers, 'The Vale of Trent,' *E.H.R.*, Supplement 3, (1957). 59–60.

[7] In 1804 there were five or six small mills, but by 1833 only three remained. It has been pointed out that attempts to establish large mills in the town before the turn of the century had floundered. S. D. Chapman, in a forthcoming article 'The Transition to the Factory System in the Midland Cotton Spinning Industry,' *E.H.R.*, xviii. John Blackner, *op. cit.*, pp. 207, 251, 212, 74; J. D. Chambers, *Nottinghamshire in the Eighteenth Century*, (1932), pp. 88–9.

[8] See *The Nottingham Directory*, (Nottingham, 1818).

[9] For details of the technology of framework knitting see J. D. Chambers, *Nottinghamshire in the Eighteenth Century*, (1932), Appendix I; G. Henson, *The Civil, Political, and Mechanical History of the Framework Knitters*, (1831), p. 39 et. seq.

[10] *Report of the Royal Commission on the Condition of Framework Knitters*, 1845 (609) XV. 1. p. 677.

[11] F. A. Wells, *The British Hosiery Trade*, (1935), p. 57.

[12] See J. D. Chambers, *Nottinghamshire in the Eighteenth Century*, (1932), pp. 119–132.

[13] Charlotte Erickson, *British Industrialists; Steel and Hosiery*, (Cambridge, 1959), Chapter IV, Infra, Chapter X.

[14] J. D. Chambers, *Nottinghamshire in the Eighteenth Century*, (1932), p. 95; John Blackner, *op. cit.*, p. 243.

[15] F. A. Wells, *op. cit.*, *pp.* 93–94.

[16] John Blackner, *op. cit.*, p. 234.

[17] *Infra*, Chapter III.

[18] John Deering quoted in *The Victoria History of the County of Nottinghamshire*, II, 1910 ed. W. Page, p. 320.

[19] Herbert Green, *The Southern Portion of the Nottinghamshire and Derbyshire Coalfield and the Development of Transport before 1850*, p. 69.

[20] A. Redford, *Manchester Merchants and Foreign Trade* Vol. I., (1939), p. 34; *N.R.*, March 13, 1818.

[21] John Blackner, *op. cit.*, p. 23.

[22] *Nottingham Directory*, (1818) p. 18.

[23] *The History, Antiquities, and Present State of the Town of Nottingham* (Nottingham, 1807), pp. 3–4.

[24] H. Field, *The Nottingham Date Book* (1884) p. 383; Cooke's *Topographical and Statistical Description of Nottinghamshire* (1810) p. 61; Boat Cargo Tables, Trent Navigation 1800–1842; *House of Commons Select Committee on the North Midland Railway Bill* 1826, pp. 40–50.

[25] J. Priestley, *Historical Account of the Navigable Rivers, Canals and Railways throughout Great Britain* (1831); see frontispiece map.

[26] A. Cossons, *The Turnpike Roads of Nottinghamshire*, Historical Association Leaflet, no. 97 (1934), pp. 12–14.

[27] John Blackner, *op. cit.*, p. 27; G. M. Woodward, 'Nottinghamshire' (1796-8), ed. A. C. Wood, *Transactions of The Thoroton Society*, LXI, 1957, p. 39.

[28] *B.R.* VIII, 242, April 6, 1818.

[29] *Jessop & Son Sesquicentenary 1804–1954*, John Lewis Partnership publication, p. 4.

[30] See John Blackner *op. cit.*, pp. 60–61.

[31] *N.J.*, September 6, 1800.

[32] For the town's demographic history in the eighteenth century see J. D. Chambers, 'Population Change in a Provincial Town, Nottingham 1700–1800,' *Studies in the Industrial Revolution*, Essays presented to T. S. Ashton, ed. L. S. Pressnell (1960).

[33] F. C. Laird, *Topographical Description of Nottinghamshire*, (1810), p. 102; John Blackner, *op. cit.*, p. 54.

[34] *Infra*, pp. 162–65.

[35] J. D. Chamber's *art. cit.*, pp. 104–5; S. D. Chapman, 'Working Class Housing in Nottingham during the Industrial Revolution,' *Transactions of the Thoroton Society* LXVII, 1963. p. 77.

[36] *Infra*. p. 236.

[37] S. D. Chapman *art. cit.*, p. 75.

[38] J. Blackner, *op. cit.*, p. 66.

[39] *Ibid.*, p. 15.

[40] *Infra*, pp. 164–67.

[41] S. D. Chapman, *art. cit.*, p. 69.

[42] *Infra*, p. 164.

[43] H. Field, *op. cit.*, p. 341.

[44] *Second Report of the Commissioners* (*Large Towns and Populous Districts*) 1845, Report of J. R. Martin, Appendix p. 250.

[45] *Ibid.*, pp. 647–8.

[46] *First Report of the Commissioners* (*Large Towns and Populous Districts*) 1844, (572) XVII. 1., p. 645.

[47] F. and J. White, *History, Directory and Gazetteer of the County of the Town of Nottingham* (Sheffield, 1844), p. 179.

[48] *Ibid.*, p. 181; W. Dearden, *Historical and Topographical Directory of Nottingham,* (Nottingham, 1834), pp. 74–75; John Blackner, *op. cit.*, p. 23.

[49] *Infra*, pp. 167–68.

[50] See S. D. Chapman, 'The Evangelical Revival and Education in Nottingham' *Transactions of the Thoroton Society*, LXVI (1962), p. 38.

[51] *Ibid*, p. 52; *Infra*, Chapter VI.

[52] F. H. Jacob, *A History of the General Hospital, Nottingham,* (Nottingham, 1951), pp. 102–03; J. D. Chambers in *Studies in the Industrial Revolution,* ed. L. S. Pressnell, pp. 118–19.

[53] *Ibid.*

[54] W. Dearden, *op. cit.,* pp. 60–62.

[55] Thomas Bailey, *Annals of Nottinghamshire,* (Nottingham, 1853), vol. IV. 100–01, 157–58, 185.

[56] N.R., Sept. 21, 1816; Sept. 28, 1816.

[57] David Love, *The Life of David Love,* (Nottingham, 1823), pp. 140–143.

[58] *Infra,* p. 112 et seq.

[59] *N.R.,* September 28, 1816.

[60] *First Report from the Select Committee appointed to take into consideration the several Petitions which have been presented by persons employed in the Framework Knitting Trade* 1812 (247) 11. 203. p. 48; William Felkin, *A History of the Machine Wrought Hosiery and Lace Manufacture,* (Cambridge, 1867), p. 343. (Hereafter referred to as *History*).

[61] *Infra,* p. 106.

[62] *Infra,* Chap. II.

[63] *N.J.,* November 12, 1814.

[64] F. C. Laird, *op. cit.,* p. 149;

[65] *V.C.H. Nottinghamshire,* II, pp. 391–393; W. Wylie, *Old and New Not tingham,* (1853), p. 60.

[66] *V.C.H. Nottinghamshire,* II, p. 390; *N.J.,* March 27, 1815.

[67] *V.C.H. Nottinghamshire,* II, p. 406.

[68] *Ibid.,* p. 412.

[69] W. Wylie, *op. cit.,* p. 359.

[70] W. Dearden, *History, Topography and Directory of Nottingham,* (1834), p. 65.

[71] F. C. Laird, *op. cit.,* p. 149; G. M. Woodward, 'Nottingham' (1796–8), ed. A. C Wood, *Transactions of the Thoroton Society,* LXI, 1957, p. 46.

[72] S. D. Chapman, *William Felkin, 1795–1874* (unpublished M.A. dissertation, University of Nottingham, 1960), pp. 34–5.

[73] *N.J.,* June 3, 1815.

[74] *Ibid.*

[75] *B.R.,* VIII, p. 240, f.n.l.

[76] H. Field, *The Nottingham Date Book* (1884), p. 378.

[77] J. Blackner, *op. cit.,* p. 22.

[78] G. M. Woodward, 'Nottinghamshire' (1796–8), ed. A. C. Wood, *Transactions of the Thoroton Society,* LXI, 1957, p. 47.

[79] H. Field, *op. cit.,* p. 394, 398.

[80] G. M. Woodward, 'Nottinghamshire' (1796–8), ed. A.C. Wood, *Transactions of the Thoroton Society,* LXI, 1957, p. 12.

[81] See, for example, the description of the elections of 1818 by H. Field, *op. cit.,* p. 324; Thomas Bailey, a Nottingham wine merchant, giving evidence on electioneering before the Royal Commission on Municipal Corporations in 1833, said: 'I witnessed so many disgusting scenes when I was engaged as chairman of the Election Committee that I determined to give up all connection with them' (p. 81).

[82] See, D. Fraser, 'Nottingham Press, 1800–1850,' *Transactions of the Thoroton Society,* LXVII, 1963.

[83] *Art. cit.,* p. 56.

[84] For a comparative study in three other provincial towns, see D. Read, *Press and People,* (1961).

[85] Quoted by D. Fraser, *art. cit.,* p. 58.

[86] W. Dearden, *op. cit.,* p. 66.

[87] G. M. Woodward, 'Nottinghamshire', ed. A. C. Wood, *Transactions of the Thoroton Society*, LXI, 1957, p. 40.

[88] H. Field, *op. cit.*, p. 228.

[89] In 1803 there were forty-one friendly societies in St. Mary's Parish alone, with an aggregate membership of nearly thirteen hundred people. *B.R.* VIII, 35, October 25, 1813.

[90] Thomas Bailey, *Annals of Nottinghamshire*, Vol. IV (1856) p. 286; On John Blackner see J. C. Warren, 'John Blackner', *Transactions of the Thoroton Society*, XXX, 1926.

[91] See the account of the Pentridge Revolution in R. F. White, *Waterloo To Peterloo*, (1957).

[92] *Infra*, Chap. II.

[93] W. Brown, *Spirit of the Times* (Nottingham, 1822).

CHAPTER II

A BACKWARD INDUSTRY: THE HOSIERY TRADE AND FRAMEWORK KNITTERS

THE industrial revolution consisted of changes in the volume and distribution of resources, technical change being fundamental to the economic progress that took place. 'Without the inventions', writes Professor Ashton, 'industry might have continued its slow-footed progress . . . but there would have been no industrial revolution.'[1] The history of the hosiery industry during the first half of the nineteenth century demonstrates the truth of this statement, while the implications for people whose livelihood depended upon the condition of an industry which experienced little or no change in the methods of production are also apparent in an account of the life and labour of Nottingham framework knitters to 1850.

The history of the hosiery industry during the nineteenth century cannot be understood without reference to the condition of the trade at the turn of the century. Stocking frames not only produced plain socks and stockings but nearly twenty different kinds of hose which differed in style, texture, and colour, in addition to other fancy items such as mitts, gloves, and waistcoat pieces.[2] Prior to the wars with France by working diligently framework knitters were able to earn sufficient to support themselves and their families, but already in the nineties, according to Eden, only about one-third of all framework knitters in the Nottingham district could support themselves with ease.[3] Owing to the blockades of 1810-12 during the war against France foreign trade with northern Europe was disrupted, and English markets in America were also adversely affected by war with that country in 1812. A reliable estimate that Nottingham hosiers normally shipped more than 40 per cent. of their output overseas helps to explain the depressed condition of local trade during those years.[4] The closure of foreign markets, however, was only temporary and because of their long run consequences the changes which took place in the domestic market were more serious. The need for increased public revenue for military purposes necessitated rising taxation, while the war years also brought higher food prices. This pressure on real incomes might well have been connected with the appropriately austere turn in fashion which set

26

in at that time. Consumers increasingly showed preferences for plain clothing and as growing numbers of men took to wearing trousers, gaiters, and boots, fancy hosiery quickly lost its popularity. Already the prosperous times were being left behind, for changes in favour of less elaborate articles which required less time and skill in their production resulted in a reduced demand for framework knitters. Owing to the town's partial specialization in the production of plain cotton stockings the effect of the fashion changes upon the Nottingham trade was particularly adverse, for many frames which had previously been employed in making fancy silk or cotton stockings were now devoted to the manufacture of plain cotton hose, thereby increasing the competition among local producers. Whereas in 1812 two-thirds of the total number of frames had made fancy hosiery, by 1833 half the total (which was also greater than in 1812) made plain cotton hose.[5]

Even though the overall condition of the trade from 1810 was depressed, demand for some articles actually increased, yet it was precisely the production of these which the framework knitters and some hosiers sought to prohibit. These stockings, referred to as 'cut-ups' because they were cut out of a straight piece of fabric and then seamed, were considered by the majority of people in the trade to be spurious, fraudulent work. Although as a moving spirit behind the framework knitters' petition Gravener Henson opposed the production of cut-ups, he later acknowledged that they originated as a response to the change in fashion by which stockings came to be worn as underwear, a trend which gradually increased.[6] The article was not shaped like the full-fashioned hose, neither did it have a selvedge which, in the fashioned stocking, prevented the fabric unravelling should the seam give way. The fundamental difference, however, was the low degree of skill required in its production, while it was also possible to make several straight hose pieces at once. This was because fashioned or 'wrought' hose was produced on narrow frames, wide frames being used to make coarser low quality hose. Furthermore, the larger pieces of knitted fabric made on the wide frames could be cut up and made into socks, gloves, shirts, drawers, and pantaloons as well as stockings.[7]

It was partly with the intention of banning the production of cut-ups that in 1812 the framework knitters of Nottingham petitioned the government to introduce a bill 'for preventing frauds and abuses in the framework knitting manufacture and in the payment of persons employed therein.' The Nottingham hosiers, who up until the House of Commons granted permission for the Bill's introduction had refrained from taking action, applied to give evidence, and when they did so divided themselves in a predictable manner;

hosiery manufacturers producing fashioned hosiery aligned themselves with framework knitters in support of the Bill, while those
making inferior goods opposed legislation. After a debate in the
Commons the clause to prohibit cut-ups was deleted, and the Lords
rejected the Bill. Peace did not bring any solution to the problems
of either the silk or cotton hosiery branches. The trade continued to
be depressed, unemployment and underemployment continued, and
the wages of framework knitters were reduced. A number of cotton
hosiery manufacturers again petitioned Parliament to prevent cut-
ups which, they argued, were the cause of the depression. The reply
to the petitioners expressed the government's view that it could not
countenance measures whose effect might be to increase the success
of foreign competitors.[8] After 1815 although the cessation of hostilities had removed trading uncertainties French and German markets
continued to be protected by heavy import duties and high transport
costs, and aided by these conditions the cotton hosiery producers of
Saxony succeeded in extending their trade beyond the home market
and, to the loss of Nottingham manufacturers, secured the major
share in the rapidly growing American market. By 1844 Saxon
hosiery exports to that country amounted to one and a half million
dozen pairs, compared with less than half a million from England.[9]
British hosiery exports stagnated. (See Table II.)

Given the consensus of opinion among hosiery manufacturers that
domestic demand fluctuated inversely with the price of provisions,[10]
and given the comparative failure of exporters to expand sales
rapidly in the face of competition from Saxony, it follows that real
incomes were not rising sufficiently to bolster a demand for knitted
products which were too highly priced. Although population increased, the slowly rising standard of living of some sections of
society did not encourage consumers to spend more on stockings.
Even so, the popular introduction and sale of fancy goods in the
late eighteenth century followed by the commercial successes of
cheap cut-up hosiery in the first decade of the nineteenth century,
suggests the existence of a relatively elastic demand for hosiery
which, until 1850, British hosiers failed to tap. It illustrates that
even in a period of dampened consumer demand if ingenuity could
create fashion or if productivity could be raised and prices lowered,
markets could be found. Reporting on evidence taken in 1819 in
connection with the investigation of the framework knitters' complaints concerning cut-ups, the Select Committee stated that as a
result of the adoption of cut-up articles in the cotton glove trade
(centred mainly in Nottingham and Bulwell) the cost per dozen
shipped to North American markets had been halved and exports,
as a result. had increased.[11] In 1833 Felkin stated that cut-up hosiery

TABLE II

An Account, showing the Quantities (so far as the same can be given) and the Declared Value of Hosiery Goods Exported from the United Kingdom, in the Years 1814, 1815 and 1816, and in the Ten Years from 1834 to 1843 inclusive, distinguishing each Year.

British Manufactured Hosiery Goods Exported from the United Kingdom

Year	Cotton Hosiery			Linen or Thread Hosiery			Silk Hosiery			Woollen or Worsted Hosiery			Total Declared Value of British Hosiery of all Sorts, Exported
	Stockings		All other Sorts	Stockings		All other Sorts	Stockings		All other Sorts	Stockings		All other Sorts	
	Quantity Doz. Pairs	Value £	Value £	Quantity Doz. Pairs	Value £	Value £	Quantity Doz. Pairs	Value £	Value £	Quantity Doz. Pairs	Value £	Value £	£
1814	311,705	530,779	49,748	5	11	[2]	53,353	200,776		100,630	123,890	234,554	1,139,758
1815	426,071	603,062	37,674	323	518	—	71,414	239,307		205,771	250,423	182,657	1,313,643
1816	391,042	515,454	33,477	158	256	[3]	45,009	187,301		122,133	139,102	139,076	1,014,666
Annual average of period	376,273	549,765	40,299	162	262	[3]	56,592	209,128		142,845	171,138	185,429	1,156,022
1834	399,885	168,583	11,161	85	93	166	24,618	51,734	23,891	173,063	92,286	22,932	370,846
1835	367,589	172,095	9,053	—	—	983	29,478	49,330	56,496	207,014	94,447	44,725	427,129
1836	440,893	198,809	9,223	506	492	1,468	56,185	91,102	47,101	163,182	95,044	59,897	503,136
1837	295,857	141,014	7,551	229	267	1,204	32,209	61,489	26,547	74,947	42,165	36,803	317,040
1838	498,591	202,298	11,512	2	3	1,970	28,036	51,643	74,271	109,759	61,656	59,001	462,354
1839	537,046	218,678	16,351	—	—	453	24,883	48,269	127,025	175,023	92,151	68,830	571,766
1840	460,522	177,743	21,661	—	—	779	25,366	48,897	33,733	96,946	51,133	57,970	391,916
1841	426,164	156,037	12,923	52	47	2,172	26,487	38,272	45,508	135,909	64,490	62,644	382,046
1842	308,331	114,107	22,314	—	—	1,085	17,984	29,764	37,300	137,062	65,050	58,502	328,169
1843	317,691	108,152	31,975	—	—	959	14,423	24,704	63,405	147,507	68,784	51,697	349,676
Annual average of period	405,257	165,752	15,372	87	90	1,124	27,962	49,520	53,528	142,041	72,721	52,301	410,408

Source: *Report of the Royal Commission into the Condition of the Framework Knitters, XV (609), p. 83.*

exports were expanding owing to an improvement in the manner of making this type of article. He was referring to the growing practice whereby three frames were employed, each making a separate part of the knitted garment, a method which improved the fashion of the cut-up stocking. This division of labour also brought about a reduction in the cost of shirts by making it possible to work the body of the shirt separately from the sleeves, which were sewn later.[12] By 1844 slightly more than one-third of the total number of frames in Nottingham and Sneinton were making cotton gloves on wide frames and about half that number made drawers, shirts, and caps on similar frames. The remainder were divided between the production of wrought fashioned stockings and silk hosiery.[13]

Between 1812 and 1844 the number of frames in the industry rose from 29,590 to 48,482, one-half that number making plain cotton hosiery. In Nottingham and Radford the figures were 2,950 in 1812 and 4,265 in 1844; but in the cotton branch nearly 60 per cent. of the total number of frames making cotton hosiery in the east midlands were wide frames.[14] William Felkin, a local businessman who wrote extensively describing the development of the town's staple industries, estimated that each narrow cotton frame could produce about forty dozen hose annually compared with three hundred dozen on a wide frame, whereas narrow worsted frames each produced seventy-five dozen, wide worsted, one hundred and fifty dozen, and silk, thirty dozen.[15] In the light of these developments and judging from the fragmentary evidence that exists relating to the course of prices and output we must conclude that supply outpaced demand, although the fall in the prices of hosiery was also influenced by falling yarn prices and reductions in wage rates. (See Figure I.)

In his explanation of the condition of the hosiery trade during this period Professor Wells has argued that demand was stagnant. But Felkin estimated that between 1812 and 1833 the output of cotton hosiery increased by 50 per cent. to 2,380,000 dozen and reached 2,872,000 dozen in 1844, rough estimates which suggest a moderate expansion in the demand for cotton hosiery. Nevertheless, even if demand did not remain stable it persisted well below the level necessary to employ fully the increasing number of frames in the industry, for Felkin claimed that from 1812 to 1844 between one-quarter and one-third of all frames lay idle.[16] By the thirties, when the value of cotton hosiery exports was at a level one-third below that of average wartime levels, hosiers were experiencing pressure on profit margins.[17] It is true that yarn prices had fallen by about two-thirds, but wages rates had been reduced by only one-third. Meanwhile, German producers were penetrating Continental and American markets. Sluggish domestic demand might help to explain

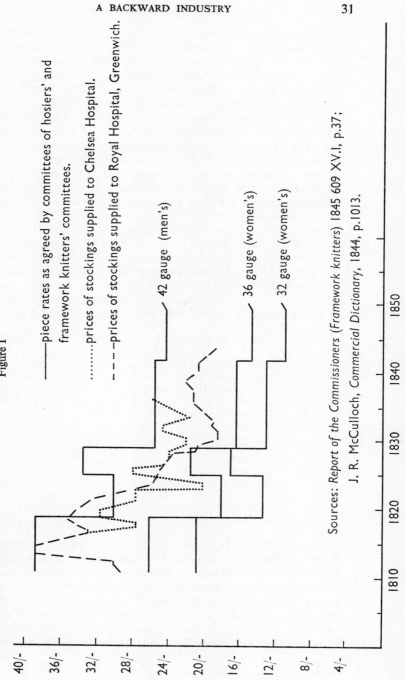

Piece rates as agreed by hosiers' and framework knitters' committees.
Prices of stockings supplied to Chelsea Hospital.
Prices of stockings supplied to Royal Hospital, Greenwich.
Sources: *Report of the Commissioners (Framework Knitters)* 1845, 609 XV, I, p. 37; J. R. McCulloch, *Commercial Dictionary*, 1844, p. 1013.

Figure I

——— piece rates as agreed by committees of hosiers' and framework knitters' committees.

·········· prices of stockings supplied to Chelsea Hospital.

— — — prices of stockings supplied to Royal Hospital, Greenwich.

42 gauge (men's)

36 gauge (women's)

32 gauge (women's)

Sources: *Report of the Commissioners (Framework knitters)* 1845 609 XV.I, p.37;
J. R. McCulloch, *Commercial Dictionary*, 1844, p.1013.

the absence of important technical changes (although the depression in the latter half of the eighteenth century had seen impressive technical developments take place); but in view of the superior performance of German producers in markets which had formerly been dominated by Nottingham hosiers, factors determining supply conditions in the industry warrant closer examination.

On the supply side, several factors contributed to render the industry largely unresponsive to market forces, for the critical failure of the trade to become a mechanized factory industry was closely related to the structure and organization of the industry as well as to the conditions of labour supply and the quality of entrepreneurs. The central feature of industrial organization was outwork. Villages within a ten mile radius housed framework knitters who were occasionally self-employed but who more often worked for the town hosiers or for local middlemen. (See Table III.)[18] The yarn was put out to be wound onto bobbins and knitted. The garment was then returned to the warehouse for seaming and finishing before being sold. The organization of trade was flexible, and the functions of hosier and middleman varied greatly. In the early nineteenth century the business of finishing and selling was largely the concern of a few merchant hosiers who could command sufficient capital to

TABLE III: *The Location of Hosiery Frames in Nottinghamshire in 1844.*

Total Number of frames in the U.K.	48,482
Nottingham and Sneinton	3,490
Radford and Hyson Green	775
Basford	518
Carlton	589
Bulwell	606
Sutton-in-Ashfield	1,968
Arnold	1,397
Hucknall	937
Mansfield	821
Kimberley and Brinsley	553

Source: William Felkin, *Extent of the Hosiery Trade and the Condition of Framework Knitters*, (1845,) pp. 14–15.

purchase yarn and finance costly finishing processes. Several of the hosiers owned more than a thousand frames each in addition to workshops and warehouses, but they were not all necessarily employers as well as capitalists. A hosier might be a merchant selling the end product, a capitalist renting frames, an employer supplying raw materials to his own frames in the warehouse, at the workshop, or in the villagers' own homes, or any combination of these. Until roughly 1812 London had been the distribution centre for the hosiery trade, and several of the Nottingham merchant hosiers disposed of their goods through their warehouses in London, the centre of fashion, while some used the services of London commission houses where agents kept them informed of market conditions. Sometime between 1813 and 1833 London lost its dominant position, and Nottingham, which during that time had become the major centre of the cotton hosiery trade, became also the principal hosiery market. This development is partly accounted for by the tendency for the hosiers to deal direct with buyers at their Nottingham warehouses or, in the case of exports, to consign the goods through commission houses.[19]

Outside the town it was unusual for framework knitters to work direct to the hosier's warehouse. The management of labour and capital in the form of frames and materials was often undertaken by a middleman employed by the hosier; however, even though it was the custom for some of the large firms to make an allowance to the middlemen, the latter were allowed complete freedom to negotiate with the journeymen whatever terms they could, while most hosiers regarded the middleman as a contractor to whom no pecuniary obligations were due. In many cases he merely put out materials to be made up and then returned the articles to the warehouse.[20] Sometimes he owned or rented a workshop and, like a master, employed journeymen and apprentices to make up materials which he obtained from yarn merchants or hosiers. In such cases, like the master framework knitter, he demanded various deductions from the journeyman's wages which in the trade were referred to as shop charges. Apart from frame rent, which was paid for the use of frames owned by the bag hosier, these charges included payment for standing space in his workshop and a charge for 'taking in' the hosiery to the warehouse. In the country districts other services were included as shop charges, such as seaming, stitching, or sewing and winding, but more often these tasks were performed by members of the framework knitter's own family, though it was usually the frameknitter's responsibility to pay for these services.[21] (See Table IV.) Similarly, the expenses incurred by the framework knitter in supplying himself with needles, oil, candles, and coals were further items which, when the factory system was later adopted, became recognized as costs of production to be met by the employer and not by the workman. The middleman rarely performed a merchanting function unless he was a bag hosier who, in addition to selling frameknitted goods of other knitters, purchased his own material and sold his own articles to hosiers and shopkeepers. Felkin estimated that in the forties up to 25 per cent. of the total number of frames which were not owned by hosiers belonged to bag hosiers who dominated

TABLE IV: *Examples of Shop Charges in the Hosiery Trade.*

Name	Location	Branch	Frame Rent		Seaming		Standing		Taking		Winding		Total	
			s.	d.	s.	d.	s.	d.	s.	d.	s.	d.	s.	d.
John Geary	Nottingham	Cotton glove	2	0			0	3	1	0	1	0	4	3
Thomas Marston	Nottingham	Silk glove	1	0			0	3					1	3
John Crew	Nottingham	Cut-ups etc.	1	9			0	3			1	0	3	0
Edward Hallam	Bulwell	Wrought hose	1	0	1	0	0	3	0	6			2	9
David Fox	Ruddington	Selvedge heel	1	9	3	9½	0	3	0	9	0	9	7	3½
John Wilson	Ruddington	Cap	1	6	2	3½	0	2	0	9	0	6	5	2½
Samuel Winters	Carlton	Wrought hose	1	0	1	3			0	3			2	6
Joseph Granger	Arnold	Wrought hose	1	0					0	4			1	4
Henry Krause	Ison Green	Cut-ups etc.	1	9			0	6	1	0	1	0	4	3
William Pickard	Sutton-in-Ashfield	Cut-ups etc.	2	0			0	3			0	7½	2	10½

Source: *Report on the Condition of Framework Knitters* 1845 (609) XV 1. p. 1006–7.

the economic life of such villages as Sutton-in-Ashfield, Arnold, Bulwell, Calverton, Woodborough, Ruddington, and Mansfield.[22]

A characteristic feature of the trade's organization was the frame rent, a sum which was customarily paid to the frame owner by the framework knitter and which was an exaction over and above the shop and standing charges. A dwindling number of knitters were frame owners, but the difficulty in obtaining supplies of raw materials made their livelihoods uncertain. With frames costing between £15 and £20 during the early years of the century, and prices of second-hand machines falling thereafter to £7 in the mid-twenties and £4 in the thirties, it was just possible for a framework knitter to save enough to own a frame, but there was often little economic advantage to be gained from frame ownership. During a depression it was in the interest of hosiers to keep their own frames supplied with work to ensure rent. To supply material to an independent framework knitter in slack periods was to encourage unwelcome competition for it was well known that in hard times he was only too willing to work at a reduced rate on the literal reckoning that half a loaf was better than no bread.[23] Thus by the beginning of the nineteenth century the numbers of independent framework knitters had declined and become a small minority.

Dominating the structure of the hosiery industry during the first half of the nineteenth century were a number of long-established large firms. The leaders in Nottingham were William Hayne & Co., Brocksopp & Parker, J. & T. Watson, H. & J. Cox & Co., Nelson & Co. and A. & J. Hadden. Among the largest were Messrs. Heard & Hurst and Hannay & Co., which together employed five thousand frames in 1833;[24] I. & R. Morley was another important firm of hosiery manufacturers which in 1844 was reckoned their equal and which by 1856 was employing more than twenty-seven hundred frames.[25] Other large firms which employed framework knitters in the Nottingham district were Thomas Carver (employing between seven hundred and a thousand frames in 1856), James Roger Allen of Nottingham, Brettle & Co., and Ward & Co., of Belper, and Barker & Adams.[26] There were also several medium-sized firms which generally followed the policies of the larger firms, while the rest of the industry consisted of small hosiery manufacturers or bag hosiers, most of whom resided in the villages. At Arnold two bag hosiers each employed about one hundred frames, but the employer of less than fifty seems to have been more common.[27]

The principals of the large and old-established firms, who were often referred to as the 'respectable gentlemen hosiers', met occasionally to discuss piece rates, but there is no evidence to suggest that they entered agreements concerning hosiery prices. In 1844 a middleman who had worked with I. & R. Morley for twenty-seven years, stated quite categorically that men of small capital were always the first to reduce wages. 'Large manufacturers', he said, 'do not like altering prices. There are others besides Morley who pay the same price year after year.'[28] That there was a difference between the pricing policies of large and small producers is evident from the manner in which the Hosiery Manufacturers' Association, which included the larger firms, sometimes supported workmen's combinations in their attempts to prevent reductions. Thomas Carver maintained that workmen in the trade relied upon Morley and himself 'to keep the market steady' by adhering to the 'price list' schedule of wage rates negotiated from time to time by hosiers and framework knitters' representatives. In 1820 leading hosiers contributed towards the stockingers' relief fund to support a strike against other producers who had reduced wages below the statement of wage rates agreed in 1819.[29] But even the agreements between the larger and medium-sized firms sometimes proved weak, and in 1819 and 1824 competition forced the leading hosiers to adopt the reductions in wage rates which were initially effected by the small firms.[30] Stimulated by the small price-cutting bag hosiers faced with a sluggish demand, competition led to an alteration in the structure of the industry, a change which was to their own detriment, for their numbers declined.

Between 1814 and 1844 the number of firms in Nottingham itself declined from one hundred and twenty-seven to fifty-six, while the number of frames increased from 2,600 to 3,490 and it was the large long-established businesses which proved most durable. This change in the industry's structure was accompanied by a shift in its social structure, for by the forties the industry contained a high proportion of hereditary entrepreneurs. Dr. Erickson has pointed out that in the 1840's all but six Nottingham manufacturers of hosiery (i.e. excluding bag hosiers and middlemen) came from the upper reaches of the social scale, a fact which indicates the presence of a closed recruitment among Nottingham hosiers. Thus during the first half of the century a superior social standing and a larger scale of operation marked out the Nottingham hosiers as a distinct group. The majority of the most prosperous were educated at Standard Hill, a local nonconformist academy, many married into respected burgess families, and the heads of the largest firms built homes in the Park, the fashionable residential district of the town.[31] Beginning in the fifties much of the capital for the factory industry was to come from this class, but the role of the merchant hosiers in the transition to factory production will be considered later.[32]

The report of the Royal Commissioners in 1845 into the Condition of Framework Knitters reveals the baleful effects of a technically backward industry upon those employed in it. Since 1810 demand had expanded slowly whilst productive capacity had increased. This development can be attributed partly to the existence of frame rent, for its attraction in providing a steady source of income had encouraged over-investment in the trade. In recognition of this fact in 1809 a number of larger hosiers led by William Hayne had tried to bring about a reduction in frame rents, but without success;[33] in 1812 members of a Select Committee were informed that it was

> customary for Gentlemen's servants who had saved £150 or £200 to pay a premium of £5 5s. 0d., or £10 10s. 0d., to learn the art and then set up after six months with 10 to 12 frames . . .[34]

Frame clubs organized by framework knitters themselves also contributed to over-capitalization in the industry. The actual amount of frame rent customarily charged between 1815 and 1849 was 9d. per week for a narrow frame below a gauge of thirty inches, and for a narrow frame between thirty and fifty inches 1s. was the usual weekly charge. During this period income from frame rent varied between 5 and 8 per cent. return on capital.[35]

The condition of framework knitters depended to a large extent upon whether they worked direct to a warehouse, through a middleman, or through a bagman. Absolem Barnett, Clerk to the Board of Guardians of the Nottingham Union and knowledgeable on the subject of social conditions, maintained unhesitatingly that, probably because they were able to give out orders for stock, men working to large manufacturers were better treated than most, and he quoted Hurst Sons & Ashwell and I. & R. Morley as model employers.[36] When trade was depressed Heard and Hurst gave out work to men, partly in order to obtain frame rent and partly to keep the frames in repair, but at times of severe depression it was their practice to suspend work rather than to stint.[37] William Hannay stated that he never took frame rent when frames were wholly unemployed,[38] while at the warehouse of I. & R. Morley a standing order prevented the distribution of materials for less than a full week's work, and rents were waived when frames lay idle.[39] Although the larger hosiers seem to have suspended frame rent when trade was bad, the bag hosiers' practice of 'spreading' was a major grievance among framework knitters in years of slack trade. By this practice a middleman, who might have up to twenty warehouse frames and perhaps ten of his own, would divide the materials distributed at the warehouse amongst all the frames, though at the same time maintaining the

level of charges. In this manner many bag hosiers insured their income from depression, especially in the villages surrounding
Nottingham where bagmen and middlemen handled about half the
high quality and three-quarters of the cheap work.[40] It was this
practice which helps to explain the depths of poverty into which so
many of the village framework knitters sank. Reasonably full employment was least likely to be experienced by framework knitters
working independent frames which were, in effect, marginal
resources utilized only in periods of very brisk trade. Most were
located in the villages where framework knitters, dependent on
middlemen for yarn and for the delivery of articles to the hosiers,
were often ignorant of piece rates paid for work at the warehouse.

'If I am a rogue and working to two or three different houses
which are giving prices,' explained a middleman master framework knitter, 'I shall tell them the lowest price and put the
difference in my pocket.'[41]

By contrast, all framework knitters making hosiery for James Roger
Allen were occasionally invited to drink tea with him and the master
framework knitters at the warehouse. On one occasion a master was
discovered to have been cheating a journeyman, whereupon Allen
confiscated the master's frames; the culprit subsequently entered the
workhouse.[42]

Besides the practice of spreading work, bag hosiers in the villages
commonly made truck payments. At Sutton-in-Ashfield many bag
hosiers kept grocers', butchers', bakers' shops, or ale houses, and
paid only in kind,[43] and similar situations existed at Bulwell, Calverton, Woodborough, and Arnold. Framework knitter George
Kendall, later to become a prominent member of the Hosiery Board
of Arbitration, observed that in two years he had received in cash
only 16s. 6d., of which 10s. 6d. was given to enable him to pay
interest on pawn tickets.

'When Saturday night came I had to turn out with a certain
quantity of meat and candles, or tobacco and ale or whatever
I had drawn as wages, to dispose of at a serious loss. I used
to take a can of ale to the barber to get shaved with, and a
can of ale to the sweep . . . I was obliged to take a pound of
candles at 7d. and leave it for the newspaper, the price of
which was 4d. I used to take my beef at 7d. per pound and sell
it to the coal woman for 5d., and any bit of sugar or tea or
anything of that kind that my employer did not sell, I used to
get from the grocer living at the bottom of the yard by swop-
ping soap and starch.'[44]

Largely because of the heavy extra charges and truck payments imposed by the bag hosiers, village framework knitters tended to fare

worse than those who lived in the town. It was common, however, for the villagers to raise potatoes on land rented from the farmers, and house rents in the country were considerably lower than those in the town.[45] Nonetheless, between 1815 and 1849 the condition of most hosiery workers in town and village was comparable with that of the handloom weavers in the northern textile manufacturing centres, although for fundamentally dissimilar reasons. For while the handloom weavers of Lancashire and Yorkshire were casualties in a process of technical change from which the industry as a whole subsequently benefited, to a large extent framework knitters were victims of technical backwardness, as their improved condition during the second half of the century showed.

Since the beginning of the century, capitalists and framesmiths had continued to invest in frames for the purpose of securing frame rents, and in 1833 were estimated to own approximately two-fifths of all frames. While capital had flowed into the industry there was to be found no shortage of the complementary productive factor as population grew, a fact of considerable importance in an industry in which it was estimated that between 1833 and 1844 wages accounted for 40 to 48 per cent. of total variable costs, while in the cotton branch labour costs as a proportion of the total were between 40 and 60 per cent. For lack of alternative employment in the outlying villages framework knitters, often with reluctance, encouraged their sons to take up the frames.[46] In 1809, at the age of fourteen, William Felkin had begun to learn how to make stockings; many years later he recalled his mother's distress,

> my mother directed me if possible to avoid ever learning to gain my bread in a stocking frame. She knew that stocking making had laid in my father's constitution the seeds of disease and of premature death.[47]

The work was often physically onerous and poorly remunerated, and the principal source of labour was from the homes of the impoverished framework knitters who first made their children perform simple auxiliary tasks until they reached the age of nine or ten after which they might learn to work a frame.

Notwithstanding a growing tendency to avoid apprenticeship regulations, especially from the early years of the century, this continued to be the normal channel of entry into the trade for many people. The justification for such a prolonged period being devoted to training as a framework knitter was open to serious question, as Felkin's experience suggests. After three months tuition at the age of fourteen he had been able to make one pair of womens' narrow hose in a day; after another three months he had doubled his rate of output and by the end of nine months he could produce three pairs daily, a weekly average of a dozen pairs.[48] Even after the repeal of the Elizabethan laws in 1814 a period of up to seven years apprenticeship was not uncommon. In 1832, for example, at the age of eleven John Parker, a Nottingham framework knitter, was apprenticed for seven years; but by 1842, according to Parker, except for the parish apprentices bound by Poor Law authorities in the villages, few were serving apprenticeships in the hosiery trade.[49] One reason which was sometimes given for apprenticing children in the trade was the parents' inability to afford the premiums required by masters in better paid crafts—for example in the lace industry; but the absence of alternative opportunities for employment, especially in the villages, and the need to supplement the incomes of father and mother to support a family are factors which largely explain the continued drift of labour into an industry which was already overcrowded.[50] 'It is impossible for a man having several children to exist without sending them to work at an early age,' said Jonathan Barber, a framework knitting father of six who became a leading Nottingham Chartist.[51]

Variations in the earnings of the framework knitters depended not only upon cyclical and seasonal fluctuations in employment, the type of employer for whom he worked, and his locality but wages were influenced fundamentally also by the class of goods made by the framework knitter, by the degree of skill needed, and by the popularity of the different articles. The production of fully-fashioned stockings made on the narrow gauge frames required manual control to fashion the stocking to the shape of the leg. Thus, compared with the manufacture of cut-ups on the wide frames which were shaped by stretching the stocking on a board, the making of wrought hose was a relatively skilled branch. The demand for wrought fashioned hose, however, was declining during the first half of the century, while the number of wide frames making cut-ups increased.[52] Some of the most highly skilled framework knitters were to be found making silk gloves and hose. Only such workmen would be entrusted with this expensive material whose fineness so strained the eyes of the framework knitters that many were obliged, after several years work in that branch, to turn to the coarser sections of the cotton trade. The manufacture of silk was located chiefly in the town, and in 1844 Nottingham was the most important centre of silk as well as cotton hosiery production, but earnings in the silk branch did not greatly exceed those of other branches. Another factor determining earnings was the regularity of employment.[53] Framework knitters making drawers and shirts could usually count on fewer days of idleness than those knitting gloves, which were essentially fashionable articles and subject to very marked fluctuations due to changes in taste as well as to the cyclical fluctuations which affected all branches.

Within the branches, earnings varied according to the pace at which the framework knitter was able — or chose — to work. As frames increased in width so the physical strength required to work them also grew. 'It tries the chest and the stomach from the constant stretching of the arms and heavy labour', said one wide frame worker.[54] The operation of narrow frames needed little strength, but the making of fashioned articles required more, although moderate, skill. After the age of forty, according to hosier John Rogers, a decline in physical energy and deterioration in eyesight commonly led to a decline in the framework knitter's ability to compete, except with boys of twelve or fourteen.[55] Ten more years saw many framework knitters reduced to the manufacture of coarse work although they could not handle the widest frames and their rate of production was relatively slow. Weekly earnings, obviously, were affected by the time devoted to labour and, like outworkers in other industries, framework knitters habitually worked irregular hours. In 1842 one master framework knitter remarked, 'They very seldom work on Monday; some, but few, not on Tuesday. On Friday they work late, frequently all night.'[56] This statement was corroborated by other hosiers, but it was also stated that many men worked steadily, when the state of trade allowed, from Monday until Saturday.

With so many variable factors influencing framework knitters' earnings it is misleading to consider their incomes in terms of averages, but without generalization it is impossible to compare their condition with other sections of the population. Until 1810, framework knitters earned about 14s. or 15s. weekly, an amount which was considered adequate to bring the workman a moderately comfortable existence in comparison with other sections of the working classes.[57] The length of the average working day was twelve or thirteen hours, but most framework knitters put aside their frames for three days each week. By 1819 the average weekly earnings had fallen to about 7s., but to earn this sum framework knitters commonly worked more than fifteen hours daily.[58] The year 1819, however, was one of cyclical depression and earnings during that time were exceptionally low. Henceforward, until 1850, framework knitters' earnings fluctuated between the levels of 1810 and 1819, but due to underemployment and unemployment, as well as to falling wage rates which were not offset by the increased productivity of the wide frames, average earnings remained nearer to the low levels of 1819. In 1833 Felkin maintained that since 1800 wages had fallen by about 30 per cent. His estimates of net weekly earnings in 1833 were between 3s. and 6s. for workmen in the worsted branch,

E

between 4s. and 7s. in the cotton branch, and from 6s. to 12s. for framework knitters making silk hosiery. Workmen in the cut-up branches, he thought, earned between 10s. and 21s. weekly. Factory commissioner Alfred Power considered that these estimates which were based upon Felkin's enquiries made in 1831, were not quite accurate for 1833. In Power's view average clear earnings of framework knitters making cotton lace on narrow frames amounted to 6s.; on wide frames it was between 9s. and 12s. . These estimates applied to men working fifteen hours daily and fifteen hours spread over Saturday and Monday. The makers of silk hose working fourteen hours daily on four days weekly, he stated, earned between 9s. and 13s. .[59] Elsewhere, Felkin lumped all framework knitters together and concluded that in 1833 their average wage was about 9s.; three years later, when the economy was booming, the figure had risen to 11s. 6d. . By 1845 average earnings had fallen to about 7s. for sixty hours labour.[60] This was partly the result of a reduction in the agreed list of piece rates that took place in 1842, and it is also partly explained by an increase in unemployment during those years. At this lower level of rates the range of earnings within the different branches of the trade was still striking in 1845.

In assessing the well-being of the framework knitting section of the population, it is important to note that the household was an integrated economic unit in which both wife and children often contributed towards family income. The common custom was for a married man to hire two or more frames, according to the size of the family.[61] One of the frames would be worked by the husband, another by the wife, and others by whichever children might be capable. The younger children were almost invariably employed in winding the cotton or silk for the frames, or in seaming the articles which had been made. Children of both sexes were put to this work often at the ages of six or seven and they frequently worked the same hours as their parents, including the frantic nightwork to complete orders at the end of the week. Their earnings varied between 1s. and 5s. weekly. Some women and girls earned similar wages by 'chevening' or embroidering hosiery, although this work was carried out in the town mainly in groups of between two and twenty under the supervision of mistresses in their homes or workshops. They worked much the same long and irregular hours as the family units and, in the opinion of the Factory Commissioner, R. D. Grainger, the conditions of those who worked as cheveners in small and crowded rooms in the lower parts of the town were worse than those of the winders and seamers in their village homes. The physical condition of outworkers in the hosiery trade was affected by the long hours of work necessary to earn a living wage, and the eye strain which accompanied especially the finest work. Felkin described the physical deterioration of framework knitters:

> they are mentally depressed and too often morally debased. Ill fed, ill lodged, ill clothed, with careworn and anxious countenances, they are a class by themselves and easily distinguishable from most others by their personal appearance.[62]

Even though Nottingham was the home of many of the most highly skilled framework knitters in the silk branch, as well as a large number of wide frame drawers and shirt makers, and although it was generally agreed that, in general, the knitters in the town earned more than those in the villages,[63] the framework knitters were to be found in 'the most obscure and wretched courts and alleys.'[64] 'I can tell a stockinger by his appearance', said a local doctor, 'there is a paleness and a certain degree of emaciation and thinness about them.'[65]

These conditions altered little between 1815 and 1850. Many framework knitting households sent children to workshops and factories to perform simple auxiliary tasks connected with lace manufacture; these tasks were similar to the winding, seaming, mending, and embroidering required in the production of hosiery, and the earnings and conditions of these auxiliary workers were much the same. In his report on children's employment in 1842, R. D. Grainger expressed the view that the seamers and cheveners of stockings and gloves, and the menders, drawers, pearlers and embroiders of lace were most in need of protection: 'The toil to which these poor children, infants some of them might almost be termed, are subject, is altogether disgraceful in a Christian country.'[66] Adult males in the lace trade, however, in terms both of their working conditions and pay, were a superior section of the community. Although lace makers' earnings fluctuated tremendously between extremely wide limits, most lace makers could earn between one-half and twice as much again as the framework knitters, although in the thirties the incomes of a small number of lace makers using narrow hand frames were much nearer to the sums earned by the majority of hosiery workers. In comparison with other sections of the working classes, an average weekly wage which did not rise above 10s. between 1815 and 1850, and which was for some years nearer to 7s., placed the framework knitters very low on the scale of wage earners, sharing a standard of living comparable with that of the hand loom weavers.[67]

The ability of framework knitters to improve their conditions depended upon the general level of economic activity, the demand for hosiery, and upon success in effective trade union organization.

The Framework Knitters' Company had been deprived of its powers to regulate the industry during the previous century, and in the second decade of the nineteenth century when depression set in, workers found themselves unable to seek redress for their grievances under the Company's protection.[68] Two alternative methods had been adopted. One was to exert direct pressure upon the hosiers through vigorous industrial action; the other was to petition Parliament for the prohibition of cut-ups and the abolition of truck payments. Neither policy brought success in the long run. The smashing of hosiery frames, which was one remarkable feature of the framework knitters' policy of direct industrial action, did not consist of random acts of devastation. The frame-breaking Luddites destroyed only those frames making cut-ups or those belonging to hosiers who were paying below agreed rates. Far from being a band of desperate men, the Nottingham Luddites were members of a secret and intelligently organized body which received the tacit support of some members of the local village populations.[69] Their leaders' identity was never revealed, but it was during this period that framework knitter Gravener Henson emerged as the leader of the framework knitters' combinations. To what extent Henson and the associations he led were implicated in the frame-smashing policy is difficult to determine. The magistrates had little hesitation in asserting that Henson was a key figure in the Luddite campaigns, but there is evidence that Henson exerted a restraining influence on the more extreme elements among the framework knitters.[70] In 1812 after the framework knitters' Bill to prohibit cut-ups had been rejected, Henson, who had been entreated by the members of Parliament for Nottingham to exercise his influence to assuage and moderate popular feeling, urged the formation of trade clubs and combinations.[71] The following year the framework knitters formed themselves into a 'Society for obtaining Parliamentary Relief and the Encouragement of Mechanics in the Improvement of Mechanism' which consisted of a federation of societies each with less than one hundred members.[72] The executive committee was established in Nottingham, while subordinate committees were located in districts in various parts of England.[73]

The society, with its intended employment exchanges or 'houses of call', its central fund for the letting of frames, travel grants for the unemployed, and relief payments to the infirm and aged, seems to have been far removed from the spirit of Luddism. Nevertheless, in 1814 frame-wrecking broke out again and the Nottingham hosiers opened a subscription to support the activities of a secret committee whose purpose was to suppress the Luddites. In the summer of 1814 the framework knitters were prosecuted under the Combination

Act when men in the silk branch were involved in an attempt to raise wages by strike action. At the instigation of the hosiers' secret committee Coldham, the secretary, who was also the Town Clerk, secured the arrest of two men after they had been seized by constables at a Society meeting. Three men were subsequently convicted of 'receiving money for illegal purposes', but they were sentenced only to a month's hard labour because, according to Coldham, it was the first prosecution in Nottingham under the Combination Act. Their slender financial resources strained as a result of the spring strike, the Framework Knitters' Society collapsed.[74] With the breakdown of the vehicle for Henson's peaceful policy the extremist faction once more assumed the initiative, although Henson launched his own counter attack upon the hosiers by successfully instituting proceedings against two hosiers for truck payments in 1816.[75] The same year frame-breaking was resumed, but the objects of the new outbreak were chiefly lace rather than stocking frames.[76] Although in view of the hostility of the authorities to workmen's combinations and the refusal of the hosiers to negotiate with the framework knitters' bodies the Luddite policy of 'sabotage and direct action' may be understood, it is difficult to concur with the claim that it was effective in improving the workmen's position.[77] According to Felkin, who was working in the trade at that time, while frames were being smashed some hosiers raised wages by up to 25 per cent., but as soon as the machine-breakers laid aside their hammers the hosiers reimposed the reductions.[78] The hosiers whose frames were attacked were those paying lower rates and producing cut-up goods, but it should be noted that framework knitters working these frames could earn more than the men making fashioned stockings.[79]

Except as a very short-term measure Luddism was foredoomed to failure. Apart from the clear impossibility of sustaining a policy of intimidation in the face of the authorities, owing to the employment of lesser skills in the production of cut-ups the practice of 'colting', or unregulated trade apprenticeships, offered easy ingress for a growing number of people as the market for cheap hosiery developed.[80] In attacking the cut-up trade the Luddites, like the petitioners, were thereby seeking to cripple the industry's growing points. Even if the Luddites had succeeded in forcing cut-ups off the market, it is unlikely that the demand for fashioned hosiery would have grown enough to generate sufficient employment to absorb all framework knitters. So long as entry into the industry remained easy and so long as alternative opportunities for a growing east midland population remained unattractive, neither Luddism nor peaceful industrial pressure through combination could be expected to advance the workers' long run interests. How far the hosiers' attitude to the adoption of machinery was affected by Luddite activity is open to speculation.[81] The total effect on local industry was small, though the smashing of lace machines in 1816 was immediately followed by the departure from Nottingham of by far the largest manufacturer who removed men and machinery to a peaceful Devonshire village.[82] This was the last of the Luddite episodes to occur in the midlands, their cessation following the hanging of six men and the transportation of three others in 1817. Looking back upon this era of violence half a century later Felkin wrote,

> The broad substratum of the whole of this wretched heap of wrongdoing was undoubtedly the hunger and misery into which the large portion of the fifty thousand framework knitters and their families were fallen, and from which they never fully emerged for the following forty years.[83]

An explanation for the conditions which bred misunderstanding and violence is not to be found in exploitation of framework knitters by the hosier class, but in the change in fashions which resulted in a reduced demand for the skills required in making fancy hosiery— unaccompanied by a compensatory rise in the demand for the makers of cheap plain stockings. Those framework knitters who owing to this change in the composition of the industry's output became redundant, together with the large numbers of workmen who found themselves underemployed, were the victims of circumstances. But in this they differed from their employers only in so far as they were poorly equipped to cope with the effects of the sudden and large scale changes in the pattern of consumption and the resulting adjustments that the market required. The future of the industry depended upon the ability of its members to hasten technical progress and to reduce the number of men employed in making stockings, but the rate of population growth and the immobility of village labour complicated this process. Few would claim that the declining profits of a wealthy hosier occasioned discomfort comparable with the hardship of the unemployed framework knitter; but to explain the poverty of framework knitters in terms of class conflict or of a system of competition[84] (which in the lace industry, for example, was accompanied by rising wages) leads to oversimplification of the complex economic and social changes which took place simultaneously.

Despite setbacks, and although Gravener Henson was in prison in 1817, leading framework knitters made renewed attempts to halt the men's declining fortunes. Following the Leicester framework knitters' modest success the same year, men in the cotton branch agitated for advances. At a meeting in September, 1817 several parish overseers met in Nottingham and affirmed their belief in 'the inalienable Right of every honest and industrious Man to live by his Labour.' A strike involving between eight and nine thousand people followed, but it gradually petered out.[85] By October the men were contemplating cooperative production, an idea which materialized early in 1818. In the hope of cutting out the bag hosiers and middle-men they established a Hosiery and Lace Mart in Clumber Street to enable independent framework knitters and small manufacturers to sell goods on better terms at clearly stated Mart rates.[86] To support an appeal for public subscriptions the men claimed that the Mart would benefit the large hosiers by making available a wide range of articles, and by providing a source of supply when their orders exceeded the hosiers' manufacturing capacity. For each frame producing for the Mart the levy was 1d. per week, and three months before the opening eight hundred frames had been registered. They were owned, for the most part, by small societies which were formed especially for the purpose of purchasing cotton and employing independent frames. The societies, consisting of framework knitters from the different branches, held their meetings at public houses, one being the Bell Inn, the headquarters of The Central Commercial Society which was one of twenty such societies in Nottinghamshire and Derbyshire. Shares in the Society to the value of £5 were purchased by weekly contributions of a shilling, the intention being that when sufficient capital accumulated a ballot for frames would be held, each share commanding one ticket in the ballot. The Society was ruled by a committee of five which appointed both a salesman and a secretary.[87] Despite high hopes, by the spring of 1818 the Mart had proved a failure. The value of goods sold each week had been less than £1,000, and as enthusiasm had ebbed subscriptions had fallen off and the Mart had run into debt.[88]

After this failure, and following Henson's release from prison in 1819, deterioration in trade and the threat of further reductions led to a plan for strike action. In that year, on the same day as the hosiers announced reductions, fourteen thousand men in Nottinghamshire, Derbyshire, and Leicestershire struck for the statement agreed by the hosiers at Leicester in 1817. In Nottingham the strike lasted nine weeks during which time framework knitters and their families endured extreme deprivation. Carrying placards inscribed with pathetic appeals, they claimed that although working over sixteen hours a day they earned less than seven shillings in a week, while some had been near to starvation for eighteen months:

> Though we have substituted meal and water or potatoes and salt for . . . more wholesome food . . . we have repeatedly retired after a hard day's labour (to put) our children supperless to bed, to stifle the cries of hunger.[89]

The hosiers met, and two-thirds of their number agreed to a revised statement of prices which contained a slight increase. This agreement was made on the understanding that parish authorities refrained from employing the unemployed in making hosiery, that 'unfair competition from irregular and truck masters should cease', and that stocking makers did not repeat their experiments in co-operative production.[90] Division in the trade was manifest in the support given to the workmen's campaign by some of the gentlemen hosiers, while there was also widespread connivance at the new statement.[91] The initial success of the Framework Knitters' Society in coordinating action in the localities, which had made the strike a partial success, inspired the formation of what was intended to be a permanent union. The initiative came from the largest branch, the two needle (narrow-frame) cotton branch of the three midland counties. Workers in the silk branch were urged to form a similar union and this was launched with the aid of contributions from eminent local citizens of the district. These bodies, it was hoped, would be able to maintain the new statement and put an end to strikes for all time. However, while unemployment existed and in the absence of financial resources, the task of enforcing higher rates of payment proved to be impossible; to the dismay of the Framework Knitters' Committee much work was taken out below statement price. One culprit was met at the warehouse by brother knitters and seated backwards on an ass, 'they decorated his hat with a label descriptive of his good qualities' and led him through the streets. The hosier who had offered reduced rates was dragged in effigy through the town behind a horse and cart, followed by a framework knitter in a blue smock who dealt to the straw villain punishment with a cat-o'-nine-tails.[92]

The eventual failure of 1819 led to attempts the following year to improve the financial structure of framework knitters' combinations, and, prompted by an experiment at Leicester, the stockingers instituted a friendly society to build up a fund for the relief of unemployed framework knitters and for those unable to find work at statement prices.[93] The fund was organized by a union embracing all framework knitters in the three midland counties, each county being divided into districts with a committee of seven for each district. Every person subscribed 3d. or 6d. weekly, depending upon age, and no allowance was permitted from the fund until three month's subscription had been paid. Arrangements were made for the names of hosiers paying less than statement prices to be circulated among the committees. The rules were sanctioned by the larger hosiers who themselves formed a committee to cooperate with the men.[94] Heard & Hurst, I. & R. Morley, Barker & Adams, and Ward,

Brettle & Ward, were among firms donating sums, which they promised should be annual, to promote the aims of the society. The body of trustees formed to manage the fund included such prominent citizens as Samuel Fox and John Gill from the Friends' Meeting House, the Reverend Richard Alliott and the Reverend Jarman, and a leading Radical, Thomas Wakefield, cotton merchant and later Mayor of Nottingham.[95] In the stagnant condition of trade, however, the workmen failed to continue their contributions, and although the parish vestry at Arnold subscribed £80 to the Framework Knitters' Friendly Society the trustees were forced to suspend operations.[96]

In 1821 leading hosiers again urged stockingers to initiate action for the enforcement of the 1819 statement, and the strike which followed was even greater in its scope than that of 1819. Again the sources of support were similar.[97] For on both occasions public appeals by the framework knitters met with a generous response from several gentlemen of the town and county of Nottingham. Contributions were received from local friendly and benefit societies and from the chapels, and sermons expressing sympathy were preached from the pulpits. A sum of £800 was in this way donated to support the framework knitters.[98] Where it was practicable, some of the gentry and farmers set framework knitters to work on their land, and the public subscription financed the employment of men in clearing and levelling land. Some of the parish authorities resolved to provide the unemployed with manual labour unrelated to the stocking frame. To supplement the public subscription the union levied working stockingers 1s. per week for two months, after which the charge fell to 6d.. The Framework Knitters' Committee, remembering the violence of the Luddites, requested those hosiers who refused to give statement price to collect their frames immediately from the framework knitters' homes and workshops; the Committee also issued specific instructions to workmen not to damage frames.[99]

In view of the difficulties of combined action in the hosiery trade, due especially to the dispersion of workers and the employment by hosiers of men in various localities, the strike of 1821 was well organized; but it was badly timed, for February and March, months when trade was usually slack, also brought a reduction in alternative employment opportunities in the building trades and in agriculture. For two months the hosiery trade was paralysed.[100] In the villages, families yoked themselves to wagons and tramped to Nottingham to deposit their frames at the warehouses and to make a desperate attempt to earn a few shillings by selling coal, gravel, and lime.[101] The Framework Knitters' Committee was resolute in its decision to gain its objective and one of its spokesmen told the press, 'We will suffer all the horrors of famine rather than work at the late prices.'[102] After two months the wage-cutting hosiers relented, but the sequel was the apprehension of Benjamin Taylor and three other committee members of the Nottingham branch of the union. All four were charged with offences against the Combination Acts, but when no adequate evidence was forthcoming the men were acquitted. However, the county magistrates warned the men that similar activity in the future would lead to their imprisonment.[103] Shortly afterwards, Taylor and the other three were arraigned again; they were accused of the same offence on identical evidence and before the same magistrates. Each was convicted and sentenced to three months' imprisonment, but at this stage the framework knitters asked the advice of Gravener Henson who told the men to appeal against the conviction. This they did, the costs being borne by subscriptions from framework knitters of the silk branch and from several gentlemen; as Henson had forecast the conviction was quashed.[104]

On his acquittal Benjamin Taylor was vigorous in reconstructing the union in order to defend the gains of 1821.[105] The temporary success was due to a brisk American demand, and Taylor realized that when this disappeared and stocks began to accumulate then price cutting would be resumed.[106] He reproached framework knitters for their lukewarm financial support of previous unions and proceeded to form a fresh committee under his own leadership to organize the stocking makers.[107] Following the request of several leading hosiers in the cotton branches in 1823, he led the stockingers of Derbyshire and Nottinghamshire in a strike to outlaw payment on account and to regain adherence to the 1819 statement price.[108] This strike lasted for two weeks, and it proved completely successful in Derbyshire, though eight Nottingham hosiers refused to submit to the men's demands.[109] Uniformity in price continued to be a vexing problem. After the settlement in 1823, the 'gentlemen hosiers' asked the committee for a guarantee that framework knitters would refuse to accept work at reduced prices. Taylor replied that orderly wage contracts were precisely the aim of the workmen's committee, but he pointed out that the hosiers also had responsibilities:

> Call a meeting of your own body, and three of the most intelligent persons shall attend it on the part of the trade to consider the great claim of abuses which extend to the trade,

a plea which was to be repeated in essence by Mundella, the hosiery manufacturer, in 1860.[110]

Lack of unity on both sides again became evident in 1824. Early in the year reductions had been forced on the men, but some months later, under the dual impetus of improving trade and the repeal of the Combination Acts, Taylor led the Three Counties Framework Knitters' Union in a strike for an upward revision of the current statement. The hosiers were divided over the issue and two statements were published, the higher statement having received the signatures of only fifteen of the larger hosiers; consequently framework knitters returned to work in some confusion.[111] This was the last strike which produced significant gains before the late forties. After the statement of 1811 piece rates had fallen until a new statement was drawn up in 1819. Following further reductions the turnout of 1821 had seen Taylor trying to regain the 1811 statement price. By October, 1825 several cotton hose manufacturers had reduced wages to the level of 1819, and in 1826 deductions followed which together amounted to 33 per cent..[112] The smaller branches, the silk glove, the cotton glove, silk hose, cotton drawers and pantaloons possessed even less power to resist the pressures of market forces and the demand for silk hosiery especially, contracted steadily. Even during the early months of 1825 strikes by the silk branch (financed largely by the proceeds of a concert at the Theatre Royal), and the cotton drawers and pantaloons branch, were failures. The Hosiers' Association, which was formed in 1825 to resist demands for higher wages, continued to press for reductions in 1826 and 1828.[113]

Similar patterns of trade union activity and seasonal and cyclical fluctuations occurred in the thirties and forties. *Ad hoc* societies were formed for specific campaigns when trade was favourable. In the event of success their existence was prolonged in order to defend any ground gained, but the lives of such societies were as temporary as the gains they secured. Subscriptions, if paid at all, were minimal, and sometimes strike appeals to the public were supplementary to levies from working framework knitters. Not until 1860 did Nottingham framework knitters stage another general strike. Meanwhile, they became involved in the wider labour movement and in Chartism.[114] Their only achievement was to persuade the Government to institute a Royal Commission to enquire into the conditions of framework knitters. In 1845 a petition with the signatures of twenty five thousand framework knitters enumerated their sufferings and grievances. Their complaints included low wages, frame rent, truck payments, the non-delivery of tickets showing the piece rates paid by the warehouse, and the importation of foreign hosiery. Showing little understanding of the basic factors which placed them in such wretched conditions, the petitioners expressed themselves in favour of the re-establishment of the old Framework Knitters' Company, with its charter of strict regulations for the conduct of trade. Furthermore, just as in 1812 and 1819 when framework knitters had complained to Parliament about the introduction of cut-up work, so in 1845 complaints were aimed at the growing number of wide frames in the industry which could produce more of the cheaper quality stockings per unit of labour or capital employed. It was stated that the craft of framework knitting was becoming debased through the production of inferior goods. In both instances hosiery workers, and indeed some hosiers, failed to realize that it was because the hosiery industry had lost much of its hold on the luxury market that some hosiers, and especially the price-cutting bagmen, were seeking to supply the needs of lower income groups who could not reasonably be expected to pay higher prices for wrought high quality goods. The introduction of lower grade articles was an effect and not a cause of the decline in the fashioned trade.[115]

The Royal Commission's final report, drawn up by Muggeridge, revealed nothing startling. He isolated what he considered to be the main problems of the trade—overcrowding and overcapitalization. He condemned the charging of frame rent as an anachronistic practice which placed a brake upon change. His recommendations included a diminution in the labour force, an extension of the trade 'by a more judicious appropriation and division of labour whereby the cost of production would be diminished,' and an improvement in design and quality of the industry's products. In effect this was a blueprint for expansion, and indeed widening markets and rising productivity through greater division of labour, technological change, and through the factory system which entailed the abolition of frame rent were the major features of change in the second half of the nineteenth century.

Even as the Report was being published the transformation was beginning to take place. After unsuccessful experiments with steam-powered hosiery frames at Loughborough in 1829, at Arnold in 1838, and at Leicester in 1840, Paget at Loughborough achieved success with an improved version of Brunel's tricoteur in 1844, and further modifications were patented in the fifties.[116] In 1845 a factory of steam-powered frames was established at New Radford, although this was another failure.[117] Nevertheless, these developments heralded the long postponed technical revolution in the hosiery trade, for the fifties were to produce innovators who transformed the trade. The erection in 1851 of Hine & Mundella's large five-storeyed factory containing the new circular frames driven by steam, marked a turning point in the history of the town's development almost as important as the economic watershed created several decades before when lace net was first successfully produced on a machine.

References

[1] T. S. Ashton, *The Industrial Revolution*, (1948), p. 94.

[2] William Felkin, *History*, pp. 434–35.

[3] F. M. Eden, *The State of the Poor*, II, (1797), p. 574.

[4] *First Report from the Select Committee (Framework Knitters' Petitions)* 1812, (247) II. 203. p. 48.

[5] F. A. Wells, *op. cit.*, p. 94.

[6] *N.J.*, March 13, 1846.

[7] *Ibid.*, pp. 95, 98, 99.

[8] *Ibid.*, p. 101.

[9] *Ibid.*, pp. 132–33.

[10] *Report from the Select Committee appointed to inquire into the several Duties levied on Imports into the U.K., with minutes of evidence*, 1840 (527) VIII. 1. p. 247.

[11] *First Report of the Commissioners on the Employment of Children in Factories*, 1833 (450) XX, 1. p. 519; *Report of the Commissioner's on the Condition of Framework Knitters*, 1845 (609) XV. 1, ev. of Colburn, p. 753.

[12] *Report from the Select Committee appointed to inquire into the grievances complained of in the Petition of the Hosiers and Framework Knitters in the Woollen Manufactory of the Town and County of Leicester*, 1819 (193) V. 401. p. 78.

[13] *Report of the Commissioners appointed to inquire into the Conditions of Framework Knitters*, 1845 (609) XV. 1. ev. of Felkin, p. 685.

[14] William Felkin 'Some Particulars of the Past and Present State and Extent of the Hoisery Trade' Appendix 3, to *First Report of the Select Committee on the Exportation of Machinery*, 1841 (201) VII. 4. p. 243.

[15] *Ibid.*

[16] *Ibid.;* William Felkin, *History*, pp. 435, 437, 463, 518.

[17] J. D. Chambers, *Nottinghamshire in the Eighteenth Century*, (1932), p. 135; William Felkin 'Some Particulars of the Past and Present State and Extent of the Hoisery Trade', p. 244.

[18] The following description of the organization of the hosiery industry is based upon the analyses of F. A. Wells, *op. cit.*, J. D. Chambers, *Nottinghamshire in the Eighteenth Century*, (1932), and upon the *Report of the Commissioners appointed to inquire into the Condition of Framework Knitters* 1845 (609) XV, 1.

[19] William Felkin 'Some Particulars of the Past and Present State and Extent of the Hosiery Trade,' Appendix 3 to *First Report of the Select Committee on the Exportation of Machinery* 1841 (201) VII. 4. pp. 244–245.

[20] J. D. Chambers, *Nottinghamshire in the Eighteenth Century*, (1932), pp. 128–129.

[21] *Report of the Commissioners (Framework Knitters)*, 1845 (609) XV. 1. p. 1033.

[22] *Report of the Commissioners (Framework Knitters)*, 1845 (609) XV. 1.

[23] *Ibid.*, p. 80; William Felkin, *History*, p. 518.

[24] In 1836 the firm of William Hannay & Co., became the firm of Cox, Horner & Hogg.

[25] *Report of the Commissioners (Framework Knitters)*, 1845 (609) XV. 1., ev. of Barnett, p. 738.

[26] *Report of the Select Committee appointed to consider the Stoppage of Wages in Hosiery Manufacture with Proceedings, Evidence, Appendix, and Index*; 1854–55, (421) XIV. 1., ev. of Street, p. 426 and ev. of Allen p. 409.

[27] *Report of the Children's Employment Commission*, 1843, (431), XIII. p. F. 13.

[28] *Report of the Commissioners (Framework Knitters)*, 1845 (609) XV. 1. p. 466. Ibid., p. 47.

[29] *Fourth Report from the Select Committee appointed to inquire into the state of the law respecting Artizans leaving the Kingdom and residing Abroad; the exportation of Tools and Machinery; and the Combination of Workmen and others to raise wages, or to regulate their Wages and Hours of Working.* 1824 (51) V 183 ev. of Benjamin Taylor p. 270; *N.R.*, September 6, 1820; *N.R.*, February 2, 1821.

[30] William Felkin, *History*, p. 445.

[31] Charlotte Erickson, *British Industrialists 1850–1950; Steel and Hosiery.* (Cambridge, 1959), p. 121.

[32] *Infra*, Chap. X.

[33] *N.J.*, September 30, 1809.

[34] *First Report from the Select Committee (Framework Knitters' petitions)*, 1812 (247) II.

[35] *Report of the Commissioners (Framework Knitters)*, 1845 (609) XV. 1. p. 59–61.

[36] *Report of the Commissioners (Framework Knitters)*, 1845 (609) XV. 1. ev. of Barnett, p. 738.

[37] *Report of the Select Committee (Stoppage of Wages in Hosiery)*, 1854–55, (421) XIV. 1., ev. of Hurst, p. 418.

[38] *Report of the Commissioners (Framework Knitters)*, 1845 (609) XV. 1., ev. of Hannay, p. 738.

[39] *Ibid.*, ev. of William Miller, p. 775.

[40] *Ibid.*, p. 69.

[41] *Ibid.*, ev. of George Chandler, p. 797.

[42] *Report of the Select Committee (Stoppage of Wages in Hosiery)*, 1854–55, (421) XIV. 1., ev. of Allen, p. 414.

[43] *Report of the Commissioners (Framework Knitters)* 1845 (609) XV 1. ev. of William Gregory, pp. 837, 993.

[44] *Ibid.*, ev. of George Kendall, p. 89.

[45] *Report of the Children's Employment Commission*, 1843, (431) XIII. p.F. 15.

[46] *Report of the Commissioners (Framework Knitters)*, 1845 (609) XV. 1. p. 118; D. Smith, 'The British Hosiery Industry at the Middle of the Nineteenth Century: An Historical Study in Economic Geography' *Transactions and Papers of the Institute of British Geographers*, 1963, no. 32, p. 135.

[47] Felkin mss. quoted by S. D. Chapman, *William Felkin, 1795–1874.* (unpublished M.A. dissertation, University of Nottingham, 1960), pp. 20–1.

[48] *Ibid.*, p. 23.

[49] *Report of the Children's Employment Commission*, 1843, (431) XIII, ev. of J. Parker, p. 89.

[50] *Report of the Commissioners (Framework Knitters)*, 1845 (609) XV. 1., ev. of Hurst, p. 760.

[51] *Report of the Children's Employment Commission*, 1843, (431) XIII, ev. of Barber, p.f. 87; *Report of the Commissioners (Framework Knitters)*, 1845 (609) XV. 1., ev. of Pinkett, p. 795.

[52] *Report of the Children's Commission,* 1843 (431) XIII, ev. of Kelk, p.f. 85; *Report of the Commissioners (Framework Knitters),* 1845 (609) XV. 1., ev. of Hurst, p. 759.

[53] *Ibid.,* ev. of Felkin, p. 691.

[54] *Report of the Children's Employment Commission,* 1843, (431) XIII. ev. of Calcroft, p.f. 89.

[55] *Ibid.,* ev. of Rogers, p.f. 83–4.

[56] *Ibid.,* ev. of Cornelius Smith, p.f. 85.

[57] *Report from the Select Committee (Framework Knitters' Petitions),* 1819 (193) V. 401.

[58] Felkin, *History,* p. 441.

[59] *First Report of the Commissioners on the Employment of Children in Factories,* 1833 (450) XX. 1. ev. of Felkin, p. 519; Power's Report, p. 554.

[60] *Report of the Commissioners (Framework Knitters),* 1845 (609) XV. 1. p. 1045.

[61] *Report of the Children's Employment Commission,* 1843 (431) XIII, p.f. 13.

[62] 'Some Particulars of the Past and Present State and Extent of the Hosiery Trade' Appendix 3, to *First Report of the Select Committee on the Exportation of Machinery,* 1841 (201) VII. 4., p. 244.

[63] *Report of the Commissioners (Framework Knitters),* 1845 (609) XV. 1., p. 685; *Report of the Children's Employment Commission,* 1843, XIII, p.f. 15.

[64] *First Report of the Commissioners on the Employment of Children in Factories,* 1833 (450) XX. 1., p. 519.

[65] *Ibid.,* ev. of Dr. Manson, p. 557.

[66] *Report of the Children's Employment Commission,* 1843 (431) XIII, p.f. 16.

[67] See a list of average weekly wages for Manchester workmen from various trades between 1820 and 1832 in E. Baines, *The History of the Cotton Manufacture in Great Britain,* (1835) p. 439; also T. C. Barker and J. R. Harris, *A Merseyside Town in the Industrial Revolution, St. Helens 1750–1900,* (1954), p. 277.

[68] F. A. Wells, *op. cit.,* pp. 111–12.

[69] See J. L. and B. Hammond, *The Skilled Labourer,* (1919), chs. 8–9.

[70] The character of Luddism in the east Midlands, and the role of Gravener Henson, are discussed in a forthcoming article: Roy Church and S. D. Chapman 'Gravener Henson and the Making of the English Working Class,' in *Land, Labour, and Population; essays presented to J. D. Chambers,* ed. G. F. Mingay and E. L. Jones (1966). For a brief account of Henson's life and thought see *infra.,* pp. 320–26.

[71] *Fourth Report from the Select Committee (Emigration, Export of Machinery, Combinations),* 1824 (51) V. 183, p. 282.

[72] J. L. and B. Hammond, *The Skilled Labourer,* (1919), p. 230.

[73] *Ibid.*

[74] *Ibid.,* pp. 230–35.

[75] *Ibid.,* p. 236.

[76] *Infra,* p. 66.

[77] E. Hobsbawm, 'The Machine Breakers,' *Past and Present,* I, no. 1, 1952, 59–60.

[78] William Felkin, *History,* pp. 233, 237, 241.

79 William Felkin 'Some Particulars of the Past and Present State and Extent of the Hosiery Trade' in Appendix 3 of *First Report of the Select Committee on the Exportation of Machinery*, 1841 (201) VII. 4. p. 244; F. A. Wells, *op. cit.*, p. 103.

80 *First Report from the Select Committee* (Framework Knitters' Petitions), 1812 (247) II. 203, pp. 16, 19; F. A. Wells, *op. cit.*, p. 95.

81 *Infra.*, p. 259.

82 *Infra.* p. 66.

83 William Felkin, *History*, p. 239; J. L. and B. Hammond, *The Skilled Labourer*, (1919), p. 243.

84 This view presented by E. P. Thompson in *The Making of the English Working Class* (1963), e.g. see pp. 530, 551, is attacked in the forthcoming article: Roy Church and S. D. Chapman 'Gravener Henson and the Making of the English Working Class' in *Land, Labour, and Population; essays presented to J. D. Chambers*, ed. G. F. Mingay and E. L. Jones (1966).

85 J. L. and B. Hammond, *The Skilled Labourer*, (1919) pp. 248–9.

86 *N.R.*, January 10, 1818.

87 *The Stocking Makers' Monitor or Commercial Magazine*, I, (October 25, 1817).

88 *The Stocking Makers' Monitor or Commercial Magazine*, VII, (March 5, 1818).

89 John Sutton, *Date Book of Remarkable Events Connected with Nottingham and Neighbourhood 1750–1850*, (1852), p. 353.

90 *Ibid.; Fourth Report from the Select Committee appointed to inquire into the state of the Law respecting Emigration, Combinations, and Export of Machinery*, 1824 (51) V. 183. ev. of Benjamin Taylor, p. 270.

91 *Ibid.*

92 *N.R.*, December 17, 1819; *N.R.*, December 24, 1819.

93 F. A. Wells, *op cit.*, p. 126.

94 *N.R.*, February 19, 1820.

95 *N.R.*, May 6, 1820.

96 *N.R.*, September 21, 1820.

97 *N.R.*, February 2, 1821; *N.J.*, February 3, 1821; *N.R.*, May 4, 1821; *N.R.*, February 16, 1821.

98 *Fourth Report from the Select Committee (Emigration, Combinations, and the Export of Machinery)*, 1824 (51) V. 183. ev. of Benjamin Taylor, p. 271.

99 *N.R.*, March 2, 1821.

100 William Felkin, *History*, p. 445.

101 *Report of the Proceedings on the Conviction of Benjamin Taylor, John Ball, William Rutherford, James Snow, part of the Framework Knitters' Committee, at Nottingham on April 30th, 1821*, p. 12; *N.R.*, March 17, 1821.

102 *N.R.*, April 30, 1821.

103 *Fourth Report of the Select Committee (Emigration, Combinations, and Export of Machinery)*, 1824 (51) V. 183, ev. of Benjamin Taylor, p. 271–2.

104 *Ibid.;* William Felkin, *History*, p. 240.

105 William Felkin, *History*, p. 366.

106 F. A. Wells, *op. cit.*, p. 125.

107 *N.R.*, August 15, 1823.

[108] *Fourth Report of the Select Committee (Emigration, Combinations, and Export of Machinery)*, 1824 (51) V. 183, ev. of Benjamin Taylor, p. 272.

[109] *N.R.*, September 24, 1823.

[110] *N.R.*, November 14, 1823; For Mundella's role in the establishment of arbitration machinery see *infra*. pp. 269–71.

[111] *N.R.*, April, 28, 1826.

[112] *N.R.*, October 12, 1825; *N.R.*, April 28, 1826.

[113] William Felkin, *History*, p. 446.

[114] *Infra.*, Chap. VI.

[115] F. A. Wells, *op. cit.*, p. 103.

[116] William Felkin, *History*, p. 490.

[117] *N.R.*, August 27, 1847.

CHAPTER III

THE RISE OF THE MACHINE-MADE LACE INDUSTRY

THE history of the hosiery industry during the first half of the nine-teenth century exemplifies the 'slow-footed progress' which indust-ries might have experienced without the important inventions which we associate with the industrial revolution.[1] The history of the machine-made lace industry shows the economic and social effects of an innovation which revolutionized an industry. The changes were less rapid and, because of the smallness of the industry, less significant than the transformation of the cotton industry. Neverthe-less, important similarities between the two should not be over-looked, for innovation in both industries was followed by falling prices and, eventually, the production of articles of improved quality. Furthermore, the rise of the machine-made lace industry exemplifies Professor Charles Wilson's statement that

> It is misleading to consider the industrial revolution merely in terms of undifferentiated commodities called cotton or woollens or iron. Such treatment obscures the fundamental fact that the need to be met was for highly specific versions of such general categories.[2]

For entrepreneurs this need for cheaper, better, and a greater variety of lace nets was important; it was equally so for the many people of Nottingham whose lives were thereby affected.

By the end of the eighteenth century Nottingham's unrivalled supremacy in the manufacture of cotton hosiery had been firmly established, and it was upon this economic base that the machine-made lace industry grew. This development is especially interesting because it owed nothing to the traditional centres of hand-made lace in the mainly agricultural communities of Buckinghamshire, Bed-fordshire, and Devon; for the first net produced in Nottingham was made not on a mechanical cushion, but on a hosiery frame. Hence, machine-made lace materialised not as the legitimate offspring of the hand-made lace industry, but as the stepchild of the hosiery trade.[3] The explanation for this lies in local conditions. Nottingham was an established commercial and framework knitting centre linked by turnpike and canal with other inland centres and ports. In the latter part of the eighteenth century, until Lancashire producers

58

forced many of them out of business, Nottinghamshire mills supplied cotton yarns to midland hosiers while mills in Derbyshire and Nottinghamshire produced silk for high quality hosiery; thus raw material for lace production was nearby, as was the river Leen which provided both power and water suitable for bleaching and dyeing. As early as 1760 Nottingham framework knitters, totally ignorant of net and lace making, were experimenting in attempts to adapt the stocking frame to lace net manufacture in order to penetrate the market for hand-made lace. The last quarter of the eighteenth century also saw the beginning of a long sequence of ingenious efforts to increase the demand for hosiery by modifying the methods of production and widening the range of hosiery goods;[4]

> 'The local development of initiative and skill had some relation, there can be little doubt,' said Felkin, 'to the spirit of enterprise rising into activity all around. Here as elsewhere, it was without pretension in the beginning but very marvellous and unlooked for in its results.'[5]

The origin of the pin, point, and warp lace trades of Nottingham can be found in the series of inventions aimed at adapting hosiery machinery for the production of fancy hosiery.[6] There were two main approaches to the alteration of the stocking frame. One involved the application of a warp to give extra threads, thereby facilitating the production of a mesh on the warp frame which could thus make both hose and lace; the other consisted of the use of 'ticklers', or points, for the mechanical selection of loops of thread so as to form meshes and patterns.[7] Based on these principles, the mechanical production of cheap and simple imitation lace nets expanded during the closing decades of the century as the new articles found favour with some sections of the public.[8] In 1781 John Morris, a hosier of Nottingham, took out a patent for the manufacture of point net which Felkin described as almost equal to any invention to appear in the trade between 1760 and 1800.[9] Point net proved to be the finest article produced on the adapted hosiery frame, and while it was far from being a perfect imitation of cushion lace it was the most popular of the simple nets. In 1786 not more than fifty point net frames existed, but by 1810 between fifteen hundred and eighteen hundred point net frames and four hundred warp frames were making lace nets in Nottingham.[10]

Before 1815 point net manufacture was already on the decline, partly because of the effect of war and also, according to a reliable contemporary, owing to the ability of French producers to make a better article more cheaply. Blackner attributed the decline of the English point net trade to excessive cheapening and coarsening of the product which, although aimed at competing with French lace in Continental markets, in effect ignored consumers' tastes.[11] Nottingham again became the centre of innovation where a spate of technical experiments, adaptations, and improvements by local framesmiths were directed at getting a thread to twist completely round a warp thread, thereby producing a twisted instead of knitted fabric. The result was a mounted bobbin which rotated in a carriage passing round warp threads so as to form twists from which a mesh could be contrived.[12] This was the basic mechanism by which bobbin net, or 'twist', came to be manufactured automatically, and the bobbin net machine, patented by John Heathcoat in 1808, was a technical breakthrough, the culmination of a series of inventions achieved mainly through the efforts of superior local framework knitters and framesmiths like the Frosts, Whitemore, Taylor, Brown, Lindley, Holmes, Flint, and Morley.[13] Outstanding among the successful inventors were John Brown, who developed the Traverse Warp machine in 1811, Clark and Mart, who devised the Pusher machine in 1812, and John Leavers, whose machine came to be the most widely used after its introduction in 1813.[14]

Heathcoat's machine inaugurated the division between hosiery and lace manufacture, and its significance is indicated by its ability to make one thousand meshes per minute compared with the five meshes per minute of the lace maker producing pillow lace by hand. Before 1823 Heathcoat's improved machines could make much wider nets at a rate of ten thousand meshes per minute, and by 1836 thirty thousand meshes per minute were achieved.[15] Heathcoat's genius lay in his incorporation of the most valuable results of previous technical inventions and experiments with his own prototypes. His 'Old Loughborough' model, patented in 1809, superseded the model of 1808, the net produced on it being wider, stronger, more regular and attractive than previous nets.[16] These latter qualities owed something to the success of Samuel Cartledge of Nottingham in developing a fine but sturdy cotton thread as a suitable material for use on the bobbin net machine. This was more elastic than linen yarn and gave a sheen to the finished product. Besides its strength and appearance, its low cost—in comparison with silk—was of major importance in encouraging greater use of cotton in the manufacture of lace nets, while the falling price of cotton yarns supplied by the Lancashire cotton mills was undoubtedly another factor enabling the bobbin net entrepreneurs to create wider markets for what had been, hitherto, chiefly an item of luxury used for the embellishment of dresses and domestic linens. Between 1812 and 1835 the price of a number 200 count high quality yarn used in making lace nets fell from an average of 19s. 1d. to 12s. 0½d.[17]

While Lancashire supplied fine count yarns and Manchester doubling mills provided twisted yarns for Nottingham lace manufacturers, some came from the local mills belonging to Wilson, Milnes, and Elliott & Mills, and from three others in the neighbourhood. In 1835 these mills together employed about seven hundred people. However, it was the Derbyshire mills with their successful history of silk manufacture which responded to the needs of the lace trade, and which began to specialise in the production of lace thread, while silk mills at Beeston and Nottingham also grew up to supply thrown silk to the trade. As the lace trade grew, the collateral operations of bleaching, dyeing, and finishing also shared in the expansion and were stimulated by it.[18]

By the application of practical chemistry the dyeing establishments of Keely and Windley made considerable advances in developing fast, bright dyes and in improving the processes of bleaching and finishing. In 1813 Samuel Hall took out a patent for a machine to be used for dressing and finishing framework knitted goods, and he turned his attention to the elimination of floss on warp nets and twist laces. Hitherto, floss on the surface of cotton had been removed by passing the cloths over red hot metal cylinders, a process detrimental to the net fabrics which were intended to be semi-transparent. In 1817 Hall solved the problem by taking out a patent for gassing, a process by which the floss was singed from the nets without harming the fabric. The gassing frames were improved and another patent taken out in 1823, by which time according to Felkin, 'the superior character of lace . . . after gassing was increasingly recognised.' Another patent for which Hall was responsible was that for the bleaching of starch, which employed a chloride in its preparation. By this process both quality and colour were improved.

Despite the attempts of manufacturers in and around Nottingham to surround their operations with secrecy, information circulated quite freely among the 'number of clever artisans who were most of them more or less known to each other'; they were members of a closely knit community 'whose great object it was to construct machines to make lace'.[19] As in other towns where the local industry was one of small units, the solitary inventor working in comparative isolation was a rarer figure than the inventive operative who rubbed shoulders with fellows in the same trade; they shared similar problems, and in some instances cooperated in the improvement of machinery. As one historian has commented, it seems that, 'no bobbin net machine can be attributed in entirety to the genius of one man,'[20] and even Heathcoat, who developed his machines in Loughborough some twenty miles from Nottingham, maintained close contact with local framesmiths. In view of the ferment of ideas and the increasingly complex nature of machinery which underwent rapid changes during the early decades of the century, it was advantageous—even essential—for entrepreneurs and inventive mechanics to be located in, or keep up close connections with Nottingham in order to stay abreast of new developments. Thus, the direction and application of accumulated local knowledge of stocking frame and associated technology to improving local products resulted in technical change: the industrial atmosphere in Nottingham encouraged industrial progress. It is significant that after Heathcoat left the area for Tiverton in Devon, he made no further important contributions to lace technology. But although Heathcoat may have underestimated the value of working in close proximity to an established lace manufacturing centre, he recognised the need for a supply of skilled workmen and he persuaded a few local journeymen to make the 500 mile trek to Tiverton on foot.[21] Likewise William Nunn, who relied upon the purchase of local ideas for his success, left Nottingham for the Isle of Wight as a large manufacturer, but after a short period of hand-powered production his firm perished in isolation.

The earliest machine-made nets were either plain, varying in types of mesh, or ornamented with simple designs.[22] The impetus for invention originated in an expanding and competitive market in which the demand for nets grew as their quality and appearance improved, and the inventors sought to construct machinery which made firmer, stronger, more even and elastic nets of greater widths. Shares in the expanding market depended upon the ability of entrepreneurs to anticipate consumer demand in devising new machinery, as a result of which several framesmiths and a few ingenious framework knitters became independent lace makers. Thus in 1768 Hammond, a Nottingham framework knitter, adapted his frame to produce a popular net. According to Felkin he succeeded in making sufficient income

> to supply the most pressing necessities, working by day and drinking by night; thus passed several years of the life of this original machine wrought lace manufacturer.[23]

Another ingenious framework knitter with somewhat more ambition was Robert Brown, who achieved much greater success as a lace manufacturer in Radford after patenting his invention in 1802.[24] John Bagley, several years after his apprenticeship to James Smith, a framesmith at Radford (during which time Bagley claimed to have received no wages for twenty weeks labour, but gained a large amount of valuable information), devised plans for constructing a versatile machine.

I resolved to act on my own account. My father lent me £10 and my wife's father £10 with which an old 'circular' was bought; the smithing in it I got done on credit. During the time this machine was getting to work, my sufferings from hunger and those of my wife . . . were intense; we were reduced to the deepest distress, so that for three months, we only ate meat once, and subsisted during several days upon water gruel without bread; my father-in-law on learning our state, assisted us to keep us from starving . . .

Earlier, Bagley had offered the plans of his improvements to a lace manufacturer but his offer was not taken up. He had then employed a smith to make the extra guide bars required for adapting circular machinery. Under an agreement to take equal shares in profits from the plan, Peach, a lace maker who owned a small leavers frame, joined him in partnership after advancing £40 and paying Bagley 25s. weekly. In due course Peach sold the invention and Bagley received nothing. It was then that he commenced production on his own account. Describing his first encounter with James Fisher, an influential lace merchant operating in London and Nottingham, who had seen the products made on his machine, Bagley said

(Fisher) sent me a note, charging me with an infringement; but in conversation said, "we want you in our employ." I engaged with him and continued there for several years; being employed in getting out new things for which they obtained patents.[25]

Bagley's account illuminates the process of capital formation in the lace industry.

The problem of securing finance was a difficult one for the inventor, especially in view of the expense of patent rights which cost between £100 and £700; moreover, additional expenses might be incurred should the inventor be forced to defend his patent at common law—sometimes against a spurious contender.[26] In the opinion of Gravener Henson, the mechanic was thereby often prevented from 'reaping the fruits of ingenuity'.[27] Furthermore, the tendency of extended patent rights, he argued, was to deter experiment and innovation. Citing the case of a man named Johnson who had modified a bobbin net machine, Henson showed that this machine was seized and Johnson imprisoned for several months before he was acquitted of the charge of infringing patent rights.[28] Intrigue and the risk that ideas might be copied led some mechanics to sell their ideas, though this did not eliminate the danger of prosecution for infringement should the inventor continue to use his improved machine.[29] Entrepreneurs were eager to secure patent rights on inventions which promised to yield high rates of return. The result was that while a few inventors succeeded in purchasing a patent independently, some relied upon the financial resources of established businessmen, though some attempted to form working partnerships using their modest capital to exploit the invention commercially without applying for patents.

An analysis of patents taken out between 1770 and 1826 reveals that of the total of forty-eight issued for inventions relating to stocking net and looped fabrics, meshed and netted fabrics, and plain and figured lace, twenty-eight were the products of local ingenuity.[30] This figure assumes greater significance when it is realized that of the remaining twenty patents, John Heathcoat at Loughborough was responsible for nine. Of the patents taken out by persons in Nottingham, eight were taken out by lace manufacturers, four by hosiers, one by a hosiery and lace manufacturer, one by a linen and woollen draper, and three by 'gentlemen'; seven were taken out by framesmiths or machine builders, and four by framework knitters. Of the latter only one became a manufacturer. He was Thomas Frost who took out a joint patent with his hosier brother, Robert, in 1783.[31] By 1800 the brothers were leading point net manufacturers. John Eaton enlisted financial support from Samuel Hague to develop his patent but the partnership proved a failure.[32] The other two cannot be traced. Of the framesmith patent holders, Thomas Taylor sold his patents and later became a partner of James Hood, the hosier, where he and Whittaker, a setter-up of lace machines, continued to experiment with machinery for making bobbin net.[33] After being financed first by two Leicester manufacturers and then by an architect in Nottingham, William Dawson of Leicester was successful in working a number of his machines in Nottingham. When his patent expired competition resulted in losses which were so great, according to Felkin, that Dawson was driven to suicide.[34]

To a large extent the rise of the machine-made lace industry depended not only upon the ingenuity of local artisans, but also upon the enterprise of men with capital who were willing to finance research with no guarantee of a return. Often the financial backers became impatient or apprehensive and withdrew support. John Heathcoat experienced two such failures in confidence before he finally perfected his machines during his partnership with Charles Lacey, a lace net manufacturer, whose function was to prepare the products for the market and dispose of them in Nottingham.[35] Of the four principal point net manufacturing firms between 1790 and 1810 —Robert & Thomas Frost, Wilson, Burnside & Watson, Maltby & Brewitt, and W. & T. Hayne[36]—the first was a family partnership of capital and inventive skill and the second was built on the capital of Watson, the hosier, who purchased the patent of Samuel Hague.[37]

The capital for the other two enterprises originated outside the hosiery trade. Thomas Maltby came from Hoveringham in Nottinghamshire, and after working at the stocking frame for some time his family financed him to commence point net manufacturing 'on a respectable scale.'[38] The Hayne brothers likewise possessed extensive landed property, and launched themselves in the 1780's by purchasing the entire manufacturing business of John Morris, including his patent. The Haynes then employed framesmiths to experiment with Morris's machinery and this led eventually to the production of a much higher quality net which laid the foundation for a rapidly expanding demand for point net.[39] Blackner states that in 1809 William Hayne was the greatest manufacturer in the town[40] and in 1812 he possessed frames to the value of £24,000.[41]

The personnel of partnerships in Nottingham changed rapidly and according to Felkin most mechanics who busied themselves with lace inventions appear to have had one or two partners in the execution of their experiments.[42] The circulation of knowledge and skill accelerated under the pressure of keen competition. Heathcoat's success with the bobbin net machine in 1809 prompted Nunn, a man of property and a large manufacturer of point net, to offer a reward to any artisan who could construct a machine which would make bobbin net. He hired a workman who had seen a copy of Heathcoat's specification and then proceeded to employ several skilled framesmiths to build thirty machines.[43] Nunn also tried to attract workmen from the Heathcoat and Lacey factory, and backed by Nunn, two framesmiths, Brown and Freeman, eventually succeeded in building a machine which Brown patented one month after he left Nunn and two years after the appearance of Heathcoat's patent. The machine did not violate outstanding patents, but when Longmire & Noble at New Radford financed Benjamin Moore's machine, Brown unsuccessfully instituted legal proceedings to defend his monopoly. According to Felkin, the decision of the court in 1816 that, 'if the invention consisted of an addition or improvement only, a patent for the whole machine was void' was greeted with great approval in Nottingham,[44] particularly by small men in the trade. The infringement of patents became more common and the accumulation of knowledge and skill made it easier to solve technical problems in the construction of more and better machines. Improved machinery continued to develop further the market for lace nets already established by the producers of point and warp lace nets, and, after the appearance of the superior nets produced on Heathcoat's 'Old Loughborough' machine in 1809 and following the legal decision of 1816, the industry proceeded to expand.

By 1815 in addition to the point net and warp lace frames there

were 140 bobbin net machines on license and more than 150 infringers of Heathcoat's patent,[45] but although the industry was un-
dergoing steady expansion, it seemed in 1816 that it might be
checked when no fewer than 55 machines valued at £10,000 were
smashed at the factory of Heathcoat, Boden & Lacey at Loughborough.[46] This destruction, which was carried out by the midland
gang of Luddites, followed a reduction of wages by one-third, a step
which the partners had thought necessary in order to meet competition from warp lace machines. In the same year, Heathcoat departed
from Loughborough to continue lace manufacturing in Devon. It is
difficult to assess the relative importance of Luddism and the competition from warp lace in determining Heathcoat's move, for that
was decided upon in 1815 when he had purchased a disused woollen
mill.[47] Heathcoat was of the opinion that the news of this intended
removal caused the attack, although the destruction of about one
thousand hosiery frames in the Nottingham vicinity during the preceding five years must have been a factor taken into account before
he arrived at his decision.[48] It is certain that the invasion of his
factory on the night of June 28, 1816 precipitated his midland exit.
Historians have called attention to the injurious effects on the local
economy of Luddite violence.[49] Felkin maintained that it 'deprived
the midland district of employment and profit derived from six or
seven hundred machines' for sixty years afterwards.[50] What is more
impressive, however, is the resilience of the Nottingham lace industry in the face of Heathcoat's departure, and the failure of the isolated Heathcoat to make further important additions to the technology of lace manufacture.[51]

Throughout the period of Luddite activity, and after the
violence of 1816, bobbin net continued to attract investment, both
through the persistent imitations and modifications of Heathcoat's
machine and through the numerous patentees who obtained licences
to own the machines for the purposes of manufacture or renting. By
1818, licences had been issued for 696 machines.[52] The following year
Heathcoat owned 147 machines and Lacey 127, the rest—apart from
machinery of the two hundred infringers—were in the hands of 164
small manufacturers or owners, of whom about eighty each owned
one or two narrow machines. But capital requirements still posed a
considerable problem, and although several hosiers had invested
capital in the net trade during the last quarter of the eighteenth century (when the hosiery industry was expanding), they were no longer
an important source of capital after Heathcoat's patent of 1809.
When net production was no longer a framework industry hosiers
appear to have lost interest, and after 1810 when the point net trade
underwent rapid contraction and the hosiery trade began to stagnate,

merchant hosiers showed reluctance to invest in a new industry where the risks of quick change and competition contrasted with the quasi-oligopolistic structure of the hosiery trade, and the partial insulation against falling profits which frame rents provided.

Until 1825 some capital was attracted into bobbin net machinery from investors outside the trade. Their role was essentially capitalist, financing the construction of new machines and renting them to machine holders who made their own nets and who sometimes employed journeymen. But the drastic fall in machine prices which accompanied the slump of 1826 led to a rapid decline in machine renting. Another source of capital during these early years of the machine-made lace industry was the partnership. For example, John Stevenson & Skipwith financed John Leavers, the framesmith and setter-up, who in 1813 successfully devised a net-producing machine which dispensed with the need for traversing.[53] But high initial capital requirements rose further, following the trend of expected returns from machinery which, due to the increasingly complicated modifications and improvements made by such men as Leavers and Lindley, necessitated increased capital outlays to commence production. The average value of the twist net machines wrecked at the Loughborough factory of Heathcoat, Boden & Lacy in 1816 was estimated at between £150 and £200. By 1823 new machines were being sold for between £500 and £700 each.[54]

These developments made it difficult for lacemakers without financial backing to become independent machine holders during the earliest years of the machine-made lace industry. Those who succeeded, however, were helped by two factors: one was the high wages earned by skilled operatives, the other was the partial restriction placed on net supply by Heathcoat's patent. In 1820 journeymen were paying premiums of £50 a year to be taught bobbin net making, a sum often in excess of the annual industrial income of most framework knitters. This amounted to placing a limit on the movement of framework knitters into the trade; but the intelligence required to master the new machines was an equally effective bar to all except the superior hosiery workers with intelligence as well as initiative. This relatively inelastic supply of skilled labour helped also to push up wages, and during the early years of the patent many bobbin net makers were earning between £5 and £10 weekly,[55] though average earnings declined after the mid-twenties. The second factor which was favourable to the rise of the independent machine holder was the practice of framesmiths and machine builders in encouraging hire-purchase.[56] The firm of Swift & Wass, for example, established in 1814, would build a machine on a deposit of £100. Twenty years later the terms were considerably easier when John

Hill, a machine builder of Lenton, accepted a £25 deposit from William Shipman on a machine costing £255. On completion of the machine in working order Shipman was to pay £100, a further £30 with interest six months after installation, and the remainder with interest twelve months hence. Three months after the agreement had been signed Shipman sold half of his share in the machine to another lace maker, and another agreement was drawn up.[57] Even after Heathcoat's patent lapsed, the profits and earnings of machine makers and assemblers, as well as machine holders, were so great that capital to finance a growing output of lace nets and an increasing amount of bobbin net machinery could be internally generated. Thus when Heathcoat's patent expired, coinciding with the cyclical upswing from 1823–25, bobbin net makers' earnings grew rapidly, and despite the inflated prices of machinery many were purchased outright or by weekly instalments. During this period a workman could purchase a second-hand machine, on various terms, for between £200 and £250, and by working it he would earn as much as 30s. daily. Moreover, during the boom years more capital was attracted from outside the trade, from professional men, landowners, farmers, and retail dealers who charged up to £120 annual rent for the hire of new machines.[58] From neighbouring counties came skilled artisans and their families; smiths and mechanics migrated from Sheffield, Birmingham, and Manchester, and during the decade 1821–31 the population of Nottingham and the surrounding parishes increased by one-third. By 1831 approximately one-half of all lace machinery was worked in the Nottingham district, while only about one-fifth was situated outside a radius of twenty miles, scattered in the west country, the Isle of Wight, Warwickshire, and elsewhere.[59] (See Table V.)

TABLE V: *The Location of Bobbin Net Machinery 1826–1862.*

	1826	1836	1862		1826	1835	1862
Nottingham	620	576		Leicestershire	278	385	
Radford	315	373		Derbyshire	78	282	500
Hyson Green	110	134		Mansfield and	356	132	
Beeston	69	202		Chesterfield			
Basford	62	257	3175				
Sneinton	80	155		West of England			
Carrington		143		and the Isle of			
Lenton	150	208		Wight	677	793	660
Elsewhere in							
Nottinghamshire		76					

Total of Machines   1436   2044   3175
in Notts.

Sources: *Report from the Select Committee on the Exportation of Machinery* 1841, (201)VII. I. Appendix 6; Felkin, *History*, p. 251; Felkin, 'The Lace and Hosiery Trades of Nottingham', *B.A.A.S.*, 1866–7, Notices and Abstracts, p. 128.

In 1826 the lace trade was caught up in the nation-wide commercial crisis. During the boom period the patentees and licensees had put into operation the most improved and speedy machinery yet developed, and the sequel to the cyclical downturn was a rapid fall in the prices of bobbin nets and machinery, and a drop in wages. Lace machines which had been sold for between £500 and £700 in 1823 and 1825 cleared the market at £80 to £150 in 1826, and between 1826 and 1832 leavers machines sold for less than £50.[60] This was due partly to the existence of wider machines which rendered the older and narrower models obsolete, and partly to the exodus of most of the outside owners who had crowded into the trade between 1823 and 1825. Hence, the drastic reduction in prices gave rise to a lively market for discarded lace machines which were put up for auction, while rented machines were offered for sale by disillusioned owners at nominal prices. (See Table VI.) Between

TABLE VI: *Prices of Lace Machinery per quarter yard width 1824–1833.*

	1824–5 £	1826 £	1828 £	1833 £
Leavers	90	18–20	12	4–6
Circular	80	15–18	15	4–6
Pusher	50–70	10–15	3–4	3–4
Traverse Warp	50–70	10–15	6	2–3

Source: William Felkin article reproduced in Andrew Ure, *The Cotton Manufacture of Great Britain* (1861) Vol. II, pp. 318–327.

1826 and 1832 at least one-third of all machinery changed hands, and in 1829, according to Felkin, among well over 1,250 owners of bobbin net machines all but eight had been originally working men, 'a tribute', as Felkin remarked, 'to their individual labour, skill, economy and foresight.'[61] These qualities enabled many machine holders and journeymen lace makers to build larger enterprises, sometimes with the support of partnerships which became increasingly common as machine renting disappeared.

For example, in 1824 John Kirkland, a machine builder who had worked for Peach, a framesmith of Radford, was taken into partnership by two lace makers, Samuel Mullen and Henry Kirkland, adding £500 to their existing capital of £2,000. The production of lace, and machine construction was to take place at the Beeston workshops where the Kirklands were in charge. Mullen was responsible for managing affairs at the warehouse in Nottingham, and matters of general policy were to be discussed at monthly meetings which all three would attend. They agreed that profits of machine building and lace manufacture should accumulate, the target capital stock of the manufacturing side of the business being £5,000. Until then John, the junior partner, was to receive a weekly salary of £4, the others each to take £5.[62] Some indication of expected profitability of investment in the lace trade is to be found in another seven year partnership agreement which was signed by two Nottingham lace makers in 1833, a time of unsettled trade and growing competition among fewer lace producers.[63] Thomas Langham put up £400 and Jacob Woodhouse was to contribute £2,500 to capital stock. Each was to receive no more than £150 per annum in salary, although Woodhouse was entitled to 5 per cent. annually upon the excess of his share beyond that of his partner; profits were to be ploughed back into the firm. The most interesting clause, however, stated that if over six months the rate of return was less than 10 per cent. upon the joint stock, Woodhouse reserved the right to terminate the agreement.[64]

The general impression is that the expansion of local industry was not held back by any serious lack of capital, although one would like to know to what extent the banks encouraged industrial growth. The Smiths' bank and the Wright's bank had been established with trading capital, the former in the seventeenth century, the latter in 1760. These were the leading financial institutions in Nottingham for many years. The Wrights, at least, extended credit to local industry[65] and throughout the numerous commercial crises of the nineteenth century neither bank closed its doors. Presumably it was for the purpose of sharing the gains from economic expansion that during the first decade of the century three new banks opened in swift succession: that of Fellows, Mellor & Hart in 1808, Fellows who was a former hosier, and Hart a silk merchant; that of Moore, Maltby, Evans & Middlemore in 1802, who were connected with lace, cotton manufacturing, building, and the law respectively; and Rawson, Inkersole & Rawson, which was formed with capital from the hosiery and net trades in 1808.[66] Rawson, Inkersole & Rawson was in existence for only nine years, leaving four banks to meet the needs of the community during the expansion of the lace industry in the twenties. Then in 1834 the first joint stock bank, The Nottingham & Nottinghamshire, was established, one leading sponsor being William Melville, a hosier, cotton merchant, and lace manufacturer. Two years later the bank of Moore & Robinson (formerly Moore, Maltby & Middlemore) was reconstituted as a joint stock bank, the principal signatories being hosiers Heard and Mills, and Henry Leaver, the lace manufacturer.[67]

The entry of large amounts of capital in the hands of single persons was a feature of the trade which soon disappeared after the expiration of Heathcoat's patent, though one exception is to be found in the career of James Fisher, the London lace merchant, who had begun his career by selling hand-made laces and later point nets which he purchased from Charles Lacey.[68] In the early years of the century the mode of selling nets in the country markets was similar to that practised by the hand-made lace makers of Buckinghamshire who hawked boxes of goods and disposed of them on the spot. Despite the growth in volume of domestic trade, until the building of the railways marketing technique remained in essence unchanged, lace merchants travelling the country sometimes accompanying up to three tons of lace which they exhibited in larger towns up and down the country.[69] Fisher and Copestake, both of whom became extensive buyers in the Nottingham lace market, at one time employed over thirty horse-drawn vehicles in their marketing organization. The London market did not depend upon such elaborate sales methods, and although large houses like Fisher's owned warehouses in Nottingham and in the metropolis, most London buyers visited Nottingham to purchase from specialist merchants dealing in finished goods. In 1823 Fisher invested a large amount of capital in plant and machinery at Radford, and by 1829 approximately one hundred machines had been installed at his Radford factory. Determined to devise machinery which would produce plain nets more rapidly and cheaply, he employed John Leavers, son of a machine builder and skilled in the construction of his uncle's leavers machines, who took out three patents during his few years with Fisher. After the partnership between Leavers (junior) and Fisher terminated, Fisher hired William Crofts as his chief mechanic who, on Fisher's behalf, between 1831 and 1834 took out eighteen patents covering thirty distinct constructions. A patent taken out by Crofts in 1835, which included nine actual improvements in the manufacture of spotted nets, cost Fisher between £4,000 and £5,000. By this patent he succeeded in monopolizing for many years the production of every article into which a spot was introduced.[70]

Unlike the London capitalist Fisher, Thomas Sewell, John Kendall, William Sneath, William Morley, William Herbert, William Gregory, Richard Birkin, and Jonathan and Samuel Burton, were all originally local working artisans, either framesmiths or framework knitters. They had gained valuable experience in the point net trades and, either in partnership with others similar to themselves or with their own capital, had become skilled mechanics before becoming manufacturers.[71] Successful though they were, not all expressed their self-confidence in quite such a sanguine manner as William Herbert who, as a result of changes of fashion, was twice forced to discontinue business, each time after amassing quite considerable profits. He finally achieved more permanent success producing black laces on a large scale. 'Turn me into Nottingham Park without money or clothes,' he is reported to have said, 'and I shall die a rich man.'[72] Skill, enterprise, and thrift were features common to these lace manufacturers of the first half of the nineteenth century, and many were directly responsible for invention and innovation in the industry. Of a total of 107 patents taken out for plain and figured laces between 1826 and 1851, seventy-two originated in Nottingham and nine in Leicestershire and Derbyshire.[73] These represented the efforts of a generation of lace manufacturers, most of whom were acquainted with point net or bobbin net from their youth.

Although localization encouraged technical progress, the mainsprings of change included an expanding market (which was itself partly dependent on technological change) and the highly competitive structure of the lace industry. Efforts to develop the domestic market for bobbin net have been referred to earlier, and the case of W. B. Carter illustrates how demand was created through enterprise and initiative. Although the larger makers each employed agents to market their output, independent lace makers relied upon a number of lace agents working on commission to secure outlets for their nets. In great competition, these men hawked the nets from warehouse to warehouse. The agents thus formed a link between the maker and the finisher, but sometimes innovations in quality and design were underestimated by the intermediaries. When the pearl edgings made by Marmaduke Miller of Basford were displayed in the hope of attracting orders, the response was unfavourable. W. B. Carter, however, a small independent lace factor who sold lace and net to country shopkeepers, was convinced that after slight improvements the edgings would sell in the fashion market, therefore when high class London houses rejected the improved edgings Carter himself undertook to market the goods. Soon he was established as a specialist in edgings in the capital cities of England, Scotland, and Ireland.[74]

Until the thirties nets were only slightly differentiated; most were plain, although some were produced as quillings, while others incorporated simple patterns such as spots and sprigs. To obtain more elaborately figured laces it was necessary to put out plain nets to runners and embroiderers who would run the pattern by hand. Nevertheless, the appearance between 1809 and 1813 of the 'Old Loughborough', the pusher, the leavers, and the traverse warp machines provided the basis for competition in the market for lace nets. Prior to the twenties the intensity of competition varied, due

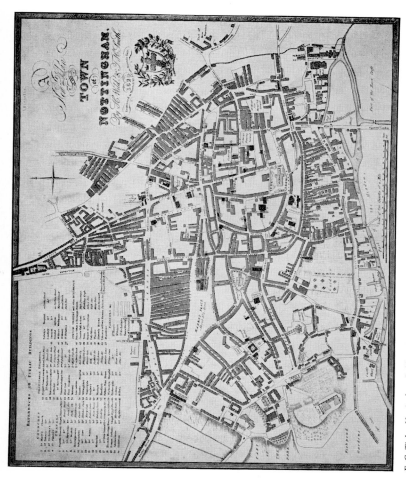

F. C. Tighe, *Nottingham Public Library*

PLAN OF NOTTINGHAM, 1825

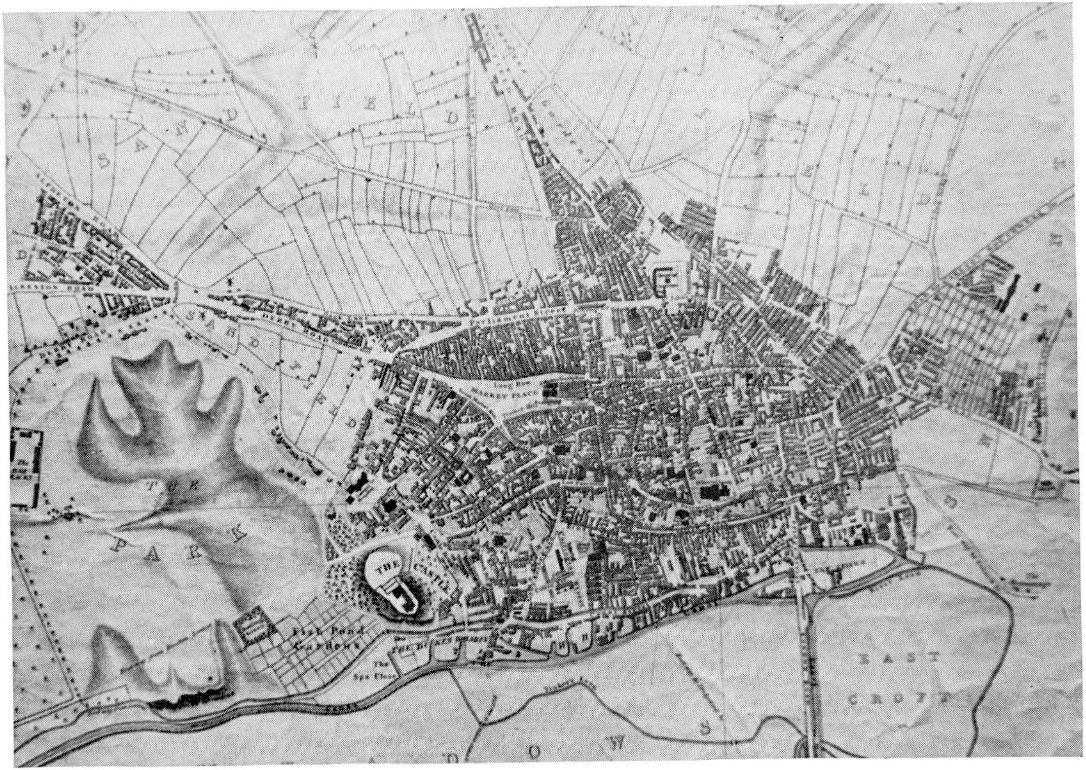

F. C. Tighe, Nottingham Public Library

to the attempts of patentees to restrict the number of licences issued, to control output, and to fix bobbin net prices. As infringements increased competition grew, and after the expiration of Heathcoat's patent in 1823, despite spasmodic experiments in large scale collusion among many sellers retailing similar articles,[75] the multiplication of small firms ensured the presence of competition.

Between 1833 and 1836 the industry became somewhat less competitive as the number of machines fell from about 5,000 to 3,600. However, these figures conceal the increase in the width of the new machines and the actual growth of total industrial capacity. The decline in the number of persons owning machinery from 1,382 to 857 during the same period, testified to the effective operation of a competitive market which allowed the manufacturers producing lace by steam power to eliminate many of the smallest narrow machine holders.[76] In 1836 approximately two-thirds of existing lace machinery was in the hands of slightly more than 6 per cent. of all machine owners, while 70 per cent. owned less than three.[77] (See Table VII.) Nonetheless, technical developments which took place

TABLE VII: *Lace Machine ownership 1831 and 1836.*

	1831	1836		1831	1836
Owned 1	700	300	Owned 7	17	15
,, 2	226	203	,, 8	19	13
,, 3	181	102	,, 9	17	14
,, 4	96	62	,, 10	12	6
,, 5	40	48	,, 11	8	7
,, 6	21	21	,, 12	6	6
			,, 13–20	5	10

Source: William Felkin *A History of the Machine-wrought Hosiery ann Lace Manufacture*, (1867) p. 341.

in the late thirties and forties to some extent slowed down this movement towards the growth of larger units of production.

Since 1795, figured as well as plain laces had been made on warp frames. With the appearance of the superior bobbin nets the demand for plain warp nets declined rapidly,[78] and in the thirties manufacturers and mechanics concentrated upon the production of more elaborate figured laces.[79] By developing various machines which incorporated the use of extra guide bars to work upon warp threads, the application of the jacquard to a lace machine, the avoidance of traversing by the carriages, and the application of rotary motion to an improved leavers machine, a number of local mechanics helped to solve many of the problems connected with the mechanical production of fancy laces. Among these men the achievements of Leavers, Crofts, Bagley, Bertie, and Draper provided the foundation

G

of technical experiment and knowledge on which Hooton Deverill, a local bobbin net manufacturer, was able to draw.[80] Thus in 1841 Deverill constructed a machine which was fundamentally an improved rotary leavers machine, but in which the new guide bar and jacquard system allowed unprecedented selectivity and control over individual threads. This enabled him to manufacture shawls, scarfs, veils, imitation pillow lace, and edgings, insertions, and other laces of intricate design.

Indeed, Deverill's machine marks a turning-point in the history of machine-made lace.[81] Prior to this date machines were designed to make a particular pattern; but after Deverill's success, new machinery, especially the leavers lace machine, became highly versatile. Writing in 1842, Felkin commented on the excellence of some of the new laces embroidered by machinery and stated that, in his opinion, the future prosperity of the Nottingham district depended upon the ability of its manufacturers and artisans to develop fully the fancy section of the bobbin net trade.[82] Designs became more varied and the range of articles produced on the new machines also grew; hence the influence of fashion in the trade increased, a development which enhanced the influence and importance of the merchants and finishers. Another result was that in the rapidly expanding fancy lace branch of the industry, where fashion was crucial in determining demand, speed in execution and the ability to alter patterns for which a given machine might be geared became essential. These factors favoured the perpetuation of the small units of production and strengthened the position of independent machine holders, while at the same time increasing the advantages of location close to existing centres of production. Thus increased localization was complementary to greater specialization. Deverill's machine was important not only because of its effect upon the quality and range of fancy laces which it could produce: of equal importance was its suitability for operation by steam power. For although, in 1829, Bailey had given the leavers machine a rotary action, it was not until the appearance of Deverill's machine in 1841, when the harmful effects of vibration upon the leavers machine were successfully eliminated, that steam power began to be widely adopted.[83]

During the third quarter of the century the structure of the industry began to alter. The boom of the twenties had given rise to increased specialization within the trade, with the separation of lace maker from machine builder, finisher, and merchant.[84] In 1825 Glover's directory lists sixteen bobbin and carriage makers and forty-six framesmiths and twist machine makers, including many partnerships such as Kendall, Sewell, Green & Co., Bird & Rumley, Wann, Jervis & Haslam, Callow & Leavers, and Manlove &

Woodhouse. In 1832 White's directory listed twenty-four bobbin and carriage makers and twenty-two machine builders, among whom Higgins & Wharton also produced steam engines. Sixteen years later Lascelle and Hagar counted only eight bobbin and carriage manufacturers, including J. Cropper and Edward Shipley, ten machine builders, and twelve guide makers. By 1854 the number of bobbin and carriage makers had increased to thirteen: there were thirty-three machine smiths, including such firms as Attenborough, Mellor & Co., Manlove & Alliott, Bailey & Hollingsworth, Joseph Topham, and Edward Whitehall, and in 1855 John Jardine laid the foundations of his famous enterprise by specializing in making insides of lace machines. Four jacquard makers were also listed. The independent specialist machine builders disappeared during the sharp fall in machine prices that occurred after the boom years of the twenties,[85] but at about the same time some merchants became machine holders manufacturing lace, while some machine holders and finishers began to market their own lace.[86]

Expanding trade in the middle decades of the century, the gradual standardization of machine design, and the greater stability in machine making led to the re-emergence of a specialist class of lace machinery builders in a manner similar to that which had occurred during the earlier period of rapid expansion and technical change. But whereas the earlier specialists had been little more than independent machine-makers the new machine-building firms of the fifties and sixties, such as Keeton & Savage, Manlove & Alliott, and the firms of Whitehall, Cropper, and Gamble, sold machines of uniform design produced in factories, and offered them to the trade on hire-purchase or for rent. This was another practice which tended to strengthen the position of the independent machine holder.

As regards finishing and merchanting, technical changes from the thirties onwards widened the range of design possibilities and called for increasing specialization to develop them. This was the function of the several firms who, through their activities which included the finishing and warehousing, and buying and selling of brown (unfinished) and finished laces, earned for the locality in which they were concentrated the description of the Lace Market. Even before the introduction of Deverill's new machine Felkin observed,

> the most sanguine can hardly appreciate how extensively the bobbin net machine may be adapted to the production of new fabrics or the attractive modifications of those already known.

By exploiting commercially their 'elegant tastes' and 'judicious designs' Felkin looked to Nottingham's lace manufacturers 'to direct fashion, instead of receiving it, and hence command sales and profits accordingly.'[87] Pattern designing thus emerged as a separate function. In 1825 there were no specialist lace pattern designers, but in 1832 White's directory listed eight, and in 1848 ten were included. Six years later Wright's directory listed seventeen, and in 1877, in addition to ten jacquard card makers, forty designers served both the lace and the newly invigorated hosiery trades. The leading pioneer in methods of designing and draughting was William Haines of Nottingham who developed a process of recording designs accurately and enabling patterns of increasing complexity to be devised on the drawing board rather than in the machine shop.[88] Another development resulting from the growth in the range of lace articles was the practice of commission agents who handled single lines.

Felkin had stressed the importance of design during the middle thirties. Manufacturers, he claimed, were

> beginning to acknowledge the connection between the perfection of their goods and the cultivation of the fine arts on correct and scientific principles.[89]

Aware of the need to lead and create fashion and to influence demand for fancy lace, the local press became the vehicle for a campaign led by Felkin to establish a school of design in Nottingham which would serve both the lace and hosiery industries. Other manufacturers and merchants, notably William Vickers, and the Town Council supported the idea and finally the scheme materialized. The School of Design was opened in 1843 and was financed mainly by private subscription, although the government also granted an annual subsidy of £150.[90] Hitherto the prevailing practice for merchants and merchant finishers had been to visit London where they selected patterns from among the French articles and had them copied.[91] Henceforward Nottingham began to produce its own designs and the sale of laces was made easier by the success in 1844 of William Taylor, a local stationer, in taking accurate paper impressions of lace designs.[92]

In the Lace Market the merchant finishers attempted to gauge the potentialities of fabric and design; indeed the whole industry depended to a great extent upon the skill with which they interpreted, anticipated, and sometimes influenced changes in fashion. Another factor contributing towards the revitalization of the trade was the injection of skill, capital, and enterprise by a number of immigrant Jews during the middle thirties. Having quit the great commercial centres of Europe to which Nottingham merchants regularly shipped lace and hosiery, such men as Warburg, Weinburg, Jacoby, Stiebel, Alexander, and Heymann brought to the Nottingham lace market zeal and vision, capital and a willingness to risk it, worldwide connections and commercial judgment, without which, it has been claimed, a great deal of Nottingham lace would never have been called into existence.[93] In 1834 Lewis Heymann from Mecklenburg-Schwerin together with Alexander, a merchant formerly living in Hamburg, established the lace house of Heymann & Alexander, and a shipping house was founded by Moritz Jacoby the following year. Simon, May & Co., was the creation of Jacob Weinberg who was sent to Nottingham by Phillip Simon in 1849.[94]

Greater specialization and vertical disintegration in the third quarter of the century were accompanied by innovations in technique which improved the quality and range of articles made on the lace machine. While the manufacture of lace curtains, pioneered by Lewis Heymann in the forties, opened up an entirely new branch of trade, the tremendous variety of laces which appeared in the market brought a rapid expansion of the fancy lace branch. From Hall's bleaching and dressing enterprise in Basford, a locality where bleaching establishments were concentrated to ultilize the waters of the Leen, came technical improvements in both spheres, while another firm, Manlove & Alliott, developed a centrifugal drying machine.

The establishment of the Penny Post in 1840 and later the Parcel Post, and the opening of the Midland Railway through Nottingham in 1839–1840 were two developments important to commerce which tended to quicken the pulse of trade. The improvement in communications brought London buyers into closer contact with the Lace Market in Nottingham and unified the home market.[95] As a consequence orders became smaller and more frequent, requiring more rapid execution (especially in the fancy branch), with the result that lace makers were more often obliged to incur the expense of putting new patterns on their machines. Merchants and finishers, on the other hand, were able to hold back orders until the last moment in order to lessen their own risks in the market. As the holding of inventories in a fashion trade also brought risks, these changes tended to add to the advantage of flexibility enjoyed by the small unit of production.

Industrialization and economic expansion led to urban growth; the town, however, was the framework within which an expanding industry obtained the gains from specialization, while auxiliary and complementary industries could operate more efficiently. Given this localization, individual plants could specialize in a smaller range of products and functions. Economies of urbanization also included improved transport facilities, a broader and more flexible labour market with appropriate skills, numerous auxiliary business services like banking, insurance, and brokerage, and a greater availability of information on trade matters. But not all gains from spatial concentration were due to the economies which small and medium-sized firms could secure without expanding their scale of operations. Heathcoat, for many years the largest lace manufacturer in the country, succeeded in conducting a thriving business some two hundred miles from the acknowledged centre of the industry. This was partly due to his outstanding entrepreneurial ability, and to that of his agent in Nottingham, William Felkin, and partly because of the early lead which his bobbin net patent secured. From the early years of the century Heathcoat had owned and managed a vertically integrated plant, finishing and marketing his own plain net, and thus created his own internal economies. As we have noted, however, Heathcoat's contributions to lace technology were insignificant after his removal to Tiverton. It may therefore be relevant to argue that in addition to gains in efficiency due to the orthodox external economies obtainable in Nottingham, other external benefits were to be found. These derived from the localization of industry in and around an urban centre where an 'industrial atmosphere', to use Alfred Marshall's phrase, might generate forces favourable to innovation.[96] Richard Birkin, the leading merchant who was also a large machine holder manufacturing fancy laces, also appears to have felt this when in 1841, in his capacity as representative of the trade, he remarked,

> it is not the machines themselves in which the value exists, but the great practice we (in Nottingham) have had, and the ideas we have from being congregated together, that enable us to apply our various improvements to the machines . . .[97]

Although it is impossible to assess the effective contribution of the Nottingham Society of Inventors to technical progress, its formation under the chairmanship of bobbin net maker Gravener Henson received the support of a number of local mechanics and machine owners. Although the society met for only a few years before its dissolution in 1831 (owing to lack of funds), Henson maintained that it had been successful 'by drawing the attention of the population to inventing.'[98] A survey of inventors during the period of industrial revolution suggests that they were members of a more closely-knit society than is popularly supposed.[99] The origins and development of the machine-made lace industry during the late eighteenth and early nineteenth century also lends support for a generalization which seeks to establish a relationship between localization and technical progress. However, this refers only to the creation of conditions favourable towards technical experiment, while allowing the positive stimulus to innovation to be found in other conditions affecting supply and demand. In a period when in many industries the small unit of production was typical, the external economies of urbanization reflected an important function of the industrial town.

References

1 T. S. Ashton, *The Industrial Revolution*, (1948), p. 94.

2 C. Wilson, 'The Entrepreneur in the Industrial Revolution in Britain', *Explorations in Entrepreneurial History*, VII, 3, (1954), p. 138.

3 D. E. Varley, *A History of the Midland Counties Lace Manufacturers' Association*, (Long Eaton, 1959), pp. 1–2.

4 See D. M. Smith,' The Silk Industry of the East Midlands,' *The East Midland Geographer*, 1962, no. 17; F. A. Wells, *op. cit.*, pp. 91–93.

5 William Felkin, *History;* p. 85. D. E. Varley, *op. cit.*, p. 45.

6 *Ibid.*, p. 92.

7 For the technical details of lace machinery see D. E. Varley, *A History of the Midland Counties Lace Manufacturers' Association*, ch. 2.

8 John Blackner, *op. cit.*, pp. 230–32.

9 William Felkin, *History*, pp. 103–06.

10 John Blackner, *op. cit.*, p. 232; William Felkin, *History*, p. 139.

11 *Second Report from the Select Committee on Postage* 1837–8, XX, Part II, ev. of Gravener Henson, p. 213; John Blackner, *op. cit.*, p. 235–6.

12 William Felkin, *History*, p. 171; See D. E. Varley, *op. cit.*, pp. 16–17.

13 Referred to by William Felkin in his *History*.

14 William Felkin, *History*, pp. 208, 271, 292.

15 William Felkin, 'The Lace and Hosiery Trades of Nottingham,' *Journal of the Statistical Society*, XXLX (1866), 540.

16 William Felkin, *History*, pp. 168–69, 171 *et. seq.*

17 T. S. Ashton, 'Some Statistics of the Industrial Revolution in Britain,' in *Essays in Economic History*, III, ed. E. M. Carus Wilson (1962), p. 248.

18 William Felkin, *History*, pp. 300–05; See also D. M. Smith 'The Silk Industry of the East Midlands, *The East Midland Geographer*, 1962, no. 17; I am indebted to Mr. S. D. Chapman for drawing my attention to the importance of the Derbyshire Silk Mills.

19 William Felkin, *History*, p. 156.

20 D. E. Varley, *op. cit.*, p. 4.

21 W. Gore Allen, *John Heathcoat and His Heritage*, (1958), p. 73.

22 *Ibid.*, p. 19.

23 William Felkin, *History*, p. 135.

24 *Ibid.*, p. 157.

25 *Ibid.*, p. 372; A list of inventive artisans with whom Fisher was connected is included among the Fisher mss.

26 *Place Mss.* 27807, Letter, Henson to Place May 31, 1825; Barbara M. D. Smith, 'Patents for Invention,' *Business History*, IV, 2 (June, 1962), 111.

27 *Second Report from the Select Committee on Postage* 1837–8, XX, II, ev. of Gravener Henson, p. 214.

28 *Place Mss.* 27807, Letter, Henson to Place May 31, 1825.

29 *Ibid.*

30 B. Woodcroft, ed., *Supplement to the series of Letters Patent and Specification of Letters Patent for Inventions recorded in the Great Seal Patent Office and granted between . . . 1617 and . . . 1852 . . .* (1858). 1. 935–46.

31 William Felkin, *History*, p. 141.

32 *Ibid.*, p. 113.

33 *Ibid.*, pp. 173–77.

34 *Ibid*, p. 148.

35 *Ibid.*, pp. 183, 205.

36 *Ibid.*, p. 140.

[37] Gravener Henson, *The Civil, Political and Mechanical History of the Framework knitters in Europe and America,* (*Nottingham,* 1831), I, 382

[38] William Felkin, *History,* p. 140.

[39] *Ibid.,* p. 139.

[40] John Blackner, *op. cit.,* p. 237.

[41] *First Report from the Select Committee* (*Framework knitters' petitions*), 1812, (247) II. 203, Appendix 5, p. 16.

[42] William Felkin, *History,* p. 183.

[43] *Ibid.,* p. 215.

[44] *Ibid.,* p. 223.

[45] *Ibid.,* p. 245.

[46] *Ibid.,* p. 237.

[47] J. L. and B. Hammond, *The Skilled Labourer,* (1919) p. 242; W. Gore Allen, *John Heathcoat and his Heritage* (1958), p. 71.

[48] Heathcoat's letter to the Mayor of Tiverton is reproduced in W. Gore Allen, *op. cit.,* Appendix I, p. 216.

[49] J. D. Chambers, *EHR,* Supplement 3, (1957), 60.

[50] William Felkin, *History,* p. 242.

[51] *Infra,* pp. 77–78.

[52] William Felkin, *History,* p. 248.

[53] *Ibid.,* p. 271.

[54] *Ibid.,* p. 333.

[55] *Ibid.,* p. 334.

[56] *Penny Magazine,* Supplement 1843.

[57] *N.P.L. Archives* M 8832/2 Agreement May 16, 1833.

[58] William Felkin, *History,* pp. 333–34.

[59] *First Report of the Children's Employment Commission 1833,* (450) xx. 1., p. 189.

[60] William Felkin, *History,* p. 333.

[61] *Ibid.,* pp. 339–41.

[62] *N.P.L. Archives,* M 8827/2 Articles of Co-partnership November 17, 1824.

[63] *Infra,* p. 96.

[64] *N.P.L. Archives* M 8833/2 Deed of Co-partnership, November 11, 1833.

[65] *Infra,* p. 145.

[66] J. M. Hunter, 'Sources of Capital in the Industrial Development of Nottingham,' *East Midland Geographer,* XVI (1961), pp. 34–36.

[67] A Nottingham branch of the Manchester, Northern and Central Bank which was opened in 1834, was wound up three years later.

[68] William Felkin, *History,* pp. 320–37.

[69] D. E. Varley, *op. cit.,* p. 57.

[70] For the career of James Fisher see William Felkin, *History,* Chapter III, pp. 320–330.

[71] William Felkin, *History,* p. 152. Although in the trade the lace finisher described himself as 'manufacturer' (even though he owned no machinery) the term manufacturer is reserved throughout the text for a machine owner or 'machine holder' making lace. Some firms also combined the manufacturing and finishing of lace.

[72] William Felkin, *History,* p. 152.

[73] B. Woodcroft, *loc. cit.*

[74] D. E. Varley, *op. cit.,* p. 58.

[75] *Infra,* pp. 94–97.

[76] William Felkin, *History,* pp. 340–344.

[77] *First Report of the Children's Employment Commission,* 1843, (431) ev. of William Felkin, p.f. 49.

[78] William Felkin, *History,* pp. 149–50.

[79] *Ibid.,* p. 363 *et. seq.*

[80] D. E. Varley, *op. cit.,* pp. 22–29.

[81] William Felkin, *History,* pp. 360, 363.

[82] *First Report of the Children's Employment Commission,* 1843 (431) ev. of William Felkin, p.f. 52.

[83] William Felkin, *History,* p. 554; D. E. Varley, *op. cit.,* pp. 20–27.

[84] William Felkin, *History,* p. 509; D. E. Varley, *op. cit.,* pp. 49–50.

[85] William Felkin, *History,* p. 334.

[86] *Ibid.,* p. 552.

[87] *First Report of the Children's Employment Commission,* 1843 (431) ev. of William Felkin, p.f. 52.

[88] D. E. Varley, *op. cit.,* p. 30.

[89] *First Report of the Children's Employment Commission,* 1843 (431) ev. of William Felkin, p.f. 52; D. E. Varley, *op. cit.,* p. 30.

[90] *N.R.,* October 20, 1846.

[91] *N.R.,* August 19, 1842.

[92] William Felkin, *History,* p. 554.

[93] For a lucid analysis of the Nottingham Lace Market see D. E. Varley, *op. cit.,* pp. 52–90.

[94] C. C. Aaronsfield, 'Nottingham Jewish Lace Pioneers,' *Nottingham Guardian Journal,* April 19, 1954.

[95] D. E. Varley, *op. cit.,* p. 86.

[96] See Alfred Marshall, *Industry and Trade,* (1920), pp. 284–287, p. 350. Referring to the significance of the 'industrial atmosphere' to be found in industrial towns, he commented '. . . good work is rightly appreciated, inventions and improvements in machinery in processes and the general organization of the business have their merits promptly discussed; if one man starts a new idea it is taken up by others and combined with suggestions of their own and thus it becomes the sources of further new ideas.'

[97] *First Report from the Select Committee on the Laws affecting the Exportation of Machinery,* 1841 (201) VII. 1., ev. of Richard Birkin, p. 179.

[98] *Second Report from the Select Committee on Postage,* 1837–8, XX. Part II, ev. of Gravener Henson, p. 214.

[99] J. Jewkes, D. Sawyer, and R. Stillerman, *The Sources of Invention,* (1958), p. 67.

CHAPTER IV

A PROGRESSIVE INDUSTRY: GROWTH AND FLUCTUATION IN THE MACHINE-MADE LACE TRADE

BETWEEN 1809 and 1850, the new machine-made lace industry grew both in terms of the capital and labour that it employed, and the output produced. It is extremely difficult, however, to quantify this change, except by using very approximate estimates of the size of the industry in that period.[1] The number of licensed bobbin net machines in 1818 was 970, and it was known that in 1819 at least 200 machines infringed Heathcoat's patent. The number of warp frames making lace in 1815 was approximately 400, and a few point net frames were still in use. Thereafter, bobbin net machinery increased to 2,469 in 1826, rising to 5,000 machines seven years later. After this date the increased construction of wider and faster machinery prevents a comparison of these figures with those of later years. The number of machines fell to 3,200 in 1843, rising to 3,500 by 1855. The productive capacity of these wider machines with faster actions, however, was much greater than that of the larger number of machines which were operating in former years. During a period of steadily falling prices, Felkin's estimates of the value of machine-made lace output showed a rise from approximately £1·9m. in 1831, to £3·1m. twenty years later, the latter figure including about £700,000 accounted for by warp lace. In 1856 the value of total lace output was estimated at £4·8m. and by 1862, £5·1m.

Employment figures for the industry are equally difficult to determine, and contemporary estimates probably err wildly. For example, it is difficult to believe that in 1834 an industry based upon 5,000 bobbin net machines, which probably needed no more than 7,500 operatives to work them, employed between 150,000 and 200,000 persons altogether, although it is true that several thousand women and children found employment as auxiliary workers and, often on a part time basis, in the ancillary branches of the trade as needle women and finishers; hundreds more men made and maintained machines. In 1851 Richard Birkin estimated that 133,000 persons were employed in the industry, while the census returns for the same year showed that in Nottingham, where approximately 70 per cent. of all bobbin net machinery was located, nearly 10,000 men, women, and children found employment in the lace industry; owing to the large amount of partial employment in the industry this is almost certainly an underestimation, but it is impossible to calculate an accurate figure.

The initial expansion of the machine-made lace industry took place after the factory system had already been adopted in other sections of the textile industry. The warp lace branch, which for many years was unaffected by this form of organization, continued to be conducted in a similar manner to that in the hosiery industry until the few remaining hand warp lace machines disappeared sometime after 1840.[2] The bobbin net industry was also influenced by the mode of organization in the hosiery trade, but the payment of frame or machine rent to one's employer, which had long been a practice peculiar to that trade and to the warp lace branch, did not develop. Prior to the expiration of Heathcoat's patent, industrial organization revolved around capitalists leasing machines to machine holders who either worked the machines with relatives or employed journeymen.[3] From the beginning a number of independent machine holders also belonged to the trade, making nets and paying wages, even though the only employee might be a relative; the independent machine holders also relied upon yarn merchants and commission agents to supply them with raw material, orders, and credit.[4] After the commercial crisis of 1826, the capitalist figure whose interest in the trade was merely financial largely disappeared, while the reduction in the number of machine owners during the thirties was also accompanied by an increase in the number of factories producing lace nets on machines propelled by steam power.[5]

However, the factory did not become characteristic until after 1850. From the introduction of the bobbin net machine, a few entrepreneurs had concentrated large numbers under one roof, but not until 1816 was power used to produce bobbin net. In 1831 there were twenty-two factories housing the industry's one thousand power machines.[6] By 1836 at least seven more had been added, while there were also forty large workshops, most of which contained less than fifty hand machines. The typical unit of production, however, was the small workshop which in Nottingham was often to be found in the upper storeys of substantial houses near the town centre, though during the thirties and forties many of the new dwellings with long windowed attics which were built in the adjacent villages housed lace makers and their families.[7] So long as hand-operated machines could survive competition, which was possible until the late forties, the lace machines were suitable for attic and workshop use. In 1833 the four largest lace factories in the Nottingham district were those which belonged to John Kendall, whose factory was in Canal Street, Thomas Sewell and Jonathan Burton at Carrington, and James Fisher at Radford.[8] These were still among the largest factories visited by the Factory Commissioner in 1841 when Fisher's factory was under the management of Robert Leavers. Kendall, whose factory contained thirty machines, also employed a manager, William Gregory, who later set up on his own. Sewell, who shared a factory building with Jonathan Burton, owned twenty-eight machines, while Jonathan Burton owned forty-three, and his brother, Samuel, who moved into a factory at Sherwood, owned twenty-seven. At New Basford the lace manufacturing partnership of Biddle & Birkin managed a factory which contained twenty hand-operated machines in addition to twelve driven by steam power. At Thomas Robinson's factory, which was also located at New Basford, twenty-two machines were under the supervision of his manager John Sisling, while William Astill owned thirty-three machines in his factory at Carrington.[9]

The application of steam to lace machinery proceeded rapidly between 1840 and 1860, and the fact that this process occurred when an independent machine-owning class already existed, together with the economies of specialization to be gained from small-scale production, resulted in the development of the 'stall system'.[10] Capitalist machine-owners built factories in which their own machines were placed, while extra space was rented to other machine holders who either worked the machines themselves or employed lace makers. An example of this system is afforded by William Herbert's lace factory, which in 1842 occupied one hundred people. He owned two factories of five and six storeys respectively, both having steam power and gaslight,[11] and they were let partly to machine holders from whom he received £800 annually. On a more modest scale William Stanton, having decided to work his machinery by steam power, reached an agreement with two lace makers situated opposite to extend a shaft underground across the street from his factory to theirs, so as to enable them to rent power, the annual charge to vary with the width of their several machines.[12] In 1842 Taylor's factory at Broad Marsh housed the machines of twenty-three owners, each of whom owned between one and ten machines. Messrs. Hall's factory at New Lenton, in addition to their own thirty-one machines contained fifty more which belonged to four other lace making firms.[13] Most manually operated machines located in workshops belonged to the workshop proprietors, and only when competition from steam power became serious did the independent machine holders move from the attic workshops in their homes into factories where they were able to rent steam power. Thus although the number of factories increased from twenty-nine or thirty in 1836, to one hundred and thirty 'larger factories' in 1865, the small production units and the independent producers remained.[14] Their existence continued to be a dominant feature of the fancy branch, just as the large unit was characteristic of the plain net branch. In both branches, however, by 1861 handpowered production of machine-made lace was virtually extinct. According to Felkin, in that year no more than ninety machines of this type were making lace.[15]

Whether a factory contained the single proprietorships and other small firms, or whether it contained the machines of a single employer, the hours of work were determined by the steam engine which, in most factories, ran for twenty hours from 4.0 a.m. until midnight, or as in a few cases, for twenty-four hours daily. In those cases where power was leased it was in the interest of the independent machine holder to work the same hours, and there is no evidence to suggest that shorter 'power hours' were available for hire. In most factories the engine stopped on Saturday evening at six or eight, but several engines ran throughout Friday night to make up for stoppages which may have occurred during the week. In almost all cases the working day was divided into four shifts so that each man worked a ten or twelve hour day in alternate shifts lasting five or six hours. The hours worked by men operating the hand machines, which accounted for a majority until after 1850, were most irregular. The wider machines like the power machines were usually worked by two sets of men, but the narrow machines were single handed in order to compete. By 1841 few narrow lace machines were employed, and most men worked between eight and ten hours daily. Idleness on Monday and sometimes Tuesday was commonly made up through nocturnal labour at the weekend and as one witness remarked, 'when they can sell, the men work the machines night and day.'[16]

The occupational dangers attached to lace making were small. Even in the factories serious accidents rarely occurred, and most injuries consisted of little worse than crushed fingers. Neither was the physical labour involved in operating power machines at all onerous, for the operative's function consisted of minding machinery and watching the work in progress, rectifying errors when they arose, and adjusting the delicate mechanism of bobbins, carriages, and springs. But the operation of wide hand machines, especially those not worked by rotary motion, required considerable strength as well as skill. The use of any method for the manufacture of lace caused a deterioration of eyesight resulting from the constant control of a machine between nine and twelve feet wide, containing between 2,600 and 3,600 bobbins which moved through the guide threads a hundred times a minute.[17]

Child and female labour was of great importance to the trade, as it was in other textile industries. In the actual process of lace making it was customary for a shift team working each machine to consist of one man, and a youth or a boy who might begin at about the age of thirteen. In the workshops rotary hand machines were turned by youths and boys, a laborious task which relieved the lace maker from the perpetual motion of feet and hands. In factories and workshops, the two separate processes of winding thread onto the bobbins, and of threading the bobbins, thereby replenishing a machine with yarn, were both performed by women and children.[18] Again, the tasks were not physically demanding, but the manner in which lace manufacture was customarily organized required threaders and winders to be available for work throughout all the four daily shifts. This was especially true of the threaders, most of whom were boys, for upon their function depended the ability of the lace maker to continue manufacture after one piece of material had been completed and came off the machine.[19] The Factory Commissioner described the evils under which the threaders suffered:

> Sometimes they will make a round to see if the piece is about to come off, sometimes they have a notice sent to them it will be off at such and such an hour, and they go accordingly at the appointed time.[20]

It was clear, however, that it was usual for the lace makers to send for a number of children at all hours of the night and day, and with minimum warning; it then depended on the number that appeared how long the operation would take.

A large number of children, mostly girls, were employed in finishing processes which were performed outside the factories and machine shops in workshops and homes. These were the lace runners who embroidered the lace, the drawers who pulled out the threads which held the individual widths of figured lace together, the pearlers, hemmers, and menders, whose needle work enabled them to supplement family incomes. In 1833 Alfred Power was especially dismayed by the plight of the lace runners. In his opinion the lace runner was, 'the most skilful, the hardest worked, and the worst paid of all operatives connected with the lace trade.'[21] Their long hours of work—usually fifteen or sixteen each day except for the late afternoon closing on Saturday and the respite on Sunday—were slightly longer than those of the other warehouse and workshop employees. Finally, the processes by which lace was bleached or dyed were also carried out in part by women and young girls, and likewise lace dressing. This process, by which the bleached or dyed lace was dipped in starch and dried to stiffen the material thereby giving it greater body, entailed working in one of the town's large warehouses where, in order to dry the lace, the temperature was maintained at extremely high levels.[22] The result, as the town's medical authorities pointed out, was a most unhealthy atmosphere for work.

Giving evidence before the Factory Commissioners, Felkin was asked to state his opinion on the question of extending the Factory Act to the lace trade. He claimed that the practical result of this would be to act as an incentive to wide hand-operated machine owners to retain hand power. He forecast that in the event of the Factory Act being applied to lace, the resulting diminution in the output from power machines (as a result of the curtailment of working hours) would be supplemented by hand machines, thereby delaying the extension of power. Felkin also stressed the folly of legislation which would restrict the hours of labour on a particular *mode* of manufacturing, while the majority of the population would continue to consent to labour excessive hours for deficient wages in domestic employment.[23] In his report Power stated that he considered legislation unnecessary, as the services required of the children involved were 'precarious and occasional rather than continuous and constant.' When they returned to report again ten years later, the Factory Commissioners discovered that conditions in both lace and hosiery trades were virtually unchanged from those prevailing in 1833.[24] For the hosiery trade, Rogers, Morley, Heard, and Carver expressed themselves in favour of restrictions being placed upon child labour, and Carver insisted that if the hours of work for children were restricted, then provision should be made for their proper instruction and education, 'or greater evils are to be apprehended.'[25] Boys began winding at the age of five or six, and worked the same hours as men. Girls began to seam at seven or eight years and worked from 7 a.m. until 10 p.m. At some of the lace factories rules were laid down prohibiting the threading of machines outside certain hours, but even with these restrictions children were kept until ten or eleven at night and required again at four or five the next morning. Most children, however, were employed by small owners of hand machines and often they would visit shop after shop at all hours of the night to carry out their tasks. There was generally no provision made for them to sleep, although they were often sent for at three or four in the morning and would thread a machine, wait, thread another and so on until eleven, twelve or later at night. 'It is in such instances no exaggeration to affirm', stated the Report, 'that these boys are, in a Christian country, treated as if they were mere brute animals.'[26] Treatment in factories was said to be rather superior to that met in the workshops, where the mechanics, and not the principals, contracted with the parents and paid the children wages. Grainger's verdict on the threaders and winders was that there were 'no children who are subject to such uniform hardship.'[27] The condition of women and children employed in the workshops and private houses drawing, mending, purling, hemming, and embroidering was only slightly less wretched.[28] One very disturbing feature of the Report was the discovery that many working mothers were in the habit of administering diluted opium to silence their children's cries. This mixture, asserted by local doctors to have proved fatal on several occasions, was called 'Godfrey's Cordial'. When finally the Commissioners drew up their report, it proved to be an indictment, not of the few local factories but of the small workshops where hosiery and lace auxiliary workers toiled under first, second, or even third hand mistresses. In the domestic workshops of Nottingham, ill-ventilated, damp, and overcrowded, were to be found appalling demoralisation, filth, and poverty. 'In comparison with these wretched places', wrote the Commissioners, 'factories are Elysiums.'[29] But unhappily these conditions did not concern a small number:

almost all the children of the labouring classes in Nottingham are engaged at a very early age in one or other of the several branches of the lace manufacture or hosiery trade . . . as soon as they can tie a knot or use a needle.[30]

A minority of power machine owners objected to applying the Factory Acts to children in the lace trade on the grounds that unfair advantage would be given to hand machine owners who would be beyond reach of the Act. This had been Felkin's view in 1833. In 1842 conflicting aims produced a frustrating stalemate. To legislate on factory hours would leave the vast majority of women and children outside the law and would probably increase the number of domestic workers. Meanwhile, suffering and hardship continued. 'The children', Felkin observed ruefully, 'suffer from scrofula, indigestion and defective eyesight . . .'.[31] Felkin, who was alive both to the interests of business and society, welcomed the temporary inconvenience that would be caused by shortened hours of labour for children. He was confident that readjustments would take place speedily so as 'to secure to all the fair interests of trade and the just claims of humanity'. On this subject the leading hosiers also agreed. The opposition by the few power owners, however, could not be ignored, and it was feared that the effect of regulating existing factory labour in the lace trade might be to check the extension of

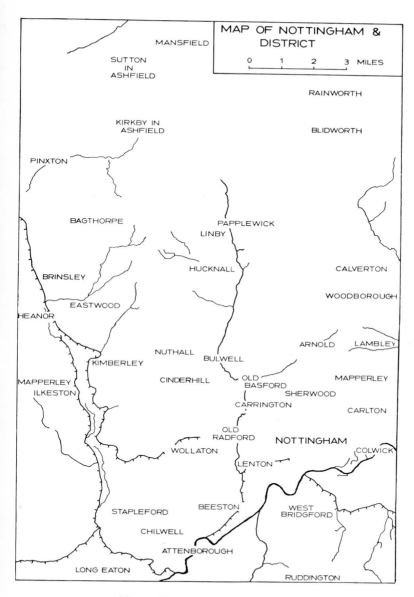

MAP OF NOTTINGHAM AND DISTRICT

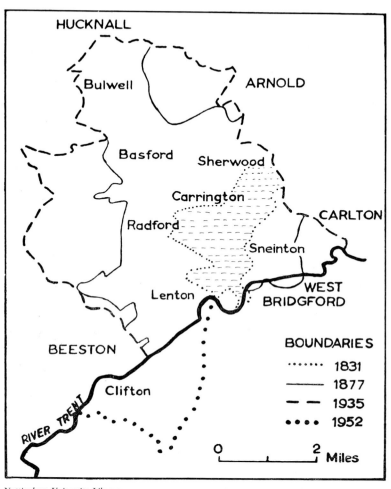

PLAN SHOWING THE NOTTINGHAM BOUNDARIES IN 1831, 1877, 1935 AND 1952

steam power. The Report of the Commissioners stressed this fact, making it plain that because lace manufacture could not yet be described as a factory industry legislation must be postponed.

Those lace workers, whose hours on duty (as distinct from actual hours of work) were the longest, and whose rewards were lowest, were thus denied the protection secured by women and children who performed comparable tasks in the cotton industry. Lace makers earned more and worked less than these groups, though the shift system prevents a direct comparison between their customary nine-and-a-half hours work on five days a week and five hours on Saturdays, or the sixty-one hour week in a few factories, with the considerably longer hours normally worked in factories and workshops in other trades. Not until legislation passed in 1860 were the hours of Lancashire cotton textile workers limited to sixty a week, and forty years passed before the working week was reduced to fifty-five-and-a-half.[32] Moreover during an average working week of between fifty-two-and-a-half and sixty-one hours, many lace makers earned sufficient to place them among the higher paid section of the industrial working classes.[33]

Between 1815 and 1837 their average weekly wages declined from 25s. in 1829 to 16s. in the depressed year of 1837, but throughout these years most lace makers earned enough to afford a standard of comfort which was much higher than that of their fellow townsmen in the hosiery industry. An exception was the dwindling number of lace makers working narrow hand machines. In 1834, when their average wages were only 8s., Felkin described them as 'a body of industrious but poor men who cannot maintain their families working all hours.'[34] Although there was little hope of improvement in the condition of this section of the industry, after the depression of 1837-8 innovation and expanding trade aided in reversing the steady decline in wages. Felkin estimated that the average lace maker's wage in 1844 was about 18s., though as in earlier years some earned as much as 40s.. When lacemakers organized the British Union of Plain Net Workers in 1846, they planned to allow sickness benefits and unemployment grants, the sizes of which were to depend upon whether the member's normal weekly wage was 16s. or 20s., another indication of the level of earnings in the industry.[35] By 1860 lace makers were earning between 20s. and 35s., . . . 'a rate of wages', Felkin commented, 'calculated to secure the means of health, comfort, and most of the ordinary conveniences of life . . .'.[36] In 1836, women employed in the trade earned an average weekly wage of 6s., children earned about 2s.. By 1860 children could earn between 3s. and 5s., and women, between 10s. and 16s.. Thus, while the changes that took place during the two decades after the com-

H

mercial crisis of 1837 transformed the industry, the benefits which resulted from technical innovation and improvements in economic organization were shared by employees.

Estimates of average earnings conceal the wide variations in wages and employment that arose out of cyclical fluctuations in economic activity, for, as their presence shows, the course of economic change was far from smooth. This was especially true of the machine-made lace industry which experienced its first spectacular fluctuation between the year when Heathcoat's patent expired in 1823 and the commercial crisis three years later which brought to an abrupt end the general economic boom. During these years, the complete freedom to invest in bobbin net machinery coincided with expanding foreign trade and easy credit conditions which encouraged domestic capital investment.[37] The combination of these two factors—the lapse of the patent and the economic upswing— together resulted in such a volume of investment in the lace industry that for many years excess capacity presented serious problems both for employers and workmen.

Attempts to solve these problems followed the example set by the patentees in 1819, a year of widespread depression in the textile trades.[38] The patentees had then formed a Mart Association whose purpose was to build up a fund from which to purchase lace nets from subscribers at guaranteed prices. To this fund 165 machine-owning members subscribed, their individual contributions depending on the size and number of machines in the owners' possession.[39] A further measure aimed at supporting the price of lace nets was a periodic stoppage of machinery which was also organized by the Mart Association, while in the same year a Deed of Restriction included an agreement among the patentees to withhold further licences.[40] However, nearly one-quarter of all existing lace machinery (excluding warp lace machines) belonged to infringers, over which the Mart Association possessed no control. According to Felkin, the price of nets was pegged slightly above that of the competitive market, but as restrictions on new machinery laid down by the deed were ignored, the higher net prices led to the construction of more machines; as these came into operation lace net prices resumed their downward trend.[41] During that depression journeymen bobbin net makers had appealed to machine holders to extend aid to the unemployed. They requested the independent machine holders to support their resistance against the proposals made by some of the larger manufacturers which, if they were adopted, would shift some of the production costs on to the journeymen. They also endeavoured to persuade the independent machine holders that the proposals concealed a conspiracy aimed at engrossing machinery into the hands of the large manufacturers. The change suggested was that the mode of payment which was customary in the hosiery trade should be adopted in the lace trade, the journeymen should pay rent for a machine and also meet the expenses of auxiliary work. To this form of contract the journeymen refused to agree.[42] Indeed, only a short time after the journeymen had been on the defensive, as a result of changes in economic conditions manufacturers were bidding keenly for their skills, the effect of which was to transform bobbin net makers and mechanics into an artisan aristocracy. The construction of lace machines reached such a level that in 1823, when Heathcoat declared his intention of applying for an extension of his letters patent, a meeting was called to mobilize opposition to this proposal which many feared would seriously injure the local economy. However, the patent lapsed, and the next few years brought a rapid increase in the size of the industry. In 1820 slightly more than a thousand bobbin net machines existed; by 1826 their number had increased to nearly two thousand five hundred.[43]

Notwithstanding his sometimes prolix literary style, it would be difficult to improve upon William Felkin's colourful account of the boom of those years, for his description successfully communicates the excitement which, evidently, contemporaries experienced:

Everything combined to lead the people in Nottingham and its neighbourhood to expect golden times when the patent shackles were removed. In consequence, through the years 1823 to 1825, a time of unparalleled prosperity, capital flowed into the business abundantly from bankers, lawyers, physicians, clergymen, landowners, farmers, and retail dealers, in order to construct new lace machinery. That which was already at work could be sold for three times its cost. Every available smith and mechanic on the spot was hired, and the wonderful wages offered, speedily attracted smiths and mechanics from far off towns. Day labourers came from the plough and strikers from the forge, for some of the latter got £5 to £10 a week. Birmingham, Manchester, and Sheffield engineers and tool-makers met on one common ground; but houses were too few to lodge them; bricks doubled in price, and building land sold for £4,000 an acre. Thousands of pounds were wasted in paying enormous weekly wages to people pretending to construct machinery, the movements of which they could not comprehend; and tens of thousands of pounds were drawn from speculators for machines, which, even if well constructed, could not possibly repay them their outlay. The inflation of the public mind was universal and became a sort of local epidemic—a mania, acquiring the name in after years of the "twist net fever". The whole community was athirst for gain, and became intoxicated. Nothing like it had ever been seen before in that trade or probably in any other. Those who actually wrought in the machines had an opportunity to realise large sums of money. The provident generally, as was natural, put their gains in a part or the whole of a machine, paying for it by weekly instalments; thus becoming partly or wholly their own masters. The self-indulgent spent their time and money in a constant round of alternate work and pleasure. They would ride on horseback to and from labour, and having taken their shift at their machines, refresh themselves with a pint of port or claret on their return. Not a few of these spendthrifts were receiving parish pay or aid from public benevolence within the following ten years. The minds of many of the more ardent smiths and other mechanics became bewildered and overpowered, in the endeavour to overcome the difficulties presented by this intricate class of machinery, and they fell into insanity. When the speculative national frenzy of 1825, which had countenanced this more limited mania, collapsed in 1826, the effect in Nottingham and the district around was fearful. Visions of wealth and cherished schemes for grasping fortunes suddenly, were dissipated almost in a day. Many not in the trade, as well as some who were, lost all their means and fell into hopeless poverty; some died from despair; others went into self-imposed exile; a few destroyed themselves.[44]

A sober recollection in tranquillity by one of the local dandies inspired the following song:

With rum and gin and brandy we made the people stare,
And horse and gig so handy O, to take the morning air,
And then with single-breasted coats and spanking new top boots
And pockets lined with one pound notes we were the merry shoots

The bobbin and the carriage hands they scarcely would look down,
Or bend their portly bodies for to pick up half-a-crown;
And if it had but lasted long, I think they wouldn't stoop,
To poor beaf steaks and onions, but they'd dine on turtle soup.

The Cobbler left his soles and heels and wouldn't be so mean
As stick to wax and tatching ends, but bought a twist machine;
The tailor left his board and goose, the miller left his grist,
Tag rag and bobtail all got loose, to get into the twist.

And servants left the mop and broom and wouldn't go to
place,
But set their dainty hands to work to purl and mend the lace.
But to tell the long and short of it, and so to end my song
Amongst so many twisters, Sir, they've twisted it too strong.[45]

Before the end of 1825 the optimism of manufacturers and workmen was reversed. By September the buoyancy in the lace trade had
begun to diminish. The third week in December jeopardized the
town's prosperity when the general speculative mania collapsed.
There was an immediate run on the four Nottingham banks, three
of which had figured among the largest note-issuing houses in the
country, but their reputation for prudence and good management
helped to prevent failures. Recognizing the importance of maintaining the level of confidence in the town, manufacturers and tradesmen met under the Mayor's chairmanship to express their 'perfect
reliance in the solidarity and safety of each and every one of the
Nottingham banks', while declaring their intention to receive the
bank notes 'with the most perfect satisfaction.'[46] The large amount
of unsound paper money in general circulation, which had resulted
from the ease with which credit could be obtained prior to the crisis,
created a commercially dangerous situation for merchants and
manufacturers having connections with the large London commercial houses. It enlarged the possibility of an extensive disruption
of trade and credit, accompanied by widespread unemployment.
Repercussions from the stoppage of the firm of Banks, Gould, &
Banks of Cheapside, London, for example, involved manufacturers
in uncertainty and losses.[47] Fortunately, the notes of firms were met
promptly by the banks in cash, with the result that apprehension
concerning their stability was shortlived and the minor panic
ended.[48] Locally, many people were of the opinion that the action
of tradesmen and manufacturers in affirming confidence in the banks
had been the main reason why Nottingham suffered less than other
towns of comparable size.[49]

The short term effects of the crisis were less serious than those
which took slightly more time before the full implications of the
investment boom became apparent to the trade. For although the
speculative mania had been the characteristic feature of the general
boom, especially that centred upon South American schemes, considerable capital investment had taken place.[50] One result was that
many factories operated at less than full capacity and much
machinery lay idle. This was especially true of the cotton industry
in which workers and manufacturers faced falling prices until, in the
middle thirties, demand caught up with supply.[51] A similar situa-

tion existed in the lace industry, in which there was a duplication of the sudden and severe depression that occurred in the cotton industry following the commercial crisis in the winter of 1825–6. Inventories were immediately placed on the market and net prices fell drastically. Many machine owners who had invested in new machinery rushed to move out of the trade, liquidating capital in order to recoup losses due to depreciation in the value of idle machinery.[52] As a result, machinery prices followed the downward course taken by lace. Leavers machines, which had been purchased for £700 in 1823, were sold for £150 only three years later,[53] and this downward movement in the prices of lace nets and lace machinery continued, interrupted only by short pauses in the middle thirties and forties. Thus the crisis of 1826 marked the beginning of a period in which the trade experienced the consequences of speculation and overcapitalization, and machine owners, independent machine holders, manufacturers, and workmen were forced to meet these problems.

As early as September, 1825 after the peak in net prices and machinery had passed and signs of a softening market had already appeared, machine holders reconstructed a Mart Committee and attempted to restrict supplies of net and machinery, this time by setting a daily limit of eight on the number of hours machines should be worked and by the distribution of printed price lists.[54] Gravener Henson called together a meeting of workmen in the bobbin net trade and a committee was appointed to levy 6d. weekly from each man employed. This was used to relieve the unemployed and to defend wages, while to the same end the men resolved to cooperate with the machine holders in restricting output. The stint was intermittent until February and it met with little success.[55] Fears of the effects of increased construction of machinery and general overproduction through the operation of improved machines for longer hours were coupled with growing apprehension concerning illicit exports of machinery and the emigration of skilled artisans to the Continent. As long before as 1814 a committee of bobbin net makers, which included Gravener Henson, had taken steps to restrain the smuggling of machinery overseas.[56] In 1823 Henson travelled to France to investigate the nature and size of the machine-made lace industry there. At Calais, St. Quentin, and Lisle he discovered Englishmen building the outsides of bobbin net machines, assembling them, and producing nets, and at Rouen he encountered Leavers, himself, with many of his journeymen; indeed, many of the bobbin net makers in France were known to Henson and several were frequently in Nottingham to keep abreast of improvements in the trade. Henson argued that the export of the delicate 'insides' of machines, which might cost about £200, was a matter for serious concern, for although only Englishmen were as yet able to build, assemble, and operate them efficiently, the next generation of Frenchmen, benefiting from the instruction of English artisans with English machinery, would then be able to build a completely independent machine-made lace industry.[57] For this reason Henson firmly opposed the free movement of artisans and machinery. The Board of Trade continued to refuse licences for machinery exports, but smuggling did not cease. When the trade suffered another depression in the early thirties a committee was again formed in an attempt to check the growing competition from France based on English men and machines.[58]

Meanwhile, output restriction absorbed the attention of the trade and the lapse which followed the temporary recovery of net prices in 1827 led to the establishment of another Trade Committee in 1828. The initiative lay with the journeymen whose earnings were suffering, and in November between one thousand five hundred and two thousand of their number met and advocated a stint on output. The following month manufacturers within a radius of twenty-five miles of Nottingham drew up a plan to limit output.[59] At Tiverton Heathcoat, one of the largest machine owners, also gave his assent to the scheme. Machine-owning members raised a fund of £6,000 and the operations were directed by twelve power and twelve hand machine owners presided over by William Felkin, Heathcoat's lace agent in Nottingham.[60] The aims of the Committee included the limitation of entry into the trade, the prevention and exposure of frauds, and the regulation of working hours of existing machinery. Normally during periods of brisk trade machines were worked between twenty and twenty-four hours daily by four alternate shifts of workmen; under the Committee's regulations daily working hours were reduced to twelve. For several weeks the voluntary restriction was effective, although James Fisher refused to cooperate,[61] and when in April the Mart Committee drew up a quasi-legal Restriction of Hours Deed by which it sought to consolidate its informal authority and to penalize members for violating the articles of the restriction agreement, a majority of power and hand machine owners gave their assent. It was doomed, however, when more than one-eighth of the machine owners refused to cooperate, for the Committee had agreed that unless seven-eighths of all machine owners agreed to sign the Deed, it should not become effective.[62] Nevertheless, the informal twelve hour restriction continued until June, when an attempt to limit hours of work to ten led to a revolt of the larger manufacturers. In an attempt to placate them the Mart Committee proposed a return to twelve hours restric-

tion, but by this time the trade was in disarray, and, despite the
journeymen's petition drawn up by Henson urging its continuance,
the Trade Committee dissolved.[63]

Judging from the evidence presented before the Factory Commissioners in 1833 by William Felkin and others, it seems that the
Committee's authority was more nominal than real, and that its
dictates were obeyed only so long as those working hours prescribed
were generally acknowledged by manufacturers to be most advantageous for all.[64] It seems more probable that the individual owners
and holders considered their interests separately, withdrawing from
the Mart when the 'general feeling' as to what was good for the trade
clashed with what the individual manufacturer thought most beneficial to his own condition. In the absence of evidence which might
suggest their reasons, one can speculate that the larger manufacturers were probably low cost producers—their factories housed
power machines—with superior marketing organisations. The
twelve or so larger producers employed their own agents who sold
brown nets in the lace market, while smaller producers and machine
holders were largely in the hands of about two hundred commission agents to whom they were often indebted for credit in purchasing their material.[65] In fierce competition, these agents then circulated the finishing warehouses offering the nets for sale. The small
men wanted stable prices beneath an umbrella of price and output
control; the larger producers preferred to 'let trade find its own
level.'[66] Nevertheless, despite the disenchantment of the large manufacturers, Felkin maintained that the restriction of hours in 1828–29
succeeded at least in slowing down the fall in the price of unfinished
plain net.[67]

In 1830 Felkin was called to chair a meeting of machine holders
who wished to revive the limitation of hours, but after two weeks
the attempt was abandoned.[68] The following year the journeymen
re-formed their union and refused for a time to work more than
twelve hours daily.[69] In 1834, another year of depression in the lace
trade, separate associations formed by different branches of the
trade sought to restrict working hours and to regulate sales and
output by setting up Marts after the style of the Marts of 1819–23.[70]
In 1835 one thousand three hundred plain net machines worked
only eight hours daily, until a sudden revival of demand led to the
committee's dissolution.[71] Reflecting upon the shortcomings of
restriction, Felkin noted that during the 1828–29 stint six hundred
and fifty new machines of greater power had been built, and that
machine owners' profits had been raised by £240,000; his verdict
on the experiments in collusion was that financial losses 'may
account for but cannot justify these departures from the laws of

demand and supply.[72] The effort of the trade committee to support prices were unsuccessful. (See Table VIII.)

TABLE VIII: *Prices per square yard of Finished Plain Net 1813 to 1856.*

	s.	d.		s.	d.
1813	40	0	1830	2	0
1815	30	0	1833	1	4
1818	20	0	1836		10
1821	12	0	1842		6
1824	8	0	1850		4
1827	4	0	1856		6

Source: William Felkin, *Journal of the Society of Arts*, IV (1856), p. 483.

One factor which the trade found it impossible even to attempt to control was the high rate of obsolescence of lace machinery. Machines were often liable to be superseded by others, either in consequence of improvements, which succeeded each other in rapid succession, or by changes in fashion.[73] During the thirties obsolescence occurred on a huge scale and between 1833 and 1836, according to Felkin, the number of machines fell from 5,000 to 3,600. The reduction in the number of machine owners from 1,382 to 857 mainly affected independent machine holders who, with their capital tied up in machinery, had financed yarn purchases on credit and who had found themselves unable to meet their debts when commission houses and finishers reduced their purchases. Between 1831 and 1836 more than 500 owners of one, two, and three machines either reverted to journeyman status or quit the trade.[74] The causes of this development were twofold. As the experiments in collusion showed, for several years following 1826, owing to the existence of excess capacity in the industry, plain net was overproduced. As profits and wages steadily declined, competition successfully eliminated the less efficient producers. Felkin held the view that this downward pressure on incomes during the thirties 'forced the progress of invention onwards with unusual rapidity', and as wider and faster machines left the mechanics' workshops, competition grew even more fierce. So firmly convinced were many people of the obsolescence of slow and narrow machinery, that in 1833 and 1834 between five and six hundred machines of this type were broken up.

'Many of these', wrote Felkin, 'were thrown piece-meal out of the windows of the upper rooms in which they had been worked into the neighbouring streets, not being thought worth the trouble of carrying downstairs, though they had cost a few years before several hundred pounds a-piece, and were still in good working condition'.[75]

Thus, as competition ensured that rising productivity showed in lower prices rather than higher profits, several hundred narrow traverse warp, narrow straight bolt, and narrow circular machines were sold for scrap. Only a few years after these machines had cleared the market for £2,000,000, their value in 1836 was estimated at no more than £15,000.[76]

For a number of local smiths and mechanics the cry of the Nottingham street merchant, 'Old rags and twist machines to sell', encouraged enterprise and not despair. The upswing in the economy which had begun in 1832 had not been of sufficient magnitude to ease the burden of excess capacity, but the peak reached in economic activity in 1836 provided favourable conditions for introducing to the market new and fashionable lace nets. These were produced on some of the modified scrap machines which, after only a few pounds expenditure by skilled mechanics, had regained value. In 1836 Felkin referred to tenfold increases in the market value of machines which only three years before had been sold as scrap iron.[77] The beginnings of mechanized production of fancy lace nets by use of the jacquard was important in several respects. Successful adaptation of the old narrow machines, and the favourable reaction to the slightly more varied lace nets which they produced, resulted in the modification of several hundred machines formerly idle or making plain nets.[78] In 1836 nearly one-third of all machines were making the new articles which were more expensive than the plain nets, but whose appeal to fashion-conscious consumers at home raised the proportion of output sold in the domestic market from about 25 per cent. in 1832 to about 60 per cent. ten years later.[79] Meanwhile, some of the modified narrow machines also became obsolescent, as machine smiths constructed new and wider machinery incorporating recent technical improvements. Between 1836 and 1842 nearly five hundred machines were scrapped, many small owners capitulating in the face of powerful competition from the growing number of factory producers, and more machine-owning lace makers swelled the ranks of the journeymen.[80]

Although the extension of steam power in Nottingham lace factories was detrimental to small machine owners making plain net on machines worked by hand, the factories were best able to compete with the rapidly expanding Continental industry.[81] Foreign competition in overseas markets was growing. In 1833 the British lace industry began to feel the effects of a 50 per cent. duty which the French Government had imposed on lace imports, for as a result that market had become almost impossible to penetrate.[82] In the same year journeymen, independent machine holders, machine owners, and manufacturers joined together to support Gravener Henson and William Felkin in a renewed attempt to prohibit the export of machinery. Two committees were formed. One was to discover machines intended for export and to take measures for their seizure before they left the country, the other was a financial committee to receive, manage, and disburse funds subscribed for this purpose.[83] According to Felkin, within a month every principal house in the trade signified its adherence to the movement. Response from the journeymen was similarly enthusiastic. Henson drew up a memorial to the Lords of the Treasury, signed by owners of more than three thousand machines and by four thousand workmen. The petition referred to the increase in the number of bobbin net machines in France which had risen from one hundred to two thousand in ten years:

> Frequently the whole machines and almost in every case the inner and more delicate parts have been made in this neighbourhood, some houses employing 30 to 70 hands each in fabricating them.

The Manchester Chamber of Commerce agreed to cooperate in the prevention of exports of textile machines. The Board of Trade had consistently refused to grant licences for the export of lace machinery, but the Government failed to prosecute infringers of the law prohibiting the export of machinery or parts of machinery. The committee resolved to take the initiative. Following a favourable decision in the case of King v. Faber, in which net machinery due for export had been seized, on Henson's authority the committee took possession of other machinery which was being dispatched abroad by the London merchant, Faber. He promptly instituted action against Henson for illegal seizure. Henson conducted his own case, but the funds of the committee were soon exhausted and the campaign to prevent exports of machinery was abandoned.[84] Thereafter, beginning in 1838, the Board of Trade granted licences to the majority of applicants and in that year alone more than sixty lace machines were licensed for shipment to Europe.[85]

While agitating for the prevention of machinery exports, Felkin and Henson drew up another petition against the importation of foreign lace, a gesture aimed particularly against France. In the depressed year of 1834 the memorial, signed by two thousand five hundred persons, was submitted to the Board of Trade.[86] The reply stated that although the Government desired reciprocity it could not be forced, and the situation continued whereby cotton thread could be exported but net could not.

In 1837 the dislocation of trade with America, where a large proportion of lace exports were directed, caused an acute depression in the lace and hosiery trades.[87] Anglo-American trade rested upon an intricate framework of credit between manufacturers, importers, exporters, and discount houses, as did the trade with other countries. In this trade the most important figure was the commission merchant, and the failures of such merchants involved manufacturers and independent lace makers in losses, resulting in the unloading of bankrupt stock on the market, and a downward pressure on prices. During the commercial crisis of 1837 Felkin estimated that half the hosiery and more than half the lace machinery stopped working.[88] In January the lace trade was already suffering a steep fall in prices, and a meeting of hand and power owners was held at the Durham Ox to discuss what steps might be taken to alleviate the situation. Richard Birkin, one of the largest manufacturers of lace in Nottingham, questioned the advisability of a stoppage which had been suggested by Aulton, manager of Kendall's factory. Birkin preferred a restriction to a stand as the latter, he argued, would involve the subsequent unemployment of many families. He urged the necessity for unanimity and cooperation. Birkin, who owned power and hand machinery, considered that the worsening in trade was intensified by rivalry between power and hand machine holders, and advocated some sort of joint action to put the trade on a sounder footing.[89] Birkin and Felkin were appointed members of a Trade Committee to carry into effect a stint of machinery which was to be worked only during daylight hours. This appeal for restriction, however, was not taken up. Lace houses continued to fail, and in April the lace trade was said to have been 'all but at a stand'. Felkin reported that some houses did not make a single entry during a whole month,[90] and as the prolonged depression displayed little sign of abatement, employers and operatives showed serious concern for the way in which the economy might be revitalised.

In April, 1838 Ichabod Wright, together with a number of lace and hosiery manufacturers, attempted to establish a Society for the Protection and Encouragement of the Trade in Nottingham and its vicinity which, in effect, represented a renewed effort to stem the flow of skills and machinery overseas. This was an issue, however, on which opinion was divided, and the proposed society failed to command adequate support.[91] In the same month Gravener Henson called a meeting of artisans and makers of machinery in the hosiery and lace trades. He explained that it was desirable to investigate the causes of distress and trade depression and, with special reference to the lace and hosiery trades, to consider the effect of protected European economies on the British free trade economy. For these objects he proposed to form an Artisans' Chamber of Commerce; it was to consist of no more than ten members from each branch, half of whom were to be masters or machine owners and the rest journeymen. The employers' Chamber of Commerce having disintegrated after a brief existence between 1835 and 1837, Henson suggested that hosiers and lace manufacturers should be persuaded to form an association for the better management of the trades, to regulate wage agreements and to undertake commercial action.[92]

Abortive though the Chamber proved to be, the proposal illustrates the initiative and willingness of an intelligent artisan to co-operate with employers in trade matters. At the second meeting the Chamber's Chairman was John Barratt, who was later to become a member of the Nottingham Working Men's Association. Despite the lace makers' scepticism ten members had been appointed to the Chamber Committee. Master framework knitters in the plain silk trade had kept aloof, apprehensive of the hosiers' opinions; the majority of other framework knitting branches had appointed members and likewise the machine makers and smiths. The intended functions of the Chamber included most of those set out in the rules of the Manufacturers' Chamber three years before—to handle inventions, communicate with official bodies, consider technical education, enforce commercial law, and to act as a source of information.[93] At the next meeting the Committee revealed its findings concerning the causes of depression. Over-taxation, the Corn Laws, and competition among manufacturers were considered secondary. To obviate the evils of unfair competition it was agreed to petition the House of Commons for the enactment of a law to establish boards of trade of masters and men which would enforce uniform wage agreements within separate industries. An additional and primary cause of distress, the Committee concluded, was the lack of political representation by the majority of the population,[94] a view which was to be reiterated throughout the country with increasing intensity during the next ten years. The formal articulation of this feeling in the Nottingham Artisans' Chamber in 1838 helps to explain why some of the Chamber's supporters soon became absorbed in the Chartist movement whose tide of popularity was then beginning to rise.

References

[1] See William Felkin, 'Facts and Calculations illustrative of the present state of the Bobbin-Net Trade', September, 1831; 'Statistics of the Bobbin-Net Trade', August, 1833; 'Statistics of the English Bobbin-Net Trade', January 1836; These are reproduced as appendices 4–6 in the *First Report of the Select Committee on the Laws affecting the Exportation of Machinery* 1841 (201) VII. 4. pp. 245–261; Account of the Lace (and Hosiery) Manufacturers, in *First Report of the Children's Employment Commissioners* 1863 (3170) XVIII 1. pp. 234–236; William Felkin *History*, pp. 250, 337, 395.

[2] *Report of the Commissioners on the Condition of Handloom Weavers* 1840. XXIV. pp. 353–355.

[3] D. Varley, *A History of the Midland Counties' Lace Manufacturers Association* (Long Eaton, 1959), p. 42.

[4] Felkin's statistics in *First Report of the Children's Employment Commission* 1843. (431) XIII, p.f. 53; *N.R.*, April 17, 1829; October 6, 1829.

[5] D. Varley, *op. cit.*, p. 35; William Felkin, *History*, pp. 340–344.

[6] William Felkin, *History*, p. 340.

[7] *Ibid.*, pp. 338–341; *First Report of the Children's Employment Commission*, 1843 (431) XIII, p.f. 3; *First Report of the Children's Employment Commission*, 1833 (450) XX. 1, p. 369.

[8] *Ibid.*, p. C.1. p. 44; *Ibid.*, ev. of Felkin, p. 383.

[9] *First Report of the Children's Employment Commission*, 1843 (431) XIII., pp.f. 7–f. 29.

[10] A description of the stall system appears in *The Penny Magazine*, March, 1843. XII.

[11] *N.R.*, October 21, 1842.

[12] *N.P.L. Archives* M 8851/2 Agreement, March 25, 1843.

[13] *First Report of the Children's Employment Commission*, 1843 (431) XIII, pp.f. 9–f. 10.

[14] 'The Lace Trade and the Factory Act' reprinted from the *New Quarterly Review* (1860).

[15] *First Report of Commissioners on Employment of Children etc. in Trades and Manufactures not already regulated by Law, with appendices*, 1863 (3170) XVIII. 1., p. 235.

[16] *First Report of the Children's Employment Commission*, 1843 (431) XIII., pp.f. 3–f. 4.

[17] *Ibid.*, p.f. 4.

[18] *Ibid.*, p.f. 3.

[19] *Ibid.*, p.f. 5–f. 6.

[20] *First Report of the Children's Employment Commission*, 1833 (450) XX. 1., Report of Alfred Power, p. 370.

[21] *Ibid.*, p. 457.

[22] *First Report of the Children's Employment Commission*, 1843 (431) XIII. ev. of Edison, p.f. 58; f. 11.

[23] *First Report of the Children's Employment Commission*, 1833 (450) XX. 1., p. 50.

[24] *Ibid.*, p. 547.

[25] *Appendix to Second Report of Commissioners for inquiring into the Employment and Condition of Children (Trades and Manufactures) with Reports and Evidence from Sub-Commissioners* 1843 (431) XIV. XV. 1., p.f. 84.

[26] *Ibid.*, p.f. 8.

27 *Ibid.*

28 *Ibid.*, p.f. 10.

29 Quoted by J. D. Chambers, *Modern Nottingham in the Making* (Nottingham, 1945), p. 11; *Second Report of the Commissioners (Large Towns and Populous Districts)*, 1845 (610) XVIII. 1., pp. 611–12.

30 *Second Report of Commissioners on the Employment of Children (Trades and Manufactures)*, 1843 (431) XIV. XV. 1. ev. of Samuel Whitchurch, p.f. 62.

31 *Ibid.*, ev. of Felkin, p. 171.

32 W. Ashworth, *An Economic History of England, 1870–1939* (1960), p. 193.

33 *Report of the Commissioners on the Condition of Framework Knitters*, (1845) XV. 1. ev. of Felkin, p. 702; William Felkin, 'The Lace and Hosiery Trades of Nottingham,' *J.S.S.* XXIX. 1866, p. 537.

34 William Felkin, *History*, p. 344; *N.R.*, April 4, 1834.

35 N. H. Cuthbert, *The Lace Makers' Society, A Study of Trade Unionism in the British Lace Industry, 1760–1960*, (Nottingham, 1960), p. 28.

36 William Felkin, 'The Lace (and Hoisery) Manufactures' in *First Report of the Children's Employment Commission*, 1863. (3170) XVIII. 1., p. 236.

37 A. D. Gayer, W. W. Rostow, and A. J. Schwarz, *The Growth and Fluctuations of the British Economy, 1790–1850*, I. (1953), p. 205.

38 *Ibid.*

39 William Felkin, *History*, pp. 248–250.

40 *Ibid.*

41 *Ibid.*, p. 334.

42 *N.R.*, January 27, 1826.

43 William Felkin, *History*, p. 337.

44 William Felkin, *History*, p. 332.

45 Quoted by John Sutton in *Date Book*, p. 34.

46 *Report from the Secret Committee appointed to inquire into the expediency of renewing the Charter of the Bank of England, and into the System on which Banks of Issue in England and Wales are conducted.* 1831–32 (722) VI.1. p. 34.

47 *N.R.*, February 24, 1826.

48 *N.R.*, December 17, 1825.

49 Leicester, for example, with a similar economic structure was badly affected. A. Temple Patterson, *Radical Leicester* (Leicester, 1954), p. 140; John Sutton, *Date Book*, p. 398.

50 A. D. Gayer, W. W. Rostow, and A. J. Schwarz, *op. cit.*, p. 205.

51 J. D. Chambers, *The Workshop of the World* (1961), p. 31.

52 William Felkin, *History*, p. 332; *N.R.*, April 21, 1826; *N.R.*, January 6, 1826.

53 William Felkin, *History*, p. 333.

54 *N.R.*, October 4, 1825.

55 *N.R.*, December 23, 1825; *N.R.*, January 6, 1826; *N.R.*, February 11, 1826.

56 *Fourth Report of the Select Committee on the Emigration of Artizans and Machinery*, 1824, (51) IV, ev. of Gravener Henson, p. 275.

57 *Ibid.*, pp. 274–82.

58 BT.6.151.

59 *N.R.*, November 28, 1828.

60 William Felkin, *History*, p. 334; *N.R.*, December 12, 1828.

61 *N.R.*, January 9, 1829; *N.R.*, February 6, 1829; *N.R.*, February 20, 1829; *N.R.*, February 29, 1829.

[62] *N.R.*, April 3, 1829; William Felkin, *History*, p. 337.

[63] *N.R.*, July 17, 1829; William Felkin, *History*, p. 337.

[64] *First Report of the Children's Employment Commission*, 1833 (450), XX. 1., p. 371.

[65] William Felkin, *History*, p. 521.

[66] *N.J.*, April 4, 1829.

[67] *First Report of the Children's Employment Commission*, 1833 (450) XX. 1., p. 371.

[68] William Felkin, *History*, p. 243; *N.R.*, December 31, 1830.

[69] William Felkin, *History*, p. 243.

[70] *N.R.*, July 18, 1834; *N.R.*, December 5, 1834; *N.R.*, January 23, 1835.

[71] William Felkin, *History*, p. 345.

[72] William Felkin, 'The History and Present State of the Machine-Wrought Lace Trade.' *Journal of the Society of Arts*. 1856. IV., 184, p. 482.

[73] *First Report of the Children's Employment Commission*, 1843 (431) XIII, p.f. 2.

[74] William Felkin, *History*, pp. 341–2.

[75] William Felkin, 'Statistics of the Bobbin Net Trade', in *First Report of the Children's Employment Commission*, 1843 (431) XIII, p.f. 50.

[76] *Ibid*.

[77] *Ibid*.

[78] *Ibid*., p.f. 52.

[79] *Ibid*., p.f. 53.

[80] *Ibid*., p.f. 2.

[81] *First Report of the Children's Employment Commission*, 1843 (431) XIII. ev. of Astill, p.f. 24.

[82] William Felkin, 'Statistics of the Bobbin Net Trade', in *First Report of the Children's Employment Commission*, 1843 (431) XIII, p.f. 53.

[83] William Felkin, *History*, p. 352.

[84] *Ibid*., p. 355.

[85] BT 6.151.

[86] *N.R.*, August 1, 1834.

[87] William Felkin, *History*, p. 376.

[88] *Ibid*.

[89] *N.R.*, February 3, 1837.

[90] *N.R.*, April 14, 1837; William Felkin, *History*, p. 345–46.

[91] S. D. Chapman, *William Felkin, 1795–1874* (unpublished M.A. thesis, University of Nottingham, 1960).

[92] *N.R.*, April 16, 1838.

[93] *N.R.*, April 27, 1838.

[94] *N.R.*, June 22, 1838.

CHAPTER V

POVERTY AND THE NEW POOR LAW

ARISING from changing techniques of production and fluctuations in demand, insecurity was one of the major problems of the new urban industrial society. Fluctuations in trade, finance, and industry were exacerbated by the difficulty of accurately forecasting demand in distant markets and by the weakness of financial institutions. The local community was especially vulnerable to cyclical fluctuations, for its members depended for their livelihood upon the export-oriented lace and cotton hosiery industries.[1] Furthermore, the unique character of the town's staples as articles susceptible to the caprice of fashion also contributed to conditions of unstable employment. The responses to such circumstances by the working classes in Nottingham were similar to those in many other manufacturing centres, and took the form of the proliferation of friendly societies, political protest meetings, the growth of trade unions, and Chartism.

The reactions of the local aristocracy towards these developments were likewise typical of contemporary upper class attitudes. After the disastrous Peterloo episode which took place in Manchester in 1819 when eleven people died, a huge public meeting was held in Nottingham. As in other towns up and down the country, the speakers expressed sympathy for the Manchester men and women, protesting against the actions of the Tory government and the authorities who were immediately responsible for the massacre. Alarmed by these developments in the context of the current political unease, the Nottinghamshire aristocracy and gentry arranged for troops to garrison Bromley House. The Duke of Newcastle, the Duke of Portland, Earl Manvers, Lord Middleton, Sir J. B. Warren, Admiral Sotheron, M.P. and between thirty and forty county magistrates met at Shire Hall to pass a resolution condemning all 'Radical Reformers' and their subversive practices. This resolution was printed in the newspapers together with advertisements urging all Magistrates to enforce the Six Acts (the repressive measures passed by the government immediately following Peterloo) 'with promptitude and energy'.[2] The year 1819 was notable not only for the political repression that occurred; it was also a year of acute cyclical depression, a fact not unconnected with the accompanying political developments. An 'index of social tension' devised by one student of this period has led him to conclude that only twice between 1790 and 1850 did social tension reach higher levels than in 1819.[3] Qualitative evidence supports the view that 1819 was a year of extreme deprivation in Nottingham whose staple trades were so dependent upon the markets in which dislocation had brought on depression accompanied by widespread unemployment.

In that year destitute framework knitters and their families paraded their suffering in the streets of Nottingham. With a donation of £500 the Duke of Newcastle, Lord Lieutenant, set up a fund which was intended to enable the unemployed to emigrate to Cape Colony; the Duke of Portland and Earl Manvers donated comparable sums. Eventually three hundred wretched families left English shores under this plan, but on the whole the Duke's scheme met with lukewarm response among framework knitters who referred to it as transportation.[4] The Duke considered the plight of the framework knitters to be unfortunate but, in his capacity as a guardian of law and order, he thought it impracticable to interfere with their condition. Of the stockingers who in 1819 turned out and demonstrated against poverty he commented that they were 'orderly, peaceable and I must say reasonable, but still they have entered into a conspiracy and therefore cannot be entitled to any legal assistance.'[5] He issued an address counselling patience: 'let me beg of you to bear up manfully and make the best of whatever you consider an indifferent lot.'[6] The following year Mr. Rolleston, one of the county magistrates, declared that the gentlemen of the county disapproved of the framework knitters' trade union; shortly afterwards, the three committee members of the Nottingham branch of the Three Counties Union together with the Leicester delegate were convicted of conspiracy and were each given prison sentences of three months.[7]

Following the depression of 1819 the commercial crisis which took place in 1826 was also accompanied by unemployment and distress. The annual turning points of British trade cycles as calculated by W. W. Rostow show subsequent troughs to have occurred in 1829, 1832, 1837, 1842, and 1848.[8] The Nottingham textile trades were seriously affected each time, and, except for 1832, public relief committees were formed to help the unemployed during the recessions. A committee also operated in 1839.[9] Between 1819 and 1841 an aggregate sum of nearly £23,000 was contributed to such public relief funds[10] which were, in effect, a form of out-relief financed by voluntary subscriptions. It was insufficient, however, to achieve more than temporary mitigation of extreme hardship cases. This was the chief shortcoming of charity: it could afford only temporary relief and was not designed to stimulate efforts to devise institutions which might cope with some of the problems of an industrial society. Nevertheless, while the number of charitable bodies in Nottinghamshire rose from 51 in 1840 worth £4,806 to 124 worth £8,003 ten years later,[11] a number of local inhabitants made practical attempts to reduce the element of insecurity in the lives of the working classes, to improve the social environment, and to nourish cultural amenities. A small and heterodox group of conscientious professional and business men, comprising humanists and Evangelicals, men from both the established church and more especially from the nonconformist chapels, now began to concern themselves with the social consequences of industrialization. During the early years of the century the paternalistic approach in the form of public subscriptions, charity, and allotment schemes was in evidence at the same time as the philosophy of self-help was beginning to influence attitudes towards the alleviation of distress. Wrights, the bankers were associated simultaneously with paternalistic and with less traditional measures. During the depression of 1840 Major General Sir Charles Napier, who himself supported local efforts to relieve hardship, wrote, 'there is one family here that would save a city from God's wrath . . . a better fellow (referring to Ichabod Wright) never rolled in riches as he does.'[12] Of John Smith Wright it has been said, 'in his hands wealth was a trust.'[13]

It was with the intention of bolstering the workman's feeling of independence by forming a savings bank that in 1818 a group which included the Wrights, Thomas Wakefield, John Gill, and John Barber, established the Nottingham Savings Bank. By 1830 it catered for 4,127 depositors who held in aggregate nearly £94,000. Of these members 2,677 held £15,264 in deposits of less than £20, and 856 held £25,612 in sums smaller than £50.[14] By 1831 there was a larger number of provident societies in the town, many of which, like the Benevolent Society founded by Samuel Fox, were sponsored by religious bodies, while almost every dissenting congregation in Nottingham had its friendly society.[15] In 1837 information concerning the earnings and savings of persons applying for relief from public funds threw light on the extent to which the Savings Bank and friendly societies were fulfilling their proposed functions.

This information grew out of the endeavours of the 1837 Relief Committee to alleviate the widespread suffering in the town. Felkin, one of the Committee members, issued printed questionnaires to persons applying for assistance from the public subscription. Of 1,100 returns distributed, 1,043 were returned fully completed. Of these, 452 came from framework knitters, 498 from lace makers and ninety-three from frame-smiths. The returns showed that of the 1,043 men not one was a depositor at the Nottingham Savings Bank.

Ninety framework knitters and 128 lace makers were members of sick clubs, three framework knitters and four lace makers belonged to a provident society and eleven hosiery workers and nine lace operatives were members of the Oddfellows Society.[16] Thus, a slightly higher proportion of lace makers belonged to friendly societies. Felkin observed that the rate of wages did not materially influence the desire to belong to these clubs, though there was a greater tendency for married men with larger families to become members.[17] In some instances, probably because of working wives, men with large families had succeeded in supporting their families for as long as men with smaller families. Felkin's conclusion as to the reason why emergency public subscriptions and charities were necessary was a general lack of diligence and thrift among the working classes. He regretted that many sick clubs were ineptly managed and implied that the practice of such societies of meeting in public houses might in some way be connected. This view was endorsed by Absolem Barnett (by that time overseer of the Nottingham Poor Law Union), who regarded ale house clubs with decided scepticism.

'In most instances,' he claimed, 'the funds are inadequate to the promised payments, partly because a considerable portion is drunk in ale . . . The Club is an allurement to the ale house: love of company combined with love for liquor is occasion for a periodical debauch.'[18]

In Felkin's view the results of the investigation confirmed his suspicions that the working classes were failing to recognize the importance of prudent economy and foresight.[19] Felkin's regret that savings banks and sick clubs were seldom used is understandable, but want of diligence and thrift was not the only reason for the working class poverty—as Felkin himself realized. He was well aware of the necessity for expanding trade to raise the level of employment, and it was upon these grounds that he opposed the freedom to export machinery.[20] The sample of household budgets that Felkin presented at the Inquiry into the Condition of Framework Knitters in 1844 indicates that for many people there was little margin for investment in some form of insurance, friendly society, or savings bank. Between 1s. and 2s. 6d. was normally spent each week on rent and a similar amount on coals in the winter, after which in several families the amounts left for food and clothing varied between 6d. and 3s. per head per week. The very slight difference between the number of framework knitters and lace makers affiliated to benefit clubs suggests that higher pay, and not membership of friendly societies, was the main reason why few lace makers were reduced to such extreme and prolonged poverty as enveloped so many framework knitters. If we are to believe Gravener Henson, some artisans in the lace industry even migrated backwards and forwards between Nottingham and Calais in order to escape cyclical unemployment.[21] Indeed, the acquisition of skill, as many of the best and most intelligent framework knitters who had become lace makers recognized, was almost certainly the soundest form of insurance. With the low normal expectation of life, sickness and death were hazards accepted with equanimity.

Savings banks and friendly societies represented similar approaches to the problems of cyclical unemployment and poverty; likewise the method adopted by the Nottingham and District Visiting Provident Society, which, with the support of several leading citizens, was established in 1835 on the model of those at Manchester, Liverpool, and other large towns. The aim of the Society, like that of the Savings Bank, was to stimulate self-help among the working classes by encouraging weekly contributions which were collected regularly by the visitors, and on which there was a small return financed by a private subscription. It was also hoped that habits of industry, cleanliness, and sobriety, as well as economy, could be nurtured by the visitors.[22] In the first year of its operations just over £1,100 was collected from 1,350 subscribers, and despite difficulties in securing adequate numbers of visitors the work of the society continued throughout the forties.[23]

While the Savings Bank, friendly and provident societies achieved very limited success, there was growing local interest in a more traditional form of safeguard against depressed trade—the possession of a plot of land. In the early forties James Orange, sometime joint-pastor of Salem Chapel and historian of Nottingham, was beginning to canvass his ideas for a cottage garden plan.[24] Alone and unpaid, Orange expended enormous energy addressing various local bodies and engaging in a sustained publicity campaign conducted through the correspondence columns of the press. In an essentially paternalist pamphlet published in 1841, 'A Plea for the Poor', Orange expounded his ideas in detail. His intention was to transplant a measure of peasant husbandry to the midst of industrial society. For many years framework knitters had worked their allotments in the outlying villages, but Orange wanted to benefit working men in the town. After much individual campaigning he was appointed to the post of travelling agent for the Northern and Midland Counties Artisans' and Labourers' Friend Society. This was formed in 1842 in an endeavour to translate general sympathy for the condition of working men and their families into a practical scheme for aid. In effect, Orange's Cottage Garden Plan and the policy of the Labourers' Friend Society were the same: 'to encourage industry, education, temperance and morality.' The treasurer of the local

branch organized by Orange, was another dissenter, Thomas Wakefield, and other directors included the nonconformist hosier, Richard
Morley, and lace manufacturer, Jonathan Page.

The first step was to obtain land and divide it into allotments of
one-quarter of an acre, an area which Orange considered to be no
more than supplementary to an industrial occupation. It should
support a small family for about thirteen weeks, sufficient 'to carry
them through any necessity which may be forced upon them in a
depression of trade or a time of sickness.' Orange conceived the
traditional allotment system as a form of social insurance, but he
was also convinced that it would relieve workmen from utter dependence upon industry and so indirectly improve their bargaining
power. Orange maintained that the workhouse system under the
new Poor Law tended to destroy self-respect, liberty, and independence, qualities which his Cottage Garden Plan aimed to promote.

The two chief problems connected with the allotments scheme
were those of obtaining land and enlisting support from local landowners. In the industrial villages land was fairly easy to come by,
while a conviction that allotments might have an improving influence
upon the working classes brough a cooperative response from members of the landed class. In these villages gentlemen and clergy were
willing to act as directors on the local Labourers' Society Committees, where their presence was necessary not only as a symbol
of the Society's respectability but also as form of security for payment of rent. Observers in 1843 claimed that already they detected
the improving effects of allotments among framework knitters in
the Nottingham area, 'instead of frequenting the pot house . . . they
work early and late in the gardens . . .'. The Earl of Chesterfield was so certain that the incidence of poaching on his estate had
decreased since more time had been lavished upon garden culti-
vation, that he allowed the Society twenty additional acres. Felkin
said that in 1844 the allotments were much sought after, and that
those at Arnold were particularly well cultivated and yielded good
crops. Here, he observed, 'the cottages of the holders are improving
in cleanliness and comfort and the ale house keepers begin to complain.[25] However, some villages were less fortunate. When landowners were unwilling to support Orange and his scheme and declined to act as guarantors to encourage others, there were often too
few persons of substance who could be requested to form the local
committee. Orange related that societies at Beeston, Lenton, Radford, Sneinton, Hyson Green, and Radcliffe had been abandoned
because of the impossibility of recruiting directors. All of these
parishes, except one, were close to Nottingham where, owing to the
demand for industrial and house building sites, land prices were

high. Furthermore, the Burgess Rights Committee refused to grant the Society's requests for the use of a few acres of the town's common land. Without land the Nottingham Society could make no progress, and in the town itself the only allotments available were those which the Corporation rented for £25 an acre, but which only the better paid artisans and tradesmen could afford.

Similar to Orange's Cottage Garden Plan was the so-called Chartist land scheme which by 1843, according to a report from the editor of the *Nottingham Review,* had been received with enthusiasm at Arnold where, he said, sick clubs were withdrawing funds from savings banks and investing them in land. Fields had been purchased with the aim of dividing them into small plots to be rented to Chartists at a low rate. In 1846 two branches of the Chartist Land Company were founded in Nottingham, and in the same year the first allotment of land was granted when a Radford lacemaker, Charles Tawes, rented two acres at O'Connorville, near Watford. This was the occasion for a spate of correspondence printed in the *Nottingham Journal,* the *Nottingham Mercury,* and the *Nottingham Review.* The first two papers printed letters which, for the most part, were critical of the land scheme and the Chartists in general; the *Review* allowed space to Tawes himself, who claimed that despite his hardships he did not regret going. By 1849 Nottingham was the sole contributor in the Midland Counties, and after a parliamentary commission of inquiry the National Land Company wound up in 1851.[26] Thus the Chartist land plan was a failure, while the Cottage Garden Plan succeeded in increasing the number of allotment holdings in the Nottingham district; by 1853 it is estimated that there were some seven thousand such cottage gardens in and around Nottingham, though not all were the fruit's of Orange's scheme. Laudable though his intentions might have been, in the context of an industrializing society in which urban land values were rising rapidly the Cottage Garden was impracticable as a measure intended to combat poverty and cyclical unemployment.[27]

Whereas the sponsors of such schemes might be accused of looking to the past to find a solution to these social problems, no such charge could be levelled against the men who framed the Poor Law Amendment Act of 1834.[28] This was intended to create a system appropriate for relieving poverty in an industrial society in which the labour supply would become more responsive to the market mechanism of supply and demand. However, like the supporters of the allotment schemes, the legislators neglected to analyse the causes and nature of poverty, with the result that the Act failed to provide a solution to the problem of poverty due to cyclical unemployment.[29]

Under the new Poor Law a Central Board with a network of

elected local Guardians replaced the purely parochial basis for relief; henceforth the only relief to be given was to be restricted to workhouse inmates, and that relief was to be made as disagreeable as possible by stringent discipline and minimal expenditure on food and amenities. These changes, introducing the principles of the workhouse test and 'less eligibility' on a national scale, were intended to alter completely the system which determined the treatment of the poor. It is significant, therefore, that in 1838, giving evidence before the Select Committee on the Administration of the Poor Law Amendment Act, one of the Guardians stated that the system of giving relief in the Nottingham Parish of St. Mary had changed little as a result of the Act.[30] In the two smaller parishes of St. Peter and St. Nicholas the effects of the Act were more noticeable, because the principle on which relief had been offered there was 'no principle at all.'[31] The reason for this situation was to be found in the reforms of Absolem Barnett, who had been appointed full time Assistant Overseer to St. Mary's Parish in 1819[32] and who, since that time, had built upon the experience of his predecessors. Influenced by other Nottinghamshire reformers at Bingham and Southwell, Barnett gradually evolved his own policy for the relief of poverty.

In his first year of office in 1819, one of depressed trade and high unemployment, an inter-parochial Vagrant Office had been established to which were referred all vagrants seeking relief.[33] In part this reflected the inadequate accommodation of the three parochial workhouses, which had been constructed to hold altogether six hundred-and-sixty persons.[34] In 1811 the overseer of St. Mary's Parish had offered out-relief to applicants who were then immediately set to sweep streets for a modest payment, although this quickly exhausted the overseer's funds. In 1819 Barnett adopted a similar procedure when the unemployed flocked to the workhouse for aid, and seven hundred able-bodied men were employed laying drains and water courses, repairing the banks of the Trent, and paving and metalling roads. The employment was financed from a public relief fund and Barnett paid wages which were deliberately fixed at less than the average that could be earned in comparable employment.[35] This policy of temporary out-relief was criticized by George Nicholls, overseer of Southwell Parish, but he subsequently acknowledged the differing problems faced by industrial and rural parishes.[36] However, this important point became lost in the controversy over poor law policy in which the Rev. J. J. Becher, the Rev. Robert Lowe, Nicholls, and Barnett took part.[37] Under the influence of this local debate and the experiments which accompanied it at Southwell and Bingham, Barnett soon emerged as one of the progressive Nottinghamshire officers who sought to secure poor law reform on the basis of less eligibility.[38] Administration of poor relief in Nottingham before 1834 was 'progressive' in other ways besides the application of the labour test in time of acute distress, and the food, lodging, and assistance provided by the visitors connected to the Vagrant Office. Since 1813 a medical department offering free vaccination for children of the poor had been attached to St. Mary's workhouse, and in 1834 some twenty five hundred patients were receiving treatment at a cost to the parish of between 2s. and 2s. 6d. per head.[39] This, together with the establishment of a fever ward in 1813, resulted in a measure of separation of classes, another detail included in the 1834 Act. Barnett carried this further with the opening of a parish school where some of the pauper children were taught. In order to reduce the probabilities of undesirable influence the school was established outside the workhouse and was responsible for the provision of food, instruction, and employment.

When poor law reform was discussed during the investigations being carried out by the Royal Commission, Barnett made his own contribution to the controversy in a pamphlet on 'The Poor Laws and their Administration.' In it he advocated the concentration of local authority for the administration of poor laws in the hands of the elected overseers and their paid assistants, whose duty it would be to suggest that inspectors should be appointed to ensure that this authority administered the law satisfactorily.[40] He also suggested that it might be possible for small parishes to unite in employing an Assistant Overseer, and urged the abolition of the law of bastardy, whose treatment of the unmarried mother he thought to be unnecessarily harsh. Giving evidence before a Select Committee in 1838, Barnett, in his official capacity in St. Mary's parish, stated that since 1819 he had seldom employed able-bodied poor.

Between 1819 and 1826 there had been no extraordinary call for assistance from Poor Law authorities. Although framework knitters had been involved in strikes in the winter of 1820–21 the next five years saw tremendous expansion revolving around the machine-made lace industry, while the concomitant influx of population to Nottingham had given an extra filip to the local building industry, making it easier for unemployed framework knitters to find labouring work. After 1825, owing to the existence of a larger urban population and the recent expansion of an industry and ancillary trades acutely affected by seasonal and overseas markets, the problems connected with cyclical unemployment assumed increasingly serious proportions. During the depression of 1826, when more than three hundred persons were admitted to St. Mary's Workhouse, the highest number since 1821, unemployed framework knitters and mechanics were set to relaying pavements in the market place. They were paid from a public subscription of £3,000 and the Corporation consented to allow five acres of land to be enclosed and used by the churchwardens and overseers of St. Mary's parish for the expressed purpose of employing the poor.[41] Presumably this was the major exception to his general practice between 1819 and 1833 to which Barnett had referred. In 1834 the labour test was again applied and the able-bodied were set to work.[42]

In the context of general industrialization, the altered economic and social structure of the town in the thirties and forties rendered large scale cyclical unemployment a much greater threat than hitherto. Barnett had succeeded in applying the principle of less eligibility in connection with the labour test and to some extent had relieved local poverty, but when the Poor Law Amendment Act came into operation all forms of out-relief were prohibited. The irrelevance of the new law to an industrial society which, by its denial of out-relief to its able-bodied poor, ignored the role of cyclical unemployment in creating poverty, became apparent when its provisions were enforced in the depressed years of 1837 and 1838. In 1836 the parish workhouses of St. Nicholas and St. Peter were closed, and the parishes consolidated with that of St. Mary to form the Nottingham Union. The same year representatives were elected to serve on the first Board of Guardians, twelve from St. Mary's parish, six from St. Nicholas, and six from St. Peter's. The rather tame elections saw the return of existing Overseers of the poor of the three parishes, with the result that a body of no marked political colour was entrusted with the responsibility of administering the new law.[43] Absolem Barnett was elected as master of the workhouse, clerk to the Board of Guardians, and principal relieving officer. Immediately following the election of the Board of Guardians, and the formation of the Union an order was issued prohibiting out relief to able-bodied male paupers, a premature development in comparison with other unions.[44]

The St. Mary's Vestry no longer controlled the administration of the Poor Laws, but its members resolved to watch closely the guardian's behaviour and after appointing Barnett as honorary Vestry clerk they insisted on receiving reports of the Board's proceedings. Early in 1837, as the number of unemployed began to swell owing to the dislocation of trade with America, complaints were brought to the attention of the Vestry. Committees were set up immediately to investigate the efficiency of administration under the new poor law and the condition and functioning of the workhouse. Although the results of the committees' inquiries into economy and efficiency were not reported, after conducting a thorough examination the third committee concluded that the workhouse diet was adequate, praising the school and nursery. It complained only of cramped sleeping quarters, for although the official capacity of the St. Mary's workhouse was five hundred persons, more than six hundred were crowded inside.[45] The same month in which the Committee's report vindicated the conduct of the guardians, their term of office expired and nineteen of the twenty-four newly elected Board served for the first time.[46] With a number of leading political figures as representatives, including the local Whig leader Thomas Wakefield, and Richard Sutton and John Hicklin, the *Review* and *Journal* editors, during the second year the Board became a forum for political debate which crystallized over the issue of a new workhouse.

In the spring of 1837 it became evident that St. Mary's workhouse would be unable to accommodate applicants if the depression grew worse. When the Board met in April it was resolved

> that in the present state of trade in Nottingham it is inexpedient and impracticable to carry out the full regulations of the Poor Law as to outdoor relief.[47]

The Board recommended that the relieving officer be instructed to give relief to able-bodied men during the present pressure in such urgent cases 'as on due enquiry shall appear to require immediate relief.' The Poor Law Commissioners rejected this proposal, expressing the hope that the efforts of private individuals would prevent the necessity of relaxing the clause prohibiting out-relief,[48] an admission, in effect, that the new Act was not designed to cope with temporary unemployment. In May the guardians had re-opened St. Nicholas' workhouse as a hospital, and a number of old people occupying parish houses were given money for alternative accommodation and told to quit, their houses to be converted into a nursery. To reduce pressure on the workhouse, persons having settlement more than ten miles from the Union were refused relief, a decision which caused much hardship, for almost half of the applicants had settlements outside the three Nottingham parishes.[49] After repeated remonstrances, in August the order prohibiting outdoor relief was eventually suspended, but until then private efforts attempted to alleviate the distress.

Mayor Richard Morley, the leading hosiery manufacturer, called a public meeting and formed a relief committee. In less than three months £5,000 had been paid to more than one thousand able-bodied unemployed for work done under the direction of the Corporation Chamber and Bridge Estates Committees.[50] Exhaustion of the Relief Fund was followed immediately by an increase in the number of applicants to the workhouse which in January, 1838 held no fewer than nine hundred and nine persons.[51] One of the visitors complained,

> take an ordinary door off its hinges, lay it on the floor, and on the surface of that door is given the house room of five persons in Nottingham Union Workhouse . . . In such an ill-ventilated overcrowded building the separation of various classes is impossible.

However, the visitors declared that they considered a total separation undesirable and approved of the prevailing practice whereby married couples, and parents and children were allowed to meet.[52] Eventually, in August, 1837 the Commissioners had suspended the order which prohibited outdoor relief, and in the hard winter of 1837–8 family men were employed by the Union for wages paid partly in bread and potatoes. The guardians also erected a wooden shed in which food, consumed on the premises, was distributed to persons applying for relief.[53] Nicholls, the Poor Law Commissioner, criticized this departure from the test and the less eligibility principle.[54]

It was against this background that in November, 1837 at a meeting which lasted for eight hours, the guardians discussed the question as to whether Nottingham should have a new and larger workhouse. The rise in poor rates, from £11,628 in 1836 to £21,139 in 1837,[55] rendered any decision to spend more money on a new workhouse a controversial one, but purely political animosity intensified the rift between the Whig pro- and Tory and Radical anti-workhouse factions, a fact which was reflected in later Board and municipal elections. The question was in abeyance during most of 1838 as pressure on the workhouse eased, but the winter months of 1839 brought another depression which was accompanied by local unemployment on a scale comparable with that which had occurred in the winter of 1837. The medical report presented to the Board of Guardians by Dr. Watts in October, 1839 drew attention to the growing prevalence of disease and fever in the town. Many of the poor whom he visited outside the workhouse seldom ate meat and lived mainly on bread and tea, with perhaps an occasional herring, though inmates were well fed daily.[56] Even so, rather than submit to the degradation of becoming a pauper it became common, according to Sutton, for many of the poor to sell all their belongings rather than enter the workhouse. Nevertheless, in November, 1839 though fifteen hundred unemployed persons begged the Mayor to provide work few families applied to the workhouse for relief.[57]

Once more the Board of Guardians received the consent of the

Poor Law Commissioners to suspend general orders and grant temporary outdoor relief.[58] Framework knitters with two or more children were employed on some form of outdoor work, and, at the discretion of the relieving officer, unemployed persons belonging to the Union who had been employed hitherto in the staple trades were to be provided with two meals daily. Sir Charles Napier who had recently been stationed in Nottingham expressed his horror at the starvation and poverty suffered by over two thousand people in the town, and he, Ichabod Wright, William Felkin, and Richard Morley opened another public subscription. Under the direction of Mayor William Roworth, a committee was formed to provide work for the unemployed and to distribute food and blankets to deserving cases visited by the Committee.[59] Soon more than five hundred able-bodied poor were set to work on Mapperley Plains. As chairman of the Committee, this experience brought about a reversal of Roworth's views on the new Poor Law. He was a Whig and had originally favoured the principles underlying the new law, accepting the workhouse test as the keystone of the system. However, when he became directly involved in meeting the needs of the poor he soon became an ardent advocate of the continuance of out-relief. He maintained that the tendency of the new law, in practice, was towards permanent pauperization, or at least to make it difficult for people who had been inside the workhouse to regain independence. Roworth was also a bitter critic of the guardians' management of the Nottingham poor.[60]

On his election to the Chairmanship of the Relief Committee, William Roworth had called the attention of the guardians to the excessive amount of destitution which had come to the notice of the Committee of Visitors. At its second meeting, when a resolution was passed to the effect that relief should be extended to females, Roworth stressed that an increasing section of the population was being relieved out of funds which Absolem Barnett had previously denied would be necessary under the new law.[61] Barnett had insisted that the law would work without outside pecuniary assistance, a view which was doubtless influenced by the fact that the bulk of his experience since 1819 had been during the period when the lace industry had expanded rapidly.

The guardians' reluctance to raise rates in order to finance enough outdoor work for all who applied to them, necessitated the refusal of labour tests to a number of able-bodied unemployed.[62] Roworth attacked the situation by which one man was almost the sole arbiter on the distribution of relief while at the same time filling two other offices, for Absolem Barnett was clerk to the Board, superintendent registrar, and relieving officer. The result, argued Roworth, was that duties in his latter capacity tended to be neglected, resulting in much privation and suffering. He quoted several instances where refusal of relief or lack of visiting had been succeeded by illness and starvation.

'There are many evils produced by withholding temporary relief', he wrote, 'and however justly it may be deprecated as a general system to give outdoor relief, yet from my own knowledge of the way in which it has been withheld in Nottingham it has produced the greatest distress among the industrious poor and brought on disease which would have caused death, had not others provided that which the Relieving Officers ought to have given.'

Because of the deficiencies in administration, the poor law in Nottingham, he claimed, was administered neither according to the old law nor the new.[63] Nicknamed by the poor, 'Absolute Barnett', Roworth referred to him as the 'best hated man in Nottingham.'[64]

A stranger to the town endorsed Roworth's contention that hardship was inflicted on the poor. During his stay in Nottingham, Major General Sir Charles James Napier knew of an old man suffering from starvation who, on applying for relief, was told to return a few days later. According to Napier, had not Roworth fed the man he would have died shortly thereafter. Napier also reported a scene he witnessed at the Police Office where he encountered a pretty young woman with two children in her arms and hardly able to move, so close was she to childbirth; she said her husband was a hod man looking for work and that she had entered the town that morning to find him. 'She had no acquaintance, no shelter, was wet, half dead with cold and about to be delivered in the streets,' but her application for admission to the workhouse was refused.[65]

It would be unfair to contrast Roworth and Barnett in terms of good and evil. Both were Evangelicals and their lives show that they were genuinely concerned with the problems of poverty, pauperism, and unemployment. Both had applauded the introduction of Chadwick's new Poor Law. Barnett adhered to the Benthamite principles involved and was prepared to carry out the articles of the new law to the letter—though in 1837 he pointed out that while the Poor Law Commissioners' regulations did not permit outdoor relief, the unrepealed Elizabethan Poor Law did. Barnett also received the assurance through Gulson, an Assistant Poor Law Commissioner, that this rule would be relaxed, should it prove necessary in response to local requests.[66] Barnett considered the hardship involved a reasonable price to pay for the nice rearrangement of social forces which would, he was confident, benefit the community in the long run. He argued that Christian principles should provide the basis for legislative remedies, 'they must supply moral restraint and virtuous stimulants and afford room for principles and for the gradual improvement of 'social intercourse'.[67] After the first hand experience of Barnett's rigid application of the Act, Roworth felt obliged to reject the new poor law on humanitarian grounds. He also deplored the need for public charity to offset the deficiencies of the new poor law and the conditions brought about by the guardians' partial abdication of their responsibilities. The debate on the merits and disadvantages of the workhouse system and the administration of the new poor law continued, while the provision of a new workhouse became a major local issue. Wakefield, Felkin, Fox, and Carver supported the campaign for a new workhouse on humanitarian grounds;[68] Richard Sutton, on the other hand, was opposed to the idea. He supported the principle underlying the new poor law, but opposed the expenditure of public funds on a new workhouse. Sutton also argued that the guardians should be allowed to exercise greater discretion in applying the labour test during periods of great distress.[69] The Rev. W. J. Butler, Rector of St. Nicholas, was a bitter opponent of the new poor law but, appalled at the overcrowding, he urged the erection of a new workhouse.[70]

The argument in favour of such a policy was a regurgitation of the reports of inspectors and visitors to the existing workhouse;

> 'something must be done or humanity will be outraged', said one report, 'in some parts of the house inmates could not be said to live, they only vegetate.'[71]

In spite of alterations to the existing structure and the utilization of temporary and other buildings, this state of affairs persisted. In his history of Nottingham, James Orange commented:

> The manner in which the poor, both in the workhouse and out of it, are cooped up is unhealthy and demoralizing and utterly at war with every principle of popular interest.[72]

The antagonists defended their views on the grounds that a new workhouse would mean a heavy burden on the rates, which were already colossal. Nevertheless, the humanitarians and Whig party members held a majority in the Board of Guardians, and against embittered opposition determined to press on with the commissioners' policy and build.[73]

The winter of 1841 caused much discomfort to the framework knitters, many of whom, wearing tattered garments, exhibited their meagre forms, pinched with cold and hunger, in the streets of the town. Yet another public subscription was opened, and two thousand destitute persons who had refused to apply to the workhouse were fed on soup and bread.[74] The state of the workhouse met with a continued barrage of criticism, but an election of a fresh Board of Guardians altered the distribution of power. Although the outgoing Board had begun the building on York Street of a new workhouse which was to accommodate a thousand persons, a Tory and anti-Poor Law majority dominated the new Board which refused to countenance continuation of the house or the habitation of any part of the completed wings.[75] Nassau Senior paid a visit to the Union and attended a Board meeting at which he asserted that the Nottingham workhouse then in use was positively the worst he had ever seen, quoting instances where seven or eight children slept in one bed. The guardians offered to move some of the inmates to St. Nicholas' Workhouse which had been closed by the commissioners in 1836, but Senior objected. The guardians argued that they could not be considered responsible for the debt outstanding so long as the workhouse was not in use.[76] Shortly after Senior's visit, the guardians flouted his directives and opened up parts of the new workhouse, removing some of the children and aged couples to St. Nicholas'. They also resolved to extend out-relief, and immediately four thousand five hundred persons qualified.[77]

Conditions inside St. Mary's deteriorated. An official medical authority reported on the grossly overcrowded conditions which prevailed in the winter of 1842 when he described the ward for old and infirm men as

> one of the most wretched places I ever entered. One of the doors opens into the same narrow passage and immediately at right angles with the entrance of the common privy, while against the outside of the opposite wall are erected the common urinals for the men and boys, hence this wall is completely saturated . . . It is dark and close and dirty and quite unfit for residence of human beings . . .

The sleeping apartments and beds for girls were very damp owing to their situation above the washhouse, and the day ward which contained forty married men was known as the 'Black Hole of Calcutta', a dismal garret twenty feet by seventeen feet by eight feet high.[78] After inspecting the buildings the commissioner immediately issued an injunction decreeing a maximum of two hundred and forty persons in St. Mary's and ninety in St. Nicholas' workhouses.[79]

The battle between guardians and commissioners continued, the guardians resenting bitterly the central authority in London and becoming alarmed at the Union's growing indebtedness. In February, 1842 no less than a quarter of the Nottingham population was in receipt of relief in some form or other.[80] On the plea that it would decrease rates and increase the comforts of the poor, the guardians requested the commissioners to dissolve the Union of parishes, but met with refusal.[81] The reaction of more than half the guardians was to declare their intention of resigning, but it was then discovered that this would be illegal and they fulfilled their term of office. By this time money was being spent on pauper inmates, able-bodied men working on the Forest, and able-bodied men to whom no test whatsoever had been given. In April the new Board of Guardians found that the Union was £3,400 overdrawn at the bank, in addition to the £4,000 which they had borrowed in order to pay for the completion of the new Nottingham workhouse.[82] Throughout the three months following May in 1843, the average number relieved inside was six hundred, for which part of the new workhouse was utilised. The authorities were victims of the situation, though the suffering was borne by the unemployed, aged, and sick.

Disgust with the new poor law, whose harshness was symbolized by the workhouse, appalling living conditions, unemployment and poverty, reinforced the general dissatisfaction of the working classes in Nottingham.[83] It is significant that Chartism in Nottingham received most support from framework knitters, a submerged class whose economic, social, and physical inferiority was generally admitted.[84] Without protection of the Factory Acts they could hope for no reduction in hours; on the contrary, they must hope for ever more work in order to earn a bare subsistence wage. The effort to obtain unity for collective trade action was almost invariably doomed to failure. The trade was divided into branches according to articles of manufacture and because it was so difficult to reconcile the claims of the different branches, each varying in numbers and its hold on the market, formulation of a general policy for the trade was impossible. Added to this, the scattered locations of framework knitters encouraged the formation of local unions in each small village, but further confusion arose when more than one hosier employed men in the same locality. Hence the difficulty of effective strikes, which in a stagnant industry could not, in any event, be expected to improve trade.

Compared with the hosiery industry, in which framework knitters rented frames from the hosier, there was considerable vertical mobility in the lace industry.[85] The stall system offered to skilled artisans the opportunity to become machine holders, while some became large manufacturers, and in normal years bobbin net makers worked fewer hours and earned on average twice the wage of framework knitters. In 1834, one of the worst years for lacemakers, only narrow hand machine operators (a rapidly dwindling group) were earning as little as eight shillings weekly, the normal average wage

K

of most framework knitters. Conditions of work in the two industries offer another contrast slightly favourable to lace workers. Much of the lace production took place in more recently built larger workshops, and, especially from the forties onwards, in the new steam-powered factories. It is true that auxiliary lace workers, who were mainly women and children, endured appalling working conditions similar to those of framework knitters. Women and children, however, remained outside the political arena, and the numerical strength of Chartism depended upon the support it could elicit from the adult male population. The position of the male operatives differed in the two industries. Not only were there many small independent owners of lace machinery, but the journeymen lace operative was a skilled artisan in an industry which, although subject to erratic fluctuations, was nevertheless expanding, and the lacemaker was therefore in a stronger position from which to bargain with his employer. In 1828 the first of a series of joint actions had been taken by machine holders and journeymen by which they agreed to restrict output with the aim of halting a fall in prices. In the same decade, intermittent experiments in trade unionism occurred in connection with the National Association for the Protection of Labour, the Grand National Consolidated Trades Union, and other general trades unions, and after a shortlived response to the revival of the N.A.P.L. in 1846, a permanent union of lacemakers was established finally in 1850.[86]

With recognition of their weakness, and seeking strength in working class solidarity, local framework knitters' societies were inspired to action between 1829 and 1834 by the idealism of Doherty's National Association for the Protection of Labour.[87] The Association was a large federation of organizations linked by a common goal, and as it spread from the Lancashire districts into the midland textile areas it enrolled existing trade societies. The movement in Nottingham was not confined to the poorly paid semi-skilled workers. Although framework knitters' societies were the mainstay of the trades union movement in the town during these years, bobbin net workers, smiths, filers, turners, iron moulders, and bobbin and carriage makers each formed unions in order to enrol as members of the local branch of the National Association. Although it could not be termed a widely popular movement, in comparison with its strength in other towns, the support in Nottingham was nevertheless impressive. In 1831 the Nottingham Union of Trades ranked as the second largest contributor to the Association's funds, and was the only well-organized district outside Lancashire.[88] The National Association disintegrated in the midlands late in 1831, as Nottingham stockingers expressed disappointment with the lack of

Association support for their own campaigns.[89] Frustrated by
administrative squabbles which occurred at the Manchester headquarters, in 1833 the Nottingham Bobbin Net Union enrolled in
the Secret Order of the Operative Trades Union, while hosiery
workers resolved to revive the cotton stockingers' union covering the
three midland counties.[90] In the same year working class leaders,
Robert Owen prominent among them, gathered up the remnants of
the National Association and established the Society for National
Regeneration.[91] The aim of the Society was to obtain an eight hour
day, without wage reductions, through a general strike; but although
a National Regeneration Society was established in Nottingham,
the Trades Union retained the allegiance of the villagers. With its
transformation into The Grand National Consolidated Trades
Union early in 1834, more lodges opened at Radford, Basford, and
Arnold, and in March, 1834 two thousand trades unionists took part
in a demonstration on the Forest to protest against the sentence of
transportation passed on the Dorchester labourers.[92] Soon afterwards
the Trades Union collapsed.[93] The lives of the N.A.P.L. and the
G.N.C.T.U. were shortlived, but the enthusiasm with which local
unions embraced them presaged the support which Nottingham
workmen subsequently rendered to Chartism. Between 1838 and
1850 Chartism and direct trade action alternated as the vehicles of
working class protest; and because of the political strength of
framework knitters in Nottingham, many of whom had served
apprenticeships with freemen and who were therefore entitled to
burgess rights including a parliamentary vote, Chartist success
showed at the polls.

Following the establishment of the London Working Men's
Association in 1837, the Nottingham Working Men's Association
was formed in January, 1838 when nearly 10 per cent. of the local
population was receiving relief inside or outside the workhouse.[94] In
March of the same year depressed trade had resulted in the shutting
down of 1,155 houses including many retail shops, some of them in
Market Place. Families were being forced by circumstances to
live as rooming tenants, while pawnbrokers were unable to accept
the amount of property offered in pledge, much of it, in consequence,
being virtually thrown away by forced sales in the streets.[95] Through
a series of letters printed in the *Nottingham Review* the N.W.M.A.
attacked the new Poor Law with its 'bastilles' and 'tests of destitution',[96] and in July, 1838 the Association called a meeting to present
the People's Charter and the National Petition for the approval of
working men and women. The handbills which were circulated to
publicize the meeting began:

Join our ranks oppressed brothers,
You once obeyed your country's call,
The right you gained you gave to others
Press forward now for rights for all.[97]

During the ensuing decade the Chartist movement became a focus for sections of the community who were dissatisfied with existing social and economic conditions and who saw greater political power as an instrument for securing radical change. In 1847 the Nottingham electorate chose Feargus O'Connor, the colourful Chartist leader, as one of its parliamentary representatives, and thereby gave the Chartists their only major electoral victory. This achievement adds further interest to an analysis of the nature and strength of Chartism in Nottingham.

References

[1] See Assistant Commissioner Wylde's evidence in the Poor Law Commissions published *Reports on the Operation and Administration of the Poor Laws*, 1834, App. A. Reports of Assistant Commissioners, Part II, p. 126A.

[2] Thomas Bailey, *Annals of Nottinghamshire*, (Nottingham, 1853), IV, 307–08.

[3] W. W. Rostow, *British Economy of the Nineteenth Century*, (Oxford 1948), pp. 123–5.

[4] *House of Lords Committee on the Poor Laws*, 1831 (pub. with the Reports of the Poor Law Commission as a separate volume, 1834), ev. of Becher, p. 309.

[5] *N.R.*, September 4, 1819.

[6] Quoted in J. L. and B. Hammond, *The Skilled Labourer, 1760–1832* (1919), p. 251.

[7] *N.R.*, May 5, 1821.

[8] W. W. Rostow, *op. cit.*, p. 33.

[9] Thomas Bailey, *op. cit.*, pp. 310, 348, 368, 401, 414, 423.

[10] *Ibid.*

[11] *Accounts and papers, Tables of Revenue Population and Commerce* 1840 XLI; 1850 XLI.

[12] Quoted in A. C. Wood, 'Nottingham 1835–1865,' *Transactions of the Thoroton Society*, LIX (1955), 57.

[13] Thomas Bailey, *op. cit.*, p. 451.

[14] John Sutton, *Date Book*, p. 342; *Accounts and Papers* XLI. *Tables of Revenue Population and Commerce of the U.K.*, p. 8.

[15] *N.R.*, January 21, 1831.

[16] William Felkin, *Remarks upon the Importance of an Enquiry into the Amount and Appropriation of Wages by the Working Classes* (1837), pp. 5–9.

[17] *Ibid.*, p. 7.

[18] Absolem Barnett, *The Poor Laws and Their Administration*, (Nottingham, 1833), pp. 7–8.

[19] William Felkin, *Remarks upon the Importance of an Enquiry into the Amount and Appropriation of Wages by the Working Classes*, p. 8.

[20] *Second Report from the Select Committee on the Exportation of Machinery with minutes of ev. 1841* (202) VII. 1. 265, ev. of Felkin, pp. 141–75.

[21] *Second Report from the Select Committee on Postage*, XX, Part II 1837–8, ev. of Gravener Henson, p. 217.

[22] *N.R.*, July 10, 1835.

[23] S. D. Chapman, *'William Felkin, 1795–1874'* (unpublished M.A. thesis, University of Nottingham, 1960), p. 102.

[24] The following account is based on R. A. Church, 'James Orange and the Allotment System in Nottingham' *Transactions of the Thoroton Society*, LXIV (1960).

[25] William Felkin, *An Account of the Machine-wrought Hosiery Trade, its Extent and the Condition of the Framework Knitters*, (Nottingham, 1845), p. 23.

[26] *N.R.*, October 24, 1856.

[27] See also Chapter XII for further consideration of these problems.

[28] S. E. Finer, *The Life and Times of Sir Edwin Chadwick*, (1952), p. 69.

[29] A. Briggs, *The Age of Improvement*, (1959), pp. 278–279.

[30] *Twenty-second Report of the Select Committee on the Administration of Relief under the Poor Law Amendment Act* 1837. (446) XVII, Part II, p. 515; *Third Annual Report of the Poor Law Commissioners,* 1837 (546–1) XXXI, pp. 11–15.

[31] *Ibid.*

[32] *Ibid.,* ev. of Barnett, p .521.

[33] H. Field, *The Nottingham Date Book 1800–1884,* (Nottingham, 1884), p. 329.

[34] John Blackner, *op. cit.,* p. 401.

[35] Absolem Barnett, *op. cit.,* p. 12.

[36] J. D. Marshall, 'The Nottinghamshire Reformers and their Contributions to the New Poor Law,' *E.H.R.,* 2nd Series, XIII no. 3.

[37] See J. D. Marshall, *art. cit.,* pp. 387–394.

[38] *Ibid.,* p. 386.

[39] T. H. Smith, *Hints to the Churchwardens and Ratepayers of St. Mary's Parish Nottingham,* (Nottingham, 1834).

[40] Absolem Barnett, *op. cit.,* pp. 74–79.

[41] *Ibid.,* pp. 54–58.

[42] *Twenty-second Report from the Select Committee of the House of Commons on the Administration of Relief under the Poor Law Amendment Act,* 1837 (446) XVII Part II, ev. of Barnett, p. 519.

[43] *Ibid.,* ev. of Barnett, p. 522.

[44] *N.R.,* June 24, 1836.

[45] *N.R.,* March 17, 1837.

[46] *Ibid.*

[47] *N.R.,* March 31, 1837; *N.R.,* May 15, 1837.

[48] *N.R.,* May 12, 1837; *N.R.,* May 15, 1837.

[49] Copy of Report from Mr. Gulson on the Subject of Distress in Nottingham (1837) in *Accounts and Papers* LI p. 197.

[50] *N.R.,* May 26, 1837; *N.R.,* June 2, 1837.

[51] *N.R.,* January 26, 1838.

[52] *N.R.,* November 10, 1837.

[53] *N.R.,* December 3, 1841; *N.R.,* September 8, 1837.

[54] Sir George Nicholls, *A History of the English Poor Law* (1854), II, 330.

[55] *N.R.,* November 17, 1837.

[56] *N.R.,* October 4, 1839; William Felkin, *History,* p. 376; For details of the workhouse diet in 1840 see the menu reproduced in J. D. Chambers, 'Victorian Nottingham,' *Transactions of the Thoroton Society* LXIII, (1959), 7.

[57] *N.R.,* October 4, 1839; November 22, 1839.

[58] *N.R.,* November 22, 1839.

[59] *N.R.,* November 29, 1839.

[60] W. Roworth, *Observations on the Administration of the New Poor Law in Nottingham* (Nottingham, 1840), p. 52.

[61] Roworth, *op. cit.,* pp. 37, 70.

[62] Roworth, *op. cit.,* pp. 61–62.

[63] *Ibid.*

[64] *Ibid.,* pp. 61–2, 69.

[65] W. Napier, *op. cit.,* p. 11.

[66] *Twenty-second Report from the Select Committee of the House of Commons on the Administration of Relief Under the Poor Law Amendment Act,* 1837 (446) XVII Part II, p. 526; *Third Annual Report of the Poor Law Commissioners,* 1837, pp. 11–15.

67 Absolem Barnett, *op. cit.*, p. 80.
68 *N.R.*, November 6, 1840.
69 *N.R.*, March 9, 1838.
70 See W. J. Butler, *op. cit.*
71 *N.R.*, September 6, 1839.
72 James Orange, *History and Antiquities of Nottingham*, (Nottingham, 1841), II, 912.
73 *N.R.*, June 26, 1840.
74 *N.R.*, November 26, 1841; John Sutton, *Date Book*, p. 480.
75 *N.R.*, December 3, 1841.
76 *Ibid.*
77 *N.R.*, February 4, 1842.
78 *Ibid.*
79 *N.R.*, February 11, 1842. There were 692 paupers in St. Mary's workhouse.
80 *N.R.*, February 18, 1842.
81 *N.R.*, February 4, 1842.
82 *N.R.*, March 4, 1842.
83 *Infra*, Chap. VI.
84 *Supra*, p. 43.
85 *Supra*, p. 69.
86 *Infra*, p. 293.
87 G. D. H. Cole, *Attempts at General Union*; *A Study in British Trade Union History 1818–1834*, (1953), p. 19, *et. seq.*
88 *Ibid.*, pp. 20, 183–86; *N.R.*, February 11, 1831.
89 G. D. H. Cole, *Attempts at General Union*, p. 43.
90 *N.R.*, October 25, 1833; *N.R.*, February 1, 1833.
91 G. D. H. Cole, *Attempts at General Union*, p. 109.
92 *Ibid.*, p. 122; *N.R.*, February 21, 1834; *Report of the proceedings of the Public Meeting on Nottingham Forest on Monday, March 31st, in regard to the sentence passed on six members of the trades union at Dorchester*, a pamphlet published by the *N.R.*, (Nottingham, 1834).
93 G. D. H. Cole, *Attempts at General Union*, pp. 136–49.
94 *N.R.*, January 26, 1838.
95 William Felkin, 'Statistics of the Labouring Classes and Paupers of Nottingham,' *Journal of the Statistical Society*, IV, (1839), pp. 457–59.
96 e.g. *N.R.*, March 9, 1838.
97 *N.R.*, July 27, 1838.

CHAPTER VI

CHARTISM IN NOTTINGHAM

FOUR of the six points of the Charter—manhood suffrage, vote by ballot, annual parliaments, and abolition of property qualifications for membership of Parliament—received the support of the Nottingham Working Men's Association as the political measures most likely to lead to the abolition of poverty. Such political reform was presented to the local working classes as 'the means by which they could furnish their houses, clothe their backs, and educate their children.'[1] The most active members of the local Chartist organisation from the movement's early years were James Sweet, a newsagent and hairdresser who kept a shop in Goose Gate, James Woodhouse, framework knitter, and John Barratt, lace maker, though at the outset the Committee also included William Burden, a lace maker, a tailor named Cornelius Fowkes and two framework knitters, Benjamin Humphries and George Woodward.[2] Shortly after the first meeting Jonathan Barber, another framework knitter, and the Rev. George Harrison, a preacher from Calverton, became leading figures in the local movement, likewise James Sowter, a cordwainer. Later, Henry Mott a currier, William Hemm a mechanic, and David Heath a solicitor's clerk were numbered among the loyal and active Chartist core. From the outset the Chartist cause attracted support from outside the working classes. When in November, 1838 a petition was sent to the Mayor, requesting that a Chartist meeting should be permitted on the Forest, those who had signed included persons from a wide social spectrum: silversmith and surgeon, baker and bookseller, stonemason and shoemaker, corn dealer and clerk, policeman and medical practitioner, victualler and coffee house keeper, dyer and draper, needlemaker and grocer, hosier, manufacturer, gentleman, and newspaper proprietor.[3] But only one of these petitioners appears later as an active Chartist connected with the Nottingham organization.

In September, 1838 James Sweet harangued a crowd estimated at two thousand people at Lee's Close off Carlton Road. Speaking of the low wages of stocking makers, he claimed that in Nottingham they were unable to purchase the necessities of life.

'If they cannot get these', he would ask, 'is it right that they should remain in their present condition? How is it', he continued, 'that those who work get little or nothing and those who do not work, live in fine houses and own extensive parks?'[4] In March of the following year George Harrison, the Calverton preacher, adopted a similar approach in a different style. Making frequent references to the Bible, he assured his audience that in preaching against tyranny and oppression he was only treading in the footsteps of Joel and Nehemiah.[5]

Indeed the year 1839 was an eventful one in Chartist history. During the closing months of 1838 the Three Counties Framework Knitters' Union had reviewed, but although the possibility of strike action against the hosiers was discussed, by the end of March, 1839 framework knitters were struggling against wage reductions. Many lace workers were also thrown out of employment.[6] The public meetings called by the Chartists during 1839 became occasions for public focus upon working class grievances, and it is significant that the first speaker of national reputation to be invited by the N.W.M.A. was Richard Oastler, the vehement Tory opponent of the new poor law. In his address he advised workers to have arms to add force to their petitions, and warned property owners: 'The whole social system is on the brink of ruin. You cannot subdue the people. It is yours to grant, they are waiting to receive . . .'[7]. At a mass meeting held on March 29th, George Harrison delivered an invective, threatening the rescue of any Chartist leader who might be imprisoned.[8] Fortified by such aggressive oratory, William Hall, on behalf of the N.W.M.A., requested Dr. Wade, the radical Warwickshire vicar who was Nottingham's representative at the convention, to abstain from any opposition to the majority of the convention favouring physical force. Wade's reaction was to resign, explaining his reasons in a letter to the N.W.M.A.

'The cry of arms without previous moral opinion and union of the middle classes with you', he wrote, 'would only cause misery, blood and ruin to yourselves, your wives and children.'[9]

It was at this point in the spring of 1839, when the potentialities of Chartism as a threat to society were so uncertain, that a new general was appointed to preside over the northern command of which Nottinghamshire was a part. Until the end of March the post had been held by Lieutenant-General Sir Richard Downes Jackson, K.C.B., a sound and respected officer. When news of his appointment as Commander-in-Chief of the British Forces in America reached the Duke of Newcastle, the latter described Jackson as 'sensible and provident . . . and ever ready'; he requested that he should not be removed, seeking to avoid the appointment of Major-General Sir Charles Napier who was known as a Radical in politics.[10] Although he received reassurance from Lord Russell that there was no danger of insurrection, the Duke's suspicion of reformers remained. Early in May of 1839 the Duke was actually deprived of his office as County Recorder because of the indiscreet vigour with which he had objected to the appointment of the Ruddington landowner, Mr. Paget, to the county bench. He felt that as Paget was a dissenter and a man of 'violent political convictions' (he became Whig Liberal M.P. for Nottingham in 1856), he was therefore unsuitable for such a position of responsibility.[11]

Despite the Duke's misgivings, Major-General Sir Charles James Napier was appointed, taking up his command in April, 1839. The fact that the Duke of Newcastle opposed Napier's appointment might suggest that Jackson had been more inclined to view reforms in a similar perspective to the Duke. If that is so, then in view of his subsequent handling of the Chartists in Nottingham Napier's appointment was of considerable importance, allowing, as he did, the moderate element to dominate the local movement throughout. Nevertheless, judging from Newcastle's surprise when a body of Metropolitan Police and a troop of Cavalry were dispatched to Mansfield in February, 1839, the persons who most seriously misjudged the threat to public order were the Duke of Portland and Edward Unwin, one of the county magistrates.[12] During 1839 both wrote several times to Lord John Russell to warn of an imminent Chartist outbreak,[13] yet on examination of the evidence these fears are seen to have been without foundation.

Napier's appointment coincided with an acceleration of Chartist activity in preparation for the presentation of a National Petition to Parliament in July, the time chosen to demand that the Charter become law. Subsequently, beginning in May, Sunday meetings were held regularly on the town's outskirts at the Forest or on Bulwell Common. Each followed a similar pattern. James Woodhouse, chairman of the local committee, would read aloud the political sermons of the Rev. J. R. Stephens, the former Wesleyan minister, which usually dealt with the injustices and cruelties resulting from the new poor law. Occasionally the assembly would sing a Chartist hymn and a working man might offer a prayer.[14] Eventually the Duke of Portland and the county magistrates became alarmed, formed an Association for the Protection of Property and requested Lord John Russell to equip the force with a hundred muskets. They also urged him to delay his withdrawal of the Metropolitan Police who were then stationed in Mansfield. At Whitsun the same year, local Chartists organized a large demonstration to be held at the Forest where Feargus O'Connor was to speak. This was at a time when delegates from the Chartist Convention were touring the country, many of them delivering militant speeches, and under this influence the county magistrates issued a warning:

> all peaceable and well-disposed persons are requested to remember their presence at any such meetings not only involves them in great responsibility and risk and gives countenance to the proceedings, but also may render them liable to severe punishment indiscriminately with the guilty parties.[15]

The county magistrates also enrolled four hundred special constables to patrol areas adjacent to the town at Sneinton, Radford, Carlton, Calverton and Bulwell, in addition to the more distant villages of Arnold and Sutton.[16]

Despite the warning, O'Connor's absence, and a blinding hailstorm, the meeting attracted a huge crowd. J. Bronterre O'Brien, the popular Chartist figure, addressed the assembly, which dispersed after electing James Woodhouse as the Nottingham delegate in place of Wade, and having affirmed its confidence in the Convention.[17] A drive was then undertaken to widen the appeal of Chartism, and handbills were distributed addressed to the shopkeepers, publicans, and other retailers of Nottingham and the vicinity, saying:

> we are far from thinking that the Retailers are a useless portion of society, their interest and our own is the same: unless the working classes are well paid for their labour, the Retailers cannot exist as a respectable body, but that they must share the same fate as the working classes. We therefore call upon you Fellow Countrymen to assist us in this righteous struggle . . . come forward to the assistance of the People's delegates. So shall the working classes form one phalanx which Despotism cannot penetrate.[18]

This was a position which, for reasons which cannot be ascertained, was to be reversed completely a year hence. A few weeks after this meeting Napier commented,

> 'the people here have changed their tone: instead of pikes and physical force lectures, they make it a religious question and have political sermons,' adding that nevertheless, 'the causes of Chartism remain, the spirit is abroad and vigorous.'[19]

The Charter was rejected on its presentation to Parliament on July 12th, 1839, and as a protest the Chartist leaders called for the observance of a 'Sacred Month' to begin on August 12th. That day and the following two were to be national holidays for all Chartists, although the decision to strike was left in the hands of the local Associations.[20] With an eye for dramatic climax, on both Sundays preceeding the 'Holiday' Nottingham Chartists decided to attract public attention by attending *en masse* the Church of St. Mary, where General Sir Charles Napier and his troops were accustomed to worship.[21] The news of this demonstration, according to Napier, occasioned considerable local alarm.[22] The intention of the Chartists in this strategy was to discountenance both the Established Church and the congregation, and to embarrass the military authorities. Two of the local Chartists had expressed suspicions concerning the connection between the Church and the 'inhuman, immoral and un-Christian Act' of 1834;[23] besides, the Established Church was an institution which symbolized privilege and was identified with Toryism and aristocracy. Likewise, the military authorities were identified as the natural enemies of vigorous reform movements, the tools of a government seeking to prevent change. It was recognized that St. Mary's Church was incapable of accommodating simultaneously both troops and a large Chartist contingent, but the Chartists marched to church at the head of Napier's men. As the double procession rapidly filled the available pews, Napier issued orders that if any soldier was unable to gain admission he must remain outside until the end of the service, and thereby what might have been an ugly situation was prevented.

As the national holiday drew near the Chartists held meetings in the Market Place almost every evening. Those held during the week regularly attracted between two and five hundred people, those at the weekend drew up to three thousand. In his journal Napier commented on the speeches he heard on these occasions, some of which he thought 'outrageous', and others 'good sense'.[24] Although Mayor John Wells considered a speech made on August 5th by a Mr. Black from Arnold adequate grounds for prosecution, he saw no reason for apprehending the speakers.[25] By contrast, one county magistrate was alarmed by the same proceedings and wrote to Rolleston to inform him: 'it is too bad of the town magistrates not to interfere.'[26] At the insistence of the county magistrates the Mayor issued a proclamation forbidding any mass demonstration on the first day of the holiday. The day passed quietly;[27] but the following day between five and six hundred men—chiefly framework knitters—assembled at Market Place. Led by James Woodhouse, with a female upon his arm, the crowd followed, and singing Wesleyan hymns they marched four abreast to the Forest collecting people *en route* and trying, without success, to persuade factory workers to join them. At the Forest Barber addressed the throng: 'I hope those who have got arms will keep them and those who have not will procure them as soon as possible'. The meeting dispersed when the mayor, Major-General Napier, and several magistrates arrived, although Nixon, one of the county magistrates, was heckled and jostled as he read the Riot Act. The dragoons waiting nearby were not called.[28] The following day all public houses were closed and meetings forbidden, but again several hundred Chartists assembled on the Forest in the company of about two thousand spectators. As on the previous day the meeting was interrupted by magistrates and police, and when crowds began to re-assemble on the market place, magistrates, police, and special constables dispersed them. Subsequently Woodhouse and three others were apprehended on charges of riotous assembly.

Similar demonstrations took place in the villages but there, in contrast with the equanimity shown by magistrates in the town, the county magistrates anticipated open violence. On the first day of the Holiday, Napier and the military had been called to the town's outskirts to disperse troublemakers. Napier recorded the episode:

> I rode out ordering dragoons to follow me. Mr. N—— (Need) and I found the mob which would not notice us and marched on. Old N—— put on his spectacles, pulled out the Riot Act and read it . . . to who? Myself and about a dozen old women looking out at their door to see what we were at. We came back, found another mob and ordered it to disperse. Mr. N—— told me to disperse it. I laughed, the dragoons laughed, the young women of the mob laughed . . . Hardly home however when a second call came, then a third, a fourth; each time we were paraded in order of battle and each time were laughed at; so the day passed in great excitement.[29]

This encounter followed a series of minor episodes which had given rise to exaggerated fears in the minds of the Dukes and the county magistrates. Reports of men learning to march with hedge stakes had been dispatched to Lord John Russell by the Mansfield magistrates as early as February, 1839, and special constables had been sworn in because of a conviction that the Chartists were armed.[30] At the request of the Duke of Portland a body of Metropolitan Police was also stationed in Mansfield. Five hundred and thirty-six special constables were sworn in for six months and, on behalf of the magistrates, the Duke of Newcastle requested arms from Lord John Russell.[31] Russell refused.[32] As the Whitsun demonstration approached, the Association for the Protection of Property applied for one hundred muskets with which to equip the force, while the Duke of Portland renewed his efforts to persuade Russell to allow the Metropolitan Police to remain. He also engaged thirty men at his own expense and placed them under the drilling orders of Inspector Martin of the Metropolitan Police.[33] Russell, pressed once more for arms, dispatched cutlasses and pistols, much to the dismay of the magistrates who continued to clamour for muskets and bayonets.[34] Twice in July Edward Unwin, the Mansfield county magistrate, disturbed secret Chartist meetings; one of them he discovered at three in the morning when armed men were drilling.[35]

At another meeting, held at Sutton at 9 a.m., about five hundred men listened to

> a sort of ranting preacher who after giving out a hymn preached to them for an hour holding up the aristocracy and middle class to destruction (sic) and drawing parallels from the scriptures.

When Unwin attempted to read the Riot Act he was jeered and pelted with stones; when pistol shots were fired he became alarmed and wrote to Russell, 'a degree of terror prevails which I can scarcely describe in adequate language.'[36] The Duke of Portland told Russell that a ' "reliable informer" ' had warned him of a Chartist outbreak which would take place within seven days.'[37] On the eve of the national holiday Napier wrote,

> The silly magistrates of Mansfield are in labour and a troop of dragoons has gone off to deliver them of their fears: the old Duke of Portland is played off by a spy.[38]

The following day crowds assembled in Mansfield and between eight hundred and a thousand men marched into the village, refusing to disperse until threatened by the military. On oath, several admitted to having hidden arms at Sutton.[39] The magistrates acting for Sutton-in-Ashfield duly issued a warrant for searching the house of Joseph Broyen, but because they failed to specify the illegal purpose for which they believed the arms were kept Broyen succeeded in sueing them for illegal action.[40] However, the day's events led to the arrest of thirty persons, seven of them receiving prison sentences which ranged between one and nine months.[41]

In Nottingham itself arrests were made on the second day of the holiday when magistrates, police, and special constables dispersed the forbidden meeting. Woodhouse and three others had been apprehended on charges of riotous assembly, but, after reprimands, all were discharged on sureties of £100 for Woodhouse and £50 and £25 the others.[42] In retrospect, after the publicity and preparation of the preceding weeks, the national holiday had been an anticlimax. The open air mass meetings were discontinued, and late in 1839 the Chartists began to rent a vacant chapel in Riste Place, Barker Gate, which was subsequently referred to as either the Chartist or Democratic Chapel. Here, newspapers were available to readers, although the chapel's principal uses were as a lecture hall, a place for regular general assembly, and as a committee room.[43] Small gatherings still met in public houses, and at about this time, following the Wesleyan type of organization, Chartists formed themselves into cells of ten meeting weekly with committee members appointed from their own number.[44]

As in some other Chartist strongholds, there seem to have been occasional efforts to surround the Nottingham branch of the movement with an aura of religion. Speakers were sometimes referred to as 'preachers' and their speeches as 'sermons'. George Harrison, the Calverton preacher, and the Rev. Linwood were *bona fide* practising ministers of religion, and likewise the Rev. Passmore Edwards, but Harrison was the only minister who figured among the leaders. Chartism has sometimes been interpreted as an involuntary non-conformist working class surge of popular agitation;[45] but this should not be confused with the consciously contrived politico-religious nature which the movement sometimes assumed. At times the Chartists used the bald ritual of hymn and sermon as a device by which the crowds might more easily become emotionally involved with the Chartist philosophy, a feature not peculiar to Nottingham. Even so, the hymns were only occasionally sung at meetings and the sermons were, in fact, political speeches with a sprinkling of religious references. One can only conjecture whether it was by chance or by design that the Chartists chose a former centre of working class evangelicalism as their regular meeting place.[46]

The lull in popular Chartist activity, which lasted from late August until the end of 1839, was broken when, partly due to unseasonable weather coming on top of depressed trade, local economic conditions deteriorated. This, together with the insurrection of the Monmouthshire Chartists in November, 1839 and the trial which followed, inspired the renewal of regular mass Chartist gatherings in Nottingham.[47] The plight of the local working classes in the winter of 1839–40 was recorded with evident compassion by Napier, who wrote of the extreme deprivation of two thousand people then receiving assistance from the Relief Committee. 'It is quite horrible to see them and to know that many who are not seen to beg are still in greater want. And again,

> the poor starving people go about by twenties and forties begging but without the least insolence; and yet some rich villains and some foolish villains choose to say they exact charity. It is a lie, an infernal lie.[48]

The early days of 1840 brought news of arms in Nottingham and one of Napier's riflemen was fired upon. Napier acknowledged that some Chartists were bent on fomenting trouble by exploiting the prevailing dissatisfaction, and when, during the second week in January, a rumour was circulating that Nottingham was to be involved in a general rising to begin at Sheffield, Napier was on the alert.[49] On the days immediately following the Sheffield disturbances on January 12th Napier remained at the Police Office[50] with the magistrates, civil and military forces. Workmen in Nottingham met the coaches from Sheffield to discover whether the rising had taken place,[51] but the coachmen had nothing to report. During the early days of January Chartist sentinels walked the streets of Nottingham, but there was no clash with the dragoons who, for the rest of this month, patrolled the town each evening after dark.[52] Meanwhile, Roworth and Napier were making efforts to impress upon the wealthier classes that the new poor law offered inappropriate means of relieving public distress and that immediate and large scale charity was urgently needed.[53]

Just how imminent was open violence in Nottingham in 1839–40? After the resignation of Wade as local representative to the Convention his replacement, James Woodhouse, who was considered by the *Review* editor to be a reliable man, maintained that he and the rest of the N.W.M.A. supported reason, law, justice, and order, and despite the few inflammatory speeches made in that year, mainly by visiting speakers, Lord John Russell, basing his assessment of the local situation on the reports received from the Police Inspector at Mansfield, had assured the Duke of Newcastle that there was little danger of insurrection.[54] The *Review,* which was one of the major influences on local working class attitudes, while endorsing the principles of Chartism, was consistent in its emphasis on the folly of physical force, and at no time did it appear unduly alarmed. Troops had been stationed in Nottingham, not because it was expected to be a centre of disturbance but because its location between Manchester (where in the summer of 1839 the main Chartist uprising was anticipated) and London meant that troops from Nottingham might be used to check the proposed march on London from the north.[55] At no time throughout the period did Napier anticipate open conflict in the locality. He was disturbed by the sale of gunpowder, but after careful investigation he concluded that the total amount in the hands of the local populace was very small. 'I do not believe that there are many in the town disposed to mischief'; but he nevertheless recognized that the county magistrates would become nervous, especially when they received the report that a shot had been aimed at a dragoon in Nottingham.[56] The few 'outrageous' speeches he had heard delivered in the market place failed to alarm Napier, and in December, 1840 he completely discounted rumours of a Chartist plan to take possession of the barracks.[57] Even when Napier discovered that one of his riflemen, an able and trusted man, was attending all the Chartist meetings he showed little anxiety, and requested to deal with the situation by inviting the soldier to dispute the aims and methods of Chartism. The Home Secretary forbade this lest the debate should receive publicity and Napier's radical views embarrass higher authorities who were less sympathetic to reform.

'My whole success, or hope of it', wrote Napier, 'rested on my being known to hold the man's own opinions, and only differing as to the means taken to give them effect.'[58]

During these years another reforming body began to take root in Nottingham, namely the Anti-Corn Law League. Even before its local appearance James Sweet had defined the Chartists' attitude to it as one of hostile competition. Political reform, he argued, was a necessary pre-condition for Corn Law Repeal, and the Anti-Corn Law League was merely a middle-class self-interest group which was unconcerned with fundamental reforms to the political and social structure of society. 'Let the Corn Law repealers become Chartists' became the cry,[59] and when a general meeting of the Anti-Corn Law Association was called in January, 1840 to inaugurate a grand recruitment campaign, Sweet and Woodhouse urged Chartists to attend. The *Review* editor, himself a free trader, reckoned that about two-thirds of the assembly were Chartists and it was these who proceeded to punctuate an uproarious meeting with cries of 'Charter! Charter!' The meeting closed, when, after a motion had been passed calling for the abolition of the Corn Laws, an amendment was proposed by Woodhouse in favour of the Charter, an amendment which was carried with an overwhelming and vociferous majority.[60] Sutton criticized the Chartists for repelling the middle classes and urged an alliance of Chartists and Anti-Corn Law supporters in agitation for free trade and parliamentary reform. The attitude of local Chartists, however, like those in other regions, continued to be hostile, and more meetings were sabotaged.[61] So boisterous was one League meeting held in October, 1841 that the mayor barred future Corn Law meetings from the Exchange rooms.[62]

Although the Nottingham Association did not become part of the national League until January, 1844, free trade slowly gained wider acceptance.[63] In July, 1841 dissenting congregations joined together for a day of humiliation and prayer on account of general distress 'engendered by iniquitous restrictions on trade, notably the Corn Laws.' Extracts from the Report of the Committee of the House of Commons on Import Duties were quoted from the pulpit and Adam Smith was used as text.[64] When, instead of repeal, news of the passage of Peel's sliding scale reached Nottingham, effigies of Peel and Buckingham were burned in the streets.[65] The disappointment of free traders created renewed vigour in the local movement and when, in December, 1842, the Midland Counties Anti-Corn Law League was founded, six Nottingham representatives were present.

Besides the vocal campaign aimed at Anti-Corn Law supporters, another local offensive was launched in 1840 against the middle

L

classes in a pamphlet entitled 'An Address to the Working Classes of England', in which was elaborated a 'moral force' plan for defeating 'the parasites of society'.[66]

> The power that oppresses us is supported by the middle class shopkeepers. If we cease to deal with them they will become poor and lose their vote and will have to labour for their bread honestly. They will cry out for Universal Suffrage and Cheap Governments. Thus, by ceasing to spend our money in the shops of our enemies we have destroyed their power; by spending in shops of our own and our friends we will have increased our own strength and added to our comfort . . . . Who can deny the right of the working man to form joint stock companies to increase their wealth by the profits of their own consumption?

Under the rules of the Society capital was to be provided by the issue of an unlimited number of shares of not less than 10s. each; the company was to be managed by a committee of twelve, of which four were to retire each month. A storekeeper was appointed to superintend the 'People's Store', but although two stores were opened, one in Nottingham, the other at Mansfield, there is no trace of their subsequent history. Neither is it clear whether the 'Nottingham Cooperative Society' had Chartist connections, although in 1840 Society members held weekly meetings in the chapel at Riste Place. Also open to speculation is the possibility of a connection between the foundation of the local society and the series of three lectures delivered by Robert Owen at the Theatre Royal in that year, though the existence of a co-operative society in Hyson Green as early as 1830 indicates that cooperation was not a novel idea in the Nottingham district in 1840.[64]

The Chartist attack on the anti-corn law group petered out after 1842, and with Sutton's continuous editorial campaign in favour of radical reform and corn law repeal several Nottingham Radicals with Chartist sympathies decided to embrace free trade. In 1845 even James Sweet and Henry Mott, another local Chartist, made public their approval of free trade in corn,[68] but it is clear that on their list of priorities political reform came first. It is difficult to judge the effect of this conversion of a handful of Chartists and several Chartist sympathisers to the cause of free trade. Neither Sweet nor Mott became actively involved in the local Anti-Corn Law League, and none of the free trade campaigners in Nottingham more than sympathized with Chartist aims; none were connected with the local Chartist cell. On these grounds it is unlikely that the lull in Chartist activity in Nottingham between 1843 and 1846 was the result of an absorption of effective Chartist leaders into the crusade for abolition of the corn law.[69] Improved economic conditions and the accompanying reversion to trade union activity by the main body of Chartist followers explains the chronology of Chartist activity.

Before this pause, the years 1841 and 1842 had brought such distress that in December 1841 a public relief fund had been established to alleviate suffering, and when in February. 1842 the Nottingham guardians resolved to waive the test and extend out-relief, forty-five hundred people qualified immediately.[70] Against this background O'Connor received a tumultous welcome on his arrival in Nottingham. Hundreds of poverty-stricken men and women travelled on foot from as far as Mansfield and Sutton-in-Ashfield to greet him.[71]

> From the railway station a huge procession moved into the town . . . First came a man mounted on a grey horse, with the Chartist colours (green) tied over it, and marshalling the way. Next came four beautiful green wreaths suspended from an upright pole with cross-bars, and then a large green silk flag bearing the inscription "Annual parliament—universal suffrage —vote by ballot—no property qualification—payment of members—our cause is just." Beside it was a plain pink flag. A band of music here was stationed. Next came a number of small flags borne by children and then a large green flag with the inscription "Feargus O'Connor, the Friend of Equal Rights and Equal Laws". Two small flags green and pink with "Feargus O'Connor" on them. A number of small flags came next and then likenesses of Oastler, O'Connor, and Emmet framed into a triangular shape, and mounted on the tops of poles, presented a gay appearance; surmounting them were caps of liberty, made of crimson satin, and embroidered imitation pearls. Next came another band of music, and behind it the carriage and four greys containing O'Connor standing up, with Dean Taylor and other friends of the Chartist cause behind him. Mr. Sweet occupied the box. A number of flags and flys drawn by single horses full of women and men followed. Next came a large banner with the bootmakers arms on it . . . The next flag bore the inscription "They have set up Kings but not by me—God is our King—Him will I obey!"

Chartists from Carrington and Ilkeston were also part of the procession and bands from Sutton and Heanor added to the general air of festivity.[72] Some of the excitement caused by O'Connor's visit spilled over into the elections which took place in the same year, the occasion when local Chartists sought to make their presence felt as a political force.

With some three thousand freemen swelling the Nottingham electorate, a large proportion of whom were framework knitters, small tradesmen, artisans of various kinds, and even labourers, the local franchise, like that in Coventry, was wider than in most towns at this time.[73] One result of this participation by the working classes in local politics was that Nottingham had become renowned for its rowdy campaigns, as well as for corruption, intimidation, and violence. The events of 1831 had strengthened the popular image of Nottingham as a centre where Radical rowdies held sway, while at the same time they indicated the presence in the town of large numbers of Radical supporters, many of whom would subsequently listen with interest to Chartist demands for reform.

In September, 1830 Thomas Wakefield and John Heard organized a petition in support of the Reform Bill. The hopes of the twelve hundred Radicals who signed the petition were shared by many more, as the reception given to the news of the Bill's rejection in October, 1831 showed.[74] At a public meeting held in the Market Place the formal motions of protest gave way to window smashing and pillage, and the offices of the *Nottingham Journal* were attacked. The reading of the Riot Act failed to quieten the excited crowd, many of whom were in Nottingham for Goose Fair. Accompanied by police, the militia, and several hundred extra constables who had been especially sworn in, managed to beat off many attacks on property. When a mob turned in the direction of the Castle, however, the police were left behind. The Duke of Newcastle, the unpopular owner of Nottingham Castle, was a symbol of the forces seeking to prevent reform, and, although he had long since resided elsewhere, an attack on the Castle was symbolic of an assault upon the principles for which he stood. The crowd surged into the building, tore tapestries from the walls, wrecked the furniture, and finally scattered fire-brands to complete the devastation. They left the Castle a blazing monument of destruction, the cries and shouts of the crowd applauding their magnificent arson. The next day Lowe's silk mill at Beeston was razed by fire. At the gates of Wollaton Park the Wollaton Yeomanry stood by with cannons, and the Hall itself was garrisoned with colliers. When the invading mob stormed the gates the Yeomanry charged, taking several prisoners. Later in the Market Place, the inevitable cockpit, an irate hussar fired at random and wounded one of the crowd. The emotional temperature then fell and no further incidents occurred. When finally the Bill became law the next year, the jubilation and excitement was unsurpassed; brass band music, bonfires, fireworks, and public sheep roastings were included in the programme of entertainment on the day appointed for formal celebration of what proved to be an increase in the national electorate by about 50 per cent. Even so, only one Englishman in twenty possessed the voting privilege, and in Nottingham the immediate effect of the Reform Act was to reduce slightly the size of the electorate.[75] Reform had little noticeable effect upon the representatives which the town elected to send to Parliament. For some time before 1818 the aristocratic Tory party, which until that year had succeeded in securing one of Nottingham's parliamentary seats, had been jointly opposed by dissenting Whigs and Radicals. From 1818 onwards the Whigs held both seats, and not until the entry of the Chartists into the political arena was that alliance against the Tories disturbed.

At the bye election of 1841, caused by the death of General R. C. Ferguson, one of the two Whig M.P.s, the Tory candidate John Walter, editor of *The Times,* was returned as M.P. for Nottingham, a result which in a traditionally Whig stronghold was quite remarkable. This victory reflected the intensity of local anti-poor law feeling, for the Whig candidate, Sir George Larpent, was much more radical than Walter and had been equally vehement in his condemnation of the new poor law. Nevertheless, Larpent was unable to dissociate himself from the Whig legislation of 1834. Walter's invective directed at the new poor law, unlike that of Larpent, had proved acceptable to the Nottingham electorate, but even so Larpent was defeated by only a narrow margin. Shortly afterwards a general election was called, and John Walter and T. B. Charlton of Chilwell as Tory candidates opposed Larpent and the other sitting Whig, Sir J. C. Hobhouse. The major issue was free trade, and although the Chartists had supported Walter in the previous bye election, largely, it seems, merely as a gesture of protest against the new poor law and the government, in 1842 their allegiance reverted to the Whigs. Both Whig candidates were returned, but only to have their success threatened by a petition to the House praying that, on grounds of corruption, the election should be declared void. In order to spare the town embarrassment the Tories, who possessed a comparable record of corruption, agreed with the Whigs to a private arrangement whereby at the following election, when Larpent retired from politics, Walter would take Larpent's seat unopposed. The discovery of this discreet compromise led to the setting up of a parliamentary enquiry, and in July, 1842 a new election writ was issued. The ensuing election was accompanied by rioting and disturbance which coincided with renewed Chartist demonstrations in the second half of 1842. Furthermore, the radical element in the local Whig party joined forces with the Chartists to support the candidature of Joseph Sturge, the Quaker reformer, on a platform which included five of the Charter points—he did not advocate payment of members—in addition to free trade, a tax on property alone, the separation of church and state, and the abolition of capital punishment.

The bye election took place in August, shortly after a second Chartist petition had been rejected by Parliament, and in the same month as local Chartists resolved to demonstrate in sympathy with the strikers in Lancashire. O'Connor's presence in the town in August intensified the excitement, but whereas in February O'Connor had denounced Sturge as a middle-class knave, he now led the campaign in support of Sturge, assisted by Thomas Cooper, the Leicester leader, and P. D. McDouall, the Chartist demagogue. John Walter was supported by J. R. Stephens whose imprisonment had followed a change in political affiliation. The encounter of such redoubtable adversaries in a town already noted for corrupt and violent political contests reached a tumultous climax on the night preceding the election when O'Connor and McDouall set up a wagon in the centre of the Market Place: Stephens and Walter rested theirs at the upper end. The crowd which assembled to witness and participate in the proceedings were reckoned at between sixteen and eighteen thousand people and they were not disappointed by the evening's entertainment.

> Contrary to the advice of Mr. Sturge and the Conservatives who beheld the proceedings from a window of Bromley House and protested unavailingly against it, the waggon placed for that gentlemen's friend was seized by the surrounding people and wheeled up to within fifteen yards of the other . . . An indescribable scene of confusion followed. Standing erect with his arms folded in an attitude of calm defiance, Stephens was the object for some minutes of the loudest execrations and the fiercest epithets. His waggon was surrounded by a number of blues who repaid the hisses and hootings which assailed Stephens, but they were overpowered by numbers. From words they came to blows; O'Connor jumped from the waggon and headed a charge that drove everything before it. The orator Stephens and his associates took refuge in the Bell Inn while the victorious party took possession of the vehicle from which they had driven them.[76]

Sturge was narrowly defeated, but the support accorded him by many prominent radical Whigs including Frearson, Gill, Vickers, Cullen, Wells, Paget, Bean, Felkin, and Sutton is a measure of the influence of Chartism upon local Whigs, for although none would describe themselves as Chartists, in fact, their political philosophy was almost identical with that embodied in the Charter. Sturge was defeated because, in the face of extensive bribery by Walter, he had

refused to resort to similar tactics. Subsequently, Walter was unseated when charges of bribery were proved. The moral victory,
therefore, belonged to the Chartists.[77]

Although the Chartists achieved some measure of success in the
local political arena in 1842, efforts to use industrial action to
further political reform were a conspicuous failure. The Plug Plot
strikes which took place in Manchester early in August, 1842 inspired Chartists in Nottingham to organize their own campaign to
obtain 'a fair day's wages for a fair day's work', though they
stressed that they were concerned with effecting a moral and not a
physical revolution. Delegates from the various trades—framework knitters, lace makers, smiths, dyers, stonemasons, joiners, and
tailors—agreed to embark upon a nine days' strike.[78] The first
major meeting to begin the strike was fixed for August 19th at
5 a.m. The magistrates forbade it, but Chartists assembled nevertheless, and an outside speaker began a harangue. The magistrates
interrupted the meeting and dispersed the crowd which reassembled
at 10 a.m. and was again broken up, this time by police. A milling
throng of some six or seven hundred then proceeded to march
through the town, calling at the factories to bring out more men on
strike. Police again swooped upon them and the Riot Act was read,
although at one point it was snatched from the hands of the
magistrate and ripped apart. Reinforcements arrived, several arrests
were made, and the crowds dispersed.[79] The following day throngs
assembled and made their way towards Radford to pursue their
turn-out tactics, but they met with little sympathy from the factory
workers and the authorities arrested some two hundred marchers.
The climax was reached on the fourth day when five thousand
Chartists assembled on Mapperley Hills. At the instigation of the
county magistrates a strong military force captured four hundred
men, who, handcuffed and bound, were marched to the House of
Correction, their captors being pelted with stones. Of those taken
into custody about one hundred and fifty were discharged promptly
on entering into £5 recognizances not to disturb the peace, while
twenty-four were sentenced to periods of hard labour ranging from
two to six months.[80]

So ended the affair later remembered as The Battle of Mapperley
Hills. The editor of the *Review* frankly condemned the authorities'
actions.

> Those arrested were a complete farce (sic) . . . Imagine . . .
> poor starving defenceless men seated at their hard begged-for
> meal (sic) . . . to be surprised and surrounded by dragoons and
> police and dragged to gaol through the streets of their town,
> when they are not committing the shadow of an illegal act.[81]

Sutton was correct in his assessment of the significance of the demonstrations. At Calverton, framework knitters had resolved to strike against a reduction in wages, 'and never to return to work until the Charter becomes the law of the land'. On the day before the giant demonstration of August 23, two thousand Chartists, mostly framework knitters, had surged into Nottingham from the villages, and many of those detained by the police during that demonstration could say nothing more about their presence than that they only wanted 'a fair day's wage for a fair day's work.'[82] These were the sort of people who provided the body of support for the twenty-five Chartist Associations that existed in and around Nottingham and Derby in 1842.[83]

Failure of industrial action and moderate success in the local political sphere helps to account for the Chartist quiescence until 1847; but equally important was the improvement in trade beginning in 1843. The chapel in Riste Place continued to open for newspaper reading, and meetings were held regularly.[84] In 1844, according to the *Review,* local Chartists were alert still,

> scattering themselves about the town and neighbourhood, professing to teach the great doctrines inculcated in the scriptures, and to show that these doctrines were not incompatible with the spirit of Chartism, but rather that the principles of the Charter were those inculcated by the New Testament.[85]

One final dramatic attempt to obtain the Charter was yet to be made, but this did not occur until 1848. During the interim, the Chartist core remained active but subdued.

The strength of local Chartism was again revealed at the election in 1843 when Thomas Gisborne, who declared his support of the six points in the Charter, was nominated as the Whig candidate. He duly defeated John Walter, junior, but subsequently it became evident that Gisborne was not as radical as local Chartists had believed—although it is significant that he had considered a Chartist platform to be necessary to bring him victory at the polls—and his vote against the Factory Bill and the Nottingham Enclosure Bill caused Chartists to censure his political conduct.[86] Three years later Feargus O'Connor reappeared on the local scene to conduct a vigorous campaign against 'the do-nothing kid glove reformers', calling upon the men of Nottingham to show their disgust with Whiggism. The programme which O'Connor laid before the electors was hardly that of an orthodox Chartist. One major plank was a plan for increasing land ownership among workmen, and indeed in August, 1847 Nottingham Chartists were contributing £100 weekly to the Chartist Allotment Society.[87] As for the rest of his programme, there was little mention of Chartism. He advocated the separation of church and state, nonsectarian education, and a property tax. He condemned the Spanish marriages, and criticized the government for failing to aid Ireland and for contemplating the endowment of the Roman Catholic priesthood. It is evident that O'Connor was anxious to avoid alarming those Radical electors who might abstain. Gisborne and Hobhouse did little more than apologize for their previous political inertia. Hobhouse had already represented Nottingham for thirteen years, and local Whigs tended to dismiss the possibility of defeat, an attitude that was reflected in a display of apathy at the poll. They overlooked the general unpopularity of aristocratic Whiggism, while Gisborne's failure to honour his previous election promise to meet the electors annually also rankled. As for Walter's programme, this remained secret. He relied entirely upon his father's reputation to bring him victory, and not once did he appear in Nottingham. Even so, Walter topped the poll with O'Connor second, nearly five hundred votes behind. O'Connor had triumphed to the delight of Chartists everywhere.[88]

His success was partly due to personal popularity in Nottingham, but mainly to the support which he received from local Tories who were seeking revenge for the broken agreement of 1841. He was aided further by Radical abstentions, especially among nonconformists, who welcomed O'Connor's proposals concerning an education system which recognized sectarian differences and who, on the other hand, were suspicious of increasing control of education given to the Anglican Church, a policy implied in recent government proposals for education.[89] Another factor which helps to explain O'Connor's victory was the plight of the lower middle classes, the shopkeepers, small tradesmen, and publicans of Nottingham, who, because of the extent of depression, were said to be suffering to a far greater extent than ever before.[90] In the spring of 1848 the *Review* editor remarked that Chartism had attracted considerable middle class support.[91] Thus despite the defection of Whigs over education measures and the local Whig-Tory feud, there is still reason to believe that the balance of political power in Nottingham was somewhat further to the left than in much of the country.[92]

In 1847 deteriorating economic conditions led once more to a reactivation of the fluctuating Chartist rank and file which had synchronized in 1837–39 and 1841–2 with economic depression and unemployment. Ichabod Wright spoke of his helplessness in the face of the financial crisis of 1847:

> Customers used to come to me for assistance and I said No, the law forbids me now. You must turn out your hands. I cannot assist you any longer under the law of 1844.[93]

He was referring, of course, to the Bank Charter Act and Wright became the leader of the Nottingham Association for Currency Reform. In May, 1847 more than one thousand people were in the workhouse and more than three times that number received out-relief.[94] High food prices aggravated the situation, and for a period the workhouse diet consisted of bread mixed with Indian meal and flour; cheese and beer allocations were discontinued for three months.[95] Outside the workhouse high bread prices caused a few incidents, and as groups of poverty-stricken workers congregated on the market place the authorities alerted the Yeomanry lest serious rioting should break out. When the price of corn fell in June, mobs assembled outside bakers' shops in Nottingham, Basford, and Arnold in anticipation of a reduction in bread prices. When local bakers cut prices by only a fraction, shop windows were smashed and bread was stolen.[96]

It was against this background that the Chartist bellman had convened a meeting of all unemployed in order to discuss the extent of hardship.[97] The depression continued into 1848, and by April one thousand six hundred inmates packed the newly-completed workhouse.[98] In the same year Ichabod Wright conducted an investigation into the amount of distress in the town. He discovered that much furniture and clothing was being pawned and children were absent from school because they simply had no clothes.

'A starving man', he concluded, 'does not discuss the principles of the party he may join, he only hopes by their means to better his condition which he believes cannot be worse.'[99]

Wright went on to express surprise that there had been no violent demonstrations and said that he did not blame the working classes for holding Chartist views. The curate of Trinity Church affirmed that during the past year less than half of the workmen in his parish had been employed full time and with considerable perspicacity added:

They enlist under the cause of the Charter because such is at present the standard of discontent. Any other name or object holding the same position would secure equally their attachment.[100]

It was to focus local attention upon their standard of discontent that large meetings in support of the Charter took place prior to its presentation at Westminster on April 10th. .[101] On that date local authorities took precautionary measures. Four troops of Yeomanry Cavalry under arms were stationed at Trent Bridge, Gamston, Wollaton, and Gedling, and soldiers were posted inside the town gaol. In addition to the normal police force (in Nottingham the police-population ratio was very low at only one policeman to nearly forty-five hundred persons),[102] sixteen hundred special constables equipped with staves were sworn in to act as general patrols. Thinking it probable that in the event of attack the gasworks would be the first objective, workmen were stationed there and provisioned to withstand a seige. Barricades were erected and walls loopholed, while chains were suspended across the street in front of the gate and boiling tar prepared in readiness.[103] Apprehensive shopkeepers, whose shop fronts overlooked Market Place, boarded up their windows and locked up before the huge meeting took place. Between five and six thousand people crowded into the square to listen to James Sweet whose tone was, as always, pacific, saying, 'I would impress upon every Chartist the necessity of being a police officer;' even McDouall failed to exhibit his customary revolutionary ardour; instead, he reiterated the plan for cooperation and exclusive dealing.[104] The crowds dispersed and the shopkeepers removed their shutters. The danger of serious local disturbance was imaginary. Nationally, enthusiasm for the cause ebbed, and locally the Chartists began to lose ground.

It is pertinent to ask why, despite the manifest strength of Chartism in Nottingham, its character never became revolutionary, and why violence, though anticipated by some in 1839, 1842, and even 1848, did not occur. The reasons which explain this situation include both the nature of local Chartism and the attitude and behaviour of the authorities. Both in 1839, and in 1842, the local Chartists themselves were divided over policy when national leaders called for industrial action. Apart from the loyal supporters, whose number it is difficult to guess, the rank and file could not be counted upon to act in solidarity. On neither occasion would the lace workers in the factories turn out to please the rest, and while Chartist leadership in the town was in the hands of moral force men like James Sweet, in the villages, according to Martin, the Metropolitan Police Inspector, the Chartist clubs had no clear designs, object, or leaders on which to build an effective movement.[105] As for the authorities, the possibility of violent outbreaks in 1839–40 was reduced by the policy of Major-General Sir Charles Napier, a stern but sympathetic guarantor of law and order.

'If the mob break the peace', he wrote in the summer of 1839, 'I will break their heads, we will have no burnings, no disgraceful proceedings which the honest part of the Chartists deprecate.'[106]

Determined to keep the peace, nevertheless he considered the Chartist cause a just one: 'The people should have universal suffrage—it is their right. The ballot it is their security and their will and therefore their right also.'[107] Despite the entreaties of an alarmed

Duke of Portland to arrest O'Connor in order to prevent a general uprising of which he claimed to have proof, Napier acted with moderation and tact.[108] When Lord Normanby urged Napier to offer a reward of £200 for the man who fired at the dragoon, his reaction was, 'let us shut our mouths and the thing will be un-noticed,'[109] and Napier's handling of the Chartist March to St. Mary's Church contrasted with the conduct of the county magistrates in the Battle of Mapperley Hills in 1842.

In the summer of 1839 Napier commended the town magistrates' behaviour. He said that they had acted with great propriety and good sense[110] and on the occasion of the National Holiday the same year he wrote, 'the magistrates here want to act rightly but have been bullied by the county magistrates into a proclamation against meetings . . .; this is unwise.'[111] Having been persuaded to take this measure 'the town magistrates endeavoured to do their duty with a conscientious regard for justice, all seemed to act with a strong sense of good humour and good feeling . . .' Throughout this episode Napier had urged the town magistrates not to prohibit meetings and to refrain from interference because 'the poor people when left alone have no desire for disturbance.'[112] In January, 1840 he reported seeing Chartist sentinels in the streets, but although he knew they were armed with pistols he advised the magistrates not to meddle with them.

> 'Seizing these men could do no good:' he wrote, 'it would not stop Chartism if they were all hanged: and as these offered no violence why starve their wretched families and worry them with a long imprisonment? I repeat it Chartism cannot be stopped. God forbid that it should: what we want is to stop the letting loose a large body of armed cut-throats upon the public. The magistrates, happily, agreed with me.'[113]

In Mansfield and in other towns precipitate action taken by magistrates had heightened local feeling, and in Sheffield it had led to bloodshed.[114] Napier worked harmoniously with the town magistrates, whom he praised enormously for their understanding of the nature of Chartism and for the sympathy which they showed in dealing with the Chartists. In January, 1840 Napier and Mayor William Roworth together organized a public subscription to relieve poverty, and Napier estimated that one-quarter of the eight hundred beneficiaries were Chartists.[115] It was for Roworth, too, the 'zealous temperate and active magistrate', that Napier reserved his highest praise.

'My firm belief' he wrote, 'is that it (Nottingham) has been saved by the good heart and good sense of Roworth the Mayor more than anything else.' Elsewhere he acknowledged his 'active benevolence and watchfulness',[116] and he considered Roworth and John Smith Wright to be two of the 'noblest works of God.'[117] Shortly before his departure Napier wrote in his journal:

I like Nottingham, the poor people are good and were they fairly treated they would be perfectly quiet . . . Thank God we have had no row and not a drop of blood has been spilled.[118]

When General Sir Charles Napier and his troops moved to Cheshire from Nottingham in 1840 the understanding and tact of the magistrates was still a relevant factor contributing to local peace in 1841–42. But after 1842 the nature of Chartism in Nottingham began to alter. The insignificant physical force elements became increasingly isolated from the main body of moral force Chartists. At the same time the latter came to embrace free trade which they had formerly considered to be a purely middle class interest—and therefore suspect. On the other hand an increasing number of middle class Radicals found themselves supporting many, if not all, of the six points of the Charter, even though they continued to describe themselves as Radicals. This latter feature of Chartist history in Nottingham becomes increasingly apparent after 1846, when Corn Law repeal was achieved. Shortly after the petition of April 10th, 1848 the *Review* editor remarked:[119]

. . . nor is the influence of Chartism confined to the working classes; on the contrary it has made and is making much way among the moneyed and middle classes who are alike smarting under the scourge of class legislation . . . .

His assessment of local feeling was borne out at a meeting which took place a few days after these comments were made.

On the initiative of a number of principal manufacturers and tradesmen, Mayor John Heard called a meeting to consider the extensive poverty which still existed in Nottingham. Admission was by circular sent to leading figures of local political parties—including the Chartists—and the immediate concern of the assembly was the drawing up of a petition urging Parliament to take active measures to end the depression. It is significant that all of the manufacturers and traders who originally pressed the Mayor to convene the meeting had volunteered to act as special constables during the recent political crisis, convinced that they must 'repress any attempts at political change by other than peaceful and constitutional means.'[120] Nevertheless, they felt compelled to show sympathy for the evident suffering of the working classes and to join with them in calling on the government to act and take steps to revive economic activity, or at least to alleviate suffering. The Rev. Brooks of St. Mary's Church wanted to see permanent soup kitchens established, and his proposal for a state allotment system drew much applause. The Rev. Carpenter supported Felkin's plea for tax reforms, the abolition of indirect taxation, and a heavy tax on income from land and capital. Ichabod Wright took advantage of the occasion to bring before the meeting the views of the Nottingham Currency Reform Association which he had instigated in the same year. The Bank Act of 1844 and the restriction which it placed on note issue, he argued, was a major factor producing depression; the currency laws should be repealed to allow the economy to expand. Sweet and McDouall spoke on behalf of the Chartists and, inevitably, attributed the situation to the failure to extend the franchise. This sentiment was echoed not only by the Rev. Passmore Edwards, a local dissenting minister, but also by William Taylor, a Whig stationer, who had enrolled as a special constable during the emergency. He supported a more flexible middle class attitude towards the Chartists, accepting the principles set out in the Charter but criticizing the 'dogmatic and arbitrary manner' of Chartist agitation:

> If Chartists would, in the spirit of moderation and candour, attach some importance to others and pay less attention to the speeches of their leaders, then by going along with the middle class they would obtain the Charter before many years had elapsed.

Others expressed themselves in favour of an extension of the suffrage.

Two months later, local Radicals formally rejected the Whig party, and under the banner of the People's League resolved to organize Radicals in Nottingham with the aim of obtaining universal suffrage. At an inaugural meeting in June, 1848, Hart, Fox, Gill, Beecrofts, Knight, Parkin, and Walter shared the speaker's platform with the Chartist trio, Sweet, Harrison, and Roberts.[121] The speeches revealed general agreement to accomplish political change 'by moral, legal, and Christian means.' But towards the end of the meeting a disagreement arose over the wording of a motion of confidence in the Charter. Radical speakers were howled down, but the hecklers failed to carry their own motion and the meeting ended in confusion.[122] Thus the formation of a broad Radical front was temporarily frustrated by the uncompromising attitude of Chartist supporters. Nevertheless, it seems clear that after the repeal of the corn laws, while middle class Radicals had continued to press for political reform, the Chartist leaders, who with few exceptions had always urged moral force agitation, were moving nearer to an alliance with them. Anxious, no doubt, to preserve their identity, a splinter group of physical force Chartists met in May under the leadership of the framework knitter, Jonathan Barber, but its numbers were few and none of the Chartist leaders took part. James Sowter, a cordwainer, and Blind Peter, referred to as 'a well-known local Chartist', were the only other persons named at future meetings, which consisted chiefly of vain boasts concerning the possession of arms.[123] Shortly after the first two meetings of this group, James Sweet presided at a meeting in the company of Thomas Kyd, a member of the Chartist Executive, and Harrison from Calverton. At this meeting Sweet spoke at length urging the wisdom of peaceful agitation.[124]

Not only were Chartist leaders and Radicals drawing together while the small physical force minority became estranged from the main organization and its loyal supporters, but also the rank and file, of whom O'Connor spoke when he was in Nottingham in 1850, finally deserted the Chartist cause.

'When trade was bad', said O'Connor, 'the operatives cried out to be led: but when trade improved and they had 8s. or 10s. a week in their pockets they became indifferent to politics at the very time when they were best able to maintain agitation.'[125] This cyclical support for Chartism had its counterpart in the fluctuating strength of trade unions, and, as in other towns, a counterpoint of Chartist agitation and trade union activity set the predominant pattern in the history of working class movements.

For the hosiery trade the years between 1836 and 1843, covering two peak years in Chartist activity, were times of almost unrelieved depression, during which trade union activity disappeared. Improvement in the lace trade in 1840 produced a short-lived lacemakers' union, and more than four hundred female outworkers employed as lace runners struck, but without success.[126] During 1842, societies were formed for information and assistance to intending emigrants, and the young men of the town were said to be gripped in a fever of emigration which at this time affected working men and women throughout the country, and whose flow continued for the next few years.[127] With the return of buoyant trade conditions early in 1843 framework knitters' unions revived, and a series of strikes took place.[128] This was followed by an attempt to establish a general union of hosiery workers to be called The United Company of Framework Knitters of Great Britain and Ireland.[129] Two years later this union enrolled in Doherty's National Association of United Trades for the Protection of Labour, and by 1847 there were branches in the villages of Radford, Basford, Hyson Green, Carlton, Daybrook, and Arnold.[130] In 1846 the lace makers also formed a union to affiliate with the N.A.P.L.[131]

The commercial crisis of 1847 and the accompanying unemployment brought the demise of the National Association, the disappearance of local unions, and the formation of a Nottingham branch of the National Charter Association, whereas an upturn in economic activity in the spring of 1849 saw a reversion to direct trade action. Moreover, the defection in 1849 of the rank and file who had provided the numerical strength of cyclical Chartism proved to be their final renunciation of faith in the movement. During the early months of 1849, the editor of the *Review* remarked upon the frequency of meetings among framework knitters who were determined to take advantage of expanding trade[132] and some of the Chartist leaders became involved in the strikes of 1849–50. Apprehensive that the strikers might apply to the workhouse for relief on the plea of being unable to find employment, hosiers furnished the clerk of the Board of Guardians with a list of shops where frames were idle for lack of men willing to work at the rates paid during the winter of 1848.[133] James Sweet called a meeting of ratepayers and organized a public subscription with which to support the strikers. 'A stockinger', he declared, 'is so transparent, you might read a newspaper through him.[134] At Arnold ratepayers formed an association on a similar model to aid the union in its campaign, the committee including among its members a farmer, a surgeon, and a school teacher; societies were also set up at Carlton and Lambley.[135]

The erosion of massive support for Chartism occurred soon after the anticlimax of 1848. Local Chartists were evidently becoming increasingly frustrated by the fruitlessness of petitions, and in 1848, Harney, Nottingham's representative on the Chartist Convention,[136] stated that this was the last petition in which Nottingham would agree to take part. By contrast local enthusiasm for O'Connor's National Land Company, although moderate, was slower to disappear than elsewhere, and during the closing months of 1848 Nottingham was the sole contributor in the north midlands. A few years later the Company was defunct.[137]

As a movement with great numerical strength, Chartism in Nottingham was a spent force but the local leadership had always been in the hands of men who did not contemplate revolutionary action and who were prepared to work for political reform within the context of the existing structure of society. Moreover for men like Sweet, Chartism was only a phase in a career devoted to championing political democracy and social justice. Thrice elected to the Town Council (in 1854, 1858, and 1864), he continued to promote these causes. David Heath, who became a solicitor, followed a similar path in local politics, and George Kendall, who was connected with the Sutton Chartists, subsequently played an important role as trade union leader on the Hosiery Board of Arbitration.[138] The occasional meetings of 'Ultra Chartists' or 'Ultra Democrats'

NOTTINGHAM MARKET PLACE, NOTTINGHAM, 1837

continued in 1849, but social evenings with songs and recitations took the place of hymns and invective.[139] Not only had the articulate and constant adherents to the principles of Chartism shed the extremists and the fluctuating protest groups, but the orthodox Radical movement in Nottingham was absorbing some of the Chartist elements, and from 1849 onwards Chartism continued to be a notable influence in local politics. Local Chartism had drawn its major strength from the chronically depressed framework knitters of the town and the surrounding villages. In Nottingham the contrasting responses of an artisan class of lace operatives and semi-skilled framework knitters emphasized the complex nature of the 'working classes.' Separated by differences in earnings, regularity of employment, working conditions, mobility, and status, the lace operatives were a superior class to workmen in the hosiery trade, although auxiliary workers in the lace trade and even some lace makers had applied for public assistance during the most vulnerable years. Even so, these contrasts help to explain why the Chartist call to all working men to strike in 1839 and 1842 drew no response from men working inside Nottingham lace factories.

During the Chartist years there had existed complicated and changing relationships between Chartists and the various elements which made up the middle classes. Although the local movement was led by a barber and stationer, in the early forties there was antipathy between Chartist and 'middle class shopkeepers', and a general cleavage between the working classes, which included a high proportion of framework knitters, and the upper middle classes which included the majority of hosiery employers and local councillors. Hosiers refused to abolish frame rent, and the Corporation, as the body responsible for law and order, was necessarily at pains to prevent outbreaks of violence. Such attitudes often appear to have run counter to a large reserve of grudging but sincere middle class sympathy for a body of long suffering humanity with real and material grievances. In the Nottingham area Chartists *en masse* tended to be equated with framework knitters, and their predicament warranted sympathy; but as an organized movement with overtones of social idealism and associations with physical force. Chartism inevitably courted middle class suspicion, if not hostility, despite the repudiation of physical force by the majority of local Chartist leaders. Nevertheless, although they might reject the appellation 'Chartist', a considerable number of middle class Radicals supported the Chartists' political programme. In 1842 Lord Rancliffe had declared himself in favour of annual parliaments, universal suffrage, vote by ballot, no property qualifications for members and the payment of members.[140] William Cripps and

M

Samuel Bean, both leading local businessmen, had nominated Sturge as parliamentary candidate in 1842, and among those who voted for him were Aldermen Vickers, Frearson, Cullen, Wells, Paget, Gill, Felkin, and Sutton.[141] There is no evidence that these Radicals were ever referred to as Chartists, and the only local figure who might possibly be considered of even slightly comparable social standing who readily identified himself as a Chartist was David Heath, the young clerk working in a solicitor's office, who appeared late on the Chartist scene.

After the upheavals of 1848, the local Radicals resolved to sever their connections with the moderates of the Whig party. At the same time the repeal of the Corn Laws and the return of brisk trade after many years of depression in the hosiery industry combined to create a more favourable climate, one which enabled the working classes to view the future with a measure of optimism. The Nottingham lace and hosiery trades participated in the general upturn in economic activity. Furthermore, local developments (in particular the increased availability of desirable land in Nottingham as a result of belated enclosure) stimulated investment in construction of all types. Employment opportunities for unskilled labour improved, and retailers began to benefit from local expenditures. Weary of failures and the constant friction between physical and moral force advocates, the Chartist leaders turned their faces towards conventional political pressure, while others looked once more with enthusiasm and determination to the resurrection of trade societies.

The Chartist demonstrations were not repeated during the cyclical fluctuations that occurred during the two decades after 1848. Economic expansion in the fifties witnessed the appearance of the Lace Makers' Society, while in the hosiery industry some came to regard arbitration as a new solution to working men's problems. The prosperity of the early fifties was real (though there was unemployment among lace makers in 1853–4), but so was the depression of local industry after the nationwide commercial crisis of 1857. As in 1847, Nottingham banks stood firm, but there were numerous business failures, and the depression was accompanied by a large amount of unemployment and short time working in both lace and hosiery trades. The Lace Makers' Society opened a special subscription for its unemployed members, urging the rest to spread work.[142] In November eight thousand unemployed gathered to demonstrate.[143] The Board of Guardians submitted a request to the Poor Law Board for the suspension of the prohibitory order regarding out-relief, but without success. The guardians proceeded to distribute out-relief nevertheless, but only to families in which there were more than two children.[144] As the number of applicants to the workhouse increased some were set to work as labourers on the Forest. Financed from chapel donations, a group of local preachers formed a relief committee and opened kitchens at which free soup was available to warm the hungry bodies of the destitute during the winter of 1857–58.[145]

Despite an improvement in trade in the spring, and a rapidly growing home demand for bonnet fronts of lace, political developments in America adversely affected trade, and as a result the winter of 1860–61 again saw hundreds of lace and hosiery workers unemployed, as did the winter of 1862–63.[146] Owing to the dislocation of the major export market for Nottingham staples, which was also the source of supply of her raw material, and to speculation in the price of cotton which caused extreme fluctuations, the resulting uncertainty checked industrial expansion.[147] Crowds of the unemployed bearing placards with the inscription: 'Willing to Work, But not to Starve' paraded the streets, and people flocked to the two soup kitchens, one set up by the preachers, the other by Major William Parsons' Relief Committee which included three leading lace manufacturers, Birkin, Heymann, and Berenhart.[148] Half the framework knitters at Arnold were reported to be out of work, and public meetings were held there at which the speakers railed against those employers and bagmen who were charging full frame rent.[149] In the same year, the war between Prussia and Denmark disrupted trade with the North German ports, and the winter of 1863–64 affected employment in the lace and hosiery industries. The soup kitchens were re-opened and bread was sold without profit.[150] Framework knitters in Nottingham formed an Emigration Association, and in March 150 persons set sail for New Zealand. Of those left behind, two thousand applied to the workhouse during the closing months of 1864.[151] The next year saw an improvement in the employment situation, but another commercial crisis in 1866 caused a brief setback. Thereafter, however, the great cyclical upswing culminating in the unprecedented boom of 1869–72 generated a high level of employment and brought growing prosperity to the town.

Unlike the lean years of the previous two decades, the winters of hardship between 1857 and 1865 were unaccompanied by even a suspicion of public disorder. Richard Birkin stated that he was impressed by the manner in which acute deprivation was borne 'without manifesting angry feeling which formerly accompanied distress'.[152] During these years there was but little mention of the Charter in the town; but even if most Chartists in Nottingham were now referred to as 'the more advanced Radicals',[153] the Chartist core continued to be a recognizable Radical pressure group despite a superficial anonymity. Indeed, in 1872 James Sweet still called himself a

Chartist, as did George Harrison and David Heath during the municipal elections of 1867.[154] In February, 1854 George Harrison was elected delegate to the proposed Labour Parliament, which was to consist of elected representatives from various trades who would proceed to 'legislate represent and protect the rights of labour.'[155] But by the middle of 1855 the Parliament had disintegrated. At meetings held in 1855 issues in national politics came under discussion, and in 1857 Ernest Jones was nominated as Chartist candidate for a Nottingham seat.[156] In the spring of 1858, a well-attended meeting passed a resolution which called for manhood suffrage, vote by ballot, no property qualifications for members, greater equalization of constituencies, and a reduction in the duration of Parliament to three years. In December, 1858 Sweet, Mott, Heath, Councillor E. P. Cox and James Saunders took the platform, with Councillor E. Hart in the chair. Cox delivered an address advocating Chartist principles, and at a similar meeting which took place in March 1859 Henry Mott referred to the People's Charter, 'which must yet be the fabric on which the constitution of the country must be raised.'[157] In the same year, after its cost of £100 had been subscribed by Nottingham Chartists,[158] a statue of O'Connor was unveiled in the Arboretum. Two years later a Tory-Chartist alliance managed by Sweet, Heath, and Mott succeeded in securing the return of Sir Robert Clifton, who defeated the Conservative Whig candidate Lord Lincoln.[159] This action by the Chartists was instrumental in precipitating the split between the Radicals and Conservatives of the Whig party, which, after the foundation of a reformed Liberal Registration Association,[160] went so far as to produce an Independent Society in 1865.[161] 'The more advanced Radicals', or erstwhile Chartists, agreed to work for reform from within the Liberal organization, and together with the orthodox Radicals they succeeded in obtaining one Radical nomination alongside one Whig candidate in subsequent elections. The election of 1861, therefore, except for the success of David Heath as town councillor representing St. Ann's Ward in 1863, marks the end of separate and direct Chartist involvement in local politics.

In general, Chartism was strongest in two kinds of places; in old centres of decaying or contracting industry like Trowbridge, and in new or expanding single industry towns like Stockport.[162] The character of Chartism was also distinctive in those established regional centres possessing traditions of Radical politics, where there was little factory production, and where the social structure was flexible. In such cities as Birmingham and Manchester the Radical tradition tended to favour attempts at political accommodation between Chartist and reformers; furthermore, in Birmingham vertical social mobility, resulting from the character of industrial organization in local trades, reduced the amount of friction often associated with large-scale factory production.

Nottingham was the long-established centre of a stagnant industry; it was also the centre of a new and expanding industry. But the former rather than the latter produced the support for Chartism. Because of the nature of the machine lace industry much of its labour force was highly skilled. Moreover, in the largest branch of lace production the small unit continued to be the most efficient. The existence of social mobility (as in Birmingham), and the superior condition of a group of skilled operatives (as in Newcastle), tended to draw lace workers out of the Chartist orbit. The Radical and nonconformist tradition may help to explain the gradual convergence of Chartists and Radicals and indeed, as in Leicester, the ideal of an alliance between the middle class Radicals and the working classes never lacked an advocate throughout the whole period. Before such an alliance was achieved, differences in nomenclature tended to conceal common aims. In effect it was only after the relegation of Chartism to the wings of the political stage that significant success was achieved. By that time, however, by a process analogous to osmosis, local Radicalism had absorbed much of the Chartist programme in much the same way as had happened in Leicester, Glasgow, and Leeds. Henceforth, orthodox reforming bodies resumed the limelight of the political stage, while the trade unions began to expand their activities in a more limited sphere.

References

1 *N.R.*, September 7, 1838.
2 *Address of the Nottingham W.M.A. to the People of England on the New Poor Law*, (Nottingham, 1838), p. 16; *N.R.*, July 28, 1843.
3 *N.R.*, November 9, 1838.
4 *N.R.*, September 7, 1838.
5 *N.R.*, March 29, 1839.
6 *N.R.*, December 7, 1838; *N.R.*, September 25, 1839; William Felkin, *History*, p. 453.
7 R. Oastler, *Letter to . . . the County of Nottingham*, (Nottingham, 1839).
8 *N.R.*, March 29, 1839.
9 *N.R.*, April 12, 1839; *N.R.*, June 7, 1839.
10 F. C. Mather, *Public Order in the Age of the Chartists*, (Manchester, 1959), p. 154.
11 *Ibid.*, p. 55.
12 Inspector Martin to H.O. February 27, 1839, *H.O. 40/47*; Inspector Martin to General Ferguson at Leicester, March 6, 1839, *H.O. 40/47*.
13 e.g. Letter of Duke of Portland to H.O., February 27, 1839, *H.O. 40/47*.
14 *N.R.*, June 7, 1839. Napier commented on the Chartist gatherings which resembled religious meetings, W. Napier, *Life and Opinions of General Sir Charles Napier*, (1857) II, 10, 49.
15 Handbill, *H.O. 40/47*.
16 County Magistrates to H.O., May 21, 1839, *H.O. 40/47*.
17 *N.R.*, May 24, 1839; W. Napier, *op. cit.*, p. 10.
18 Handbill, *H.O. 40/47*.
19 W. Napier, *op. cit.*, p. 52.
20 R. G. Gammage, *The History of the Chartist Movement* (Newcastle-on-Tyne, 1894), pp. 147–48.
21 An account is given in A. C. Wood, 'Nottingham 1835–1865,' *Transactions of the Thoroton Society*, LIX (1955), 53.
22 W. Napier, *op. cit.*, p. 61.
23 J. Barratt, W. Burden, *Address . . . to the People of England*, (n.d.), pp. 3–16.
24 W. Napier, *op. cit.*, 69.
25 John Wells to H.O., August 4, 1839, *H.O. 40/47*.
26 Knight to Rolleston, August 8, 1839, *H.O. 40/47*.
27 W. Napier, *op. cit.*, 71.
28 J. F. Sutton, *Date Book*, p. 456; *N.R.*, August 16, 1839.
29 W. Napier, *op. cit.*, p. 71.
30 Inspector Martin to H.O., February 27, 1839, *H.O. 40/47*.
31 Magistrates to H.O., March 8, 1839, *H.O. 40/47*; Duke of Newcastle to H.O., April 13, 1839, *H.O. 40/47*.
32 F. C. Mather, 'The Government and the Chartists,' *Chartist Studies*, ed. Asa Briggs, (1959), p. 377, f.n. 4.
33 Magistrates to H.O., May 14, 1839, *H.O. 40/47;* Portland to H.O., May 15, 1839, *H.O. 40/47*.
34 Magistrates to H.O., June 6, 1839, *H.O. 40/47*.
35 Unwin to H.O., July 13, 1839, *H.O. 40/47*.
36 Unwin to H.O., July 16, 1839, *H.O. 40/47*; Unwin to H.O., July 17, 1839, *H.O. 40/47*.
37 Portland to H.O., July 17, 1839, *H.O. 40/47*; Martin to H.O. March 6, 1839, *H.O. 40/47*.
38 W. Napier, *op. cit.*, p. 70.

[39] Parsons and Benn to H.O., August 13, 1839, *H.O. 40/47*.

[40] Memo. of Duke of Portland and three county magistrates, November 7, 1840, *H.O. 40/55*.

[41] Parsons and Benn to H.O., December 17, 1839, *H.O. 40/47*.

[42] *N.R.*, August 30, 1839.

[43] *Nottingham and Newark Mercury*, November 15, 1839; *N.R.*, February 5, 1842; *N.R.*, September 9, 1842.

[44] R. F. Wearmouth, *Some Working Class Movements of the Nineteenth Century*, (London 1948), p. 130.

[45] *Ibid.*, p. 177.

[46] I am indebted to Mr. S. D. Chapman for this information concerning the history of Salem Chapel, Riste Place.

[47] *N.R.*, January 12, 1840; *N.R.*, February 28, 1840.

[48] Quoted in A. C. Wood, 'Nottingham 1835–1865', *Transactions of the Thoroton Society*, LIX (1955), 57; W. Napier, *op. cit.*, p. 93.

[49] *Ibid.*, p. 107.

[50] Mayor Roworth to H.O., January 14, 1840, *H.O. 40/55*.

[51] F. C. Mather, *Public Order in the Age of the Chartists*, (Manchester, 1959), pp. 23–24; W. Napier, *op. cit.*, pp. 92–93.

[52] J. F. Sutton, *Date Book*, p. 468; *N.R.*, January 17, 1840; W. Napier, *op. cit.*, p. 109.

[53] *N.R.*, December 12, 1839.

[54] *Supra*. p. 130.

[55] W. Napier, *op. cit.*, p. 33.

[56] General Sir Charles Napier to H.O., January 1, 1839, *H.O. 40/58*.

[57] W. Napier, *op. cit.*, pp. 69, 72.

[58] *Ibid.*, pp. 54–55.

[59] *N.R.*, September 28, 1838.

[60] *N.R.*, January 10, 1810.

[61] See Lucy Brown 'Chartists and the Anti-Corn Law League', *Chartist Studies*, ed. Asa Briggs (London, 1959), p. 361.

[62] *N.R.*, March 5, 1841.

[63] *N.R.*, January 26, 1844.

[64] *N.R.*, July 10, 1841; *N.R.*, February 19, 1830.

[65] *N.R.*, January 7, 1842.

[66] *An Address to the Working Classes of England on the System of Exclusive Dealing and the Formation of Joint Stock Companies by a Member of Nottingham Cooperative Store*, (Nottingham, 1840).

[67] *N.R.*, July 3, 1840.

[68] C. Holmes, 'Chartism in Nottingham' (unpublished B.A. dissertation University of Nottingham, 1960), p. 43.

[69] An argument presented by C. Holmes, *op. cit.*

[70] *N.R.*, February 4, 1842.

[71] *N.R.*, February 25, 1842.

[72] *Ibid.*

[73] John Prest, *The Industrial Revolution in Coventry*, (1960), pp. 28–29.

[74] For a vivid contemporary description of the events in October see J. F. Sutton, *The Nottingham Date Book 1750–1850*, (Nottingham, 1852), pp. 424–429. For the background to the Duke of Newcastle's unpopularity see J. M. Golby, 'The Political and Electioneering influence of the Fourth Duke of Newcastle', (unpublished M.A. dissertation, Nottingham, 1961) pp. 218–223 and Appendix B. For subsequent electoral history see A. C. Wood, 'Nottingham 1835–1865', *Transactions of the Thoroton Society*, LIX (1955).

[75] J. D. Chambers, *Modern Nottingham in the Making*, (Nottingham, 1945), p. 28.

[76] H. Field, *The Nottingham Date Book 1800–1884*, (Nottingham, 1884), p. 456.

[77] C. Holmes, *op. cit.*, pp. 83–84.

[78] *N.R.*, August 19, 1842.

[79] *N.R.*, August 26, 1842; J. F. Sutton, *Date Book*, p. 487.

[80] *N.R.*, October 21, 1842.

[81] *N.R.*, September 21, 1842.

[82] *N.R.*, August 9, 1842; *N.R.*, August 26, 1842.

[83] D. Read, 'Chartism in Manchester', *Chartist Studies*, ed. Asa Briggs (1959), p. 51.

[84] *N.R.*, September 23, 1842; *N.R.*, December 23, 1843.

[85] *N.R.*, July 19, 1844.

[86] C. Holmes, *op. cit.*, pp. 84–85.

[87] *N.R.*, August 13, 1847.

[88] C. Holmes, *op. cit.*, pp. 85–87.

[89] *Ibid.*, p. 89.

[90] I. C. Wright, *Evidence as to Distress in Nottingham and the Neighbourhood*, (Nottingham, 1848), p. 12.

[91] *N.R.*, April 14, 1848.

[92] J. D. Chambers, *Modern Nottingham in the Making*, (Nottingham, 1945), p. 38.

[93] *Report of the Select Committee of the House of Lords on the Bank Charter Act*, (1848), ev. of I. Wright, p. 329.

[94] *N.R.*, May 21, 1847; *N.R.*, June 25, 1847.

[95] *N.R.*, May 21, 1847.

[96] *N.R.*, May 14, 1847; *N.R.*, June 4, 1847.

[97] *N.R.*, May 14, 1847.

[98] *N.R.*, April 7, 1848.

[99] I. C. Wright, *Evidence as to Distress in Nottingham and the Neighbourhood*, (Nottingham, 1848).

[100] *N.R.*, April 21, 1848.

[101] *N.R.*, April 7, 1848; *N.R.*, April 14, 1848.

[102] F. C. Mather, *Public Order in the Age of the Chartists*, (Manchester, 1959), p. 134.

[103] J. F. Sutton, *Date Book*, pp. 509–510.

[104] *N.R.*, April 14, 1848.

[105] Martin to H.O., April 9, 1839, *H.O. 40/47*.

[106] W. Napier, *op. cit.*, p. 69.

[107] *Ibid.*, p. 63.

[108] *Ibid.*, pp. 88–89.

[109] *Ibid.*, p. 107.

[110] *Ibid.*, p. 57.

[111] *Ibid.*, p. 71.

[112] *Ibid.*, pp. 71–72.

[113] *Ibid.*, p. 109.

[114] R. F. Wearmouth, *Some Working Class Movements of the Nineteenth Century*, (1948), pp. 116–117.

[115] *Ibid.*, pp. 112–113.

[116] Napier to H.O. January 1, 1839, *H.O. 40/58*.

[117] W. Napier, *op. cit.*, p. 123.

[118] *Ibid.*

[119] *N.R.,* April 14, 1848.

[120] *N.R.,* April 21, 1848.

[121] *N.R.,* June 23, 1848.

[122] *N.R.,* June 23, 1848.

[123] *N.R.,* June 2, 1849; *N.R.,* June 9, 1848.

[124] *N.R.,* June 16, 1848.

[125] *N.R.,* September 6, 1850.

[126] *N.R.,* August 14, 1840; *N.R.,* August 21, 1840.

[127] *N.R.,* January 21, 1842; *N.R.,* February 4, 1842; *N.R.,* February 18, 1842; J. H. Clapham, *An Economic History of Modern Britain* (Cambridge, 1930), I, 489.

[128] *N.R.,* September 9, 1842; *N.R.,* February 24, 1843; *N.R.,* June 23, 1843.

[129] W. Felkin, *History,* pp. 468–69.

[130] *N.R.,* August 29, 1845; *N.R.,* February 5, 1847.

[131] W. Felkin, *History,* p. 378.

[132] *N.R.,* February 2, 1849.

[133] *N.J.,* January 26, 1849.

[134] *N.J.,* January 16, 1849.

[135] *N.R.,* May 4, 1849; *N.R.,* May 25, 1849.

[136] A. R. Schoyen, *The Chartist Challenge, A Portrait of Julian Harney,* (1958), p. 162.

[137] *N.R.,* January 19, 1849.

[138] *N.R.,* July 29, 1842.

[139] *N.R.,* January 12, 1849; *N.R.,* February 2, 1849; *N.R.,* November 9, 1849.

[140] See A. C. Wood, 'George Lord Rancliffe 1785–1850', *Transactions of the Thoroton Society,* LVII (1953), pp. 48–65.

[141] *N.R.,* February 18, 1842; *N.R.,* August 5, 1842.

[142] *N.R.,* November 27, 1857.

[143] *N.R.,* November 6, 1857.

[144] *N.R.,* November 20, 1857; *N.R.,* November 27, 1857.

[145] *N.R.,* January 8, 1858.

[146] W. Felkin, *History,* p. 397.

[147] W. O. Henderson, *The Lancashire Cotton Famine, 1861–65,* (Liverpool, 1933), pp. 20–25.

[148] *N.R.,* April 24, 1863; *N.R.,* May 29, 1863.

[149] *N.R.,* May 8, 1863.

[150] *N.R.,* March 18, 1864; *N.R.,* January 22, 1864.

[151] *N.R.,* March 4, 1864; *N.R.,* December 16, 1864.

[152] *N.R.,* November 7, 1862.

[153] *N.R.,* March 18, 1859; *N.R.,* December 10, 1858.

[154] C. Holmes, *op. cit.,* p. 124.

[155] *N.R.,* February 10, 1854; Minutes of Lace Trades Society 1851–53, March 4, 1854.

[156] C. Holmes, *op. cit.,* p. 117; *Infra.* p. 218.

[157] *Ibid.,* p. 118.

[158] *N.R.,* August 26, 1859.

[159] *Infra,* p. 219.

[160] *Infra,* p. 219.

[161] See A. C. Wood, 'Nottingham 1835–1865', *Transactions of the Thoroton Society,* LIX (1955), pp. 58–60.

[162] The frame of reference for this section is *Chartist Studies,* ed. Asa Briggs, (1959), Chapter I.

CHAPTER VII

PROBLEMS OF URBAN EXPANSION: ENCLOSURE, THE RAILWAY, AND MUNICIPAL REFORM

CHARTISM ebbed as economic conditions improved; indeed in terms of the increase in employment opportunities that accompanied expanding trade the working classes had some cause to rejoice. Nevertheless, with each spurt of industrial growth and the related rise in urban population, the downward pressure upon living standards intensified as overcrowding increased and public health deteriorated. Manifestations of this process became evident in the rising death rates of Manchester, Liverpool, and Glasgow between 1820 and 1840.[1] In terms of its size and rate of population growth, its economic structure and scale of industrial expansion, Nottingham could not be classed as one of Britain's major industrial cities, yet in 1844 it was found to be comparable, in some respects, with the great northern industrial centres:

> 'Some parts of Nottingham are so very bad', wrote J. R. Martin, 'as hardly can be surpassed in misery by anything to be found within the entire range of manufacturing cities.'[2]

Such a situation was not merely the result, as it was elsewhere, of a phenomenally rapid rate of population growth. Between 1821 and 1831 the spectacular boom in the lace industry had been accompanied by an influx of people from the neighbouring counties, but the rate of expansion of the urban population was only slightly above that of the national average. Even then, barely 50,000 people lived in Nottingham, and 53,091, ten years later.[3] The situation in Nottingham was nearly parallel with that which existed in Coventry, a town slightly larger than half Nottingham's size in 1831, and where, although the rate of population growth was considerably less than that in Nottingham, large numbers of artisans dwelt in crowded courts and slums.[4] At Leicester, which was comparable in size with Coventry and with Nottingham in its economic structure, the inferior housing was appreciably superior to that in Nottingham;[5] for unlike Coventry and Nottingham the growth of Leicester had not been retarded through lack of building land. Both in Coventry and Nottingham the power of freemen among the electorate who opposed enclosure had serious indirect effects upon urban development. This explains why Nottingham, a medium-sized

162

industrial town which in 1842 a local surgeon could describe as basically 'a healthy town,'[6] contained within its boundaries some of Britain's worst slums. These 'rookeries' were one aspect of urban development which had provoked public criticism from such prominent local figures as Thomas Hawksley the Nottingham Waterworks engineer, and Absolem Barnett, eleven years before. Equal concern was expressed over the continued dependence of the town upon only two industries, a situation which, they argued, had its origin in common with the housing problem. That common origin was the postponement of enclosure.[7]

The town was almost surrounded on three sides by open land. The Castle grounds and the Park were the Duke of Newcastle's property, the Colwick lands were owned by Mr. Musters, while Wollaton belonged to Lord Middleton, and though smaller landowners had sold plots, making possible the development of suburbs a short distance from the old town, so long as the large landholdings were withheld from the market, the existence of common land hindered the easing of land shortage.[8] The Corporation owned one-third of the open fields, which comprised six hundred and fifty-four acres of land surrounding the town, but in deference to the views of the burgesses or freemen of the borough the Corporation had long withheld its assent to the land's enclosure. For three months each year these Sand and Clay Fields were commonable to the local burgesses at the rate of three head of cattle or forty-five sheep per burgess, while the Meadows, which were divided in two, East Croft and West Croft, were likewise commonable for one month annually on payment of 2s. 6d. per cow and 3s. per horse. The exercise of these rights had declined over the years and in 1832, for example, only about two hundred burgesses were reported to have grazed animals on the commons.[9] In his capacity as lord of the manor, the Corporation owned both the Forest and Mapperley Common, and these one hundred and eighty-one acres were open throughout the year. The Coppice consisted of a farm of about one hundred and twenty acres which were let annually for a rental, and the piece of land known as Hunger Hills which was divided into burgess parts and used as gardens. Altogether, therefore, the Corporation commanded jurisdiction over fourteen hundred acres of unenclosed land.

Since 1787 there had been intermittent agitation for enclosure from individuals from various walks of life but the power of the burgesses within the closed Whig Corporation, reinforced by the support of vested interests of slum property-owners on the Council, had proved strong enough to withstand this pressure. The burgesses, who numbered more than three thousand, comprised the eldest sons of freemen and men who had served seven years in apprenticeship

to a freeman, and in their stubborn defence of common rights—
contrary to their own best interests—at times they had destroyed
gates or fences erected on the open fields.[10] Failure to resolve the
enclosure question had hindered the physical expansion of the town
during a period of population growth which, by 1800, had already
produced a growing demand for land. Restriction on its supply led
to the erection of the meanest dwellings for the working classes
many of which were back-to-back houses built around courts.
Economical of labour, materials, and especially space, private
speculators and working mens' building societies were responsible
for the erection of dwellings which the labouring classes could
afford—the slums, in fact, which so appalled the Commissioners
who visited the town in the course of their investigations in 1844.[11]

Many of these houses were built in the decade which saw the
memorable boom in the lace trade. Three thousand dwellings were
erected between 1821 and 1831 compared with one thousand from
1811 to 1821,[12] but the steep rise in land values, a doubling in the
price of bricks, and increased labour costs made house purchase
more expensive. The rapid influx of labour attracted by the boom
led to some ingenious measures to profit from the housing shortage,
and one contemporary related the opportunism of an enterprising
butcher who ousted his prize pig from a caravan in which it was
exhibited, stationed the vehicle in his garden, and let it as a dwelling for a weekly rent of 2s. 3d.[13] Stables, garrets, and cellars were
likewise converted for habitation or for use as workshops; by 1839
Felkin estimated that Nottingham possessed up to two hundred
cellar-like, low kitchen dwellings, and about six hundred and fifty
lean-to shacks which had been thrown hastily together.[14] Between
1821 and 1831 the population of Nottingham increased by slightly
more than ten thousand, bringing the total to 50,680. It is, however,
significant that the four largest industrial villages located less than
three miles from the town also experienced a population increase
which added up to almost twelve thousand; this rise amounted to a
doubling of the aggregate village populations. Between 1831 and
1841 the town population grew by less than twenty-five hundred,
while the village populations rose by nearly eight thousand, a
rate of increase of about 36 per cent. compared with that of barely
6 per cent. in the town.[15] While 929 houses were built in Nottingham
between 1831 and 1851, at New Radford, which had a population
one-fifth as large, 1,654 were erected.[16] These two decades saw the
transformation of the villages beyond the open fields adjacent to
Nottingham, as industry and population moved into New Sneinton,
New Radford, New Lenton, New Basford, Carrington and Hyson
Green. In terms of the numbers of people which the town could

absorb, by the fourth decade of the nineteenth century, given its physical constraints, Nottingham had reached the point of saturation. (See Table IX and Figure III.)

In the 'new' industrial villages there was room for the erection of more spacious dwellings and few houses were built back to back. Furthermore the artisans who moved to the villages were lace makers and mechanics who could afford to live in dwellings superior to those available at comparable rents in Nottingham, while many of the lace makers who remained in the town in the twenties and early thirties moved into the upper rooms of substantial buildings situated in the streets which led to the Market Place, those which, hitherto, had accommodated skilled silk framework knitters whose trade had since diminished. In the villages lace makers moved into houses of three storeys which had a minimum of two rooms on each floor; these consisted of a kitchen and wash-house on the ground floor and two bedrooms on the first. The second floor usually possessed large windows at either end, thereby rendering the entire floor suitable for use as a workshop. These were the buildings which housed artisans in the 'handsome villages', to which one contemporary referred in 1832, and while they represented an improvement in housing standards in Nottingham's suburban villages, at the same time fragmentary evidence relating to the movement of rent suggests that they were also instrumental in relieving the pressure on accommodation within the town.[17]

As Hawksley and Barnett reiterated, grave social costs were incurred by retaining the open fields, but as no one was directly accountable for housing conditions and the state of public health it was only on the occasions of dramatic developments, such as an outbreak of cholera, that the voices urging reform were joined by a popular chorus. The cholera epidemic of 1832 reduced the slum dwellers of England more effectively than any reforms for many years. In Nottingham the chief nests of disease were discovered in the lower areas of the town which were badly drained, in Meadow Plats, Narrow Marsh, the Three Salmon Yards, and other places in the neighbourhood of Charlotte Street.[18] Situated near the rivers Leen and Beck, the soil in this part of the town was wet and boggy, many of the houses were built below the level of the drains and most of them were back to back. In many parts of this low-lying district where the vast majority of the town's casual poor, 'the poor tramping people', lived, there was not more than one privy to thirty or forty houses.[19] Describing this district to one of the Factory Commissioners, the assistant surveyor to the three Nottingham Highway Boards remarked: 'It is the constant custom in many of these streets for the inhabitants to empty chamber-vessels into the grates over the

Table IX: *Population Growth in Nottingham and Neighbouring Civil Parishes 1801–1871.*

Civil Parishes	1801	1811	1821	1831
Nottinghamshire	140,350	162,964	186,873	225,327
Bor. of Nottingham	28,801	34,253	42,415	50,680
Basford	2,124	2,940	3,599	6,325
Lenton	893	1,197	1,240	3,077
Radford	2,269	3,447	4,806	9,806
Sneinton	558	953	1,212	3,605

Sources: Enumeration Abstracts 1801–1841. Census of England and Wales, 1851 and 1871.

Civil Parishes	1841	1851	1861	1871
Nottinghamshire	249,910	270,427	293,867	319,758
Bor. of Nottingham	53,091	58,419	77,765	86,621
Basford	8,688	10,091	12,185	13,038
Lenton	4,467	5,589	5,828	6,315
Radford	10,817	12,637	13,495	15,127
Sneinton	7,079	8,440	11,048	12,237

Sources: Enumeration Abstracts 1801–1841. Census of England and Wales, 1851 and 1871.

sewers'; it was not uncommon for his men to remove up to three cartloads of filth from only one blocked drain, and the single factor which prevented permanent blockage of drains in that part of the town was the water which drained from the higher parts of the town after heavy showers. Those houses situated either over or by the side of privies were especially obnoxious, while along the streets dung heaps and reeking cesspools were interspersed among dwellings where typhoid and dysentry were endemic. The worst dwellings in Nottingham were the low kitchens, 'kind of cellars under ground', which, according to Barnett and Taylor, Registrar and surgeon of the Nottingham Union, housed the 'poorest of the poor'. Taylor described them as 'damp, dark, dismal, and not fit for human beings to dwell in.' They were little more than 'disease engendering holes.'[20] It is small wonder that in 1832 nearly three hundred people died of cholera, while the critical nature of the town's problem of land shortage was illustrated in the necessity for intra-mural burials.[21]

During the epidemic of 1831–2 under the energetic chairmanship of Thomas Wakefield, Radical and Unitarian, an emergency Board of Health was formed, Samuel Fox, the Quaker, a Roman Catholic Priest, the Rev. Willson, and the Unitarian Town Clerk, William Enfield, exposed themselves to the risk of infection by working amidst the disease, visiting slum tenements. The intra-mural burials during the cholera outbreak awakened fears of the effects of the noxious vapours upon people whose dwellings skirted the cemeteries, and the Board accepted Samuel Fox's offer of land to be used as a graveyard.[22] But the epidemic in Nottingham was shortlived, and when the immediate danger had disappeared the Council declined to pursue the problem of public health further. Under the circumstances the Council considered increased facilities for interments perfectly adequate—an ironic commentary, it has been noted, on the outlook of the unreformed Corporation.[23]

The major reason for the inertia of the unreformed Corporation in the face of mounting social problems lies in the fact that to a large extent councillors were victims of their own environment, for imprisoned as they were by the ideas and practices of earlier generations, the positive conception of civic responsibility was as yet unborn.[24] Moreover, even if the Corporation had possessed the will to tackle the problems of housing, sanitation, and drainage, without adequate powers and financial resources the means were also lacking. None the less, the results of an official enquiry into Municipal Corporations, published in 1833, indicated that even the limited functions that the Corporation was expected to perform were not carried out efficiently. While one might have expected that the relatively wide local franchise would have resulted in the election of a governing body more representative of the local populace than in other towns, or an assembly which, at least, would be open to the pressure of public opinion, in fact before 1835 the local governing body remained largely impervious to pressures originating outside.

Under the terms of the Charter of 1449, aldermen and councillors were elected by the burgesses. The eighteen senior councillors and the six junior councillors who together formed the Common Council were elected by the burgesses at large, but since candidates for the Senior Council could only be selected from the Livery, only the small and impotent junior body was freely elected. Hence, the Corporation virtually elected itself and, freed of much responsibility to an electorate, could behave much as it wished.[25] The result was the dominance of a clique with common ties of affiliation in politics and religion which, since the middle of the eighteenth century, had ruled the town. The councillors who belonged to this caucus were middle class Whig dissenters, most of whom, until the early nineteenth century, were traders, although the hosiers were also gaining a foothold by the beginning of the century. In 1833 it was alleged that three-quarters of the whole corporate body were drawn from three chapels, and certain families therefrom were consistently represented. Indeed, fifteen times between 1800 and 1834 the

Mayoralty was filled by one of six Evangelicals.[26] The Wakefields, Hollins, Harts, Fellows, Denisons, Lowes, and Codhams were all prominent councillors and members of High Pavement Unitarian Chapel. From the Particular Baptist Chapel in George Street, Vickers, Oldknow, Barber, and Rogers were familiar names on the Council, and at Castle Gate Independent Chapel, the third temple of dissent with the wealthiest and most influential congregation in the town, the Cullens, Knights, Allens, Prestons, Morleys, and Swanns were firmly entrenched in the Corporation.[27] Moreover, to strengthen the Whig supremacy in Parliament, the Corporation was in the habit of intervening in elections, using all its considerable power as landlord, employer, and bestower of patronage to support Whig candidates and influence voters in the same way as was its custom at municipal elections.[28] It was also alleged that the mayor and magistrates called in the constabulary only when the 'Nottingham Lambs'—the rougher element of the citizenry—were rowdy in support of the Tories. In 1820 the Corporation created several hundred new burgesses whose voting power could maintain the favourable balance of power in the face of a future Tory challenge.[29]

The spheres of activity to which the Corporation confined its extra-electoral energies were the management of property—the Bridge, Chamber, Free School, and Lambley Estates, Markets and Stalls—the regulation of privileges, and administration of charitable trusts—The Thomas White Loan Fund, Lady Grantham's Charity, the Lambley Charity, and Bilby's Hospital.[30] Accounts of the Corporation displayed before the Commissioners in 1833 revealed that no less than 35 per cent. of gross annual income was spent on management—or rather mismanagement; the distribution of one charitable trust whose annual value was £13 10s. was set down at £10.[31] Added to the accusation of maladministration of finances was the charge of extravagance, for considerable amounts of money were spent on feasting and entertainment, doubtless to relieve the boredom of inactivity. As head of the Corporation, the mayor was allowed a stipend of £315 during his year of office to 'keep table and make friends.'[32] For a long time the Corporation showed a reluctance to initiate reforms and take steps towards improving the town's thoroughfares. The only projects financed by the unreformed Corporation between 1815 and 1835 were the sewering, levelling, and flagging of the Market Place in 1826, and the widening of Chapel Bar, begun in the same year, the Council contributing £500 to the public subscription.[33] As the body responsible for maintaining law and order, in 1834 the Corporation was accused by a local printer of neglect in the prevention of crime, and it was urged to increase expenditure on the organization of its Watch.[34]

THE NEW WAREHOUSE OF HINE AND MUNDELLA, 1856

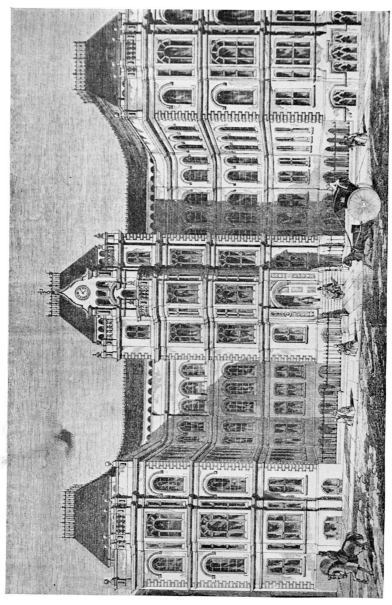

F. C. Tighe, Nottingham Public Library

THE NEW WAREHOUSE OF THOMAS ADAMS & Co.

With the slow thaw in the political structure of the Corporation after the Municipal Corporations Act in 1835, advocates of enclosure encountered greater success in gaining representation on the Council,[35] but the chief critics of the Corporation's inertia originated outside it. Thus, both Absolem Barnett in 1835 and William Felkin in 1836 condemned the burgesses for their opposition to enclosure. Felkin referred to the scarcity of land and pointed to its adverse effects upon Nottingham. High rents, he said, were causing manufacturers to seek sites in nearby villages, or settle in Leicester, Loughborough, and Derby.[36] In 1831 the Burton brothers, who owned a lace factory in Mount Street, had removed to a larger factory in Carrington. In 1838 another factory was erected at Sherwood, and although a measure of expansion took place in the lace industry in 1844 factories were erected only in Lenton and Radford.[37] In support of his argument Felkin claimed that between 1831 and 1836 the number of lace machines in Nottingham decreased by six hundred, while machinery in the surrounding district increased by the same amount.[38] The hosiery industry was also drifting away from the town. Whereas in 1812 approximately 30 per cent. of the total frames in the county were situated in Nottingham, by 1844 barely 20 per cent. were to be found in the three urban parishes.[39]

Shortly after the inauguration of the reformed Corporation in 1836, two committees were appointed to consider a limited measure of enclosure by private act of Parliament. The reports were strongly in favour of enclosure, with the proviso that freemen's rights should be protected and that there must be satisfactory town planning— an unexpectedly early indication of future policy. The Council gave its assent to enclosure late in 1837.[40] However, the General Enclosure Bill subsequently prepared by the landowners met with opposition both inside and outside the Corporation. While the landowners' committee claimed that partial enclosure would involve unnecessary expense and would be unjust to those who were excluded, the freemen accused them of trying to impede the progress of the limited Enclosure Bills for the West Croft and Lammas Fields. The Corporation resolved to petition against the General Bill, at the same time expressing its willingness to approve of a bill that would safeguard freemen's rights while providing 'ample spaces for public walks and recreation.'[41] This decision was followed by renewed opposition from anti-enclosure interests, particularly from the Freemen Rights Committee, a body formed specially to protect the privileges of the burgesses. As the petition from between five and six thousand persons opposing the bill showed, the freemen possessed sufficient electoral support to ensure that their interests were represented on the Corporation, and well represented also were

N

the interests of owners of slum property who were intent on pre-serving the acute competition for housing in Nottingham and hence the *status quo*.[42]

Meanwhile, the Board of Guardians made some attempt to ease overcrowding in the worst slums by denying relief to the inhabitants of certain localities unless they consented to be removed to another area. They met with little success. As soon as these tenants moved out, others moved in, so great was the demand for even the meanest hovels.[43] However, a fortuitous opportunity for enclosing land oc-curred in 1839 with the entry of the railway into Nottingham. This resulted in the enclosure of part of the Meadows where the Midland Station was to be built, and in July, 1839 royal assent was granted for the Westcroft and Burton Leys Act and the Nottingham Fields Act, which affected the Derby Road Lammas Fields and provided for the enclosure of fifty-two acres. This modest measure of en-closure had only a marginal effect upon local development, and not until the general enclosure act passed six years later was the town transformed. Meanwhile, a development took place which was to stimulate life in some towns and to diminish it in others; this was the coming of the railway.

In 1836 over one thousand miles were added to British railways, but Nottingham remained unconnected. Local enthusiasm for rail-way communication was slow to develop, for already the town was well provided with roads and waterways. In 1834 William Dearden's directory stated that

> few commercial towns possess greater facilities for transporting merchandise or have more direct communication with the in-land navigation of England than Nottingham.

Coal, building stone, grain, and raw materials were carried by waterways, while lace and hosiery were generally dispatched by road.[44] Nevertheless, when the Midland Counties Railway was first projected in 1833, William Felkin and William Hannay formed a local committee to support the scheme,[45] on the grounds that it would speed delivery and lower transport costs. The mainspring of financial support, however, was the association of Nottinghamshire and Derbyshire coal owners who were particularly enthusiastic about the proposed railway, viewing it as a means of destroying the mono-poly held by the canals, though equally important was the oppor-tunity of entering into competition with Leicestershire coalmasters in the Leicester Market. The Eastwood colliery owners, Messrs. Barber & Walker, had opened the subscription offering to buy shares to the value of £10,000, but although thirty-five sums of similar magnitude were promised by other coalmasters in the Erewash Valley, it was found necessary to obtain most of the capital from financiers in Lancashire.[46] A casualty of this financial deal was the coalmasters' line which was to connect the old Mansfield and Pinxton Railway at Pinxton with Leicester.

When the Bill came before the House of Commons in 1836, two petitions in favour of it were received; one came from the Nottingham Town Council, the other from 'bankers, merchants, manufacturers, traders and inhabitants of Nottingham.' Petitions opposing the measure were received from the Nottingham Canal Company, Cromford Canal Company, Nottingham Old Waterworks, and the proprietors of the Trent Navigation Company.[47] At the same time the North Midland Railway Company, which had been formed to construct a line from Derby to Leeds, viewed the Erewash Valley portion of the Midland Counties' proposed network with some suspicion as a threat of future competition to the north. In order to obtain the important through route to the south, the Manchester financiers decided to sacrifice the Erewash Extension, persuading the coal owners that this was only a temporary withdrawal of the project. The line, for which the directors received the necessary powers for construction in 1836, ran from Leicester to Rugby, forming a junction with the London and Birmingham system. The line was also to extend to the River Trent to form a junction with the proposed North Midland line from Derby to Leeds, while a branch line from Trent Junction was to bring Nottingham into the system.[43]

Served only by a branch line, and much less favourably situated than Derby where the North Midland and the Midland Counties lines (and subsequently the Birmingham and Derby lines) would join, the new project meant that Nottingham was an outpost on the railway network. (See Figure IV.) This gave rise to a considerable amount of local dissatisfaction. At a meeting of the Corporation one member received a sympathetic hearing when he reflected on the 'supineness and apathy,' which he claimed had been displayed on this matter:

'Nottingham from its geographical position might and ought to have been made a point through which the direct line of railway from south to north should pass.' The speaker continued: 'That benefit has been lost to the town in consequence of the neglect and indifference with which the subject has been treated. The neighbouring town of Derby has completely outstripped us in the race for railway advantages.'[49]

In fact, the great Northern Railway had originally planned a line from London to York via Northampton, Leicester, Nottingham, Sheffield, and Leeds, but had later revised this plan in favour of a much smaller and more practicable scheme for a link line from York to connect with the Derby and Leeds line, and the North

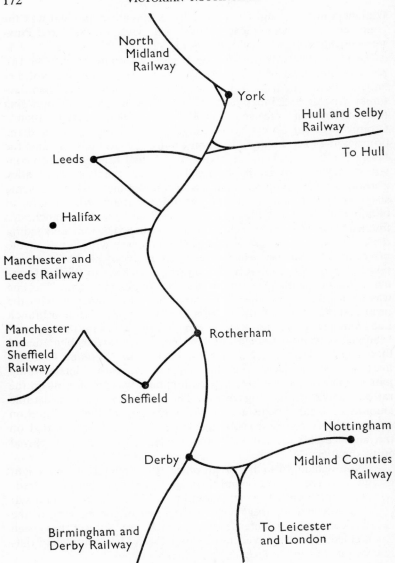

Figure II: Chiffin's Map of the North Midland, Birmingham
and Derby, and Midland Counties Railways, 1842.

Midland Railway, at Normanton. The opposition of the Nottingham Canal and Navigation Companies was no greater than could have been expected from rival forms of transport, and although little initiative or capital was forthcoming from Nottingham, the reasons for the town's comparative disadvantage can be attributed mainly to the differing opinions of the financiers who determined which lines would be most profitable.[50] Taking into consideration the location of Nottingham in relation to the known coal resources of the Nottinghamshire and Derbyshire field, and her location in relation to London and Birmingham and the adjacent industrial districts, the Midland Counties' preference for a line through Derby, despite the indignant comments that appeared in the Nottingham newspapers, is readily comprehensible. Like the motives for constructing some of the turnpikes and most canals by linking the pits with wider markets, the railways of the east midlands were designed largely to develop the traffic in coal.[51] This explains the position of Nottingham in the national transport system.

The first train left Nottingham for Derby on May 30th, 1839 taking forty-two minutes to complete the journey.[52] In the same month, the section of the line between Trent Junction and Leicester was opened, and in June the following year the opening of the line from Leicester to Rugby gave Nottingham businessmen a somewhat circuitous rail connection with London and Birmingham; not until 1880 did they obtain a main line route direct to London. The early forties saw fierce rate competition between the Midland Counties, the North Midland, and the Birmingham and Derby railway companies, and in 1843 William Hannay, a shareholder and director of the Midland Counties, seconded a motion to amalgamate with the Birmingham and Derby. The following year all three companies amalgamated to form the Midland Company with George Hudson (formerly Chairman of the North Midland) as Chairman of the Board of Directors.[53] The new company's first line affecting Nottingham was that which was built to link the town with Newark and Lincoln. It opened in 1846, at the same time providing both towns with their first railways and London connections.[54]

The transference of traffic from water to rail carriage began immediately and, although for a time the Trent Navigation and Canal Companies held their own, by 1845 the Trent Navigation Company was seriously considering a reduction of rates owing to competition.[55] Substantial cuts were made in the fifties, but the directors were obliged to pay dividends from capital. From 1847 onwards, when tolls collected amounted to less than in any year since 1808, income continued to fall. The tonnage of goods on the Nottingham Canal decreased from 12,183 in 1841–2, to 8,965 in 1845–6.[56] In that year the directors agreed to surrender to the railway and to amalgamate with the Ambergate, Nottingham, Boston and Eastern Junction Railway, which opened in 1852. By a series of Acts the Trent and Mersey (Grand Trunk) Canal, whose shares still stood at a reasonable figure, turned itself into the North Staffs. Railway Company, under which both waterway and railway were run successfully for seventy years.[57] In comparison with the improved economic potentialities enjoyed by Leicester—and especially Derby —Nottingham derived modest benefits as a result of the railway building in the thirties and early forties. Therefore, when during the economic upswing of 1845 more railway schemes were promoted, the Corporation re-opened the question of Nottingham's rail communications, and passed a resolution pledging the Corporation to make every effort to rectify the situation under which Nottingham remained a branch line outpost. Shortly after its formation for the purpose of reviewing the various railway schemes proposed by the companies, the Council Railway Committee examined no fewer than thirty-five projects which had been submitted to Parliament and which, if adopted, would affect the town.[58]

Two schemes received strong support from local businessmen. One was the Nottingham, Erewash Valley, Ambergate and Manchester Railway, whose provisional committee included directors of the Erewash, Cromford, and Nottingham Canal Companies, and Heard, Heymann, Hollins, Keely, Jackson, Swann, Alliott, and Beardsley, each of whom was either a local merchant or manufacturer. This line was intended to obtain a more direct route from Nottingham to Liverpool and Manchester by a line from Nottingham, forming a junction with the terminus of the Manchester, Buxton and Midland Junction Railway at Ambergate. It was also designed to improve the distribution of the coal, lime, and building stone resources of Derbyshire.[59] The second scheme favoured in Nottingham was the Grand Union Railway which would connect Nottingham with Grantham, King's Lynn, and the agricultural area of the east coast. Eventually the two companies amalgamated to become the Ambergate, Nottingham, and Boston, and Eastern Junction Railway Company, but although the original intention was to build a railway linking Grantham with Nottingham, only part of this project—a line between Grantham and Colwick—was constructed; by an agreement with the Midland Railway directors the Ambergate Company was allowed the use of their lines into Nottingham.[60]

The accord between these two companies stirred competition from the Great Northern Railway directors, who saw in the Ambergate line the possibility of connecting Nottingham to their own main line which ran through Grantham. Eventually, after clandestine share purchases on the part of both major companies in their efforts to foil each other's plans, and after a somewhat dramatic capture of one of the Great Northern's engines by manoeuvring it into the Midland's sheds then pulling up the lines, the disputes were settled.[61] The engine was returned, and in exchange for the withdrawal of opposition to a proposed Midland line from Leicester through Bedford to Hitchin, the Great Northern secured access to Nottingham in 1852. Frustrated in their attempt to obtain a direct route to London, five years later the Midland obtained powers to run its trains over the lines of the Great Northern into St. Pancras, the Midland line running through Leicester, and Kettering in Northamptonshire.[62] While this line was aimed at participation in the London trade, the Nottingham to Mansfield extension, which was completed in 1848, had as its intention the connection of the several rapidly growing industrial villages around Nottingham and the opening up of a section of the Nottinghamshire coal-field.[63] The extension joined the villages of Lenton, Radford, Basford, Bulwell, Hucknall, Linby, Newstead, Annesley, Kirkby, Sutton-in-Ashfield, and Mansfield. Another project which was conceived at the same time by local businessmen proved entirely abortive. This was the Nottingham Mineral Railway, designed to tap the resources of the Leen Valley coalfield which, it was hoped, would result in lower fuel prices; but the initial publicity failed to attract enough support and the plan was laid aside.[64]

In the twenty years following the opening of the Liverpool and Manchester Railway in 1829, the national economy was transformed by the railways. They were both a cause and a symbol of rapid economic change and material progress, but the social changes which accompanied this development presented a serious challenge to institutions which, by their inertia, showed themselves to be obsolete. One such outmoded institution was the closed corporation whose constitution and functions had become ill adapted to the needs of an urban industrial society. This fact was recognized in the report of the Select Committee of the reformed House of Commons in 1833; and as one of the oligarchic corporate organizations whose reform had been urged by local reformers in the campaigns which had led to the Reform Act of 1832,[65] it was inevitable that the Nottingham Corporation should be subject to careful scrutiny. The Municipal Corporations Act of 1835, however, was not conceived as a measure which would inaugurate civic reform and municipal progress. The Act was merely a logical sequel to the Act passed in 1832 in its attempt to displace self-elected and co-opted rulers to make way for elective town councils.[66] Political reforms which broadened the franchise with regard to the election of the national government were thus followed by the dissolution of over two hundred old corporations—including, of course, the Nottingham Corporation—and their replacement by municipal boroughs governed by elected councils.

The Act of 1835 was thus an instrument of municipal reform, rather than revolution. The potentialities for constructive and enterprising local government were not admitted, a fact reflected in the statute of 1835 which required of the reformed corporations only an improved and efficient management of estates and a sound plan for policing the town.[67] In Nottingham the old close body, which consisted of seven aldermen and twenty-four councillors nominally elected by freemen, was to be replaced by a Council of forty-two members elected by resident householders, although these new voting qualifications actually narrowed the municipal voting body in Nottingham from 2,880 to 2,217. Under the new Act the councillors were to elect one-third of their number as aldermen annually to replace one-third who would retire.[68]

The first election under the new Act on December 26th, 1835 brought the return of the retiring mayor and five of the six aldermen who were already in office; but of the twenty-four councillors only three survived re-election. Some of the new representatives came from outside the ranks of freemen, a trend which was to continue.[69] Nevertheless, the composition of old and new corporations was similar in occupations, religious affiliations, and political convictions. With hosiers accounting for approximately one-third of the council representatives and the rest comprising shopkeepers, a few professional men, and 'gentlemen'; and while dissenting Whigs continued to predominate, it would have been surprising had any radical change in attitude taken place. Even so, henceforward the press was allowed free access to the reports of Council meetings, and a committee which was set up to consider the question of enclosure shortly reported in favour of a limited measure.[70] However, lack of power, lack of financial resources, and lack of initiative dogged municipal progress for at least a decade after reform, and borough government in Nottingham was similar to that in most towns during this period where it consisted of 'a more or less different body of people doing the same things as before in the same way.'[71]

The items on the new Council's first agenda consisted of the appointment of two committees to administer the Bridge and Chamber Estates, and the organization of an efficient police force in place of the anachronistic watch and ward.[72] Prior to 1835 a number of constables from various wards were appointed by the justices of the peace.[73] The constables, who numbered one hundred in 1830, performed their duties only during the day, relying upon fees for payment, while because all except three constables were expected to act on a part-time basis, the constables also found it possible to continue in other employment. The responsibility for maintaining nocturnal peace lay with between forty and fifty watchmen who were paid by private subscription, but they patrolled only those streets in which the subscribers resided. In 1834 William Dearden, a local writer, remarked that the Watch in Nottingham was worse regulated than in any other town of the same size.[74] It was certainly inadequate to cope with the increase in crime that accompanied the rise in population. When the Corporation assumed control of the town's policing system, fifty watchmen were engaged to form a night force which was to function under the command of a superintendent and three inspectors; the annual cost, borne by the Corporation, was about £2,000. Between dusk and eleven, when the night watch came on duty, twelve constables were placed on patrol, while three permanent policemen were considered adequate to maintain law and order during the daytime.[75] Under such conditions the time devoted to tracking down criminals must have been small, and unless a culprit was apprehended while he was in the process of committing a crime, the possibility of discovery and capture was slim.

The threat of public disturbances in 1839 led to an increase of two evening police and five day police, and henceforth all day-police were required to be full-time employees of the Corporation. The simultaneous existence of unco-ordinated day and night forces proved to be an unsatisfactory arrangement which hindered the fight against crime, and in 1841 a re-organization of the policing system brought about the amalgamation of day with night forces under one command, the single force consisting of one inspector and twelve men to perform day duties, thirty men and four inspectors becoming responsible for night duties. In a determined effort to reduce the large number of crimes which went undetected, in 1854 the Watch Committee appointed four men and a superintendent as a detective police force. The entire police force was slowly augmented as population grew; in 1864 there were seventy-five constables, and in 1879 one hundred and eighty-eight. Following the Police Act of 1856, after which the Nottingham zone had been certified efficient, the force received a government grant of 25 per cent. of the cost of pay and clothing.[76] The extinguishing of fires was another responsibility of the Watch Committee, and it was the subject of sharp criticism in 1836 when on the occasion of a fire at the Exchange it failed in its duties to the bad state of repair of the equipment. Two years later a squad, consisting of twenty-nine suitable firemen, was selected to act as fire police under an honorary superintendent with two assistants. Two of the seven old engines were obsolete, but the rest were in good repair, and with money subscribed by the insurance companies the Fire Engine Committee also purchased one powerful new engine.[77] Another problem which still faced the Watch Committee was the delay which might be involved in moving the engines to the scene of fire. Access to the market place, for example, involved the negotiation of narrow streets eleven feet across with steep inclines, routes which, with the increasing trade of the town and the free-for-all parking of waggons and carts, often became choked even prior to the railway's appearance in Nottingham.

However, the Reform Act of 1835 had not required municipal bodies to appoint committees to deal with such problems, and not until pressure from outside the local governing body was any progress achieved in this respect. The widening of Chapel Bar, which took place between 1826 and 1833, was financed through public subscription, the Corporation donating £1,000, while Carrington Street, begun in 1829, was built by the Collins' Hospital Trustees.[78] It needed the coming of the railway to mobilize public opinion in insisting that the Council deal with the crisis which was threatening the local transport system.[79] Under the leadership of Ichabod Wright, supported by Felkin and Hannay, in 1839 an Association for the Improvement of the Town took the initiative in pressing for a solution to road and traffic problems.[80] As a result of the Association's lobbying, the Council set up an Improvement Committee to confer with the Committee of the Association. First for consideration was the area between Market Place and the railway station in the Meadows, south of Carrington Street. Taking into account expediency and expense, it was agreed that Lister Gate should be broadened and a wide street formed from its north end to the north end of High Street, but a meeting of ratepayers rejected the proposal.[81] When the Midland Railway Company pressed for a bridge to be built over the canal in Carrington Street and offered to subscribe £3,000 towards the cost of construction, the Council agreed immediately and sold land to raise the rest.[82] The bridge was completed in 1842.

In the same year, the question of improved communication between Carrington Street and Market Place was re-opened. Another Street Improvement Committee recommended the formation of a street about thirty-five feet wide, travelling in a straight line from the north end of Lister Gate to St. Peters' Square, so avoiding the narrow and highly dangerous road along Church Gate;

but the cost, estimated at £3,600, caused the Council to refer the question back to the Committee, requesting that it should consider instead a partial widening of Church Gate 'on reasonable terms.' The Committee could not accept this alternative, and again reported in favour of a new street to be paid for by the levy of a special rate by Act of Parliament.[83] To this recommendation the Council agreed, and a special rate of 2½d. in the pound was levied on properties rated at and over £7 10s. 0d. per annum. On its completion in 1846, Albert Street, one hundred yards in length, had cost £8,000 and a public subscription raised £2,000 to meet the excess expenditure over the original estimate.[84] Albert Street alone, however, was inadequate to solve the town's problems of internal communication: and merchants and manufacturers continued to complain of the absurdity of a situation where, owing to the pressure from so-called 'economists', Nottingham was forced to attempt to carry on the business of a great commercial town without the existence of adequate public thoroughfares. An editorial in the *Review* commented: 'Lanes and alleys we have in plenty—but of anything like main thoroughfares we are innocent.'[85] Old means of communications were unchanged, while the town's trade had expanded and the number of carriers, carts, and waggons greatly augmented. There was still a chronic lack of an adequate outlet from Market Place to Parliament Street, for Sheep Lane was only ten feet across; likewise Clumber Street and Chapel Bar, Pelham Street and Bridlesmith Gate, main thoroughfares though they were, were less than five yards in width.[86]

'If only words had been convertible into bricks and mortar' wrote Sutton, 'and town councillors *ex officio* architects, we might have had streets in plenty. The fact is we require so much doing that we cannot agree where to begin.'[87]

One sphere of local government in which the Council did make a modest beginning was that of subsidized municipal enterprise. In 1844, two years after Liverpool Corporation had opened baths and wash-houses, a committee was appointed to inquire into the provision of a municipal bathing establishment in Nottingham. Two months later the Baths Committee suggested that rates should finance the construction and that a small charge should cover the operating costs:

'In no other way will the same amount of money be attended with the same amount of benefit—cleanliness, health, recreation and public decorum will be promoted.' The Committee expressed the hope that the project would be adopted 'with that public spirit which its importance demands.'[88]

Two years later an Act to encourage the Establishment of Public

Baths and Wash-houses revived local interest, and in 1849 the Nottingham Corporation adopted the Act. After receiving the Treasury's consent for the appropriation of land and for the loan of £3,000, the Corporation took advantage of this departure from the principle of *laissez-faire,* and the first municipal baths and wash-houses in Nottingham were opened early in 1851. Public response was similar to that encountered by the Liverpool enterprise, the baths receiving greater support than the wash-houses. The poor, for whose benefit the wash-houses had been established, used them little, and in 1855 the Council decided to terminate its subsidy and to let both baths and washhouses annually by public tender. Not until 1878 did the Council build more public baths.[89]

Apart from the initial activity of its first three years, the reformed Council achieved little until after the Enclosure Act of 1845, but in some respects the early years were important. As stipulated by the Act of 1835 the Council appointed a Watch Committee to organize the police force, while of crucial importance for future government was the evolution of a system whereby specially appointed committees became responsible for the management of separate affairs. Although the Council was the legislative body with complete power to finance and initiate new activities, the committees were allowed complete freedom of action, assuming the function of executive bodies limited only by the power delegated to them. Increased responsibility, however meagre, involved greater expenditure, and the act of 1835 sanctioned the levying of a borough rate to supplement Corporation income. In Nottingham, as in Leicester and other boroughs, financial problems go far to explain the reformed Corporation's failure to respond to the social needs of a growing industrial town,[90] for the new Corporation inherited more than £20,000 in debts, the equivalent of almost twice its annual income.[91] Indeed, current income from property and from the supplementary rate was insufficient to meet regular expenditures until 1837–8 when there was a surplus of £615, and in order to maintain the Coppice and other estates the Council sold land in the Meadows for £1,400. The annual average surpluses during the early forties ran slightly above £700.[92]

In 1842 the Corporation appointed a Debts Committee to secure loans on mortgages, the interest charges constituting a prior charge on all Corporation property and rates. On the recommendation of the Debts Committee, loans bearing interest of more than 4 per cent. were paid off, but it was decided not to sell Corporation Estates. Seven acres of the Westcroft were mortgaged the following year for £3,000, and the Corporation advertised for loans at no more than 4 per cent.[93] Presumably it was owing to the difficulty of obtaining a loan on such terms that in the same year the Corporation borrowed £5,000 at 5 per cent. from Alderman Joseph Frearson.[94] Serious measures were taken to reduce the Corporation's indebtedness which in 1843 still stood at £20,450, and in that year land received under the Enclosure Award was sold; the Corporation Debt was finally amortized in 1853–54.[95] Preference for land sales or borrowing to raise income reflected the Council's concern that the cost of schemes should not fall heavily on one year's rates. Moreover, the policy of keeping the rates fairly steady from year to year allowed the cost of improvements to fall upon future beneficiaries as well as on current ratepayers. Nevertheless, so long as rates could be charged only on real property, the Ratepayers' Association continued to agitate against increasing expenditure.

The personnel of the reformed Corporation over the next twenty years continued to include men from prominent Whig families, many of whom had previously been members of the close Corporation, for whereas until the closing decades of the previous century the local dissenting Whig clique had been recruited from wealthy retail trading interests, before the nineteenth century had begun the merchant hosier *élite* had emerged.[96] Ashwell, Heard, Rogers, Morley, Allen and Hurst—all Whigs, dissenters, and merchant hosiers—held office under the reformed Corporation and in the forties and fifties made their contributions towards the life of the community chiefly through the Corporation and the chapels. Likewise William Hannay, Thomas Carver, John Hadden, and Benjamin Hine, who were more recently established hosiery manufacturers, played comparable roles in town life. The retailing group, which had predominated in the old close body, was less well represented, although Swann, Fox, Knight, and Barber were also members of the reformed Corporation. Occupations of other members of the Corporation during this period included various types of merchanting, the professions, and a group which began to make its impact felt in the 1850s and whose numbers gained in strength and influence thereafter—the lace manufacturers. This development brought about a significant change in the social composition of the Corporation, for whereas the majority of hosier councillors sprang from prominent local merchanting families, lace manufacturers tended to be products of a different social stratum; many were self-made men who had laid the foundations for their wealth in the boom years of the twenties.

By the early fifties the Corporation aldermen included in their capacities as chairmen of committees a number of figures who dominated Corporation affairs for some twenty years. Only four of the fourteen aldermen were hosiers, Aldermen Heard, Carver,

Wells, and Wilson; Aldermen Reckless, Cullen, Heymann, Burton, Herbert, Biddle, and Birkin were lace manufacturers, while Alderman Hart was a banker. Lace manufacturers Vickers and Herbert had served as mayor in 1844 and in 1846 respectively, and Cripps, a lace merchant, filled the office in 1847. It was during the following decade, however, that two of the town's outstanding public figures, both of whom were Evangelicals and lace manufacturers of humble origins, were first elected to that office. Richard Birkin, born in Belper in 1805, began to work a stocking frame at an early age; he later learned to operate a point net machine and became a bobbin net maker during the early twenties. In the forties Birkin became one of the country's leading lace manufacturers, first as partner, then owner of a firm which gave employment to more than two thousand people.[98] He was a member of the Corporation for many years and was mayor of Nottingham in 1850, 1855, 1862, and 1863. The following year Birkin received a silver testimonial in recognition of his services to the town, and in 1855 he retired from business, for several years thereafter devoting his time to municipal and magisterial duties until his death in 1870.[99] Although Richard Birkin and William Felkin shared similar social origins, Felkin did not reach Birkin's stature as entrepreneur, but as civic leaders both men left their marks upon the town.[100] While Birkin led the Improvement Committee, Felkin chaired the Sanitary Committee, becoming mayor in 1851 and 1852. Birkin and Felkin, although the most outstanding local figures of their type, are examples of the kind of men who began to appear as members of the Corporation from the forties onwards. Their careers and life experiences differed from those of the gentlemen hosier mayors of the two previous decades, and they contrasted too with the members of the unreformed Corporation, most of whom had sprung from established and respected trading families.

The Corporation also began to benefit from the participation in local government of a few of the Jewish lace merchants who came from Europe to live in Nottingham at the time of political upheavals in the late forties.[101] Despite some local inhibitions in 1857 Lewis Heymann became the town's first foreign mayor in Nottingham. Heymann, like several of the wealthy Jewish merchants and manufacturers in Nottingham, worshipped with the Unitarians.[102] Indeed, one is struck by the extent to which dissenting and business interests were represented on the Corporation, and while it cannot be claimed that the fusion of these produced a combination as fruitful as that in Birmingham,[103] in Nottingham, too, religious ethics and business sense were, to some extent, the source of inspiration and practical driving force for civic progress. But change in Nottingham was slow, and though a sense of civic duty and responsibility to the community began to develop, often only after permissive legislation had been passed by the central government did progress occur.

The first indication of significant progress made by reforming influences in the new Corporation might be seen in the passage of the Nottingham Enclosure Act of 1845, though the Bill was promoted by an independent group of citizens, a fact which suggests that the Enclosure Bill was accepted because of the weakening of the anti-enclosure interests on the Council rather than because of the growth of reforming zeal in the latter. Renewed interest in the enclosure issue was precipitated by the inquiries of the Select Committee of the House of Commons on Enclosure, to which Thomas Hawksley gave evidence.[104] In 1844, inspired by motives of philanthropy, public spirit, and self interest, the advocates of enclosure rallied once more and proposed a new bill. The reformed Corporation, which included an increasing number of non-burgess councillors, had estranged many freemen from the Council[105] and this tended to reinforce the ascent of Tory interests in the borough, whose fortunes had improved following the Poor Law Amendment Act of 1834. Free from pressure of freemen votes and spurred on by public opinion (even the Whig leader, Thomas Wakefield, who had hitherto consistently voted against enclosure, accepted the inevitability of legislation and voted for the bill) the Corporation resolved unanimously to support the application for a General Enclosure Bill.

As a result, the Nottingham General Enclosure Act which allowed for the enclosure of 1,069 acres received the royal assent on June 30th, 1845.[106] As indicated in the Bill's preamble, the Enclosure Act was intended as an instrument of 'social, moral, sanitary, commercial, and agricultural reform.' The Enclosure Commissioners were given statutory authority to build and widen roads, and to construct drains, sewers, and bridges, while it endowed the Council with a new function inasmuch as it became responsible for the establishment and future maintenance of public walks, gardens, and recreation grounds; the management of the Races on the Forest also passed into the hands of the Council.[107] It was decided that an area of twelve acres in the Sand Field was admirably suited for an arboretum owning to 'the diversified nature of the ground and the salubrity of the situation',[108] and in May, 1852 the first visitors entered the Nottingham Arboretum at a charge of 6d. for adults and 3d. for children under fourteen. Some years later a large section of the public made it known that it resented this charge; after several petitions from public meetings the Enclosure Committee took legal advice and reluctantly abolished the offending fee, regretting that their 'ornamental Pleasure Garden . . . was to become a mere place of recreation'.[109] The campaign for free entrance had its opponents. Edwin Patchitt, Clerk to the Enclosure Commissioners, submitted petitions signed by 1,655 working men, 6,572 from the staple trades, and 2,994 ratepayers and inhabitants; all were in favour of keeping the Aboretum as a self-supporting enterprise. After further debate the Council gave its assent to the insertion of Patchitt's clause in an Improvement Act, thereby legalizing paid admission to the Arboretum on three-and-a-half days each week.[110]

Those responsible for drawing up the Nottingham Enclosure Act were enlightened in ways other than in the provision of lungs for a growing industrial town. Building standards were laid down requiring principal thoroughfares to have a minimum width of thirty feet, while each public street was to have raised pavements. Housing standards implied no further construction of back-to-backs and each house was to include a yard attached, a privy set apart, a piped water supply, and three bedrooms. Cess-pools were to be at least ten feet distant from any dwelling house, and special regulations were included in the Act to protect the local populace from various noxious trades being carried on in its midst.[111] However, apart from these minor specifications there was no plan to regulate the general pattern of development. The open field footpaths provided the Enclosure Commissioners with their starting-point which determined the basic road system; land was then allotted according to the claims of some four hundred owners and the land was developed privately as self-contained areas. There was no co-ordination of road building on the several allotments and no reference was made to basic communications within and leading out of the area; the result was a labyrinth of perfunctory streets and a jumble of buildings which quickly began to swallow up the available land.[112]

The Enclosure Act of 1845 removed one of the principal causes of overcrowding and of the concomitant evils of squalor and disease; it opened the way to attack the appalling condition of the town and to take steps to prevent future deterioration in standards of housing and public health. During the 1840's the shocking state of public health was revealed in a series of investigations and reports which showed that the cholera epidemic of 1832 had failed to generate a sustained assault upon this problem. The reports of the Parliamentary Committee on the Health of Towns, and of the Royal Commission on the State of large towns and populous Districts consisted of page after page of facts and figures disclosing the incredible extent to which human life was being wasted.[113] The areas of working class dwellings in the lower parts of the town were

still by far the worst. (See Table X.) Owing to the absence of sewerage the older streets in St. Ann's and Byron Wards were narrow,
unpaved, ill-ventilated, noisome, and damp. The stench from surface
drains, stagnant pools, and accumulated filth in Narrow Marsh,
Leen-side, and Canal Street was particularly obnoxious.

> 'There is no want of public nuisance in Nottingham', reported
> Martin; 'the entire quarters occupied by the labouring classes
> form but one great nuisance.'[114]

The only mitigating feature which the Commissioners could discover
was the town's highly efficient and cheap supply of water. This was
due mainly to the exertions of Thomas Hawksley, engineer to the
Trent Water Works. Before the reforms that he inaugurated in
1830 water was sold at a farthing for three gallons. Due to his
ingenuity about eight thousand houses containing thirty-five
thousand people, as well as a number of breweries, dye houses, and
steam engines were supplied by pipe lines night and day. By relaying water through pipes at high pressure Hawksley had achieved a
reduction of 75 per cent. in the cost of water to consumers.[115]

In the context of contemporary thought Hawksley held un-
orthodox but progressive views on the ethics and efficiency of
laissez-faire and competition. In 1844 there were three waterworks
in Nottingham, each competing to some extent with the others.

> 'The (water) companies usually obtain all they can or dare from
> the public and the public takes the first opportunity of selling
> up a rival to the existing monopoly' observed Hawksley.
> ' "That competition must do good" is a maxim of such univer-
> sal acceptance that Parliament without much hesitation, con-
> cedes the necessary powers to the proposed rival and *again
> without imposing supervision* . . . Both companies are on the
> verge of ruin . . . to save themselves a coalition ensues between
> them and dividends must be made on two capitals.'

Hawksley went further to elaborate remedies for the evils resulting from *laissez-faire*:

> a central board ought to be established for directing and
> superintending the operations of all public companies and
> bodies who derive their powers from local acts and royal
> charters,

a Chadwickian reservation which advocated the control of a
national authority in connection with public utilities. Hawksley
foresaw streets cleaned by jets and a constant water supply, and
water closets and earthenware drains in each house at a cost of less
than £5. He forecast for the future warm baths in public bath
houses for a nominal charge, even baths introduced into the houses

o

TABLE X: *Death Rates in Nottingham, 1844.*

| Ward | Population excluding inmates of public institutions | | | Death rate per thousand | Mean age at death | | | Birth rate per thousand | No. of children who died before reaching 4 yrs. expressed as % of births | Proportion of death rate to birth rate |
	Males	Females	Total		Males	Females	Total			
Park	2186	3047	5233	19·5	29·4	29·3	29·3	25·7	28·8	1-1·32
Sherwood	2417	2813	5230	20·1	20·0	28·2	24·3	28·5	31·8	1-1·41
Castle	3230	3887	7117	23·2	19·3	26·5	23·0	33·2	33·9	1-1·43
Exchange	2725	3132	5857	25·3	20·6	24·1	22·4	31·9	39·7	1-1·26
St. Mary	3172	3984	7156	26·5	18·7	24·0	21·3	39·9	35·3	1-1·5
St. Ann	5051	5469	10520	27·9	16·3	21·8	19·2	35·86	42·3	1-1·28
Byron	5117	5912	11029	30·9	17·3	18·7	18·1	37·65	44·5	1-1·22

Source: J. D. Chambers, *Modern Nottingham in the Making* (Nottingham, 1945) pp. 12–13, quoting *Report of the Royal Commission on Large Towns and Populous Districts*, 1845.

of labouring men for use of themselves and families . . .'[116] Fortified by expert knowledge and a resolute public spirit, by improving the supply of water and lowering its price Hawksley indirectly ameliorated the lot of the working men and women in
Nottingham at a time when sanitary conditions had reached a nadir.
In the history of the public health movement Thomas Hawksley
holds an important place. The success of the Water Company run
as a model of efficiency epitomised the ideals of the Benthamites,
and it has been said that this model success was a principal cause for
Chadwick's enthusiasm for private enterprise.[117] Some indication of
the measure of Hawkesley's contribution to society may be judged
by the almost complete escape of Nottingham from the cholera epidemic which in 1849 claimed so many victims in other large towns—
though the long term mortality rate was slow to fall. But Hawksley
was not merely concerned with the economic efficiency of the Waterworks; the social benefits which it produced were also important to
him.

It was likewise the public advantages to be gained from releas-
ing land for building purposes in Nottingham which explains
his continued advocacy of enclosure, a measure which Hawksley
and Felkin had long insisted must be effected before the town's
history could enter a new and expansive phase. They were thus
heralds of that transformation which, when it began after the Nottingham Enclosure Act of 1845, was sufficiently impressive to
prompt a local coinage of the phrase 'New Nottingham.'[118]

References

[1] W. Ashworth, *The Genesis of Modern Town Planning*, (1954), p. 50.

[2] *Second Report of the Commissioners on Large Towns and Populous Districts*, 1845 (610) XVIII. 1. Report of J. R. Martin, p. 250.

[3] *Comparative Account of the Population of Great Britain*, 1801–31, 1831 (348) XVIII. These figures, of course, exclude the suburban populations.

[4] John Prest, *The Industrial Revolution in Coventry*, (1960), p. 41.

[5] W. G. Hoskins, *The Making of the English Landscape*, (1955), p. 233.

[6] *Report of the Royal Commission on the Employment of Children in Factories*, (1843), (431) XIV. ev. of H. Taylor, p.f. 60.

[7] *First Report of the Commissioners appointed to inquire into the Municipal Corporations in England and Wales;* 1835 (116) XXIII. 1. Here a *Report of Evidence before the Commissioners appointed to inquire into the Municipal Corporations in England and Wales* printed verbatim for the Nottingham Constitutional Club (Nottingham, 1833) is used. Ev. of Barnett, p. 158; *First Report of the Commissioners (Large Towns and Populous Districts)*, 1844 (572) XVII. 1., ev. of Hawkesley, p. 30.

[8] See J. D. Chambers, *Modern Nottingham in the Making*, (Nottingham 1945), pp. 14–18; By the late twenties the development of the 'new' villages had begun to ease this shortage. S. D. Chapman 'Working Class Housing in Nottingham during the Industrial Revolution', *Transactions of the Thoroton Society*, LXVII (1963), p. 87.

[9] A. C. Wood, 'Nottingham 1835–1865,' *Transactions of the Thoroton Society*, LIX (1955), p. 6, f.n. 4.

[10] *N.R.*, October 25, 1844.

[11] Evidence before the Commissioners appointed to inquire into Municipal Corporations printed verbatim for the Nottingham Constitutional Club (Nottingham, 1833), p. 165; William White, *History Gazetteer and Directory of Nottinghamshire* (Nottingham, 1832), p. 194.

[12] *Comparative Account of the Population of Great Britain*, 1801–31, 1831 (348) XVIII.

[13] John Sutton, *Date Book*, p. 392.

[14] S. D. Chapman 'Working Class Housing in Nottingham during the Industrial Revolution,' *Transactions of the Thoroton Society*, LXVII (1963), p. 82.

[15] *Comparative Account of the Population of Great Britain*, 1801–31, 1831 (348) XVIII.

[16] *Ibid.*

[17] S. D. Chapman 'Working Class Housing in Nottingham during the Industrial Revolution,' *Transactions of the Thoroton Society*, LXVII (1963), pp. 78–82, pp. 85–87.

[18] H. Field, *The Nottingham Date Book 1800–1884*, (Nottingham, 1884), p. 408; *Evidence before the Commissioners appointed to inquire into Municipal Corporations* printed verbatim for the Nottingham Constitutional Club (Nottingham, 1833), p. 4.

[19] *Children's Employment Commission*, 1843 (431) XIV, ev. of H. Taylor, p.f. 60.

[20] *Ibid.*

[21] *B.R.*, IX, 73, minutes September 1, 1849.

[22] R. Mellors, *Men of Nottingham,* p. 211.

[23] J. D. Chambers, *Modern Nottingham,* p. 6; W. H. Wylie, *Old and New Nottingham,* (Nottingham and London, 1853), p. 371.

[24] Asa Briggs, *The Age of Improvement,* (1959), p. 278.

[25] *Evidence before the Commissioners appointed to inquire into Municipal Corporations,* printed verbatim for the Nottingham Constitutional Club (Nottingham, 1833), p. 10; Duncan Gray, *Nottingham Through Five Hundred Years* (Nottingham, 1949), pp. 20, 25, 64.

[26] S. D. Chapman, 'The Evangelical Revival and Education in Nottingham,' *Transactions of the Thoroton Society* LXVI, (1962) 51; John Ashwell 1804, 1814, 1820; J. H. Barber 1817, 1825, 1831; John Heard 1832, 1837; O. T. Oldknow 1847; Edward Swann 1805, 1812; William Wilson 1811, 1816, 1823, 1830.

[27] *Evidence before the Commissioners appointed to inquire into Municipal Corporations,* printed verbatim for the Nottingham Constitutional Club (Nottingham, 1833), p. 30 and Appendix 4; S. Collinson, *High Pavement Centenary 1691–1891,* (Nottingham 1891), p. 32.

[28] *Evidence before the Commissioners appointed to inquire into Municipal Corporations,* printed verbatim for the Nottingham Constitutional Club (Nottingham, 1833), p. 13.

[29] A. C. Wood, *A History of Nottinghamshire,* (Nottingham, 1947), p. 297.

[30] *Evidence before the Commissioners appointed to inquire into Municipal Corporations,* printed verbatim for the Nottingham Constitutional Club (Nottingham, 1833), p. 13.

[31] *Ibid.,* p. 6.

[32] *Ibid.*

[33] *B.R.*, VII, 333, Minutes, February 27, 1826; the cost of the latter was £900; *Evidence before the Commissioners appointed to inquire into Municipal Corporations,* printed verbatim for the Nottingham Constitutional Club (Nottingham, 1833), p. 12.

[34] W. Dearden, *op. cit.,* p. 74.

[35] J. D. Chambers, *Modern Nottingham,* p. 39.

[36] *N.J.,* August 12, 1836.

[37] William Felkin, *History,* p. 380; *N.R.,* June 4, 1858; *N.R.,* April 16, 1844.

[38] William Felkin, *History,* pp. 341–42, 437, 463.

[39] William Felkin, *History,* p. 467.

[40] *B.R.*, IX, 4, September 15, 1836; *B.R.*, IX, 7, minutes December 21, 1837. 21, 1837.

[41] *B.R.*, IX, 21, March 5, 1839; *B.R.*, IX, 21–22, minutes, April 29, 1839.

[42] For an indication of the magnitude of property interests at stake in connection with the postponement of enclosure see J. D. Chambers 'Nottingham in the Early Nineteenth Century' *Transactions of the Thoroton Society,* 1941, XLV, pp. 38–40.

[43] *N.R.,* July 10, 1840; *N.R.,* April 1, 1841; *N.R.,* February 26, 1842.

[44] *Evidence before the Lords Committee on the London and Birmingham Railway Bill,* (1831–32) CCCXI. 167, p. 32; W. Dearden, *op. cit.,* p. 74.

[45] *N.R.,* August 7, 1833.

46 F. S. Williams, *The Midland Railway: Its Rise and Progress* (1876), pp. 9–19. See also an unpublished Ph.D. Thesis by G. E. Bell *The Railway as a factor in the Location of Manufacturing Industry in the East Midlands,* (University of Nottingham 1958).

47 *Journals of the House of Commons,* 1836 XCI, p. 106.

48 C. E. Stretton, *History of the Midland Railway,* (1901) pp. 32–33.

49 *N.R.,* October 28, 1836.

50 Charles H. Grinling, *The History of the Great Northern Railway,* (1898), p. 3.

51 See John Birks and Peter Coxon, *An Account of Railway Development in the Nottinghamshire Coalfield,* (Mansfield, 1949).

52 F. S. Williams *op. cit.,* pp. 28–29.

53 *Ibid.,* pp. 33, 69.

54 G. E. Bell, *op. cit.,* p. 110.

55 Minutes of the Trent Navigation Company: Accounts of Expenditure 1841–53.

56 *Ibid.,* Board of Directors' Minutes, Nottingham Canal Company; J. A. B. Hamilton, 'The Railways of Nottingham,' *The Railway Magazine,* 1932 LXX. I. and II.

57 *Ibid.*

58 *B.R.,* IX, 45, minutes October 22, 1845; *N.R.,* November 21, 1845.

59 *Herepath's Railway Journal,* p. 675.

60 H. G. Lewin, *The Railway Mania and its Aftermath* (1936), p. 169; The line was opened in 1846.

61 C. E. Stretton, 'The History of the Nottinghamshire and Lincolnshire Line', Paper read on the occasion of Newark Brake Trials, 1875.

62 Charles H. Grinling, *op. cit.,* p. 134.

63 F. S. Williams, *The Midland Railway,* p. 88.

64 *Herepath's Railway Journal,* p. 2601.

65 Asa Briggs, *The Age of Improvement,* (1959), pp. 276–7.

66 *Ibid.*

67 *B.R.,* IX, 32, January 1, 1836.

68 James Orange, *History and Antiquities of Nottingham,* (1840), II, 897; F. and J. White, *op. cit.,* p. 122.

69 For a list of those returned see *B.R.,* IX, minutes December 26, 1835; H. Field, *op. cit.,* p. 420; F. and J. White, *op. cit.,* p. 131.

70 *B.R.,* IX, 2, February 4, 1836; Supra, p. 170.

71 W. Ashworth, *The Genesis of Modern Town Planning,* (1954), p. 70.

72 *B.R.,* IX, 3, February 25, 1836.

73 See A. C. Wood, 'Nottingham 1835–1965,' *Transactions of the Thoroton Society,* LIX (1955), pp. 38–40.

74 W. Dearden, *Historical and Topographical Directory of Nottingham* (Nottingham, 1834), p. 74.

75 A. C. Wood, *loc. cit.*

76 *Ibid., B.R.,* IX, 3, February 18, 1836; *B.R.,* IX, 41, December 10, 1844; *B.R.,* 133, November 15, 1858.

77 *B.R.,* IX, 5, December 5, 1837; *B.R.,* 4–5, IX, February 6, 1837; *B.R.,* IX, 9, May 3, 1838.

[78] *B.R.,* VIII, 362, August 21, 1828.

[79] *B.R.,* IX, 8–9, March 26, 1838.

[80] *B.R.,* IX, 24, December 12, 1839.

[81] *B.R.,* IX, 25, February 6, 1840.

[82] *B.R.,* IX, 23, October 21, 1839.

[83] *B.R.,* IX, 36, November 9, 1843.

[84] *B.R.,* IX, 37, January 18, 1844; Stephen Glover, *The History and Directory of the Town and County of Nottingham,* (Nottingham, 1844), p. 10.

[85] *N.R.,* October 14, 1859.

[86] Stephen Glover, *The History and Directory of the Town and County of Nottingham,* (Nottingham, 1844), p. 10.

[87] *N.R.,* October 14, 1859.

[88] *B.R.,* IX, 39, August 1, 1844.

[89] D. Gray, *Nottingham Through Five Hundred Years,* (Nottingham, 1960), p. 196.

[90] A. Temple Patterson, *Radical Leicester,* (1954), p. 216.

[91] *B.R.,* IX, 9, May 2, 1838.

[92] See *Nottingham Corporation Accounts* for these years.

[93] 5 and 6 William IV 1835 Cap LXXI *An Act to provide for the Regulation of Municipal Corporations in England and Wales,* section XCII; *B.R.,* IX, 3, August 4, 1836; *B.R.,* IX, 34, February 2, 1843; *B.R.,* IX, 39, August 3, 1843.

[94] *B.R.,* IX, 35, August 3, 1843.

[95] *B.R.,* IX, 86, June 23, 1851.

[96] The personnel of the Corporation for each year 1800–1834 is given in *B.R.,* VIII, pp. 463–472.

[97] See Wright's *Nottingham Directory,* 1853.

[98] *N.R.,* February 19, 1864; William Felkin, *History,* pp. 368–9; *Nottingham and Nottinghamshire Illustrated,* (1892), p. 77.

[99] *N.R.,* November 16, 1855.

[100] For a brief treatment of the life and thought of William Felkin see Chap. XII, pp. 326–32.

[101] C. C. Aaronsfield, 'Nottingham Jewish Lace Pioneers' *Nottingham Guardian Journal,* April 19, 1954.

[102] B. B. Granger, *The Tourist's Picturesque Guide to Nottingham,* (Nottingham, 1871), p. 42.

[103] See G. C. Gill, *The History of Birmingham* (Oxford, 1952), I, 380 *et seq.* and G. M. Young, ed., *Early Victorian England* (1934), II, ch. 17.

[104] *N.R.,* October 25, 1844.

[105] F. and J. White, *op. cit.,* p. 131.

[106] *B.R.,* IX, 44, February 20, 1845; *B.R.,* IX, 45, March 4, 1845.

[107] *B.R.,* IX, 46, August 19, 1845.

[108] *B.R.,* IX, 51, August 4, 1846; *B.R.,* IX 82, September 30, 1857.

[109] *B.R.,* IX, 120, April 28, 1857; *B.R.,* IX, May 5, 1857.

[110] *B.R.,* IX, 124, June 30, 1854; *B.R.,* IX, 126, October 13, 1857.

[111] *An Act for Inclosing lands in the Parish of St. Mary in the Town of Nottingham,* (1845) 8 and 9, Vic. Cap., 7.

[112] See J. D. Chambers, 'Victorian Nottingham', *Transactions of the Thoroton Society*, LXIII, 1959, p. 10.

[113] *Second Report of the Commissioners (Large Towns and Populous Districts)* 1845 (610) XVIII. 1. Appendix p. 250; See J. D. Chambers, *Modern Nottingham in the Making.*

[114] *Second Report of the Commissioners (Large Towns and Populous Districts)*, 1845 (610) XVIII. 1. Appendix, p. 253.

[115] *Second Report of the Commissioners (Large Towns and Populous Districts)*, 1845 (610) XVIII. 1. Appendix, p. 253, and see tables submitted by Hawksley, p. 321.

[116] *First Report of the Commissioners (Large Towns and Populous Districts,* 1844 (572) XVII. 1., p. 31.

[117] R. A. Lewis, *Edwin Chadwick and the Public Health Movement 1832–54*, (1952), pp. 88, 101; J. D. Chambers, *Modern Nottingham*, pp. 9–10; see also City of Nottingham Water Department, *A Short History of the Water Works*, (Nottingham) 1930.

[118] See William Wylie, *Old and New Nottingham*, (Nottingham 1853).

CHAPTER VIII

THE REFORMED CORPORATION AND URBAN SOCIETY

THE publication, during the 1840s, of detailed evidence describing the insanitary state of the growing urban centres must have encouraged large numbers of people to concur with one of the conclusions reached by the Royal Commission on the State of Large Towns and Populous Districts which stated:

> the most important evils affecting the public health throughout England and Wales are characterized by little variety, and it is only in the degree of their intensity that the towns exhibit the worst examples of such ills.[1]

Public reaction to the shocking revelations varied, depending upon the particular circumstances in different towns. At Liverpool, where a Health Committee had existed since 1842, the Council immediately promoted the Liverpool Sanitary Act and pioneered public health improvement, although before the thirties and forties its actual achievements were limited.[2] In Nottingham the town's poor sanitary condition had already been brought to the attention of the public in the course of the longstanding controversy which related to enclosure,[3] while it had been the object of a limited inquiry in 1841 and again, on the initiative of the Health of Towns Association, in the following year.[4] Although the 1842 committee was independent of the Town Council some of its members were included, and in addition to the Reverend William J. Butler and Dr. J. C. Williams, Thomas Wakefield, William Felkin, and Henry Leaver also served on the committee. But these men were not typical of the majority of the Council members, for as one correspondent informed the Health of Towns Association in 1848, town improvement was unpopular,

> and popular men will not hazard their popularity by voting money for such purposes, though convinced of the necessity for such improvements.[5]

Vested interests, professional jealousies, and the objections of ratepayers who would have to finance reforms to improve public health provided the reformers with opposition even to the most modest proposals. In many towns the threat of a cholera outbreak was the only factor which was capable of generating sufficient concern for public health to enable the reformers to make progress, and for this reason cholera has been referred to as 'one of the beneficent influences of the nineteenth century'.[7]

Following national legislation which gave limited powers to local governing authorities to remove some of the worst public nuisances, in 1847 Alderman John Heard was instrumental in persuading the Corporation to appoint a committee to conduct a broad survey of public health in Nottingham. The Committee included Felkin, Hannay, Birkin, Biddle, Page, Hardy, and Hewitt, and together with members of the three parochial Highway Boards they drew up a report on the appalling living conditions which were then responsible for the existence of so much endemic fever in the town.[8] At the time of this enquiry, apart from the Corporation regulations concerning the working hours of 'muck majors', the Court Leet was the only local authority having any responsibilty for improving public health, and the Leet's activity consisted of nothing more than the imposition of small fines for nuisances.[9]

In its Report the Committee of 1847 emphasized the folly of leaving sanitation to look after itself, both from the point of view of public health and public expense. It drew attention to the nine hundred cases of continued typhoid fever under the care of the Nottingham General Hospital, the dispensary, and Nottingham Union, as well as to hundreds of other cases which could not be accommodated.[10] The Committee described as illogical a policy which encouraged the building of hospitals and schools while allowing squalor and insanitary conditions to persist; it stressed that energy should be directed towards the prevention of disease through vigilance on the part of public authorities, reinforced by law, rather than by the establishment of additional curative institutions.[11] Viewing it from a practical as well as from a humanitarian angle, the Committee pointed out that by supporting preventive measures the Council would be economizing on public expenditure, thereby reducing the need for such institutions, an argument which is significant inasmuch that it reflected accurately the objections to public expenditure. But an alert minority of professional experts and philanthropic laymen could not hope to convert the majority from the prevalent conviction that a direct commercial profit should accrue from any corporate activity.[12] The Committee condemned the mode of drainage and recommended the appointment of another committee vested with the authority to implement the provisions of the Nuisance Removal Act of 1846. It also recommended that the Boards of Highways for St. Mary's Parish and Sneinton Parish should consider the improvement of drainage between the two, and that with a view to improving the Leen drainage a comprehensive

plan of all sewers in the town should be made through the collaboration of the three Highway Boards. It stressed the desirability
of paving and sewering all streets, of trapping grates opening into
public sewers, and the immediate necessity of bringing public health
within the scope of its activities:

> A great responsibility rests upon this council until it has taken
> the best steps that can be suggested to rescue their fellow
> townsmen from evils so destructive to their physical and mental
> welfare.[13]

Anxious to remedy the filth and squalor of Nottingham streets,
and at the same time to avoid the interference of the Central Board
of Health in London,[14] the report of the Committee and its recommendations were adopted unanimously and a Sanitary Committee
was appointed to act. With commendable energy the Committee of
ten immediately set about the enormous task of cleaning up the
town, aided in their exertions by the Inspector of Nuisances, William
Richards, who was appointed under the Act. Two years later the
Committee reported on its activities. Reluctant to resort to legal
force, its members had acted in a 'prudent and persuasive manner',
anxious to avoid direct conflict with the jealousies, prejudices, or
private interests of either property owners, their agents, or the occupiers. The emphasis was very definitely upon the 'amicable adjustment of the interests of all', a policy which, according to the Committee's report, necessitated only a few magistrates' decisions. The
Committee was extremely careful lest it should provoke the interference of the Central Board, and 'moral pressure' was preferred to
legal compulsion in carrying plans into effect.[15] On a meagre outlay
of £150 during three years, thirty-four dwellings situated over
privies and ashpits were gutted or taken down (one of the Committee purchased property privately for the very purpose of carrying out such alterations), and several sets of privies were removed
from beneath dwelling houses and reconstructed elsewhere; pig styes
were taken from nearby dwellings, and a dozen courts and alleys
drained and paved. But the reluctance to incur expenditure necessarily retarded progress.

In 1849 cholera struck again in various parts of the country and
the modest activities of the Sanitary Committee must be accounted
responsible for Nottingham's almost total escape.[16] Though the
Sheffield Sanitary Committee received the congratulations of London
reformers on its action following the appearance of cholera in that
town,[17] the exertions of the Nottingham Sanitary Committee, which
had begun its work two years before the epidemic occurred, received
only local recognition.[18] To publicize the success of its efforts printed
reports of its progress were circulated, as if to justify its petition

against the powers which the Public Health Act of 1848 gave to the Central Board of Health in London. The Sanitary Committee and the Council hoped that by showing that the local body was capable of acting effectively, the report would vindicate their policy of complete independence from the central authority.[19] By 1848, however, although there were more than sixty towns in the country whose populations exceeded sixty thousand, barely a half dozen had made serious attempts to tackle the problem of public health.[20]

In its report the Sanitary Committee concluded that the reasons explaining the town's amazing escape from the cholera outbreak in 1849 were a constant and plentiful supply of good water; clean, dry, and well-drained streets and courts; a considerable extent of extramural burial ground; an active foresight on the part of the authorities and the provision of prompt medical aid. The report added that a co-operative public had rendered its task easier. The Committee was also convinced that, owing to its exertions and to the publicity which they received, the townspeople were beginning to absorb the rudiments of sanitary education.[21] The lodging houses, one of the strongholds of insanitary life and a principal channel through which disease and fever spread, were brought under the Committee's control in 1851 when the Corporation adopted the Common Lodging Houses Act.[22] Under this Act all common lodging houses were registered with the local authority which was also responsible for their inspection. Although the number of Irish immigrants living in Nottingham was small, many of them were to be found in such houses, huddled together in paltry dormitories without proper ventilation and light.

The Sanitary Committee continued its exertions to improve public health in the town, and between 1849 and 1852 sixty-three dwelling-houses or sets of dwellings built over privies were taken down and removed, seventy-three sets of privies were either modified or completely reconstructed, thirty-seven sets of new privies were erected and several lanes improved. Many enclosed courts were paved and drained, seven public lavatories erected, accumulations of manure were continually being removed, and unhealthy dwellings were cleansed and whitewashed.[23] The reason for submitting the report of 1852 was the threat of an inspection by officials of the Board of Health in London. Formed in 1848 under the first Public Health Act, it had received powers to appoint Local Boards of Health in towns where the death rate exceeded twenty-three per thousand. The local boards were to work under the direction of the Central Board, and it was this surrender of local autonomy which caused resentment and which precipitated considerable opposition to the bogy of 'centralization'.[24] The report of 1852 was intended to fore-stall intervention from London after the Council had received a letter from the Board on the high rate of Nottingham's mortality, pointing out that between 1844 and 1850 it had exceeded the critical rate of twenty-three by an average of three points.[25] The report on the Sanitary Committee's work together with the plea that the beneficial effects of enclosure upon public health were soon expected to show, persuaded the Board not to interfere. Further threat of intervention disappeared in 1854 with the demise of the Central Board. Four years later, when the Local Government Act made it possible for local authorities to obtain increased powers for the purpose of carrying out town improvements, the Council quickly transformed itself into a Local Board of Health and in that capacity assumed powers which had formerly belonged to the parochial Highway Boards.[26]

In the same year, the Council issued regulations which were to be observed in the erection of private dwellings.[27] Further regulations were stipulated in provisions included in the Enclosure Act. Houses built on enclosed land were not to adjoin others on more than two sides, and must be provided with a garden or yard of not less than thirty square feet, three bedrooms, a lavatory, dust-pit, and water supply, and walls not less than nine inches thick.[28] Many people, including the editor of the *Review,* considered that these stipulations required the erection of houses which working men would be unable to afford, and this would have been true had the standards been adhered to. In fact, some five hundred back-to-back houses and trade premises lacking adequate drainage facilities were built in the Meadows in the fifties, and while London looked to the Metropolitan Association for improving the dwellings of the industrial classes and the Society for Improving Conditions of the Labouring Classes to help alleviate her housing problem, in Nottingham, as in some other large provincial towns, private building societies and other local bodies tried to ease the situation.[29] In 1852 a group of councillors and their colleagues had formed a branch of the Association for the Improvement of Dwellings of the Industrial Classes. The honorary secretary of the Association was Richards, the Sanitary Inspector, and after the purchase of about five thousand square yards of newly enclosed land off St. Ann's Well Road, ninety dwellings were erected.[30] However, the insistence on charging rents at market levels (three shillings weekly) meant that these houses were beyond the means of the lowest income groups.

The principle that measures should be economically sound irrespective of their social benefits was subscribed to by a vast Victorian Liberal public, and this view permeated municipal government during the period. Even so, in 1851 Nottingham was already levying an improvement rate of 2½d. in the pound.[31] Under the Local Government Act, the repair, scavenging, and improvement of the highways, the widening and formation of streets, the fire service, and all sanitary improvements were to be financed from one general district rate. When it was first imposed in 1860 the total rate was set at 1s. 1d. to produce an income of £11,176; in 1864 the rate was increased to 1s. 6d., rising to 1s. 8d. in 1870.[32] As the amount and value of property assessed for local taxation grew, the revenue from the steadily rising rate grew more rapidly than the rate increases indicate. The value of rateable property in the three parishes of Nottingham rose from £161,000 in 1853 to £264,008 in 1866 and to £448,166 in 1878. But so long as rates were limited to real property, and so long as the rise in rental values of occupied real property failed to reflect the growth of real wealth due to industry and commerce, ratepayers were likely to bear most of the cost of municipal progress.[33] Income from the Chamber and Bridge Estates, market stallages, and fines, which in the fifties and sixties amounted to about one-third of the total income, made some contribution towards meeting the expenses of government and town improvement. But as in the cities of Bristol and Liverpool, whose much greater corporate wealth permitted their corporations more latitude in their expenditures, the level of the rates were a perpetual source for dispute, while the Ratepayers' Association exerted its influence towards a policy of strict economy in local government.[34]

The dominance of the philosophy of civic economy was partly reflected in the very gradual rise in the general district rate until after the extension of the borough boundaries in 1877, while the determination to prevent rates from rising produced competition between the various committees delegated to conduct affairs in different spheres. Thus in its Annual Report for 1869 the Highways Committee complained that for many years the preoccupation with checking the rise in rates had resulted in a reduction in its share of corporate income, but at the same time the Committee had been under increasing pressure from the Council to improve streets and sewerage more rapidly.[35] Nottingham's indebtedness increased from the middle of the century, and the Corporation debt, which amounted to £4,700 in 1851, rose to £36,130 in 1861, to £132,713 in 1865, and reached £161,486 four years later.[36] By 1872 the amount of money handled by the Council had increased fourfold in the previous fifteen years, and most of this growth in Corporation indebtedness was due to the sudden increase in street improvement.

After the completion of Albert Street in 1846 the Council's attention seems to have been absorbed by the process of enclosure.

In 1848 the Council Enclosure Committee recommended the Enclosure Commissioners to form a street from the north end of York Street to the Mapperley Hills; the result was the construction of Gorsey Close Road, completed in 1854, which became subsequently Woodborough Road. The Commissioners were also urged to build a street across the Meadows to link Trent Bridge with Carrington Street Bridge and the new Albert Street, but this was not completed before 1860.[37] The years immediately following the opening of Albert Street in 1846 brought depression in industry, but the boom of the early fifties encouraged new proposals for town improvement. Expanding trade increased traffic congestion, rateable values tended to rise, and as the long term economic outlook for the town improved, the town's businessmen councillors were less likely to be deterred from securing loans on mortgage. In 1854 the Improvement Committee proposed the formation of a new wide street between Station Street on the town's southern edge, across the main commercial district to Clumber Street, which approached Market Place at its north eastern corner. The cost of this thoroughfare was estimated by Hawksley and Wood, the town's consultant surveyors, at about £85,000.[38] The project was shortlived, for a meeting of ratepayers refused to sanction such colossal expenditure; the seven other less expensive proposals for widening a number of arterial roads were not shelved. When these were considered in 1857 only one proposal, that for widening St. Mary's Gate from Keyes Walk to High Pavement, met with sufficient opposition as to cause its exclusion from the Nottingham Improvement Bill.

After three years of preparation under the dominating influence of Richard Birkin, Chairman of the Improvement Committee, the Bill was drawn up in 1857.[39] Immediately following the adoption of the Local Government Act in 1859, which granted the powers the Council sought in their Improvement Bill, Birkin—as Chairman of the Town Improvement Committee, which was no longer an *ad hoc* Council committee—began to arrange for the construction of Victoria Street, a thoroughfare fifty feet wide which ran from Carlton Street to the Poultry, replacing Chandlers' Lane. At the same time the committee initiated a forty feet wide street from Carlton Street to Fletcher Gate and Warser Gate, Old Queen Street replacing the very narrow Queen Street.[40] Bottle Lane, which measured only nine feet across at its narrowest point, was widened sufficiently in 1863 to allow two carriages to pass. Sheep Lane and Lister Gate were widened in 1864, and the following year Market Street was opened on the previous site of old Sheep Lane. In 1869 a plan was adopted to widen the east end of Pelham Street.[41]

The expansion of Nottingham made growing demands upon its administrators. Since the adoption of the Local Government Act in 1859 the Corporation could command extensive powers for carrying out local improvements, for it was enabled to become a Local Board of Health to which was transferred powers previously exercised by the Highway Board. A committee, appointed by the Council, investigated the working of the various committees then in existence and recommended that in order to secure greater economy and efficiency they should be reorganized, reduced in size and increased in number. Under the revised arrangements there was to be the Watch Committee of nine, whose function it was to enforce good order and manage the police force, fire brigade, and hackney carriages; the Chamber Committee of seven, to manage the Chamber Estate; the Bridge Committee of seven, to manage the Bridge Estate; the Baths and Wash-houses Committee of seven, to manage these establishments; the Sanitary Committee of seven, to take charge of drainage, water supply, privy accommodation, and cleanliness of dwellings and other buildings, to take down, rebuild, or repair ruinous and dangerous buildings, to inspect food and slaughter houses, license and inspect common lodging houses, close cellars and buildings unfit for habitation and prevent smoke; the Highway Committee of nine, to take charge of the paving, flagging, channelling, levelling, repairing, sewering, and cleansing of public streets, also to water streets, remove obstructions in streets and impound cattle; the Town Improvement Committee of nine, to attend to the levels and formation of new streets, to widen existing streets, to construct new buildings, to name streets and number houses; the Enclosure Committee of seven, to take charge of public walks and pleasure grounds, to maintain the same and provide new ones; the Markets and Fairs Committee of five, to attend to Markets and Fairs and regulate the tolls and stallages payable for the same; the Finance and Bye-laws Committee to examine all accounts. The three new bodies were the Markets and Fairs, Highway, and Town Improvements Committees.[42]

Under the requirements of the Local Government Act of 1858 Marriott Ogle Tarbotton, aged twenty-seven from Wakefield, was appointed as permanent borough surveyor. This marked the beginning of thirty years of service by one of the town's most valuable professional officers.[43] His first action in office was to draw up a report on the problem of sewage and river pollution in Nottingham, with special reference to the town's sanitary condition, for despite its claims to success in preventing an outbreak of cholera in the town in 1849, cases had since been reported in Nottingham in 1850, 1854, and again in 1865.[44] In each instance measures were taken to prevent the disease from spreading and the outbreak was confined to one or two neighbourhoods; but apart from emergency measures undertaken under the immediate threats of cholera, the Sanitary Committee had pursued a policy of piecemeal improvement in the manner which they had adopted in 1847, using its added powers granted under the Nuisance Removal Act of 1855. Although the Highway Committee was responsible for the condition and drainage of streets, the Sanitary Committee found itself unable to carry out its own responsibilities in ensuring adequate cleanliness, drainage, water supply, and privy accommodation of dwellings, without becoming involved in the larger question of the town's general drainage and sewerage system. The Highway Committee likewise considered this to be one of the town's most pressing problems from the standpoint of public health.

In its report for 1858, after pointing out that

'the foul and offensive state of the water in parts of the Nottingham Canal' was 'mainly caused by the water of the River Leen which is contaminated by the sewage of the districts lying to the west of this town being carried into the Canal',

the Sanitary Committee drew the Council's attention to the greater powers which could be obtained for local improvement under the Local Government Act passed in that year.[45] It is quite probable that members of the Sanitary Committee hoped to benefit from the guidance and advice of a Medical Officer of Health, an optional appointment under the 1858 Act. But despite the recommendation of a special committee of the Council which had considered the Act's provisions, such an appointment was not made.[46] However, the appointment of a full time surveyor in the person of Tarbotton proved to be of considerable value to the Sanitary and Highway Committees, and in 1860, a year after Hawksley had reported on drainage and sewerage on the line of the Leen, Tarbotton submitted his first report. Deploring the absence of an accurate plan of the town and neighbourhood which showed the levels of works and sewerage, his report showed in particular the defective condition of the Leen culvert, which had first been covered in 1830, to which the high mortality rates of Narrow Marsh and Leen-side were attributed. Four years later, a special committee set up to consider taking action in cooperation with other local bodies agreed with Tarbotton who had written:

The neighbourhood of Nottingham shows the mischief resulting from the present state of things . . . impure liquid matter from the manufactures and population of Old Lenton flows into the River Trent about a mile and a half above the point at which a large part of the water supply of Nottingham is now drawn . . .

P

the River Leen which passes through this town . . . is now foul
and offensive by reason of its conveying part of the sewage of
Nottingham and the whole of the sewage of an extensive and
populous higher district over which the authorities have no
control and flows with the rest of the sewage of Nottingham
into the parish of Sneinton and thence into the River Trent.[47]

Tarbotton's Report had also revealed the lack of efficient sewerage in the Meadows locality, for which the Enclosure Commissioners
were mainly responsible. Many streets in this low marshy area were
without drainage or pavement,

the streets are raised above the flood level but many of the
lower storeys of the houses which are used as dwelling rooms
are not raised above the ordinary level of the ground and are
consequently on the level at which the sewers must be laid
and are liable to be flooded and rendered permanently damp.[48]

When the Enclosure Commissioners made their final award in 1865,
some of the streets in the hands of the Commissioners still remained
unfinished. Anxious that the streets be dealt with, the Highway
Committee pressed for an Act to end the power of the Commissioners and to enable the local Board to complete the public streets
and force completion of private roads, levying property occupiers to
defray expenses. Provisions included in the Nottingham Improvement Act of 1867 allowed this plan to take effect.[49] Four years later,
having provided sewers to serve the public streets in the enclosed
area, the Highway Committee turned its attention to the completion
of internal sewerage in the older part of the borough.

By this time, the idea of establishing an integrated sewerage
system for the Nottingham area had become firmly established in
the minds of Tarbotton and members of the Highway and Sanitary Committees. In 1864 Nottingham and Birmingham sent a
joint deputation to the Home Secretary to urge the creation of
regional drainage boards with sufficient powers necessary to prevent
river pollution, and to arrange for sewage to be deposited at sewage
farms.[50] The general problem of drainage was again thrown into
relief by an outbreak of cholera in the town in 1865 and a local
typhoid epidemic in 1868. Beginning a chain of events similar to
that which had occurred in Birmingham ten years before,[51] the
initiative of Earl Manvers and John Musters Esq., the principal
proprietors of lands bordering on the Trent on Nottingham's eastern
boundaries, forced the town authorities to act. Following Tarbotton's
recommendations, the Council had approved the preparation of
plans to avoid the use of the outfall above Wilford, bringing the
sewage from Lenton through Nottingham via existing sewers, which
then discharged the town's sewage into the River Trent at Sneinton.

In 1868 the agents of Manvers and Musters complained that the volume of sewage entering the Trent from Nottingham was detrimental to the health and comfort of the inhabitants of Sneinton, Colwick, and Holme Pierrepoint, and that it had injurious effects upon their own estates.[52] Because the new plan permitted the continued flow of sewage into the Trent, the riparian owners resolved to reinforce their protests with the threat of legal action. Their agents advised the Nottingham Board of Health to obtain the co-operation of other neighbouring boards in adopting a better scheme for sewage disposal. Unless, after a reasonable time had been allowed, the Nottingham Board were able to effect a remedy, the matter would be taken to the courts.[53]

After a second communication from the landowners three years later the Highway Committee invited the local authorities of the parishes of Radford, Lenton, Basford, and later Bulwell to join with the Board of Health in Nottingham in discussing the question of pollution in the Trent and Leen rivers, for which each local body bore some responsibility. As a result of this meeting a Nottingham District Sewage Utilization Board was established uniting the several authorities, while in the same year the Nottingham and Leen District Sewage Bill was framed and drafted. In 1872 the Bill 'for securing the purification and preventing the pollution of the Trent and Leen' received the royal assent and became law.[54] The Board immediately began to tackle the problems which arose from the different methods of sewage disposal in use by the smaller authorities, and, by using the powers contained in the Act, to put into operation the plan for making a system of sewage irrigation to farm lands at Stoke Bardolph. The sewage farm at Stoke Bardolph opened in 1880. The circumstances surrounding the Council's action may be deplored, but when the responses of other municipal bodies in similar situations are compared with those of Nottingham and Birmingham the achievements of the two midland towns are impressive.[55]

Owing to the danger of frequent flooding in the lower parts of the town the foul state of the Trent was another matter which caused concern, and when the construction of a new bridge came under discussion in 1868 Tarbotton stressed the importance of altering the site of the bridge.[56] The question of building a new Trent Bridge had been opened in 1852, a year of serious flooding. In that year the Estates Committee had brought the dilapidated state of the existing bridge to the attention of the Council, but when civil engineer Sir William Cubitt submitted his report, recommending the erection of a new bridge which would cost between £25,000 and £35,000, the Council dropped the matter. Fifteen years later Tarbotton received a request to report on the bridge. He stated that the bridge was inadequate to cope with the rapidly increasing traffic and that the structure was so unsatisfactory that repairs and alterations to improve its condition would be impossible. So unequivocal was his report and so forceful his conclusion that a new bridge must be built, that within three years the new Trent Bridge, which was located lower down the river than the old one, was already carrying traffic.[57] Tarbotton's estimate of £30,000 as the cost of construction, added to an outstanding debt of more than £150,000, increased the financial difficulties of the Council, and was one factor which led the Council to reconsider the general question of municipal finance.

The Nottingham Improvement Act of 1867 included clauses securing the transfer of funds of the Flood Road Trustees which were due to the Corporation under an earlier agreement. Other clauses enabled the Council to increase its borrowing powers in order to pay off debts incurred by the Enclosure Commissioners, as well as to meet expenses of road and sewer construction.[58] The town's expansion which accelerated during the unprecedented boom of 1869 to 1873, and the outbreak of cholera in Nottingham in 1871–2 made increasingly evident the need for much greater powers if the Council was to make serious efforts to tackle the town's public health problems, to improve the road system, to coordinate urban development with neighbouring districts, and to improve recreational amenities. As early as 1842 a member of the respected Nottingham family of solicitors, William W. Enfield, who succeeded his father as Town Clerk in 1845, had stated the view:

> While towns are allowed to raise large rates for paving, draining, watching, and lighting the streets, and for houses of correction . . . why should they not be enabled to raise limited rates for the mental and bodily improvement, and education, and entertainment of the inhabitants, by providing places of recreation, museums, libraries, school rooms &c?[59]

However, this vision of a civic renaissance was slow in becoming accepted by a sufficient number of councillors to transform it into reality. The various committees still found difficulty enough in persuading the Council and the Finance Committee to accept their recommendations concerning expenditure on health and street improvements.

The Finance Committee which, like that in Liverpool, consisted of the chairmen of all other standing committees, was in the strongest position to influence the town's development.[60] As committee chairmen tended also to be aldermen, the composition of the aldermanic body was an important determinant of the quality of municipal government. From the establishment of the Finance Committee in 1860, its members included Aldermen Birkin, Cullen, Vickers, Page, and Reckless—some of the town's leading lace merchants and manufacturers who combined with their business abilities a measure of public spirit. In the same category were Aldermen Heymann, Felkin, Herbert, and Biddle, hosiery manufacturers Heard and Carver, Hollins the cotton spinner, and the colliery and brickyard owner, Thomas North. It has been said of Sheffield's industrialists that 'the range of their gifts was narrow',[61] and that most Birmingham councillors during this period were recruited from 'the unprogressive tradesmen class—many of them worthy in their way but of limited ideas . . .'; they were men unaccustomed to dealing with large sums of money, a feature which was reflected in their approach to town government.[62] Neither of these remarks could have been made concerning Nottingham's business *élite* which, encouraged by national legislation, during the third quarter of the century left its mark upon the town. One important factor which helps to explain the quality of local leadership was the tradition of public service which, though limited in scope, had been handed down from the old Corporation; membership of the old governing body carried with it a measure of social prestige which was lacking in the councils of Birmingham and some other industrial towns.[63] However, in other historic corporate towns, like Liverpool[64] for example, it seems that tradition and an accompanying prestige similar to that which was to be found in Nottingham survived political changes, and ensured that men of ability would serve on the Council.

This special neutralizing influence of tradition upon local politics would seem to have been of greater significance for government in Liverpool than in Nottingham. For in Nottingham a Whig Party caucus, controlled by radical Liberals, continued to dominate the Council after municipal reform—although repercussions of the poor law controversy after 1838 had increased the numerical strength of Tories on the Council until in 1844 they came within one vote of securing the election of seven new aldermen which would then have given the Tories a majority on the Council.[65] Thereafter, the Tories lost ground and the Whig-Liberal caucus resumed its dominant position in municipal government; moreover, so long as the Council elected the aldermen, the Whiggish aldermanic domination continued. Party political rivalry, therefore, was a less powerful influence upon the course of municipal progress in Nottingham than pressure from the ratepayers (whose sanction was needed before the Council could take legislative action) and the various sections of opinion within the governing party. Not even the appearance at the hustings of Nottingham's Independent M.P., the popular Sir Robert Clifton, during the municipal elections of 1865 when he spoke in opposition to the ruling clique, could overthrow the local caucus,[66] and not until the election of an enlarged Council for the newly extended borough did a serious reduction in the monopolistic control of municipal government in Nottingham seem remotely possible.

One might speculate that such a situation, where political control lay firmly in the hands of one party, and where, for the most part, municipal affairs were allowed to cut across party lines while a handful of leading local figures directed policy, produced better government than would have otherwise occurred. In Liverpool, municipal progress largely coincided with periods of stability when political controversy was minimal,[67] while in Birmingham the conviction grew that

> whatever the disadvantages of non-party government in local affairs, Birmingham needed party direction to destroy sloth and construct new policies.[68]

But party control by itself could not ensure progressive government without the existence of an enlightened, able, and vigorous party leadership, capable of initiating new policies appropriate for the solution of local problems, and willing to respond to stimulus and encouragement from national legislation and central authorities.

Significant municipal progress in Nottingham dated from the fifties, after the Enclosure Act had presented the town with opportunities which other manufacturing centres might envy. Already in 1833, for example, an observer in Sheffield had reported that that town was 'singularly destitute of anything in the nature of public walks or space.'[69] The opportunities for planned development of the newly-enclosed areas in Nottingham were almost totally neglected, though some of the provisions in the Act reflected a measure of enlightenment on the part of the Council. Later, through the adoption of the Local Government Act in 1859, Nottingham Town Council also showed its awareness of its responsibilities in promoting 'the health, comfort and improvement of the town'[70] while the subsequent Improvement Act of 1867 was evidence that improvement would continue. In the field of recreation, provisions included in the Enclosure Act had secured for the town parks and open spaces, but not until 1867, after twenty-six other towns had established public libraries under the Free Libraries Act of 1850, did Nottingham resolve to follow their example.

Another indication that the scope of municipal government was widening was to be seen in the growing number of towns which were acquiring their local water and gas supplies; by 1870 no fewer than sixty-nine local authorities owned their own waterworks,[71] the enterprise for which Nottingham Town Council had made the first of several unsuccessful bids in 1854. The year 1872 saw the preparation of another Improvement Bill which sought powers for compulsory purchase, consolidation of the borough and district rates, the taking over of town lighting from the *ad hoc* Town Lighting Committee, and the purchase of land outside the borough for recreation purposes; it also included provisions dealing with improvements in housing and sanitation.[72] The new powers which the Council sought to acquire under the Improvement Bill—the creation of a regional sewage board, the construction of the new Trent Bridge, the establishment of a public library, and renewed efforts to acquire the town's gas supply—together indicated the scope and direction of the Council's activities in the following twenty-five years. The inclusion in the Nottingham Improvement Act of 1874 of powers enabling the Corporation to create debentures and issue stock[73] was also an indication that lack of finance was not to prevent the progress of Nottingham's civic transformation.

In their social character the men who led the Council in early and mid-Victorian Nottingham differed from their predecessors who had controlled the unreformed Corporation for so many years; most of the men whom the new industrialists employed also differed in many respects from those who worked for the gentlemen manufacturers. Until about 1860 these four sections of the community were the principal socio-economic groups whose existence accounted for the town's unique social structure during this period, containing, as it did, elements in common with both Birmingham and Manchester.[74] Like Manchester, Nottingham possessed something akin to a capitalist aristocracy, and before the adoption of the factory system in the hosiery trade the gulf which separated the framework knitter and merchant hosier was often much greater than that between the Manchester cotton manufacturer and his workmen at the mill. Reference in the trade to the 'respectable gentlemen hosiers' is indicative of the social standing of the large hosiery manufacturers, while master framework knitters who employed journeymen were much nearer in status to the journeymen framework knitters than to the hosiers. This social hierarchy reflected the economic fact that whereas it was sometimes possible for a framework knitter to become a middleman or bag hosier, prior to the changes in technology and organization during the middle decades, hosiers were recruited from a narrow social stratum. In the machine-made lace industry the social distance between employers and workmen was much less than in the hosiery trade, and the free social intercourse that occurred among the many small lace manufacturers, independent lace makers and lace operatives, machine builders, framesmiths and mechanics was similar to that which arose out of somewhat similar economic relationships at Birmingham where, as in Nottingham, with a modicum of initiative and a small amount of capital, the skilled workman could become self-employed or an employer of other men. A comparison between the social origins of hosiers and lace manufacturers in the middle decades reflects the differing degrees of social mobility present in the two industries. After the fifties, as hosiery production moved into factories and as the proportion of the local population employed in the lace industry increased, opportunities for social advancement improved, though at the same time the trend towards factory production in one section of the lace industry, as well as in the hosiery and engineering industries, influenced the town's social structure, bringing it some degree closer to that of Manchester. Two more factors which influenced social relationships in Nottingham were the importance of women in local industries and the strength, especially among the middle classes, of nonconformist religion.

It is only possible to speculate whether the employment of large numbers of females endowed the women of the town with greater independence of spirit as well as economic freedom. William Felkin held the view that the presence of so many working women in the town was having detrimental effects upon family life, and commented on the unfitness of many young women to become wives and mothers after having worked all their lives, knowing nothing of running a home and bringing up a family.[75] These fears were echoed by other public figures, while some attributed other social evils to the large amount of female and child labour in the town. Archdeacon Wilkins, Absolem Barnett, and a local police inspector testified to the large amount of prostitution and general immorality present in the town, especially among juveniles. In Barnett's view a principal cause of 'demoralization' was the ease with which young persons of both sexes could mingle together in the streets at night after leaving the workshops, and the almost total absence of parental control. Barnett added:

> in many instances, a portion of the earnings allowed to young persons, affords the means of indulging irregular desires. Another circumstance which causes the children and young persons to go into the streets is the crowded and wretched state of their houses.[76]

Police inspector Samuel Wilkinson too deplored the unchaperoned association of young persons employed as threaders and winders at all hours of the night; and he, like Barnett, drew attention to the large number of juvenile prostitutes and thieves. He argued that there was a direct relationship between the poor state of trade and the level of these particular crimes.[77] Wilkinson placed great stress upon a general lack of religious principles and education as causative factors:

> Certainly at least one third of this population have no moral and no religious feelings whatever: grossly ignorant (*sic*) and consequently very profligate. They have had no education; they go to no place of worship; they are kept in restraint only by the strong arm of the law, and live without God in the world.[78]

The truth of his contention that the mass of the labouring section of the community disregarded religious worship was borne out by the religious census of 1851 which showed that in most manufacturing cities, churches and chapels relied upon the middle classes for their support. However, in Nottingham, where the index of attendance was 57·7 (a figure surpassed only by Leicester among towns of comparable or larger size)[79] religion might conceivably have exerted more than a merely marginal influence in promoting harmonious relations between men of humble origins, who were aspiring to a higher social status through wealth, and members of the town's old and respected families. Congregations which included merchant hosiers, bankers, men from the professions, and lace manufacturers were important social forces which influenced social organization. People from this section of the population, together with a number of Jews and persons without religious affiliations, were also responsible for enriching town life by their participation in the town's social activities.

Outdoor recreation could be enjoyed by people of all classes, and during the first half of the century few town dwellers were so fortunate in this respect as those who lived in Nottingham. It was this feature of early and mid-Victorian Nottingham which often impressed the town's visitors and was a source of local pride.

> 'How delightful it is', wrote one contemporary, 'when wearied with the bustle and noise of business to escape from the narrow streets filled almost to suffocation with buildings, and to spring over the bridge near the Navigation Inn, bursting at once upon nature, arrayed in her richest verdure, and the spirit refreshed . . .'[80]

When Samuel Collinson, a stockbroker, came to live in Nottingham in 1845, an evening walk soon became his regular habit.[81] After this date, however, when the commons were enclosed and the land had been acquired for building development, the town's abundant open spaces for recreation began to dwindle. Nevertheless, the opportunity to retain some land for public enjoyment was not ignored, for the Nottingham General Enclosure Act of 1845 included provisions under which specified areas were to be set aside for this purpose. The Town Council was henceforth responsible for the maintenance of seventy-seven acres of the Forest for race course, cricket grounds, and walks on the edge of the town.[82] In the Meadows the Council formed the Queen's Walk which was described by Wylie as 'a right royal avenue', and like other recreation walks it quickly became a favourite place for a stroll. Part of the land earmarked for recreation was turned into the town's first public park, which, when it opened in 1852 as the Arboretum, covered twelve acres of land in close proximity to the town centre. It was designed by the same person who had laid out the Victoria Park in London, and it included refreshment rooms built in the style of the Crystal Palace as well as gardens and walks. Soon it was a centre for military and quadrille band concerts, and various kinds of outdoor exhibitions and displays.[83] Five years after its opening the admission charges were abolished after fierce public debate,[84] and in the same year Samuel Collinson noted with regret that as a result of this step 'the Arboretum seems to be merely a huge playground for young girls and boys'. In 1858 another public recreation ground was opened near Millstone Lane, and Lewis Heymann furnished the park with a gymnastic apparatus as a gift to the town. St. Michael's recreation ground was completed in 1860, and in 1873 plans were drawn up for making walks and a public garden on the northern Trent embankment.[85]

For those people in search of exercise and solitude rather than excitement, dispersion was more likely to bring pleasure. A popular spot for artisans and their wives at Easter and Whitsun was Clifton Grove where, 'to the tune of fiddle, harp, or accordian, they (would) trip the light fantastic', and several decades were to pass before the journeys to such haunts as Wilford, Beeston Meadows, Wollaton, or Newstead would lose their rural character.[86] Indeed, the advent of the railway encouraged the practice, followed by Samuel Collinson and his wife, of travelling by train to a pleasant spot and returning thence on foot. The Railway Companies were quick to recognize the popular appeal of the train excursion. As soon as the Nottingham to Leicester link was completed, in 1840 a committee of the Nottingham Mechanics Institute met with the cooperation from the Company in discussing arrangements for an excursion outing.[87] For half the regular fare the Company ran special trains for guaranteed parties and in the summer of 1845, in addition to the special excursions to London and coastal resorts, the Midland Company ran a trip to Calais and Boulogne, the train leaving Nottingham early on Monday morning and returning the following Thursday. Excursions of a different kind were also becoming more common after 1850. In 1865 Hine and Mundella, directors of the Nottingham Manufacturing Company, introduced their policy of treating employees annually by chartering an excursion train for a trip to Thurgarton and Hoveringham ferry house. Here several hundred people were entertained with brass band music, and after taking part in sports events they dined before returning to Nottingham.[88] It became the custom for other firms to treat employees in a similar fashion, and the ferries at Hazelford and Wilford were also popular locations for the works outing. One of the most exotic of these excursions was that of Messrs. Dunnington, a firm of hosiery manufacturers. It took the form of a weekend gypsy party at which the participants camped in tents, sat around camp fires, danced and sang. The next day, dinner at the Smith's Arms in Lenton followed a cricket match.[89]

The popularity of cricket in Nottingham had grown tremendously since 1815, one indication of this being the publication in 1830 of 'A Correct Account of all the Cricket Matches played by the Nottingham Old Cricket Club from 1771 to 1829 Inclusive,' a fifty-three page pamphlet which sold for a shilling. Reprinted in 1835, when it was also brought up to date, and again in 1853, when J. F. Sutton added accounts of the games played since 1835, the manual included an account of the game played against Sheffield in 1822 when Nottingham had fielded twice the number of their opponents, but later the town's reputation appears to have improved, and by the middle thirties Nottingham was considered by some to possess one of the best provincial clubs in the country.[90] In 1835, the first year of the regular county matches, the poet, William Howitt, was among the several thousand spectators who watched eleven of the Nottingham club play the Sussex eleven. The game took place at the cricket ground which was situated within the race course on the Forest. Howitt described the assembled crowd on the grassy slope which overlooked the ground:

> all up the forest-hill were scattered booths and tents with flags flying, fires burning, pots boiling, ale barrels standing, and asses, carts, and people . . .

The cries of vendors selling apples, nuts, and ginger beer, and the appropriate noises signifying delight or despair were the only sounds to break the normal hush of suspense which prevailed throughout the game.[91] Four years later, in 1839, the location for the town's important matches became the new cricket ground by the Trent Bridge Inn. It was established by the Inn's proprietor, William Clarke, whose venture was doubtless intended to boost trade as well as to sustain his own interest in cricket. Clarke, Nottingham's great slow bowler, was the first to organize and captain a representative Nottinghamshire County eleven and he also played for an all-England team.[93]

In the 1850s Nottingham was the home of cricketers of a sufficiently high calibre to represent England; the town could also point to its popular prize fighter, William Thompson, alias Bendigo, who by defeating Tom Paddock became the English champion. After his retirement he drank heavily, but after his conversion by a temperance preacher Thompson himself addressed local temperance meetings. Such a colourful figure could hardly fail to stimulate interest in the sport of prize fighting.[93] Less spectacular, but nevertheless an endless subject for conversation, were the most recent exploits of the enthusiastic angling fraternity, for fishing continued to enjoy enormous popularity along the Trent; in 1858 William Bailey caused a stir in fishing circles when, in two and a half hours on a cold April morning, he landed twenty-two fish weighing a total of sixty-five pounds.[94] A feat which aroused similar interest was that performed by Charles Westhall, one of the town's leading athletes who, in 1848, covered seven miles in slightly less than fifty-eight minutes to win a purse of £20. With the intention of promoting amateur athletics, in the same year he completed the distance of twenty miles in three hours.[95] Indeed, both walking and running sports gained in popularity during the middle decades, the athletics meetings which were held at Trent Bridge attracting large crowds. The desire to perform as well as to watch sport which did not require the same degree of energy as foot racing, helps to explain the formation of an archery ground within Nottingham Park in 1867, and also the success of the town's bowling clubs.[96] Moreover, as most bowling clubs were located at public houses, refreshment enhanced the pleasures of exercise, and the sporting inquisitions after the games had ended could proceed over jugs of ale. At the Wellington Bowling Club, which was adjacent to the Castle on the banks of the river Leen, the ancient caverns in the Castle rock were transformed into dining rooms where skittles, quoits, and other equipment for indoor sports were provided for patrons' entertainment.[97]

Horse racing was still the sport of persons of high estate, though it was well supported by people from less elevated social ranks, and on two days twice each year in spring and summer, the Nottingham races continued to attract nobility and gentry to the town. Under the Nottingham Enclosure Act the management of the races and the course, which was on the hitherto unenclosed Forest, was held in trust for the public by the Council. Henceforward, the races were held under the Council's aegis, and the profits arising therefrom were devoted towards the improvement of the meetings and for the purpose of general public recreation.[98] When Samuel Collinson spent a day at the races in 1856 he noted that

> the humbler classes were much gayer than others at the race
> meeting, good humoured groups sat on the green turf, joking,
> laughing, passing round mugs of Nottingham ale . . .

Instead of the former traditional cockfights after the final race, a fireworks display was held in the Arboretum.[99] The year of Collinson's visit coincided with an attempt by the Council to end the spring meeting, but pressure from outside the Council, which included a memorial requesting that the interests of the country gentlemen should be considered, persuaded the Council to rescind the resolution.[100] More favourable was the Council's attitude towards the provision of a rifle range for the use of the Robin Hood Rifle Corps.[101] Formed in 1859, when the movement of French troops into Italy caused some apprehension in England, local volunteers came forward to drill under the command of Lieutenant Colonel Charles Ichabod Wright. The war scare passed and the Rifles became an association of men who met together for training and recreation.

For many people the climactic event in the local calendar was still Goose Fair. William Howitt recorded his impressions of Goose Fair in the thirties. Two or three days before its opening large caravans arrived in the town carrying wild beasts, theatricals, dwarfs, giants, and other 'prodigies and wonders.' Nottingham became the destination for

> 'all sorts of wild and peculiar-looking people . . . all kinds of
> strollers, beggars, gypsies, singers, dancers, players on harps,
> Indian jugglers, Punch and Judy exhibitors, and similar
> wandering artists . . .'.

Preceded by the mace bearer and to the accompaniment of trumpet fanfares, members of the Corporation marched to the market place to proclaim the opening of the Fair. The mornings were taken up with business, the afternoons were devoted to entertainment. The first afternoon was popularly called 'gig fair', because it was the custom for the 'smart people' to drive to see the pleasure fair, while the second day, according to Howitt, brought the 'very genteel' folk when one might see 'country families of good standing mingling in the moving mass of Vanity Fair.'[102] By the fifties, although the Fair lasted still for eight days and was one of the principal holidays of the year, it was rapidly becoming mainly a pleasure Fair.[103] During the 1852 Fair crowds of people who thronged the streets around the market place were entertained by the antics of clowns and hurdy-gurdy girls, and by the gyrations of a dancing bear. Theatrical groups pitched their tents in Market Place and showmen set up their booths; the Royal Caledonian Waxworks had travelled from

St. Andrews for the occasion, one of its attractions consisting of a 'Scottish triumvirate of barbarous bagpipers blowing might and main'. Bazaars offered a wide variety of goods for sale, 'from tripe and oysters to fiddlers and flageolets, toffee and ginger bread, nuts and brandy snaps,' and among the shooting galleries 'scientific machines' would test the height, weight, and strength, of a curious public.[104] Many of the residents of dwellings overlooking or in the immediate vicinity of the market place awaited the annual Fair and other visiting amusements with apprehension, as they anticipated the 'noise and disorder, destructive to all peace and comfort' which invariably accompanied the entertainers. The Town Council received complaints of

> 'annoyances, nuisances and injury to morality' caused, they argued, by the travelling theatres. 'Shows together with low theatrical exhibitions', they said, were placed 'immediately before our houses . . . We think we are correct in stating that these annoyances are usually occasioned by establishments of the most objectionable order, more especially the large penny Theatrical Booths which we believe degrading in Character and demoralising in their influence . . .'[105]

Prompted by such representations, in 1852, on the grounds that she was an 'unnatural exhibition', the magistrates refused to allow a site on the market place for the display of a bearded lady; subsequently she displayed her unusual appearance in the Assembly Rooms which, by this time, had become a social centre used by the 'humbler classes.'[106]

Balls at the Exchange still attracted genteel society, but the life of Samuel Collinson, as recounted in his diary, reminds us that people from the professions and others of similar social standing sought much of their entertainment in private, at dinner parties and at other intimate social functions. Nevertheless, it was largely due to support from these social classes, which included people with education and a comfortable income, that the cultural life of Victorian Nottingham was lively and vigorous. Thus in 1824, Thomas Wakefield, Richard Morley, Francis Hart, Ichabod Wright, and the Reverend William Butler were founder-members of the Nottingham Literary and Scientific Society whose members met in Bromley House until 1836 when the Natural History Museum moved there. Samuel Collinson was one of the group which in 1837 formed the Nottingham Literary and Debating Club, and members of the Secular Society, which was established in 1852, met each Sunday to read lectures and essays, sometimes sponsoring public lectures.[107] Similar programmes were organized by the Nottingham Literary and Philosophical Society which was established in 1869.

The Mechanics Institute, though originally intended by a number of leading middle class citizens to promote education among the town's artisans, also became a cultural centre. Here, Charles Dickens gave recitals, Fanny Kemble performed readings from Shakespeare, Jenny Lind sang, and evening concerts were popular.[108] Their popularity was due, no doubt, to the numerous amateur musical societies that existed in the town. The Anacreontic Society, which had been formed in 1792, was still flourishing sixty years later; the Harmonic Society, formed in 1829, the Choral Society, which sang at St. Mary's Church, the Amateur Musical Society, and the Sacred Harmonic Society formed in 1856, together suggest the existence of a lively circle of amateur musicians and vocalists in Nottingham whose talents the vocal classes held at the Mechanics Institute sought to encourage. The Nottingham Glee Club, established in 1836, gave regular local concerts which brought renown throughout the midland counties, and its reputation was due in a large measure to the efforts of John Farmer, a glee singer who was a great favourite with local audiences. His son, Henry Farmer, was reputed to be the best musician in the town and his compositions and concert performances won for him national acclaim.[109]

Early Victorian Nottingham, according to a contemporary, was 'the land of lyrics as well as lace,'[110] and possessed a literary circle of some merit. In addition to its historians, Gravener Henson, William Felkin, and James Orange, its writers included Robert Millhouse, Kirke White, Philip Bailey, William Power-Smith, Thomas Miller, Charles Hooton, Thomas Ragg, and William and Mary Howitt.[111] Several of the poets, whose work often appeared in the columns of the local newspapers, found inspiration in the rural beauty which surrounded the town, but Mary Howitt's novel, '*Little Coin, Much Care*', written in the early forties, demonstrates that the social and economic changes that were taking place did not (unlike the novel) pass unnoticed. The theatre in Nottingham, after considerable popularity earlier in the century, lacked support during the middle decades. Thomas Manley, one of two lessees who ran the theatre from the early years of the century until 1840,[112] had sought the support of people who enjoyed legitimate drama rather than mere spectacle, but even this conservative policy failed to overcome the moral disapproval of the dissenting middle classes.[113] Although its interior and exterior were refurnished under John Saville's management which began in 1845, in 1851 the *Nottingham Journal* referred to it as a 'much neglected place of entertainment.' In 1865 the theatre closed its doors, but they reopened two years later to admit the public to the Alhambra Music Hall. The new Theatre Royal, which had seating accommodation for twenty-two hundred people, was promoted as a joint stock company by John and William Lambert and opened in 1866.[114]

In 1840 the theatre management had requested the presence of a policeman at each nightly performance, but the demands on the town's police force during the Chartist campaigns were rising rapidly and it could ill afford to commit one of its members to permanent theatre duty.[115] In 1854, however, a newly appointed force of detectives was detailed to attend the courts so as to become familiar with the town's habitual criminals and to learn about Nottingham low life.[116]

During the middle decades of the century the gradual rise in real incomes was accompanied by a proliferation of public houses and shops which sold beer and gin. Between 1832 and 1842 the number of hotels, inns, and beer houses in existence increased from two hundred and twenty-five to two hundred and sixty-seven; by 1864 the figure was four hundred and six, and the ratio had risen from one establishment to every two hundred and twenty inhabitants, to one for every one hundred and ninety people.[117] Nottingham also had a high illegitimacy rate. Between 1850 and 1859 the proportion of illegitimate births in each one hundred births was 10·4 in Nottingham, 9·07 in Basford, and 7·98 in Radford, compared with 7·4 at Coventry and 5·05 at Birmingham.[118] Showing concern for the condition of the large numbers of young persons, especially young women, who had moved to the town from neighbouring counties in search of employment, in 1862 William Felkin commented:

> The temptations are very powerful to go into the dangerous company found in music and dancing saloons and ill-regulated licensed victuallers and beer houses of which there are too many.[119]

This development was the subject of several petitions from the town's temperance bodies appalled by the 'vast amount of drunkenness' in Nottingham. When the Public House Closing Act was passed in 1864 an enthusiastic Watch Committee, supported by pressure from other groups in the town, persuaded the Council to ignore the memorial submitted by the Licensed Victuallers' Association, and to adopt the Act; henceforward, public houses were required to close between one and four each morning.[120] Spurred on by religious and temperance bodies, during the following decade the Watch Committee, the local vanguard of Victorian respectability, redoubled its efforts to rid Nottingham of drunkenness and vice, while demands for a drastic reduction in the duration of Goose Fair began to receive the Council's serious consideration; from 1876 the Fair was limited to five days.[121]

Since 1815 the two Nottingham newspapers, the *Journal* and the

Review, had been joined by others.[122] The *Nottingham Gazette* had lasted less than a year ceasing publication in 1815, an indication that its extreme Tory views could find little support in the town. In the 1820s a number of orthodox Whigs combined to produce a newspaper which would express views less radical than those which regularly appeared in the columns of the *Review.* But the *Nottingham Herald,* whose first appearance was in 1825, lasted only two years. The *Nottingham Mercury* also commenced publication in 1825 and Thomas Wakefield, the town's leading Whig politician, and one of the newspaper's principal promoters, used the newspaper as his mouthpiece in his campaign in opposition to enclosure until shortly before his bankruptcy in 1847. Thomas Bailey purchased Wakefield's interest in the *Mercury,* but his reluctance to align himself with either major political party resulted in a rapid decline in circulation, and the newspaper was discontinued in 1852. During its early years the *Mercury* achieved a foothold in the market with a weekly circulation which in the late thirties averaged sixty thousand copies. This compared with the *Review's* circulation figure of about seventeen thousand per week, which does not appear to have suffered, in the long run, from the *Mercury's* competition, though they were both within the same broad political spectrum. The *Journal's* figures for this period were about eighteen thousand copies weekly. However, the *Mercury* editors failed to increase their paper's circulation beyond sixty thousand, except for one year in 1846; the next year the figure fell to thirty-four thousand, and in 1850 to thirty-two thousand. Indeed, both major newspapers experienced a decline in circulation during these years. The reason for the *Journal's* decline was the unpopularity of Bradshaw's decision to accept Sir Robert Peel's conversion to free trade and to reject the policy of protection which had been advocated in Bradshaw's own editorials. Peel's *volte face* and the *Journal's* reaction to it also explain the appearance in 1846 of the *Nottingham Guardian.* This was promoted by a number of the Nottinghamshire country gentry and the Reverend W. J. Butler was the paper's first editor, protection forming an important frame of reference for the *Guardian's* views. However, in 1849 the newspaper was purchased by Thomas Forman and after the political crisis had abated, the *Journal* began to increase its circulation once more. Two more newspapers commenced publication during the fifties; the *Nottingham Advertizer* was on sale between 1853 and 1860, and *Stevenson's Daily Express,* a news sheet which kept the public informed of the progress of the war in the Crimea, appeared in 1855, continuing until the termination of hostilities in the following year. Daily publication was the policy adopted by the proprietors of the *Nottingham and Midland Counties*

Q

Daily Express when it was first published in 1859, and two years later the *Nottingham Guardian* was transformed into a weekly publication. In 1870, the *Nottingham Review* was amalgamated with the *Nottingham Daily Express,* and the *Nottingham Evening Post* first appeared in 1878.

While local newspapers split over national political issues, local political parties were equally affected by divisive factors. The Whiggish control of municipal government was threatened for a short time during the controversy revolving around the construction of a new workhouse, but after 1844 the Whig majority on the Corporation rose again. Nottingham's parliamentary seats, however, did not survive the resurgence of support for the Tory Party; for the Tory revival, together with Radical sentiment stimulated by opposition to the new poor law, was sufficient to terminate, temporarily, the Whig dominance. In 1841 the Tory, John Walter, had secured one of the town's two seats, but in 1843 Whigs had retrieved it. In 1847, however, the two Whig candidates found themselves at the foot of the poll.[123] At the general election of 1852, a Tory-Chartist alliance proved sufficiently firm to secure John Walter's return, albeit in second place, to the Whig candidate, the Honourable Edward Strutt; but the strength of the alliance was inadequate to elect Charles Sturgeon, the rather feeble Chartist contestant.[124]

With the elevation of Strutt to the peerage in 1856, one of the Nottingham seats became vacant, and although the Chartist leader, Ernest Jones, received a favourable reception in Nottingham, he stood aside and endorsed the candidature of Charles Paget, the Radical Ruddington landowner. During the general election of the following year, which was fought mainly on the issue of Palmerston's policy in China, Jones was nominated, and in his campaign he opposed the Chinese war and advocated moderate reforms at home. Jones suffered defeat largely owing to his stand against the government, though the defection of framework knitters from the Chartist side also showed at the polls. In the election of 1859, Jones stood against two popular candidates, Paget and Mellor for the Whig-Liberal Party, and Walter and Bromley for the Tories, but Paget and Mellor were successful, thereby restoring the traditional Whig supremacy in Nottingham. Even in victory, however, the Whigs were divided owing to the dominant influence on municipal and national politics wielded by the Whig caucus, which continued to secure majority representation on the Council; the views of the radical Liberal faction carried little weight, with the result that conservative Whigs tended to receive nomination. Because this local ruling middle class clique of party heads customarily held exclusive meetings at room number thirty in the Exchange building, 'Number Thirty' became a symbol of oligarchic rule in Nottingham, and at the bye election of 1861, caused by Mellor's elevation to the judicial bench, an attempt to confound 'Number Thirty' produced a lively contest.

From the late forties Chartists had moved into the orbit of Liberal Party politics, but so long as the Whig coterie called the tune, radical influence was doomed to be ineffective in terms of the political complexion of parliamentary candidates. In 1861 Number Thirty chose as one of its parliamentary candidates Lord Lincoln, the twenty-eight year old son of the Duke of Newcastle and a former Tory, a choice which exasperated the radical wing. The other candidate who appealed for the support of the electorate was Sir Robert Clifton, a gambling squire with historic local connections whose brilliant oratory, panache, and wit assured him of popular support at the hustings. He stood as an Independent candidate favouring moderate extension of the franchise, secret ballot, and the abolition of compulsory church rates, but the somewhat weak political basis of his programme was strengthened by the intervention of the Chartist trio, Sweet, Heath, and Mott, who seem to have taken control of Clifton's campaign and transformed it into a sustained political attack upon the methods, philosophy, and existence of the caucus at 'Number Thirty'.[125] Several factors account for the success of this assault which brought Clifton victory. Possessing an attractive personality and the common touch, Clifton commanded the potential for political success, and in the hands of James Acland, his election agent, formerly a lecturer with the Anti-Corn Law League, Clifton became identified as a selfless protagonist of social, intellectual, and even moral progress in contrast with the image of the monopolistic clique which sought to dominate local politics. This explains why Clifton gained support from anti-Whigs, while abstentions within the Whig party increased his lead. Thus another Tory-Chartist alliance succeeded in defeating the Whigs though the key to this alliance was exasperation with Lord Lincoln's candidature. The depression of 1861–62 afforded an additional reason why Chartists should cast their votes for Clifton as their erstwhile leaders urged.

Frustrated by the power of the caucus, in 1865 a group of radical Whig–Liberals broke away and formed the Independent Society supporting Clifton's candidature.[126] Samuel Morley, the local hosiery employer resident in London, an orthodox Liberal and non-conformist, was the other successful candidate in this contest; but the election was accompanied by such dishonesty and corruption that both candidates were unseated after bribery was proved. At the re-election, Ralph Bernal Osborne, son of a wealthy West India merchant, was virtually sponsored by Clifton, and was successfully returned together with the Whig, Lord Amberley, Earl Russell's son.

After the extension of the franchise in 1867, when every house-holder received the vote, 'Number Thirty' adopted new tactics and a reformed Liberal Registration Association took its place. In 1871 the Liberal Registration Association adopted Charles Seely, a young member of a prosperous Lincoln family, who later became an extensive colliery owner in Nottingham; and Peter Clayden, a non-conformist minister who appealed directly to the working classes; both were defeated. In gratitude, no doubt, for the franchise reform enacted by the Tories in 1867, Charles Ichabod Wright of Stapleford Hall was elected together with Clifton, who once more secured a comfortable majority. Two years later Clifton died, and his funeral was attended by between twenty and thirty thousand people anxious to show their affection for a well-loved local figure. The Nottingham Liberal Parliamentary Association saw in Clifton's death an opportunity to regain its political power, and at the bye election which followed the Liberal nominee, Charles Seely, narrowly defeated the Tory candidate, William Digby Seymour, Q.C. In 1870 yet another bye election occurred when Charles Ichabod Wright was compelled to resign through ill health. Seymour stood again on a platform of 'Independence and the memory of Sir Robert Clifton', supporting Gladstone's Irish land legislation and the maintenance of the influence of religious com-munities, and opposing compulsory education. The Liberals chose the Honourable Auberon Edward Herbert, referred to in the *Nottingham Journal* as an 'aristocratic Radical'. He, too, approved of Gladstone's land reforms; he also expressed sympathy with the trade unions, but he deplored militant action and restrictive laws. He was in favour of national education, reform of the Universities, a secret ballot, and the abolition of the purchase of commissions in the army. He also supported the idea of confederating the empire to give the colonies a share in responsibility. It was this programme which attracted two hundred and ninety-seven more votes than Seymour's.

Before 1860 the Liberals had championed economic liberty, and in so doing gained the allegiance of a wide section of the business community. After 1860 they paid greater attention to the lower sections of the middle classes and the upper strata of wage earners, especially in their support for non-conformist interests. But by the time it drew to the end of its term, the popularity of the Gladstone government, which had taken office in 1868, was waning. At the local level an outbreak of dissension within the Liberal ranks resulted in no fewer than four men competing for Liberal votes at the poll. The result of the local election in 1874 confirmed the

Liberal defeat at Westminster, when the two Tories, J. E. Denison, Speaker of the House of Commons, and Saul Isaac, the proprietor of Clifton Collieries, were successfully returned. The defeated contestants were two advanced Radicals, Robert Laycock and Henry Labouchere; and two Independents, Richard Birkin, who put up as a local man and supporter of Gladstone, and D. W. Heath, the County Coroner, who put himself forward as a trade union and working man's candidate.

Electoral history during the last quarter of the nineteenth century reflected the trends in national politics. In 1880 the Conservatives were defeated in Nottingham by Liberals, Charles Seely and John S. Wright. The latter was a Birmingham button manufacturer who triumphed over Saul Isaac, and John Gill, a newcomer to Nottingham. At the bye election caused by Wright's death the same year, Arnold Morley, Liberal son of Samuel Morley, was returned unopposed. Despite the reorganization of the local Liberal party machinery on the lines adopted by Chamberlain and Schnadhorst at Birmingham, in practice the real power to select party candidates was in the hands of a small, virtually self-elected, executive committee, and the four hundred delegates sent by committees in each ward were denied effective influence. The 'Four Hundred' were revised and replaced by a new central union known as the 'Eight Hundred', though executive power still lay in the hands of a clique. It was said that in spite of its defects the local Liberal Party machine was many times more efficient than the badly organised Conservative Party executive.

Under the Franchise and Redistribution Act, from 1885 Nottingham sent three members to Parliament. In the election of 1885, in the East division, Arnold Morley, Liberal, fought the imperial preference federationist H. Finch Hatton; in Nottingham South, J. Carvell Williams represented the Liberals while Henry Smith Wright, third son of Ichabod Charles Wright, was the Conservative choice. In the West division, Charles Seely met Edward Cope, a Basford lace manufacturer educated at Nottingham High School. A third candidate was John Burns who stood as a Labour candidate supporting the principles represented by the Social Democratic Federation. All three Liberals were successful, the publication of the result being met with extreme rowdyism and demonstrations of dissatisfaction. Owing to some misunderstanding, the police were ordered to charge on the crowds milling in Market Place, and baton action resulted in injuries to about one hundred and fifty people. The behaviour of the police (many of whom had been dispatched from outside the county specially to deal with the election troubles) drew much angry comment from the newspaper editors, and after an enquiry the police were charged with acting with disorderly violence. The Recorder of Lincoln also blamed the authorities for permitting so large a crowd to gather and for failing to issue warnings before the orders to charge were given. Two constables were committed for trial; each was found guilty and given three months' hard labour.

The split in the Liberal Party over Home Rule for Ireland was followed by another election in 1886, when Carvell Williams in Nottingham South lost his seat through supporting Gladstone. In the East division, Morley's majority was reduced from 991 to 160. In the West division, Seely, the Liberal, also a Gladstone and Home Rule supporter, was faced by Henry Broadhurst who was identified with the trade union movement and who had been returned for Stoke in 1880 and Birmingham in 1885. Seely, a local colliery owner, normally a popular figure, was in the unfortunate position of being involved in a labour dispute at the time of the election, and owing to this he incurred the animosity of a large number of miners in that constituency. This situation helps to explain Broadhurst's easy victory. At the general election of 1892, the balance turned against the Conservatives and Gladstone once more took office. The only new candidates in Nottingham was John Fletcher Moulton, Q.C. He stood in the Liberal interest against Wright, Conservative, who retained his seat in Nottingham South. In the East division, Morley, Liberal, defeated the Conservative, Finch Hatton, by a substantial majority and in Nottingham West, Seely, the Liberal, no longer embarrassed by an industrial dispute and backed by the local Miners' Association, triumphed over Broadhurst who lost votes because of his opposition to the eight hour day.

The country experienced another election after the Cabinet's resignation in 1895, and in Nottingham only one of the candidates who had been to the polls in 1892 appeared in 1895. This was Arnold Morley, Liberal, whose involvement in a scandal concerning bribery at the previous election had lost him much support; he was defeated by Edward Bond, a Conservative barrister of high repute. In South Nottingham, H. Cavendish Bentinck retained the seat for the Conservatives by defeating F. W. Maude, a Radical. In West Nottingham, which was controlling largely by the mining vote, J. H. Yoxall, President of the National Union of Teachers, on a Lib-lab platform gained victory over A. G. Sparrow, his Conservative opponent. In the 'khaki election' of 1900 all retained their seats. Thus during the second half of the nineteenth century the way to Conservatism had been paved in Nottingham, firstly, by the advent of 'Cliftonism', secondly, by the Liberal party split over Home Rule; and thirdly, by the rise of socialist philosophy—factors which precipitated the erosion of the city's traditional Whig and Liberal politics.

References

[1] Second Report, quoted by W. Ashworth, *The Genesis of Modern Town Planning*, (1954), pp. 31–2.

[2] B. D. White, *A History of the Liverpool Corporation, 1835–1914* (Liverpool, 1951), p. 27.

[3] *Supra*, p. 163.

[4] *B.R.*, IX, p. 29, February 4, 1841.

[5] *N.R.*, December 3, 1847.

[6] Quoted by Asa Briggs, *Victorian Cities*, (1963), p. 389.

[7] J. D. Chambers, *The Workshop of the World*, (1961), p. 181.

[8] *B.R.*, IX, 56, December 13, 1847.

[9] See *First Report of the Commissioners on Large Towns and Populous Districts*, 1844 (572) XVII. 1., pp. 30–48.

[10] *B.R.*, IX, 56, December 13, 1847.

[11] *B.R.*, 58, December 13, 1847.

[12] William Ashworth, *The Genesis of Modern Town Planning*, (1954), p. 65–6.

[13] *B.R.*, IX, 58, December 13, 1847.

[14] *B.R.*, IX, 61, May 4, 1848.

[15] While Sheffield Town Council was quick to take steps to adopt the Public Health Act of 1848. Nottingham Corporation petitioned against the powers which the Act gave to the Central Board. S. Pollard, *A History of Labour in Sheffield* (Liverpool, 1959), pp. 10–11. *B.R.*, IX, 61, May 4, 1848.

[16] Between June and September, 1849, 1,000 cases were reported at Hull 2,000 at Leeds, and 3,000 in Liverpool. S. Finer, *op. cit.*, p. 346. In Nottingham few cases occurred, *B.R.*, IX, 72, October 1, 1849.

[17] S. Pollard, *loc. cit.*

[18] *B.R.*, IX, 56, December 13, 1847; the report is reproduced in *B.R.*, IX, 77, October 1, 1849.

[19] *B.R.*, IX, 61, May 4, 1848.

[20] S. E. Finer, *The Life and Times of Sir Edwin Chadwick*, (1952), p. 296.

[21] *B.R.*, IX, 73–77, October 1, 1849.

[22] *B.R.*, IX, 86, September 22, 1851.

[23] D. Gray, *Nottingham Through Five Hundred Years*, (Nottingham, 1960), pp. 192–194; *B.R.*, IX, March 15, pp. 89–92.

[24] Asa Briggs, *Victorian Cities*, (1963), p. 40.

[25] *B.R.*, IX, 1852, March 15, pp. 89–92.

[26] D. Gray, *Nottingham Through Five Hundred Years*, (Nottingham, 1960), p. 194.

[27] *Report of the Nottingham Corporation Sanitary Committee*, 1860, p. 9; *N.R.*, June 15, 1860.

[28] Enclosure Acts 41/Geo. III Cap. 109, 8 and 9, Vic. Cap. 7.

[29] W. Ashworth, *The Genesis of Modern Town Planning*, (1954), pp. 56–57; *N.R.*, January 10, 1849; *Ex.*, July 29, 1885.

[30] S. D. Chapman 'Working-Class Housing in Nottingham during the Industrial Revolution', *Transactions of the Thoroton Society* LXVII (1963), p. 20.

[31] *B.R.*, IX, 85, June 23, 1851; In 1853, while Liverpool was resisting the imposition of an improvement rate, Leeds was levying one of 4d. in the pound. Asa Briggs, *Victorian Cities*, (1963), p. 37.

[32] *Nottingham Corporation Accounts.*

[33] E. P. Hennock, 'Finance and Politics in Urban Local Government in England 1835–1900', *The Historical Journal* VI, 2. (1963), p. 214.

[34] Asa Briggs, *Victorian Cities*, (1963), p. 37.

[35] *B.R.*, IX, 202, May 24, 1868.

[36] H. Field, *The Nottingham Date Book 1800–1884*, pp. 606–7.

[37] D. Gray, *Nottingham Through Five Hundred Years*, (1960), p. 188.

[38] *B.R.*, IX, 104, August 14, 1854; 104, October 16, 1854.

[39] *B.R.*, IX, 124–125, September 7, 1857.

[40] *B.R.*, IX, 141, October 6, 1859.

[41] *B.R.*, IX, 163, August 3, 1863; 166, October 25, 1864; 203, November 15, 1869.

[42] *B.R.*, IX, 137–138, August 15, 1859.

[43] D. Gray, *Nottingham Through Five Hundred Years*, (Nottingham, 1960), p. 194.

[44] *B.R.*, IX, 83, November 18, 1850; 54, February 5, 1855; 173, November 20, 1865.

[45] *B.R.*, IX, 133, November 22, 1858.

[46] D. Gray, *Nottingham Through Five Hundred Years*, (Nottingham, 1960), p. 194.

[47] *B.R.*, IX, 168, December 29, 1864.

[48] *B.R.*, IX, 148, December 3, 1860.

[49] *B.R.*, IX, 183, May 6, 1867.

[50] D. Gray, *Nottingham Through Five Hundred Years*, (Nottingham, 1960), p. 194.

[51] Asa Briggs, *Victorian Cities*, (1963), pp. 217–219.

[52] D. Gray, *Nottingham Through Five Hundred Years*, (Nottingham, 1960), p. 195.

[53] *B.R.*, IX, 211–213, July 17, 1871.

[54] D. Gray, *Nottingham Through Five Hundred Years*, (Nottingham, 1960), p. 214.

[55] See Asa Briggs, *Victorian Cities*, (1963), p. 239.

[56] D. Gray, *Nottingham Through Five Hundred Years*, (Nottingham, 1960), p. 191.

[57] *Ibid.*

[58] *B.R.*, IX, 183, May 6, 1867.

[59] *Children's Employment Commission* 1843, (431), Evidence from William Enfield Esq., junior, p.f. 112–113.

[60] *B.R.*, IX, 138, August 15, 1859.

[61] Asa Briggs, *Victorian Cities*, (1963), p. 34.

[62] *Ibid.*, p. 211.

[63] *Ibid.*, p. 209.

[64] B. D. White, *A History of the Corporation of Liverpool, 1835-1914*, (Liverpool, 1951), p. 17.

[65] A. C. Wood, 'Nottingham 1835–1865', *Transactions of the Thoroton Society*, LIX, 1955, p. 73, f.n.l.

[66] *Infra*, pp. 219–20.

[67] B. D. White, *A History of the Corporation of Liverpool, 1835-1914*, (Liverpool, 1951), pp. 196–198.

[68] Quoted by Asa Briggs, *Victorian Cities*, (1963), p. 211.

[69] S. Pollard, *A History of Labour in Sheffield*, (Liverpool, 1959), p. 28.

[70] Enclosure Acts 41/Geo. III, Cap. 109, 8 and 9, Vic. Cap. 7.

[71] H. Finer, *Municipal Trading*, (1949), p. 41.

[72] *B.R.,* IX, 222, November 7, 1872.

[73] *B.R.,* IX, 239, September 1, 1874.

[74] See Asa Briggs, *Victorian Cities,* (1963), pp. 188–190.

[75] Children's Employment Commission 1843 (431) XIII, ev. of William Felkin, p.f. 48.

[76] *Ibid.,* ev. of Absolem Barnett, pp.f. 46–47.

[77] *Ibid.,* ev. of Samuel Wilkinson, p.f. 46.

[78] *Ibid.,* ev. of Archdeacon Wilkins, p.f. 63.

[79] For the influence of religion in the community see chapter XIII. See also S. D. Chapman 'The Evangelical Revival and Education in Nottingham' *Transactions of the Thoroton Society* LXVI (1962), p. 36; Asa Briggs, *Victorian Cities,* (1963), p. 60.

[80] Anon., *Walks Around Nottingham,* (1835), p. 40.

[81] Diary of Samuel Collinson, *Mss.*

[82] D. Gray, *Nottingham Through Five Hundred Years,* (Nottingham, 1960), pp. 196; *B.R.,* IX, 78, November 19, 1849.

[83] *B.R.,* IX, 46, August 19, 1845; 51, August 4, 1846; 93, August 2, 1852; 82, September 30, 1857.

[84] D. Gray, *Nottingham Through Five Hundred Years,* (Nottingham 1960), p. 196.

[85] *B.R.,* IX, 133, November 15, 1858; 146, August 6, 1860; 230, September 22, 1873.

[86] B. B. Granger, *The Tourist's Picturesque Guide to Nottingham,* (Nottingham, 1871), p. 62.

[87] J. D. Chambers, 'Victorian Nottingham', *Transactions of the Thoroton Society,* LXIII, 1959, p. 8.

[88] *N.R.,* September 1, 1865.

[89] *N.R.,* August 24, 1855; *N.R.,* July 20, 1860.

[90] W. Wylie, *Old and New Nottingham,* (1953), p. 359.

[91] W. Howitt, *The Rural Life of England,* vol. II, (1838), pp. 276–277.

[92] R. Mellors, *Men of Nottingham and Nottinghamshire,* (Nottingham, 1924), p. 107.

[93] *Ibid.,* p. 299.

[94] W. Wylie, *Old and New Nottingham,* (1953), p. 359.

[95] *V.C.H.,* II, pp. 418–421.

[96] B. B. Granger, *The Tourist's Picturesque Guide to Nottingham,* (Nottingham, 1871), p. 89.

[97] W. Wylie, *Old and New Nottingham,* (1953), p. 359.

[98] *B.R.,* IX, 46, August 19, 1845.

[99] *Diary of Samuel Collinson, Mss.*

[100] *B.R.,* IX, 134, January 4, 1859.

[101] *B.R.,* IX, 147, October 18, 1860.

[102] William Howitt, *The Rural Life of England,* (1830), vol. II, pp. 251–252.

[103] W. Wylie, *Old and New Nottingham,* (1853), p. 325.

[104] *Ibid.,* p. 325–6.

[105] *B.R.,* IX, 86, June 23, 1851.

[106] W. Wylie, *Old and New Nottingham,* (1953), pp. 326, 360.

[107] *Ibid.,* pp. 348–349.

[108] J. H. Green, *The History of Nottingham Mechanics Institution, 1837–1887,* (1888), pp. 16–17.

[109] W. Wylie, *Old and New Nottingham,* (1953), p. 329.

[110] A. C. Wood, 'Nottingham 1835–1865,' *Transactions of the Thoroton Society,* LIX, 1955, p. 41.

[111] W. Wylie, *Old and New Nottingham* (1953), pp. 167–172.

[112] A. C. Wood, 'Nottingham 1835–1865,' *Transactions of the Thoroton Society,* LIX, 1955, pp. 33–35.

[113] W. Dearden, *History, Topography, and Directory of Nottingham,* (1834), p. 71.

[114] A. C. Wood, 'Nottingham 1835–1865,' *Transactions of the Thoroton Society,* LIX, 1955, pp. 33–35.

[115] *Ibid.,* p. 35.

[116] *Ibid.,* p. 40.

[117] *Ibid,* pp. 36–7.

[118] *First Report of the Children's Employment Commission,* 1863 (3170) XVIII. 1., p. 243.

[119] *Ibid.,* p. 236.

[120] *B.R.,* IX, 136, August 1, 1859; 170, March 27, 1865.

[121] *Ex.,* August 20, 1875.

[122] The following account of Nottingham newspapers to 1850 is based on D. Fraser, 'Nottingham Press, 1800–1850,' *Transactions of the Thoroton Society,* LXVII, 1963, pp. 47–62.

[123] *Supra,* p. 145.

[124] For more detailed accounts of political developments in Nottingham see A. C. Wood 'Nottingham 1835–1865,' *Transactions of the Thoroton Society,* LIX, (1955) and 'Nottingham Parliamentary Elections 1869–1900,' *Transactions of the Thoroton Society,* LX, (1956). A shrewd analysis of local electoral history between 1852–1861 is to be found in Colin Holmes, *op. cit.,* Chapter V.

[125] See A. C. Wood, 'Sir Robert Juckes Clifton, 1826–1869', *Transactions of the Thoroton Society,* LVII (1953), p. 48 *et. seq.;* and especially Colin Holmes' *op. cit.* pp. 100–109.

[126] The following account is based on A. C. Wood, 'Nottingham Parliamentary Elections, 1869–1900,' *Transactions of the Thoroton Society,* LX 1956.

CHAPTER IX

'NEW NOTTINGHAM': THE CHANGING ECONOMIC STRUCTURE, NEW INDUSTRIES AND ASSOCIATIONS

THE Enclosure Act of 1845 ushered in a period of expansion of local industry and population. The final award was delayed until 1865, but by 1852 practically all land had been allotted and most of the recipients had disposed of their sites.[1] This meant that land for building purposes appeared on the market during a cyclical upswing in the national economy, and at a time of progressive developments in the lace and hosiery industries. The extension of steam power to lace machinery and the beginnings of power production in the hosiery industry resulted in demands for factory and warehouse buildings. Between 1851 and 1856 no fewer than seventy-four factories and forty-one warehouses were erected in Nottingham.[2] Felkin reckoned that on factory and warehouse construction alone at least £250,000 was spent in Nottingham between 1849 and 1856. In 1856–57 another eighteen factories and twenty-one warehouses were built, and a further thirty-six factories and five warehouses in 1857–58.[3] A Leicester journalist wrote:

> Nottingham is become the Manchester of the Midlands . . . with regard to its warehouses Nottingham cannot fail to astonish any visitor.[4]

One building which drew high praise from the Factory Commissioners was the new E-shaped six storeyed warehouse of Thomas Adams & Co., the leading firm of lace finishers. In 1855 the five hundred employees of the twenty year old firm moved to Stoney Street where daily services were held in the chapel which had been built into the spacious new premises at the owner's request.[5] Although many of the town's new buildings were functionally superior to the old warehouses, there was ample criticism of the quality of the architecture. The dumpy fronts, odious windows, and ugly doorways offended the sensibility of the *Review* editor,

> a man may . . . ask what sort of exhibition this New Nottingham will make when its irregular streets are fully occupied by their equally irregular edifices?

Dismayed by the absence of planned location and design, Felkin favoured a general building plan similar to that which had been adopted on a small scale on the private upper-middle class Park

228

Estate belonging to the Duke of Newcastle, where, since the late twenties, houses and stuccoed villas had been erected along carefully laid out streets.[6] The increasing number of villas that appeared in the late forties was part of the general expansion of housebuilding. In Sheffield, which had a population more than double that of Nottingham, 1,845 houses were erected between 1851 and 1855; in Nottingham between 1851 and 1856, 2,101 houses were built, 768 more in 1856–7, and 653 in 1857–8.[7]

The effect of building activity upon local industry was unmistakeable. Beginning in 1849, when John Rushworth commenced business as builder and contractor, several new brickworks were opened, the largest of which were those of Thomas North at Cinder Hill opened in 1851, and of Edward Gripper, who in 1852 formed a company to manufacture bricks by steam machinery under a new patent at Mapperley, Carlton, and Basford. Messrs. Bailey & Shaw, fellmongers of Lenton, purchased land at Arnold, also to commence the mechanized production of bricks. In 1852 a contemporary estimate put annual brick production in Nottingham and district at twenty-one million, and new brickyards continued to open up.[8]

'Employment is abundant for all', wrote an observer in 1853, 'the rapid growth of the town has created an abundance of employment for labourers, builders, bricklayers, and brickmakers, all these along with the staple trades are earning high wages. Strikes are frequently threatened but are generally prevented by employers conceding what is asked . . . additional hands are flocking into the town.'[9]

However, while the master builders were willing to pay higher wages, they were not prepared to surrender their freedom to economize labour. Growing competition from Derby and Grantham contractors encouraged several Nottingham builders to introduce machinery into their yards. In 1853 the Nottingham Operative Carpenters and Joiners Society complained that some employers were using mortice machines, and were also preparing mouldings and other work with the aid of steam-driven machinery. The union notified all employers in the building trades of their decision not to handle any work (with the exception of floorboards) which had been prepared in this manner. The sequel to this ultimatum was a prolonged and bitter dispute. In the summer of 1854 the union, which commanded the support of at least two-thirds of the total number of carpenters and joiners in the district, struck against eight of the largest Nottingham firms. Following the lead of Greensmith & Lacey and C. C. & A. Dennett, the master builders retaliated by locking out all union men and obtaining non-union labour from outside the district. After nearly eight weeks the men returned to work, their opposition to the use of machinery completely destroyed.[10]

At the same time that the Enclosure Act stimulated investment in the building and brickmaking trades, it was the growing fuel needs of the railways which led to the development of the concealed Nottinghamshire coalfield (although the Nottingham factories also generated demands for coal). At the same time, extension of the railway network itself was influenced by the search for coal supplies.[11] The first major investment to be made in this field was by Thomas North, when in 1841 he leased land at Cinder Hill in Basford and sank two 7 feet pits to a depth of more than six hundred feet.[12] The opening, in 1848, of the Midland Company's railway line linking the villages of Lenton, Radford, Basford, Bulwell, Hucknall, Linby, Newstead, Annesley, Kirkby, Sutton-in-Ashfield, and Mansfield was instrumental in attracting further investment to develop the coal resources adjacent to Nottingham. Of the seventeen collieries that existed in Nottinghamshire in 1854, eight were located within five miles of the Nottingham borough boundaries. In terms of output, the largest colliery was at Babbington in Kimberley, and it was one of the three owned by Thomas North who, in 1861, held long leases of nearly ten thousand acres in the Nottinghamshire coalfield. If the disposal of the output of Babbington Colliery was typical, more than twice the volume sold in markets outside Nottingham (mainly in the London market) was consumed within the district. Of all coal carried from Babbington Colliery in 1858, canal transport moved one-half of the total sales. From North's Nuttall colliery, whose total output was about three-fifths the volume sold by Babbington colliery, nearly seven times the amount of coal carried by canal travelled by rail. The Newcastle colliery, which also belonged to North, produced slightly less than that at Nuttall and dispatched similar proportions by rail and canal. Altogether, North's three major collieries sold approximately 121,000 tons of coal in 1858; four years later, collieries throughout the county produced a total of 732,000 tons, which represented about 0·9 per cent of total United Kingdom output. In 1870 the percentage was 1·8 per cent, by which time development of the Nottingham coalfield was proceeding at a rapid pace.[13]

As the expansion of coal mining in the area shows, the local economy felt the bracing effects of general economic development in addition to investment stimulated by circumstances peculiar to Nottingham. Fluctuations in the level of general economic activity were also shared by local trades. The commercial crisis of 1857 had serious repercussions for some merchants but, as in 1847, the Nottingham banks withstood the strains on their liquidity. Nevertheless, the strong connections which Nottingham merchants and manufacturers held with the American trade, whence the crisis came, affected confidence in their credit standing, and between 1857 and 1860 no fewer than fifty-seven lace houses became bankrupt. Stocks of the bankrupts flooded the market and leading houses sold lots at discounts of up to 30 per cent.[14] The American Civil War, which resulted in the Lancashire cotton famine and a period of high and erratic cotton prices, was the main factor disturbing the lace and hosiery trades between 1860 and 1865, while the disruption of trade with Germany in 1863 and 1864 also unsettled trading conditions.[15] The termination of the war in America was followed by a boom in exports and in industrial activity at home.

A feature of the upswing was speculation in shares of the new limited liability companies which were incorporated following the legislation of 1855, 1857, and 1862.[16] One such company was the lace finishing firm of Thomas Adams, while Adams also enlisted the support of other local merchants and manufacturers who, together with the aid of Birmingham capitalists who had helped in converting Adams' business into a joint stock company, opened the Nottingham Joint Stock Banking Company whose capital was £1m.[17] The volume of business in its first year was large, and by the beginning of 1866, though a call on shares produced £10,000 of new capital, the rediscounts with London reached very high levels. Within a few days of the failure of Overend Gurneys, the new limited company, the Nottingham bank borrowed and rediscounted in London the sum of £200,000, an amount no less than the total value of its deposits. The London agents then discontinued these facilities, but the emergency assistance had already proved adequate and the bank in Nottingham showed no external signs of strain. After the crisis had passed, the directors of the Nottingham Joint Stock Banking Company decided that additional reserves were needed, and, after English banks had refused to extend discounting facilities, one of the Scottish banks with a London office agreed to lend. Despite the financial difficulties of Thomas Adams in 1868 and the fraud committed by the bank's Ilkeston agent, the Nottingham Joint Stock Bank survived the crisis and its aftermath. The policy of expansion was resumed, and not until 1878 did the figure for deposits exceed the total for loans and bills.[18] Indeed, the few years which followed the bank's difficulties ushered in economic expansion on an unprecedented scale, reaching a peak in 1873.[19]

In Nottingham an investment boom centred upon the lace and hosiery trades and the further development of engineering, brickmaking, and coal mining. Between 1869 and 1874 the number of collieries in the Nottingham district increased from seven to eighteen, while the total output of all Nottinghamshire collieries rose from 1,575,450 tons to 3,127,750 tons. It was during these years that considerable investment entered the concealed coalfield, opening up the high quality pits which were strung out along the Leen valley between Mansfield and Nottingham.[20] During the eighties, the annual total output of collieries in Nottinghamshire averaged slightly more than five and a quarter million tons; the figure for the nineties was nearly seven million tons, and in 1900 Nottinghamshire collieries together produced about 3 per cent. of the total coal output in the United Kingdom. Between 1881 and 1891 the coal industry absorbed labour at a greater rate than any other local industry, when the number of male workers in that industry in Nottingham rose from 3,035 to 5,027; in 1901 this figure had reached 5,861.[21]

The industrial expansion which took place during the second half of the nineteenth century was accompanied by population growth and a concomitant shift in occupational distribution. Between 1831 and 1841 the population of the three parishes of Nottingham had risen by approximately 6 per cent. from 50,680 to 53,091. By 1851, an increase of 10 per cent. brought the total to 58,419. At the end of the following decade the population had reached 77,765, a rise of roughly 33 per cent.[22] In comparison, the percentage increase in the aggregate populations of the neighbouring industrial villages of Radford, Sneinton, Basford, and Lenton for the same three decades were 36 per cent. between 1831 and 1841, 18 per cent. between 1841 and 1851 and about 15 per cent. for the decade ending 1861.[23] (See Table IX.)

Shortly after the Enclosure Act of 1845, before its economic effects had begun to show, Nottingham was still a manufacturing and commercial centre which was surrounded by a constellation of industrial villages where lace making had superceded framework knitting as the chief occupation. Beyond this ring of village satellites to the North, lay more villages where framework knitting predominated. The structure of employment in Nottingham and its immediate environs in 1851 is indicated by that year's census figures. The hosiery industry occupied approximately 20 per cent. of the working population, though this almost certainly excluded large numbers of part-time outworking employees. This was also true of the figures for the lace industry which gave employment to 27 per cent. of the total number of gainfully occupied men, women, and children. Silk and cotton manufacture occupied about 4 per cent. Other than these, the only two industries that employed a significant percentage of the population were the building trades, 6 per cent., and engineering (chiefly iron manufacture, frame and machine building), which at that time employed only 2·7 per cent. The re-

TABLE XI: *Population of the Villages around Nottingham, 1801–1901*

Nottinghamshire Parishes and Townships	1801	1811	1821	1831	1841	1851	1861	1871	1881	1891	1901
Mansfield	5988	6816	7861	9426	9788	10627	10225	11824	13653	15925	21445
Sutton-in-Ashfield	3311	3994	4655	5734	6557	7692	6483	7574	8523	10562	14862
Ilkeston (Derbyshire)	2422	2920	3681	4446	5326	6122	8374	9662	14122	19744	25384
Hucknall Torkard	1497	1793	1940	2200	2680	2970	2836	4257	10023	13094	15250
Arnold	2768	3042	3572	4054	4509	4704	4642	4634	5745	7769	8757
Heanor (Derbyshire)	2322	3578	4288	4743	5467	5982	4084	4888	6822	9779	12418

Sources: *Enumeration Abstracts 1801–1841; Census of England and Wales, 1851–1901.*

R

mainder of the working population employed in the manufacturing as opposed to the distributive and service trades, were engaged in the crafts of tailoring, dressmaking, and shoemaking.[24] Apart from minor deviations, the pattern of industry in the whole area of Nottingham and district (i.e. including the industrial villages of Radford, Sneinton, Lenton, Basford, and Beeston) was fairly uniform. In 1844 in addition to the many lace and hosiery manufacturers in Nottingham, there were several finishing and merchanting houses, cotton spinners, and lace thread manufacturers. There were a number of machine works including iron and brass foundries, a white lead works, an extensive marble works, and a number of tanning and currying establishments. Basford was the major location for bleaching and dyeing establishments, while at Mapperley, Sneinton, and Carlton, brickmaking was an important part of economic activity.[25]

The economic importance of women in local trades appears to have influenced the town's demographic history. At each census between 1811 and 1841, women outnumbered men by between three and four thousand. In 1841 the town's male population fell short of the number of women living in the town by 4,233. During the decade between 1851 and 1861 the excess of female labour rose to more than seven thousand, as the factories and warehouses built on the newly-enclosed land attracted persons from the neighbouring counties of Leicestershire, Derbyshire, and Lincolnshire, Huntingdonshire, and Cambridgeshire. These were the main sources of the rapidly expanding labour supply attracted by the boom that accompanied the town's renaissance.[26] Between 1851 and 1861, 6,406 migrants born beyond the county boundaries flocked to the town, while 7,230 persons born in Nottinghamshire also moved to the regional capital. The net gain from migration during this decade was 11,299, while Leicester was suffering a net loss of 5,345. The total increase in Nottingham's population was 19,346, which compared with slightly more than five thousand in the previous decade, and less than three thousand between 1831–41. The rate of increase slowed down between 1861 and 1871, when population rose from 77,765 to 86,621. In the villages immediately adjoining the town the high rate of expansion continued; (See Table XI) but while nearly half of the 1851–61 migrants came from within the county boundaries, between 1861 and 1871 only one-fifth were Nottinghamshire people.[27] Thus whereas the movement of population between 1851 and 1861 had been from the rural areas in the county to seek industrial employment in the town and its immediate vicinity (the typical pattern of internal migration in Victorian England[28]), during the ensuing ten years there was an influx of people from outside Nottinghamshire who came to live and work in the suburban villages.[29]

These demographic patterns, which persisted throughout the three remaining decades, occurred in response to the changing location of economic activity and shifts in the relative importance of different occupations. The 1871 census figures indicated a decrease in the number of people employed in the hosiery trade in Nottingham though there was a slight rise in the proportion of women attached to the industry. The overall employment in the lace trade, on the other hand, had increased, with women almost doubling the total number of men. The engineering trades, printing, and paper box manufacture had expanded, but the local population was still heavily dependent for its occupation and prosperity upon lace and hosiery. Of the total number of working males and females aged nineteen and over, approximately 18 per cent. were employed in the lace trade and 9 per cent. in hosiery. As to the employment of males aged nineteen and over, the approximate figures were 11 per cent. in lace, 8 per cent. in hosiery, 9 per cent. in the building trades and 4 per cent. in engineering.[30]

The trade directories, although not strictly accurate, also indicate definite trends in the changing pattern of industrial structure of Nottingham and its environs. These trends are concealed by the census figures which relate solely to the borough, while precise measurement of such change in terms of employment or size of unit is impossible. A comparison of Wright's Directories for 1862 and 1871 shows a decrease in the number of lace merchant manufacturers, whereas the number of lace producers doubled. The number of hosiery manufacturers remained almost unchanged; the number of engineers, machinists, frame smiths, bobbin and carriage-makers etc., rose considerably, and the number of firms engaged in engineering and foundry work increased from 115 in 1862, to 156 in 1871.[31] In 1862 John Turney, who received technical instruction at the People's College and the School of Art, founded a firm of leather manufacturers with his brother, an enterprise which became one of the leading producers of light leather in the country, and which in 1892 employed four hundred and fifty persons.[32] Beyond the periphery of greater Nottingham, the opening of new pits to meet the growing demand for coal to be used by factories and locomotives encouraged a drift into these areas, and small mining communities began to appear as, for example, at Cinder Hill, only three miles from Nottingham.[33] The increase in population in Hucknall Torkard and Mansfield since 1861 was attributed to the extension of the coal trade;[34] Hucknall had been affected by the expansion of collieries at Bulwell, and Mansfield by the colliery which was opened at Shireoaks.[35] Mining, therefore, provided a welcome alternative employment in the traditional hand framework knitting area, and framework knitters put their sons into collieries, a development which eased the transition from hand labour to machinery.

Since the Enclosure Act of 1845, the town and the neighbouring industrial villages had become firmly integrated as a single industrial complex. In 1862 Thomas Adams told the Commissioners that lace and hosiery warehouses were situated mainly in the centre of the town, whereas factories were generally to be found on the outskirts which merged with the industrial parishes, whose factories were also in the immediate vicinity.[36] This geographical distribution of economic activity was a result of the delay in passing the Encolsure Act. Economic integration was followed, in the Borough Extension Act of 1877, by the consolidation of the industrial parishes for administrative purposes, and the enlarged borough included the parishes of Sneinton, Lenton, Radford, Basford and Bulwell, in addition to Standard Hill, the limits of the Castle, Brewhouse Yard, Wilford north of the Trent, and part of Gedling. (See Figure V.) The area of the new borough was almost five times that of the three Nottingham parishes and despite the pull of surrounding industrial and mining villages (See Table XI.), the population of the enlarged town increased by just over 25 per cent. from 186,575 in 1881, to 239,745 in 1901. Expansion took place chiefly in the newly absorbed parishes of Radford, Basford, and Lenton, while the numbers of persons living in the old town decreased slightly from 113,590 in 1881, to 111,609 in 1901. The overall rise in population was due partly to natural increase, and partly to net immigration; in the decade between 1881 and 1891 about 34 per cent. of the net increase was due to migration and in the next ten years the percentage of migrants was approximately 29 per cent.[37]

Although Nottingham remained the chief centre of the lace trade, the surrounding districts attracted increasing investment, and by the close of the century the lace trade in Nottingham employed a smaller percentage of the town's male working population than it had in either 1891 or 1881. Nevertheless, there were more opportunities for women, and in 1901 no fewer than 14,701 (compared with 6,925 males) were employed in the manufacture of lace; over 30 per cent. of all working women were connected with the industry, which included a large number in the making-up trade. Similarly, in the hosiery industry in 1901 women outnumbered men by 3,944 to 2,192. Whereas in 1881, 6 per cent. of working men were employed in hosiery manufacture, in 1901 barely 3 per cent. were connected with the trade. Hosiery and lace were already being challenged by engineering and mining. In 1881 males in engineering in Nottingham accounted for 10 per cent. of the male working population, and 11·3 per cent. in 1901; but whereas in 1881 engineering consisted chiefly of the construction of lace and hosiery machinery, by 1901 cycle manufacture had become another important section, employing several thousand skilled men. The percentage of men working in coal mines was also rising. In 1881, 3,035 or 5·6 per cent. of the total male population described themselves as 'working in and about and dealing in the products of mines and quarries'; in 1901 the figure was 5,861 or 8 per cent. The building trades, which occupied a large proportion of the population in most large urban centres, employed 11·2 per cent. of the Nottingham male working population in 1901. Other occupations in the category of ubiquitous trades included food, drink, and tobacco, which in 1901 together employed 9·2 per cent. of the total working population in Nottingham (compared with 7·8 per cent. in 1881), and transport which employed 12·2 per cent. of the total working population (9·7 per cent. in 1881).

The growing importance of the transport industry as a major source of employment was not peculiar to Nottingham; it was a phenomenon which was common to other growing commercial and industrial centres at this time. The concomitant demand for carriers and cabs to provide feeder transport services to railway stations and goods yards reflected also the geographical expansion of these thriving urban centres. The town's first regular Hackney coach service was introduced in 1825, while the establishment of the first regular cab stand on Long Row in 1845 and daily omnibus services to Beeston and Arnold, which made their appearance in 1853, were portents of the growing demand for intra-urban transport as population beyond the town's periphery grew.[38] The introduction of the tramways in 1874 was another indication of this need.[39]

Although intra-urban transport could develop according to the needs of local business, until the last two decades of the century the inhabitants were resigned to the inconveniences which were due to the town's situation on a branch railway line. Prior to 1862, passengers for London were required to make an unnecessary detour of eighteen miles to Derby and back to Trent Junction. After the opening of Trent station this journey was eliminated by shunting the trains into a siding where they awaited the Derby carriages.[40] However, the general increase in goods traffic between London and the north, as indicated by the rising traffic carried on the Midland's own main line between Kettering and Leicester, encouraged the Midland to make another attempt to secure a direct entry into London. The result was the construction of an extension line between Nottingham and Rushton, near Kettering in Northamptonshire, which, when it was opened in 1880, gave Nottingham its main line London connection.[41] The significance which was attached to this development tended to overshadow the completion, in 1875, of another Midland line between Radford and Trowell. Running through the Erewash Valley, Chesterfield, and Sheffield, this line provided Nottingham with a through route to the northern manufacturing districts.[42] In 1899 Nottingham secured a second main line which carried trains direct to London, and in 1899 the Great Central Railway Company opened the Victoria Station in Nottingham.

Throughout Nottingham's railway history, local initiative, enterprise, and capital did not play an important role, until, in 1886, a group of Nottingham businessmen formed the Nottingham Suburban Railway Company.[43] Its object was to construct a railway between Nottingham and Daybrook in order to improve passenger transport facilities for some forty thousand people living to the east of the town. The Council made a preliminary grant towards costs, as did the Patent Brick Company which expected to benefit from the rail link between Nottingham and Mapperley. The Great Northern Railway Company, whose station the Suburban trains were to use, agreed to guarantee to pay the Company 3 per cent. interest on £215,000; the line opened in December, 1889. In April, 1898 the Great Northern's Leen Valley extension from Kirkby South Junction to Skegby was opened for traffic. Already, however, the electric trams both on the grounds of speed, resulting from the use of more direct routes, and cost, contributed to the decline in the Suburban's traffic.

Closely related to transport was distribution, which, with the growth of internal trade, required the employment of more productive factors. The town's food supplies continued to converge upon Market Place as the principal point of distribution. As the volume of internal trade expanded, direct transactions between producer and consumer became increasingly difficult, therefore wholesaling and retailing intermediaries grew in importance.[44] In Nottingham it was customary for wholesalers and retailers to bring their own stalls and stands which they erected on the two acre Market Place each Wednesday and Saturday. In 1841 the Corporation created a new appointment for the supervision of the work of the toll and stallage collector and the management of the growing market trade,[45] while in 1853 a market was established in Sneinton to relieve the pressure on the main Nottingham market. In the same year receipts for tolls and stallages for the first time exceeded £1,000.[46] In 1857, the Market Superintendent noted that for some time the volume of business transacted at the fairs had been declining, but at the same time he noted that every market was assuming the proportions of a fair.[47] This gave rise to congestion in the town's central area, and, like the cheese fair in 1854, the site of cattle fairs was removed to Burton Street in 1855, though the regular cattle and sheep markets continued to be held in Market Place. These markets moved to Burton Street in 1870, but so long as cattle continued to be driven through the streets to reach their destination, market days continued to intensify traffic congestion. In 1877 the Markets and Fairs Committee decided to reduce the chaos that occurred each market day when sellers crowded their stalls into Market Place, and by providing a fixed number of stalls for hire by applicants the number of market traders was restricted. One result was that for each stall to be allotted there were often four applicants, though several stalls were let to the same persons every year.[48]

The Market Place was the largest of four that existed within the enlarged borough boundaries; there was a cattle market in the southern part of the town, Sneinton Market to the east, and a very small market to the north at Bulwell. In 1889, four years after the main cattle market had removed to a seven acre site at Eastcroft, the Market Place accommodated three hundred and forty-two stalls owned by the Corporation, and twenty-eight fish stalls which were the fishmongers' own property. Fruit, vegetable, and fish whole-salers carried on their business daily, and in 1889 it was estimated that between sixty and seventy tons of produce passed through the market each week. Much of this was transported in carriers' carts from east midland villages. Most of the meat sold in the town was also supplied from an area within twenty miles radius of Nottingham, and although some foreign cattle reached the market via Liverpool and Hull four-fifths of the town's cattle supply was driven to market on the hoof.

Both in the distribution of cattle and produce, middlemen domi-nated the scene by the last quarter of the century. Farmers and market gardeners sent produce into Nottingham to be sold in the shops, but for the most part the carriers' handled their produce, disposing of it in the town, or selling in the Market Place.[49] By 1874 the regular influx of carriers' carts for the sale of produce outside the Market Place had grown to such an extent that the Corporation secured an Act to make the whole borough a market, thereby obtaining the right to charge the carriers tolls.[50] By 1889 the Markets and Fairs Committee normally expected about one hundred carts to invade the town each market day, while in the lower parts of the town the owners of small stalls which sold fried fish, potatoes, or ice cream, became almost permanent street vendors, though they were not allowed to escape a weekly charge for these concessions. Haw-kers, whose numbers were also increasing, were considered a nuisance on the crowded streets, but the central market was a source of local pride, not only on account of the volume of goods bought and sold on market days, but also because of the wide range of articles for sale: boots and shoes, old clothing, nails, second-hand music, birds of all sorts—'anything,' according to the Town Clerk, 'from a toothpick to a coffin'.

Complementary to the growing trade in produce was an expansion in the grocery trade. In 1858 Joseph Burton had opened his first store on St. Ann's Well Road; a few years later, when he described himself as a 'provisions merchant', he was attracting custom by inviting consumers to sample food before purchase.[52] In 1864 Burton opened a larger shop on Smithy Row near to Market Place, and in 1883 he took over Stephenson's fish, game, and poultry business which was also located on Smithy Row. The purchase of cold storage premises two years later, the opening of an ice-manufacturing plant in 1887, and the employment, also, of forty soft-topped delivery carts suggests the expanding scale of Burton's trade in provisions. The enterprise continued to expand by purchasing two more shops on Smithy Row in 1892 and 1894, while the firm also acquired a disused chapel in Talbot Street which was used as a warehouse. In 1896 he opened branch shops in Alfreton, Heanor, and Eastwood, and more in Coventry and Sheffield in 1898, while no fewer than seven Burton shops opened in 1900, the same year in which Joseph became the chairman of Joseph Burton & Sons Ltd.[53] More typical than the large scale multiple retail store built up by Joseph Burton was the small shop, which, in most classes of retail trade, continued to predominate into the twentieth century; but the multiples slowly gained ground as the rising standard of living brought about a growing mass demand for standard classes of necessities.[54] While multiple shops like Burton's sold a limited range of goods, the department store followed the opposite policy, furthermore, unlike the multiple store, the department store usually restricted its business to a central urban district. Like most department stores, both Jessop & Son and Griffin and Spalding began as drapery shops, the Jessop family taking over the management of a former haberdashery and millinery store in 1866, while the establishment of Griffin and Spalding dates from 1846.[55] By 1892 the latter employed two hundred people in its twenty departments, and in that year a visitor to Griffin and Spalding wrote of the disappearance of

> that exclusiveness which in former years confined each class of tradesman within narrowest limits . . . in its stead we find a whole colony of trades centred in one establishment.[56]

Although Joseph Burton began to manufacture jam for sale in

his shops, the most successful instance where a retailer moved backwards into manufacturing on a very large scale was that of Jesse Boot, who, during the last two decades of the nineteenth century, became the country's leading retailer and manufacturer of pharmaceutical goods. The modest beginnings of the vast Boot enterprise were laid by John Boot, the labourer who opened a tiny herbalist shop in Goose Gate. He died in 1860, leaving his wife and Jesse, aged ten, to carry on the business. In order to help his mother in the shop the young Boot left school, and three years later assumed sole management of the business. As he gained experience Jesse decided that he would increase sales of such articles as Epsom salts, camphor, soft soap, and bicarbonate of soda, if he could offer them to his customers attractively packed and at lower prices. The latter policy he adopted by purchasing supplies in bulk at a discount, selling to his customers on the same principle.[57] Using similar methods to those so effectively employed at that time by Thomas Beecham to sell his pills and by William Lever to sell his soap,[58] Jesse packed salts, sodas, soaps, and herbal remedies, and advertised them under his own name. He extended that policy to the marketing of drugs in 1877, when the shop front's new legend ran: 'Jesse Boot, Drugs and Proprietary Articles at Reduced Prices'.[59] Hostile to this slick and professionally unqualified entrepreneur who sold standardized drugs by brand, his competitors in the pharmaceutical trade were united in opposition towards him and the business methods with which he became identified. But Jesse remained impervious to their verbal attacks, and in 1883 launched Boots Pure Drug Company Ltd., subscribing the entire paid up capital of £4,698.[60] By that time his staff consisted of more than ten people, including a fully qualified chemist to compound prescriptions.[61] The public, however, showed some reluctance to accord 'Boots, Cash Chemists' similar respect to that which they reserved for the town's less flamboyant apothecaries, whose incessant abuse fed the public's suspicions.[62]

The volume of prescription orders might have signified the status held by any chemist within the pharmaceutical profession, but profits were indicative of commercial success, and Boot ensured the latter by beginning to manufacture, wholesale, and retail drugs, distributing them through multiple outlets scattered over the country.[63] For manufacturing purposes Boot acquired a cotton doubling factory in Island Street, while in order to facilitate the formation of several associated companies to develop the retail trade, in 1892 the trading and manufacturing functions became separate.[64] Already by 1896 sixty Boots Cash Chemists were retailing pharmaceutical products, toilet requisites, and stationery, in twenty-eight towns, an indication of the vast expansion of Boot's enterprise which took place in the twentieth century.[65] This expansion was financed mainly from profits, for in 1899 Boot held 68 per cent. of the £47,200 paid up capital, the remainder coming from outside the Nottingham area.[66] In the nineties Boot was still at loggerheads with chemists who conducted their businesses in conventional fashion, and when he engaged several qualified chemists to handle prescriptions, the Association compelled them to resign from the Pharmaceutical Society. Not until 1908 was the feud between Boot and the remainder of the trade brought to an end.[67] An innovator in marketing, Boot also built up an integrated manufacturing plant where all processes, from the preparation of the chemicals to their distribution to the retail shops, were carried out. In 1892 the factory in Island Street contained five steam printing machines, each of which produced ten thousand circulars and advertising handbills every hour; even packing cases were made on the premises. After touring the establishment, a reporter assured his readers 'there will not be found one article wanting of all the advertised specifics for all ills that flesh is heir to.'[68]

A weakness of the flesh for which Boot offered no remedy provided the basis for the second large new enterprise whose name, like Boots, was later to become identified with Nottingham. In 1862 the small retailing and tobacco concern of William Wright, which dated from 1823, passed into the hands of John Player, the son of a solicitor from Saffron Walden, and who himself had been in the retail trade.[69] Recognizing the marketing possibilities of producing packaged cigarettes and tobacco and advertising and selling them by brand, Player met with such success that he built three factories in Radford. Two of these he let as lace factories, moving into them when his scale of operations warranted the use of more space.[70] By 1889 the firm employed two hundred and fifty people (mainly women) who manufactured cigarettes, cigars, and tobacco for sale in home and in foreign markets, and by 1898, when Player occupied all three factories, one thousand people were employed.[71] The firm became a limited liability company in 1895, though a majority of the shares were taken up by the family.[72] Player's thus became by far the town's largest tobacco manufacturer, and one of the largest in the country, and as chairman of the Nottingham Tobacco Dealers' Association formed in 1878, Player was influenced in the fixing of retail tobacco prices.[73] The other manufacturers were Messrs. Robinson & Barnsdale, established in 1877, who employed two hundred and fifty persons, and who specialized in the production of cigars; Thomas Riley, who entered the trade in 1869, employed about one hundred and fifty in 1889.[74]

The third enterprise to be established in Nottingham which laid the foundations for a growing industry and provided a major source of employment was the Raleigh Cycle Company, whose location in Nottingham owed less to chance factors than that of either Boots or John Player & Sons. The building of bicycles called for mechanical skills similar to those required in the construction of lace and hosiery machinery. By the third quarter of the century local firms had already established the town's reputation as an engineering centre, and a handful of local artisans were numbered among the first cycle engineers in the country. Following its popularity in France, the sport of cycling was introduced to England in the sixties, and already in 1868 William Humber, a blacksmith moulder employed at the engineering workshops of Manlove & Alliott, was building cycles.[75] By 1875 two other men had joined Humber to form the Humber, Marriott & Cooper Cycle Company, which then employed about six mechanics at the Beeston workshops.[76] James Carver, a lace machine builder, also began to make cycles, and at the London Cycle Exhibition of 1878 he received a bronze medal for his work.[77] At the same exhibition, Humber, Mariott & Co., were awarded gold and silver medals prizes which, added to Humber's development of the boneshaker and the 'spider wheel', contributed to their future commercial success. When the demand for cycles began to expand rapidly, after the introduction of the chain driven safety model in 1879 which transformed cycling from a mere sport into a popular hobby, Humber's reputation provided a sound basis for the firm's growth.[78] On the crest of this tide of enthusiasm three local mechanics, Woodhead, Angois, and Ellis, formerly employed at one of the town's large firms, took a small room in Raleigh Street and began to produce 'solid wheeled ordinaries', tricycles, and tandems.[79] Their success encouraged expansion, and by 1887 the firm employed fifteen men; but it became clear, two years later, that a stage had been reached when a decision must be taken as to the firm's long term future, and plans were drawn up to move into a five-storeyed factory which could accommodate ninety workmen;[80] for such a policy of expansion, however, finance was required.

The story is well known how Frank Bowden, the London financier, returned to England from the far East in ill health, how he was recommended to take up cycling as a therapeutic pastime, and how successful this proved. Firmly convinced, through personal experience of the pleasure and exercise it gave, that the popularity of cycling would grow, Bowden searched for a cycle firm which offered opportunities for large scale investment, and decided upon the Raleigh Street firm. From incorporation in 1889 Bowden took charge of the administration of the business, while Angois remained chief designer and Woodhead was nominally the works manager; Ellis, by this time, had disappeared from the partnership. In 1894 Bowden bought the interests of Woodhead and Angois and hired experienced technical managers from the Humber Company.[81] Two years later two more two-storeyed workshops were built, and in 1891, when it employed over three hundred engineers, the business was said to be worth £40,000. The firm developed a large export trade, establishing connections and building up a reputation in Australia, America, Continental Europe, and India.

In 1892 the Humber Cycle Company at Beeston employed five hundred persons.[82] Between 1881 and 1891 the number of cycle firms in Nottingham increased from eight to nineteen, and in the next decade, as mechanics like James Carver (who set up as a cycle maker with £40) entered the trade, their number rose to sixty-eight.[83] This increase in the supply of cycles occurred in response to a huge and rapid expansion in demand which was stimulated by the rising popularity of cycles fitted with pneumatic in the place of solid tyres. The century closed with a veritable cycle craze.

The Humber firm had become a limited company in 1886, a greater part of the capital having been raised in London.[84] The Beeston Works were extended, while new factories were built in Birmingham, Coventry, and America.[85] Net profits of the Humber Cycle Company, the largest cycle firm in Nottingham, rose from £25,317 in 1891, to £29,663 in 1892, falling to £19,842 in the following year. Thereafter, profits rose steadily for five years reaching £62,760 in 1897.[86] In 1896 Raleigh, by this time a limited company employing eight hundred men, built a new factory costing £80,000, which, on completion, trebled the capacity initially planned.[87] The policy of Raleigh directors, however, proved too optimistic. Depreciation on investments, loss on the sale of the French business, and other losses due to a fall in the price of materials heavily stocked, led to an investigation by a committee appointed by the shareholders. The management was accused of absenteeism which had resulted in financial losses, and on the shareholders' insistence the company was liquidated and reconstructed under the same name.[88] This fresh start proved to be a success, for it coincided with an upsurge of activity in the cycle trade, and a few years later the Humber Company's departure from Beeston, after a decision to concentrate production at the Coventry works, left behind over a thousand cycle engineers in the Nottingham district.[89] Locally, Raleigh became the giant concern among a declining number of small manufacturers for the recession of 1898–9 weeded out a multitude of unsound boom firms,[90] while Raleigh's production, in 1901, of the first 'all steel bicycle' laid the technical foundation for further expansion.[91]

The workers in the cycle trade, of whom there were estimated to be five thousand in and around Nottingham in 1897,[92] had not, up to this time, belonged to a single union; some belonged to the Amalgamated Society of Engineers, some to the Filers' Trade Union, and others to the labourers' unions. After the turners' success in 1897, the filers struck successfully for an advance. The next month a branch of the National Union of Cycle Workers was formed in Nottingham, and so great was the response that two more branches were opened in swift succession.[93] Local employers viewed these developments with apprehension, and the lock-out action on the part of the national Engineering Employers' Federation in opposition to the demands of the A.S.E. for an eight hour day, prompted them to adopt the policy of the Federation and to lock out all union members, even though the Cycle Union had made no attempt to participate in the movement for the shortened workday. As trade was uncertain many employers were not greatly disturbed by the stoppage, which affected directly about a thousand men in Nottingham. During the lockout immense crowds met blacklegs from work with hooting and jeering, and the Federation prosecuted several trade unionists for assault.[94] There was a marked sympathy for the cycle workers in Nottingham, and the *Express* inaugurated a 'Nothing to Eat Fund' to assist workers and labourers affected by the dispute.[95] The Trades Council raised subscriptions and benefit concerts were arranged, but the dispute ended in a victory for the Federation and the cycle workers returned to work, even though some employers offered lower wages than they had paid hitherto.[96] Trade slowly improved, but the temporary stoppage had served to eliminate several smaller manufacturers, and this contributed to the growing concentration of the cycle industry as larger firms like Humber and Raleigh introduced improved machinery and lower prices.[97]

The rapid rise of the cycle industry made huge demands upon the supply of skilled mechanics, and the existence in the Coventry and Nottingham districts of this kind of labour helps to explain why the cycle industry developed in these towns. During the third quarter of the century machine building for the lace and hosiery trades had moved from the workshops to the engineering works, as the domestic and foreign markets for machinery grew rapidly. Nottingham machine builders, especially the firms of James Carver, Lake & Wigley, Sharman & Tilson, Humphreys & Wyer, and E. Reader, supplied almost the entire trade with machinery and, according to one prominent lace manufacturer, in 1886 all existing lace machinery in Germany had been built in Nottingham.[98] John

Jardine, the leading firm constructing the delicate moving parts of machine insides, secured a high reputation for its work both in Continental Europe and in the United States. Judging from figures in Jardine's order books only a fraction of the newly built machinery was supplied to local manufacturers, while Jardine, who employed over one thousand men and guaranteed three weeks deliveries, doubled his output between 1895 and 1905.[99] The successful performance of Nottingham machine builders was a source of complaint by some manufacturers; they could point to the Scottish lace curtain industry which had been established in 1875 with one second-hand water-powered machine and which, by the beginning of the twentieth century, dominated the manufacture of lace curtains.[100] The industry was entirely dependent upon Nottingham lace machine builders who, between 1875 and 1885, had sold more than one hundred machines to factories in Scotland.[101] During the same period, machine building emerged as a separate section of the hosiery trade, beginning with the firm established by Moses Mellor in 1844 and the opening of a factory for the production of circular machinery in 1853. Despite strong American competition, the number of machine building firms in Nottingham almost doubled between 1881 and 1891, while the invention of the seamless automatic knitting machine afforded the industry a further stimulus.[102]

Some of these firms combined the manufacture of hosiery and lace machinery with other types of engineering. The firms of Reader and Blackburn & Sons, for example, made stoves, pipes, and other houseware; J. Taylor & Sons, founded in 1852, became one of the town's leading engineers manufacturing railway and colliery equipment and steam gas engines, as did Thomas Danks & Co., while general and specialist engineers flourished in Nottingham during this period, many of the firms receiving their supply of pig iron from Stanton.[104] Wright's Directory for 1891 records eighteen civil and mining engineering firms, five gas engine makers, five electrical engineers, and five electro-platers, apart from the numerous machine-tool makers. The most extensive engineering firm in the town was that of Manlove & Alliott, the framesmiths who in 1838 had opened an engineering works which, by the eighties, employed between five and seven hundred persons. It was recognized as the largest manufacturing firm of steam laundry machinery in the country and did a great amount of work for the Corporation in connection with refuse destructors, besides the production of sugar machinery and general millwright work.[105] This firm proved to be the training ground for William Humber, and for Edward Barton who worked as a fitter and who later founded the town's huge omnibus company.[106]

Before the turn of the century there were signs of a broadening in the base of the local economy; in the last quarter of the century the foundations of three important industries had been laid in the town with the growth of Players, Raleigh, and Boots. In addition to engineering, other industries expanding in the area were the manufacture of paper boxes, cartons, and cardboard boxes and the ready-made clothing trade; lithographic printing and packaging also grew as advertising techniques developed. Apart from these (and excluding the lace and hosiery trades), the list of local industries in the Chamber of Commerce Year Book for 1914 included in the spinning and twisting of cotton, silk, and woollen yarns, bleaching and dyeing, leather, brick, tile, and horticultural pottery works, furniture and cabinet manufacture, brewing, malting, chair making, the making of mineral water, wine, and coffee essences, confectionery and sugar boiling, soap and starch manufacture, organ building, whip making, the production of lightning conductors, boot and shoe making, basket and wicker work, and the manufacture of perambulator toys, brushes, and roller blinds.[107] In less than a lifetime Nottingham had developed from a small town perilously dependent upon only two industries for its prosperity and progress to become a modern city with nearly a quarter of a million inhabitants occupied in numerous trades, members of a community who could regard with satisfaction and confidence the diversified economic base of a thriving industrial centre. The three new major firms of Raleigh, Player's and Boots assumed increasing importance in the town's economic complexion. Yet it is agreed that the firms of Player's and Boots owed their location in Nottingham to factors largely divorced from economic phenomena—although a plentiful supply of female labour was important for success. The cycle trade, however, whose development in terms of employment was of greater significance to the local economy than the other two, grew, to some extent, out of the engineering industries which themselves owed their foundation to the machine building trades. Thus the cycle engineer was the lineal economic descendant of the framesmith whose praises had been sung more than a century before.

Coinciding with the economic changes of the second half of the century was the appearance of fresh local institutions whose functions were directly related to Nottingham's growing industry and commerce. The earliest local Chamber of Commerce had existed in 1788 and an abortive attempt to form a successor in 1813 had been followed by a more successful effort in 1834, when a group of merchants and manufacturers from the lace and hosiery trades adopted the proposal revived by Felkin to form a Chamber of Commerce. Soon the Chamber's membership had reached one hundred, the chief activities consisting of submitting petitions to the government to further the interests of the lace and hosiery trades, while discussions began to consider the formation of a hosiery lace and yarn exchange in connection with a new Corn Exchange. During the depression of 1837–8, however, the Chamber's meetings were discontinued and more than twenty years passed before that body was re-established on a permanent basis.[108]

Modelled on the commercial exchanges of Manchester and Liverpool, in 1853 a group of prominent businessmen, the majority of whom were connected with the lace trade, formed the Nottingham General Exchange and Commercial Association. The Association held its meetings in the building formerly intended as a Corn Exchange, one portion of which was set aside for use as a telegraph office. After twelve months membership had reached four hundred, but the Association was little more than a social club.[109]

Its original aims were very similar to those set down by the new Chamber of Commerce established in 1860, the rules of which were based on those of the Manchester and Leeds Chambers. Apart from its general functions—to act as a representative body for the trades of the town, to benefit, protect, and express the views of the trades —the immediate problems which brought the founders together included the increasing pressure of French competition upon the lace and hosiery trades and, in particular, the imminent Anglo-French trade agreement, the application of the Factory Act to the lace trade, the question of the abolition of frame rents, the banking law, and the Bleach Works Bill.[110] The Chamber's first measure was to send a delegation to Paris for the purpose of investigating the proposed commercial agreement with France, and this was followed by a petition to the Queen requesting her to appear in lace occasionally.[111] From the beginning, the safeguarding of interests in the negotiation of tariffs with foreign countries loomed large in the Chamber's affairs. During the first decade other business included consideration of the Trade Marks Bill, amendments to Partnership Law, the Carrier's Act, and Bankruptcy Laws. Members of the Chamber also favoured some modifications to the Factory Acts as they applied to lace and hosiery warehouses. The Chamber met with much less support than had been hoped, and members who were confined almost solely to lace and hosiery interests were frequently urged to canvass for others with wider interests, a call which was repeated in the 1890's when the Mayor of Nottingham referred to the Chamber as 'an insignificant and unomnipotent minority'.[112]

In the last quarter of the century members of the Chamber watched with dismay the tariff barriers rising against British manufacturers and merchants. Traditionally Liberal, it became divided on trade policy. When answering a questionnaire issued by the Royal Commission on Depression in 1886 the Council of the Chamber affirmed a strong belief in free trade principles; but later, representatives of the Chamber pointed out that the previous resolution had come from the Council of the Chamber—which included a very large proportion of merchant interests—and not from the whole Chamber, many of whose members favoured protection.[113] Another issue which led to disagreement within the Chamber was the gravitation of smaller hosiery and lace manufacturers into the cheaper labour markets of the surrounding districts, a problem which, owing to a 'feeling of delicacy', the Chamber did not debate. This behaviour was typical of a body lacking strength in membership and conviction on policy.[114]

Following the establishment of the Chamber of Commerce, a general meeting of trade union representatives in 1861 resolved to form the Nottingham Organized Trades Council.[115] Its aim was to protect labour and at the same time to bring moral pressure to bear upon other labour organisations in the hope of infusing general sympathy between working men in different trades. The promotion of trade union principles involved the discussion of all matters brought before the committee, the appointment of delegations to employers in the event of disputes, and assistance in the printing and circulation of documents in connection with strikes sanctioned by the Council. It was emphasized that the Council claimed no powers to interfere in the internal affairs of member societies, except after invitation. In 1862 the Association of Organized Trades in Nottingham issued an address to working men:

> the condition of the working classes having . . . become beneficially changed, we hold that it is their duty to protect themselves against all undue and improper interference on the part of those to whom they sell their labour and to each other in securing an adequate remuneration and means of compatible subsistence.[116]

The address denounced strike action, but offered to give financial support when necessary; the Council saw its role as that of exerting a moral influence, rather than mounting belligerent campaigns against employers. Drawing its main support from unions of lacemakers, engineers, bricklayers, tailors, and other skilled unions, the Association had possessed twelve hundred paying members in March 1862. However, during the unsettled years of the sixties the Council was inactive, and not until the tailors' strike in London in 1867 and the strike of the Nottinghamshire and Derbyshire Miners the same year, did members of the Council make their voices heard. By 1878 the Nottingham Organized Council Executive consisted of

s

forty members who represented over six thousand men in various unions, the largest of which were the Amalgamated Society of Lace Operatives and the Rotary Framework Knitters' Society. Workmen in the building trades were affiliated to their own separate Trades Council.[117]

In 1875 the Federated Trades Council was formed, an offshoot of the Organized Council. It is not clear why the new body was established, but eventually the Organized Council merged with the Federated Council in 1884 when the Building Trades Council also united with them to form a Joint Committee.[118] To this the Organized, Federated, and Building Trade Councils, sent four, six, and three delegates respectively. The aims of the Joint Committee were:

> to afford moral assistance and sympathy to the whole of the trades in Nottingham in times of trouble, to organize trade societies for protective and friendly purposes, to bring about an amicable adjustment in case of disputes, to petition Parliament upon questions affecting the rights of the working classes and to co-operate with similar associations.[119]

It is significant that the trade unionists regrouped their forces in 1884, for that year marked the beginning of a period of widespread unemployment in the country at large. The late seventies, a period of 'abnormal development in the town'[120] reaching a peak in 1883, had been accompanied by extensive building construction which had attracted extra labour. There was a sudden slackening in investment towards the end of 1884, and the seasonal unemployment in the winter of that year was much worse than usual. In December hundreds of unemployed congregated in Market Place to request the Corporation to provide employment.[121] A memorial from the Committee of the Charity Organization Society in Nottingham was sent to the Council, reporting that its attention was directed towards

> the existing poverty and the possibility of unusually widespread and severe destitution in the town . . . during the present winter . . . There are now a large number of people who have considerable difficulty in supporting themselves and their families.[122]

As a result of this representation the Estates Committee arranged for work levelling land on Hunger Hills and the Coppice Estate. Employed on bi-weekly shifts, the men could earn a maximum weekly wage of 6s. 6d. These public works, which gave employment to between six and seven hundred men each week, chiefly from the building trades, lasted until the end of March, during which time £7,000 had been spent; even then, work had been found for only half of those who had applied.[123] Following a reappraisal of the efficacy of providing relief through public employment, the Estates Committee discontinued the system, though admitting that unemployment in the town remained and was causing much hardship. In a report to the Council the Estates Committee stressed the importance of not protracting current works; it was feared that they might have the effect of encouraging workpeople to remain in the town, though their prospects of ultimate employment might be minimal.[124]

Backed by the Trades Council and other trade societies, the building unions accused the Council of restricting local employment opportunities through its policy of awarding building contracts to firms outside Nottingham. In 1885 the contract for building the new Law Courts, Police Station, Fire Station, and Public Offices was awarded to a Liverpool firm. The Building Trades Council formally requested the Town Council to reverse the acceptance of the tender of the Liverpool firm in favour of a local employer, but the Council refused.[125] Shortly afterwards a Labour Representation Committee was formed which unsuccessfully tried to ventilate trade unionist opinion in the Council.[126] A later complaint from the Trades Council that the Liverpool contractors were using stone below standard specifications, was investigated by four architects, but the Corporation declared its satisfaction with the materials and the matter was dropped.[127] Frustrated by the apparently indifferent attitude of the Council, the men who were discharged by order of the Estates Committee in March, 1885 proceeded in a body to the workhouse, where more than thirteen hundred presented themselves to the Relieving Officer. The guardians had no alternative but to offer them the workhouse, though Gregory, a prominent lace manufacturer and Council member, dissented from this decision. One hundred and fifty-five men actually made formal application for relief and fifty-five were admitted.[128]

The employment situation failed to improve substantially throughout the year, and with the return of winter the Corporation again received requests to provide work. The official reply was that the onus of dealing with poverty lay with the poor law authority of the district, but that 'proper applications' would be considered. The Board of Guardians arranged to provide more supervised outdoor employment, and large numbers of men were subsequently put to the labour test.[129] The winter of 1886–7 was severe and brought much hardship to the unemployed. Led by a marching band, crowds of unemployed men and women straggled through the cold December streets to draw attention to their plight.[130] In January the Mayor opened a Public Relief Fund, and £2,000 made possible the distribution of soup and bread to the cold and hungry. Meanwhile, various religious bodies were busy raising funds with which to purchase and distribute blankets, soup, and bread, and the Nottingham Charity Organization also found its services in demand. In order to help those among the unemployed who could not afford the cost of advertising for work, the Nottingham Daily Express offered to insert short advertisements free of charge.[131]

In January, 1886, Sneinton Market Place became the scene for a mass meeting when two thousand persons signed a memorial praying the Council to open relief works immediately. Similar memorials were submitted by the Nottingham Social Democratic Federation, the Nottingham Magna Charta Association, and the Committee responsible for the distribution of funds raised at a Grand Theatre Concert.[132] On the whole, the views of the Council were hostile to these applications, and on a motion passed by seventeen votes to eleven the memorials from the unemployed were referred to the guardians, who stated that they were fully capable of dealing with the problem. The guardians then drew the attention of the Watch Committee to the

> apparently legalised system of begging and imposture practised by these men in parading the streets and asking alms from door to door . . . and request(ed) that this highly improper and dangerous system may be dealt with vigorously and put an end to at once.[133]

It is not surprising that such distress which accompanied periodic unemployment owing to interruptions in trade prompted contemporaries to refer to the closing decades of the century as the Great Depression. But this description belied the secular economic expansion that occurred in this period[134] and in which local industries shared.

References

[1] *N.R.,* March 13, 1852.
[2] *B.R.,* IX, 118, January 5, 1857.
[3] *Report of the Nottingham Corporation Sanitary Committee* (1857), pp. 4–5; *B.R.,* IX, 118, January 5, 1857.
[4] Quoted in *N.R.,* July 17, 1857.
[5] *First Report of the Children's Employment Commission,* 1863 (3170) XVIII. 1; C. N. Wright and W. Wylie, *The Nottingham Handbook* (Nottingham, 1858), p .79; *N.R.,* July 13, 1855.
[6] *N.R.,* May 14, 1852.
[7] *B.R.,* IX, 127, November 16, 1857; *B.R.,* IX, 133, November 22, 1859.
[8] W. Wylie, *op. cit.,* pp. 289–90; *N.R.,* December 10, 1852.
[9] *N.R.,* May 6, 1853.
[10] *N.R.,* July 29, 1853; *N.R.,* May 12, 1853; *N.R.,* May 26, 1853; *N.R.,* July 21, 1854.
[11] H. Green, 'The Southern Portion of the Nottinghamshire and Derbyshire Coalfield and the Development of Transport before 1850,' *Journal of the Derbyshire Archaeological and Natural History Society* IX, LVI (1936), p. 69.
[12] *V.C.H.,* II; p. 329, W. W. Fyffe, *Rambles Round Nottingham* I, (1856), p. 324.
[13] These figures are taken from *Mineral Statistics, 1856–1870.*
[14] *N.R.,* September 25, 1857; *N.R.,* November 27, 1857; *N.R.,* March 9, 1860; *N.R.,* July 20, 1860.
[15] W. O. Henderson, *The Lancashire Cotton Famine 1861–5,* (1934), pp. 20–25.
[16] J. D. Chambers, *The Workshop of the World,* (1961), pp. 146–7.
[17] W. F. Crick and J. E. Wadsworth, *A Hundred Years of Joint Stock Banking,* (1936), p. 263.
[18] *Ibid.,* pp. 264–266.
[19] W. W. Rostow, *British Economy of the Nineteenth Century,* (1948), p. 79.
[20] K. C. Edwards, *A Scientific Survey of Nottingham and District.* (B.A.A.S. Nottingham, 1937), p. 31.
[21] See *Mineral Statistics,* 1869–1901.
[22] *Comparative Account of the Population of Great Britain,* 1801-31, 1831 (348) XVIII; Census (1851), Vol. II, 1852–53 LXXXVI.
[23] *Census* (1861) Vol. II, 1863, LIII. Pt. 1. 265—Pt. II. 1.
[24] *Census* (1851), Vol. II, 1852–53 LXXXVI.
[25] William White, *History Gazetteer and Directory of Nottinghamshire,* (Nottingham, 1832), pp. 186–97, 470, 497, 509.
[26] William Felkin, 'Account of the Lace and Hosiery Manufactures' submitted in the *First Report of the Children's Employment Commission* (1863), (3170), XVIII. 1., p. 236.
[27] *Census* (1861) Vol. II, 1863, LIII. Pt. 1. 265—Pt. II. 1. and *Census* (1871) Vol. I, 1872, LXVI. Pt. I. 1. and Vol. III, 1873, LXXII Pt. I. 1. A percentage comparison of 72.62 in 1851–61 with 22.72 in 1861–71. The immigration figures are net of emigration of people formerly resident in Nottingham but born elsewhere.
[28] See A. K. Cairncross, 'Internal Migration in Victorian England,' *Manchester School* XVII, (1949), p. 70 *et. seq.*
[29] *Census* (1871) Vol. III, 1873, LXXII Pt. I. 1.
[30] *Ibid.*

[31] See C. N. Wright, *Wright's Nottingham Directory* (1854–1901) years 1862 and 1871.

[32] Nottingham Chamber of Commerce publication *Arts, Trades, and Manufactures,* (Nottingham, 1892), p. 33.

[33] W. W. Fyffe, *op. cit.,* p. 350.

[34] *Census* (1871) Vol. I, 1872, LXVI. Pt. I. 1.

[35] R. Mellors, *Old Nottingham Suburbs* (Nottingham 1914), p. 209; K. C. Edwards, *A Scientific Survey of Nottingham and District* (B.A.A.S. Nottingham, 1937), p. 31.

[36] *First Report of the Children's Employment Commission,* (1863), (3170) XVIII, ev. of Thomas Adams, p. 195.

[37] *Census of England and Wales* 1881–1901.

[38] A. C. Wood 'Nottingham 1835–1865', *Transactions of the Thoroton Society,* LIX (1955), p. 5.

[39] *Infra,* pp. 349–50.

[40] F. S. Williams, '*The Midland Railway*: *Its Rise and Progress*,' (1876), p. 164.

[41] G. E. Bell, *The Railway as a Factor in the Location of Manufacturing Industry in the East Midlands* (unpublished Ph.D. thesis Nottingham, 1958), p. 145.

[42] *Ibid.,* p. 140.

[43] See John Marshall, '*The Nottingham Suburban Railway*', (Nottingham, 1963), typescript.

[44] W. Ashworth, *An Economic History of England 1870–1939,* (1960), p. 128.

[45] *B.R.,* IX, 29, February 4, 1841.

[46] *B.R.,* IX, 102, February 10, 1854.

[47] *B.R.,* IX, 118, February 2, 1857.

[48] *Report of the Royal Commission on Market Rights and Tolls,* 1890–1. XXXVII. 243., pp. 314–316.

[49] *Report of the Royal Commission on Market Rights and Tolls,* 1890–1, XXXVIII. 1., p. 78.

[50] *Report of the Royal Commission on Market Rights and Tolls* 1890–1, 243, p. 315.

[51] *Report of the Royal Commission on Market Rights and Tolls* 1890–1, 1, p. 79.

[52] '*The Year of Grace*' (Nottingham, 1958), Joseph Burton & Sons publication.

[53] *Ibid.*

[54] W. Ashworth, *An Economic History of England 1870–1939,* (1960), p. 133.

[55] *Jessop & Son Sesquicentenary 1804–1954,* (1954), Illustrated supplement to the Gazette of the John Lewis Partnership.

[56] *The Nottingham and Nottinghamshire Illustrated,* (Nottingham, 1892), p. 75.

[57] H. J. Davis, *The Honoured Name,* (1931), p. 5.

[58] T. C. Barker and J. R. Harris, *A Merseyside Town in the Industrial Revolution*: *St. Helens 1750–1900,* (Liverpool, 1954), pp. 378–9.

[59] H. J. Davis, *op. cit.,* p. 6.

[60] J. M. Hunter 'The Sources of Capital in the Industrial Development of Nottingham,' *East Midland Geographer,* XVI (December, 1961), p. 39.

[61] Cecil Roberts, *Achievement, A Record of Fifty Years Progress of Boots Pure Drug Company,* (Nottingham, 1938), p. 16.

[62] H. J. Davis, *op. cit.,* p. 6.

[63] *Ibid.*, p. 19.

[64] *Nottingham and Nottinghamshire Illustrated,* (1892), pp. 92–94.

[65] Cecil Roberts, *op. cit.*, p. 21.

[66] J. M. Hunter, *art. cit.*, p. 39.

[67] Cecil Roberts, *loc. cit.*

[68] *Nottingham and Nottinghamshire Illustrated,* (1892), pp. 92–94.

[69] *History of John Player & Son,* (typescript, John Player & Son).

[70] *Ex.,* November 16, 1889; *Ex.,* September 15, 1889.

[71] *History of John Player & Son,* (typescript, John Player & Son).

[72] J. M. Hunter, *art. cit.*, p. 38.

[73] *Ex.,* April 24, 1878, *Ex.,* April 18, 1890.

[74] *Ex.,* November 21, 1889; *Ex.,* April 18, 1890.

[75] 'Manlove, Alliott & Fryer', (Reprint from *Machinery Market,* July 2, 1888; J. Lancaster, 'Some Recollections of Bloomsgrove Works,' typescript Manlove, Alliott & Fryer (1916), R. Mellors, *Men of Nottingham and Nottinghamshire,* (Nottingham, 1924), p. 187.

[76] *Ex.,* November 23, 1878.

[77] *Ibid.*

[78] H. O. Duncan, *The World on Wheels,* (Paris, 1920), pp. 298–300; M. Mellors, *op. cit.*, p. 187.

[79] Report of Woodruff at the Raleigh Company A.G.M., *Ex.,* December 12, 1891; *Bartlett's Bicycle Book,* p. 94.

[80] *Ex.,* December 12, 1891.

[81] *N.J.,* November 12, 1952.

[82] *Ibid.*

[83] *Wright's Nottingham Directory,* (1891–1901); *Ex.,* November 2, 1895.

[84] J. M. Hunter, *art. cit.*, p. 37.

[85] *Ex.,* June 21, 1895.

[86] *Ex.,* November 19, 1897; *Ex.,* December 9, 1898.

[87] *Ex.,* November 3, 1896.

[88] *Ex.,* February 13, 1898.

[89] R. Mellors, *Nottinghamshire Villages,* (Nottingham, 1916), p. 40.

[90] *Nottingham Chamber of Commerce Minutes,* January 25, 1899; *Ex.,* January 1, 1901.

[91] *Building Bicycles* (Raleigh Industries publication, 1938), p. 11.

[92] The estimate was that of a trade union officer, *Ex.,* February 18, 1897.

[93] *Ex.,* March 23, 1897; *Ex.,* April 13, 1897; *Ex.,* July 5, 1897.

[94] *Ex.,* January 7, 1898.

[95] *Ex.,* October 11, 1897.

[96] *Ex.,* November 13, 1897.

[97] *Ex.,* January 1, 1898.

[98] *First Report of the Royal Commission on the Depression of Trade and Industry,* 1886 (c. 4621) XXI, ev. of Birkin, p. 239

[99] *Nottingham and Nottinghamshire Illustrated,* (1892), p. 42; 'The Lace Trade in Nottingham and District,' (1905), *Express* reprint, p. 55.

[100] *Final Report of the First Census of Production* (1909).

[101] *Ex.,* August 26, 1884.

[102] *Nottingham and Nottinghamshire Illustrated,* (1892), pp. 48–52; John Wright, *Wright's Nottingham Directory,* 1881, 1891.

[103] *Nottingham and Nottinghamshire Illustrated,* (1892), pp. 38, 47, 48, 51, 61.

[104] *Ex.,* August 31, 1895.

105 'Manlove, Alliott & Fryer,' Reprint from *Machinery Market*, July 2, 1888; J. Lancaster, 'Some Recollections of Bloomsgrove Works' (typescript Manlove, Alliott & Fryer, 1916).

106 *Ibid.*

107 Nottingham Chamber of Commerce, *Nottingham Past, Present and Future* (1914), p. 6.

108 R. S. Fitton and A. P. Wadsworth, *The Strutts and the Arkwrights,* (1958), p. 54; *N.R.,* November 21, 1834; *N.R.,* May 22, 1835; William Felkin, *History,* pp. 344–346; See also A. G. Walton, *History of the Nottingham Chamber of Commerce* (Nottingham, 1963).

109 *N.R.,* May 27, 1853; *N.R.,* July 7, 1854; John Wright, *Wright's* Nottingham *Directory,* 1854, p. 369.

110 *Minutes of the Nottingham Chamber of Commerce,* July 6, 1860.

111 *N.R.,* May 4, 1860.

112 *Minutes of the Nottingham Chamber of Commerce,* January 13, 1867; April 24, 1862; January 11, 1864; March 13, 1864; March 19, 1867; January 13, 1868; January 11, 1869. *Ex.,* January 29, 1890.

113 *First Report of the Royal Commission* (*Depression of Trade and Industry*), 1886 (c. 4621), XXI, p. 245.

114 *Minutes of Nottingham Chamber of Commerce,* January 28, 1895; January 28, 1897.

115 *N.R.,* January 18, 1861; *N.R.,* March 7, 1862.

116 *N.R.,* March 7, 1862.

117 *Ex.,* August 28, 1875.

118 *Minutes of the Joint Committee of the United Trades Councils in Nottingham,* July 10, 1884.

119 *Ibid.*

120 *Report of the Royal Commission on the Poor Law and the Relief of Distress,* 1909 Cd. (4499) XXXVII. 1., p. 482.

121 *Ex.,* December 12, 1884.

122 *B.R.,* IX, 313, January 5, 1885.

123 *Report of the Royal Commission* (Poor Law and Relief of Distress), 1909, Cd. (4499) XXXVII. 1., p. 482; *Ex.,* December 17, 1884; *Ex.,* December 18, 1884; *Ex.,* December 19, 1884; *Ex.,* August 31, 1885; *B.R.,* IX, 315, February 16, 1885.

124 *B.R.,* IX, 317, March 30, 1885.

125 *Minutes of the Nottingham Association of Organized Trades,* April 15, 1885; *B.R.,* IX, March 23, 1885; *B.R.,* IX, 320, October 5, 1885; *Ex.,* March 18, 1885.

126 *Minutes of the Nottingham Association of Organized Trades,* April 15, 1885, November 10, 1887.

127 *B.R.,* IX, 325, May 3, 1886.

128 *N.J.,* April 1, 1885; *N.J.,* April 2, 1885.

129 *N.J.,* October 16, 1885; *N.J.,* December 12, *B.R.,* IX, 322, December 7, 1885; *Report of the Royal Commission* (*Poor Law and Relief of Distress*), 1909 Cd. (4499) XXXVII. 1., p. 482.

130 *Ex.,* June 3, 1886; *N.J.,* December 15, 1885; *Ex.,* February 10, 1886.

131 *Ex.,* January 5, 1886; *Ex.,* January 27, 1886; *Ex.,* February 15, 1886; *Ex.,* June 3, 1886.

132 *B.R.,* IX, 322, February 1, 1886.

133 *B.R.,* IX, 323–34, February 8, 1886.

134 See H. Beales, 'The Great Depression in Industry and Trade,' in E. M. Carus Wilson (ed.) *Essays in Economic History,* (1954), pp. 406–415.

CHAPTER X

THE HOSIERY INDUSTRY: TECHNICAL INNOVATION, THE FACTORY SYSTEM, AND THE BOARD OF ARBITRATION

TECHNICAL developments in the fifties and sixties revolutionized the hosiery trade. Before the few successful experiments with new machinery that occurred in the forties, the hosiery frame was identical in principle with that which had been used for more than two centuries, a flat frame of about twenty inches in width which knitted one stocking at a time. The only important modification had been the construction of the new wider frames which could run to fifty inches and make several stockings at once.[1] In 1844 wide frames accounted for a fifth of all frames, but whereas the narrow frame produced a fully fashioned article by varying the length of the courses of rows used, the wide frame was less versatile; hence narrow frames continued to produce mainly fully-fashioned hose and wide frames made unfashioned stockings, outerwear, drawers, pants, shirting, and underwear. However, so long as hosiery frames remained flat the problem of applying power to the mechanism was much greater than in other textile industries.

In 1816 Isambard Brunel, the French engineer, had built a 'tricoteur' which was the first circular hosiery frame to be worked by rotary motion. A successful innovation which was adopted commercially in Continental Europe and in America, in Britain it remained merely a curious invention. Operated by hand, the needles in this compact machine were set in a circle, instead of the usual flat arrangement as in Lee's frames; hence the machine was much better suited to rotary-powered production. But nearly thirty years elapsed before British entrepreneurs were willing to invest in it, a situation which requires explanation.[2] In 1829 Warner's of Loughborough had experimented with steam-powered rotary machinery, but had given up; in 1844 Paget of Loughborough invested in power-driven circular machinery, and in Nottingham in 1845 William Goddard, who was bankrupt two years later, built a factory for his rotary frames, although it is not clear whether they were steam-powered.[3] Nottingham manufacturers were slow to show enthusiasm for the experiments being carried out. In 1840 a tricoteur had been shown at an exhibition promoted by the Mechanics Institute held at the

Exchange Rooms it caused little excitement.[4] But when in 1849 Chevalier Claussen demonstrated the operation of a circular stocking frame of the type used at Paget's Loughborough works,[5] local hosiers were impressed by its capacity to produce twenty pairs of stockings per day, though still the powered machinery could produce only knitted fabric of uniform width which was then either cut and made up into garments, or pressed and steamed to the shape of stockings which were seamless and unfashioned.[6]

One large firm of hosiery manufacturers eventually decided to adopt it, and two years later the new five-storeyed factory of Messrs. Hine & Mundella on Station Street housed both large rotary frames and the German 'roundabout' circular machines driven by steam.[7] According to Felkin, a steam-powered circular machine could produce weekly thirty dozen women's hose, compared with about six dozen per week on a wide frame.[8] The potentialities of the new frames absorbed much of the attention of Mundella and his mechanics, and in 1854 a joint patent of Luke Barton, Hine, and Mundella rendered the wearing of seamless hose a practical proposition. The patent was for fashioning the articles produced on a rotary frame without necessitating any stoppage on the part of the operative, thereby reducing labour input and increasing the rate of production.[9] This was followed by another improvement of the rotary frame patented by Mundella and Onion, and in 1857 Mundella developed an invention which enabled a stocking to be woven with identical inside and outside facings. In 1861 Hine and Mundella purchased an American patent for striped hose.[10] Eventually in 1864 William Cotton, a hosiery mechanic from Loughborough, combined circular motion with flat by introducing a needle bar which moved vertically on the frame, thereby making it possible to manufacture simultaneously over a dozen fashioned stockings as high in quality as those produced on hand frames. The machine could also produce other types of fashioned hosiery.[11] Thereafter, the application of power to subsidiary operations was accomplished quickly. Power winding presented no problem, but Campion's sewing machine (which he developed in Nottingham in 1858) was too slow for use on low quality articles, an obstacle which was overcome in 1887 with the appearance of the overlock machine which solved the problem by seaming cheap goods mechanically.[12]

The horizons of the trade widened as innovtions led to the introduction of a greater number of styles and colours which created a new demand for fashionable stockings.[13] But the extension of mechanization and factory production was a protracted process. In Nottingham in 1865 there were 1,000 power rotary frames, 1,200 sets of circular power machinery, and 400 warp hosiery power frames, 11,000 narrow hand frames, and 4,250 wide hand frames.[14] In 1874, though the number of factories had doubled in twelve years to 129, they employed on average twice the amount of horse-power used in 1862.[15]

What was the reason for the sluggish spread of mechanization and the reluctance to adopt the factory system? When the Luddites were smashing frames early in the century, newspaper commentators had interpreted Heathcoat's removal from the midlands as a symptom of his unwillingness to risk investment in valuable machinery where violence might jeopardize capital equipment concentrated in one building. Mundella, too, suspected that Luddism had been instrumental in postponing the introduction of the factory system.[16] During the Luddite years between 1810 and 1817 there might well have existed disincentives to invest in machinery, but it would appear significant that among the evidence given by hosiers and manufacturers before the Commissioners and Select Committees between 1830 and 1870, there is no mention of Luddism as having been a deterrent to mechanization. It could be argued that prior to the factory system in the fifties the organization of the hosiery industry was adequate to meet the demands made upon it. Over-capitalization and an abundant supply of cheap labour meant that a moderate expansion of demand would be met by existing resources, and until the forties supply and demand conditions did not require a spirited search for innovation.

Between 1815 and 1844 competition had resulted in a diminution in the number of hosiers in Nottingham from 174 to 81, and in the forties about half the merchant hosiers in Nottingham were continuing businesses begun by their fathers or grandfathers.[17] Moreover the group of long-established firms, which included I. & R. Morley, Heard & Hurst, James Roger Allen, Allen Solly, Cox, Horner & Hogg, and William Gibson, Thomas Carver & Son, and James Wilson, controlled a significant proportion of the industry's output. Although new firms had entered the industry, many of them to disappear soon afterwards, it is probable that the hosiery industry had reverted more and more to hereditary leadership up to 1850. From the point of view of industrial progress this was unfortunate, because the heads of old established firms were too much influenced by the custom of the trade, and this meant the continuance of frame rent.[18] Under the existing industrial organization labour could be employed casually, involving less risk for the hosier. Moreover, when hosiery production moved into the factories, hosiery manufacturers were required to regulate employment according to the Factory Acts, while cheap labour outside the factories could work at all hours to compensate for low productivity and in order to compete effectively.[19] Until the invention of Cotton's Patent Machine in 1864, and indeed much later, narrow frames still catered for the luxury market of high quality fashioned hose, for in the fifties the early steam driven circular machines produced only unfashioned and crudely fashioned work and the wide frames continued to compete by making garments or their separate parts, despite their growing disadvantage in terms of production costs.

The existence of frame-renting also tended to deter change, for the scrapping of hand frames would have meant the cessation of frame rent. To what extent frame rent was a source of fixed income is difficult to decide. Certainly during years of depressed trade it was the custom of several large hosiers to waive rent and shop charges, though the bag hosiers' practice of spreading work was the subject for frequent complaints. That frame rent was not considered separately from income from hosiery sales and that there was no question of relinquishing it, are views strongly expressed during the forties and fifties, and it is significant that in 1854 all hosiers except one had subscribed to the expenses of organised opposition to the proposed legislation to abolish frame rent.[20] Most hosiers maintained that the existence of the putting-out system depended on frame renting, thereby implying that the factory system was a necessary prerequisite for the abolition of frame rent. Allen declared that because of maintenance and repair costs no prudent man would take any profit at all until he had received 5 per cent. on capital invested.[21] Thomas Carver, on the other hand, complained that although he had habitually conducted his business on an expected return of 10 per cent. from frame rent, between 1835 and 1845 actual returns had averaged approximately 3 per cent., and between 1848 and 1855 about $4\frac{1}{2}$ per cent.[22] This could be explained partly by slack trade and the tendency of the respectable hosiers not to spread work and charge full rent, and partly by the lower quality of the goods in which Carver specialized. Allen produced high quality hose, and the rate of obsolescence of machinery in this branch of the trade was very slow, at least until the sixties. Carver specialized in the production of shirting and drawers, and competition from wide frames had led to the large scale scrapping of narrow frames. The cost of a wide frame could be more than £100, and, in the absence of customary charges as in the case of other frames, the amount of frame rent charged was then a matter for individual decision.[23] Furthermore, in 1849 the striking hosiery workers had succeeded in obtaining a reduction of frame rents, which in some cases amounted to 50 per cent.[24] Thus even without the factory system, frame rent was beginning to lose its attraction as an avenue for investment. But before a general conversion to mechanized manufacture would take place, the rate of return from investment in factory production with steam-powered machinery needed to be significantly in excess of the return from the manufacture of hosiery by traditional methods and from frame ownership; the marginal superiority of the new methods of production needed to be considerable. For this reason the quality of factory-produced goods was important, and this explains why, even when the new machinery was being installed in some factories, members of the trade were still preoccupied with the question of the quality of hosiery that could be produced on the power machines.

In Professor Wells' view the main obstacle to change was to be found in the condition of the labour market:

> Generations of grinding poverty had almost killed the spirit of enterprise among the stockingers, and in the hosiery villages, where they lived comparatively isolated from the social and industrial life of the outside world, children followed their father's trade as a matter of course, for the main alternative, that of agriculture, offered even worse prospects.

Again:

> the extremely irregular conditions of work in the hosiery trade had reacted on succeeding generations of stockingers and produced a type of worker who was almost by nature, irregular in his habits.[25]

Furthermore, the stockinger prized his independence; to many of them the factory bell symbolized subjection, even though the new factories could generally offer superior conditions for work and shorter hours than prevailed in the workshops and sheds.[26] Even when changes began, the existing elaborate industrial organization tended to retard the adoption of steam power and the factory system in an industry which, due to the diverse character of hosiery frame products, was not necessarily more efficient in large units of production. Until the difficulties in fashioning knitted goods by power-driven machinery were overcome, factory production was an economic possibility only for the manufacturers of low quality hosiery, which the new machines were able to produce successfully. Not until 1866, two years after Cotton's Patent machine was taken up, did the firm of I. & R. Morley, the major high quality producers, construct its first factory, a large building in Manvers Street built to accommodate five hundred workers.[27]

When technological change opened up possibilities for power production in factories few of the older merchant hosiers showed the initiative for innovation. The pacemakers were a small number of existing firms, several of which were led by youthful management.[28] The minor role played by new firms in this initial transition can be explained partly by the substantial capital requirements of the new technology, for the large rotary frames cost £200 and others over £1,000. Established market connections were also important in so far as they allowed existing entrepreneurs to concentrate attention on problems of production. It has also been suggested that those firms which traded abroad facing growing competition from foreign steam machinery, particularly in German factories, were among the first to recognise the necessity of discarding anachronistic methods of production,[29] while there is evidence which suggests that among the larger firms, the least prosperous were quicker to introduce changes. The firm of Hine & Mundella exemplifies the potent formulae which served to revolutionize the trade. Begun by framework knitter, and later merchant, Thomas Chambers in the 1790s, the firm was taken over by his son-in-law, Jonathan Hine who, in 1848, took into partnership Anthony John Mundella, a twenty-three year old overseer employed by a Leicester hosiery firm. The latter's alert mind and flair for business proved beneficial not only to the partnership but also to the whole industry. His particular genius lay in recognizing instantly an invention's commercial value and in transforming it into commercial success. In 1851 Benjamin Hine prophesied that the use of machines in their new factory would lower prices, increase consumption, and consequently raise the demand for labour, and the subsequent history of the industry confirmed his forecast.[30] Supported by a growing population and rising real incomes, during the next two decades manufacturers began to experiment with new articles and fashions which attracted a growing demand in the domestic market. Abroad, population growth, improvements in communications, and reductions in transport costs opened up even wider markets, especially in Australia, South Africa, America, and India. Not only did hosiery output increase, but the declining labour force which accompanied the trend testified to a rise in labour productivity.[31] The resulting fall in hosiery prices also helped to increase sales.

Two factors hastened the shift to factory production. One was the abolition of frame rent by legislation after trade union agitation in 1874, though by this time it was recognized that the increasing concentration of production in factories was inevitable, and that the proportion of rented frames would tend to dwindle. The other was the series of Acts passed between 1867 and 1876 which extended the provisions of the Factory Act to workshops, improved the provision for elementary education, and finally made school attendance compulsory between the ages of five and fourteen, thus reducing the supply of child labour on which the domestic system largely depended.[32] In this new phase the industry did not attract capital from outside the trade, though many men migrated to Nottingham from surrounding hosiery villages to set up as manufacturers. More than in any subsequent period, in the early days of the factory system a large number of entrepreneurs began their careers as manual workers, bag hosiers, middlemen, or overlookers.[33] In order to compete with the established hosiers for the home market they were obliged to adopt machinery, and consequently the entry of many small firms during the last quarter of the century accelerated the rate of mechanization.

Initial capital requirements for the manufacture of hosiery fell after the first wave of innovation in the third quarter of the century largely owing to the increasing practice of letting out factory rooms with power supplies. Frederick Keywood, for example, was a frame-work knitter who in 1869 worked for I. & R. Morley. Later, he purchased his machinery with borrowed capital and moved to Greave's factory on Station Street, where several other similar firms were installed. At his bankruptcy in 1886 his estate realized barely £700.[34] In 1875 the Moore brothers commenced business in a room rented at Whitehall's factory; their initial capital was only £200. Several years later their father built a factory at Arnold and they borrowed money from building societies, loan clubs, and banks, in order to erect houses for employees.[35] Some men entered the trade after purchasing machinery at bankrupts' auctions,[36] and although the machinery might be obsolete, by making economies on interest, profit, and or salary, the independent proprietor found that he could survive, though often only for a limited period. Other small manufacturers purchased machinery on credit from local machine builders. The rise of a class of small independent manufacturers and the disappearance of the bag hosier middlemen was characteristic of the hosiery trade. Moreover, the distinction between large and small businesses now became one of degree rather than kind. With the disappearance of frame rent, fixed charges, deductions, and commissions owing to the Truck Act of 1874, a reliable income for the small man had disappeared. He no longer received raw material with specific instructions covering the types of goods required, but purchased it through an agent or spinner; thus what to buy, when to buy, what to make, and what price to ask, were entirely his own responsibility.[37]

The industry became increasingly competitive, and whereas it had been customary for the merchant to order direct from the manufacturer, the merchant now required manufacturers to submit samples with their prices before he placed orders. The system of long credits also accentuated the reckless competition among manufacturers and greatly aggravated the uncertainty and risks which inexperienced producers with minimal resources often had to face. Factors which explain the competitive strength, albeit temporary, of many small firms, were the employment of members of the family (a practice which often concealed the squeezing of labour costs), the weakness of trade unionism in small firms, and personal involvement in the firm's fortune. But these factors also disturbed confidence in the industry, a situation which was exacerbated by the proprietors' failure to take full account of all working expenses owing to their ignorance of costing methods.[38] Even so, some small firms did survive competition, mainly because of their ability to reduce fixed costs and also partly because an increase in the size of a firm did not usually involve greater specialization and division of labour, but rather the use of more machinery of the same type. The optimum size of the producing unit was not large, and small firms utilized the services of other specialist firms.[39] However, such small firms rarely outlived their promotors. In 1891 it was estimated that of the one hundred and five hosiery manufacturers who had begun in the industry as a whole since 1863, twenty-seven had failed, twenty-seven had shut down because of inadequate profits, thirteen had changed hands, and only seventeen were still in existence.[40]

Those who survived in this competitive period were, in general, the largest firms, most of which had merchant hosiery origins.[41] The outstanding example is the firm of I. & R. Morley, which continued to expand through the difficult years. When the Manvers Street factory was gutted by fire in 1874, and seventy-six machines were destroyed, it was rebuilt within twelve months. In the same year, one factory was built at Daybrook and another in Heanor. In 1879 another was purchased in Handel Street, and ten years later yet another at Sutton-in-Ashfield. More factories were built at Leicester, and by 1887 Morleys owned seven factories in the midland counties and employed several hundred hand workers outside[42] who made hose for the Court and for the Army, whose specifications required hand made hosiery as well as hand made shoes. As frames wore out and the aged framework knitters died, however, hand frames were slowly withdrawn.[43] The survival of the larger firms during a period of rapid turnover in manufacturing units suggests that rates of profit varied greatly between different firms within the hosiery industry. Ease of entry with borrowed capital, hired machinery, and credit attracted many small businesses, but their foundations were often insecure and the uncertainty of trade proved fatal for them. This suggests that marketing and managerial advantages rather than technical economies of large scale production largely explain the superior performance of the bigger firms.

A factor characteristic of general trade conditions during this period, but which was especially marked in the hosiery trade, was the burden of competition from foreign producers who were supplied with machinery from Britain.[44] Foreign competition was not a new phenomenon, but the German and French hosiery manufacturers were quicker to appreciate the importance of technical education for industrial progress, and in these countries government-sponsored schools were established in the chief centres of the trade. In 1867 the Nottingham Chamber of Commerce had explored the possibilities of improving technical education facilities for the hosiery and lace trades,[45] but twenty years later complaints were still being made that English institutions for technical instruction were inferior to those in Continental Europe, and that they lacked support.[46]

Like manufacturers in other industries, hosiery manufacturers interpreted the fall in prices and profits which occurred after 1873 as symptomatic of depression. Contributing to this depression of prices and profits were growing competition, the entry of new producers into the trade, and the spread of factory production; but hosiery output rose. In 1870, 129 factories in the United Kingdom employed 9,692 persons; twenty years later 24,838 persons were employed in 257 factories, and by 1901 the factory population reached 38,549. Meanwhile, the numbers of hand framework knitters declined from about 50,000 to less than 5,000.[47] These figures indicate the progress of the technical revolution in the hosiery trade. Output per head rose, while hosiery output increased from £7,795,000 in 1865, a year of exceptionally high yarn prices, to slightly more than £8 million, the steady fall in cotton and wool prices that occurred in the intervening decades concealing a considerably greater increase in the volume of output.[48] These figures also conceal changes in the quality and composition of hosiery production. The widespread adoption of power machinery coincided with an improvement in the quality of machine-produced articles, and whereas, hitherto, socks and stockings had formed the bulk of total output, by 1907 these items accounted for approximately 50 per cent., while underwear, the other major item, was valued at about £2·5 million. The relative importance of silk hosiery production had been declining slowly since the first half of the century, but the effect of the commercial treaty with France in 1860 was to further reduce Britain's hold on the contracting market for silk hosiery. The output of British silk hosiery in 1907 was almost negligible.[49]

A further change in the composition of output was the rising proportion of woollen hosiery, especially underwear, contributing to
T

total production. Falling wool prices, as Australian wool entered world markets, stimulated demand for cheaper woollen hosiery, while the efforts of Leicester hosiers to increase exports met with considerable success. Between 1866 and 1880 exports of woollen hosiery averaged less than £0·3 million, but between 1886 and 1900 this rose to £0·8 million and increased rapidly thereafter.[51] In the nineties the growing manufacture of black cashmere, plain, and ribbed hosiery enabled Nottingham to share in this expanding market, though Leicester remained the undisputed centre of the woollen hosiery trade.[52] Entrance of Nottingham hosiery manufacturers into the woollen trade was partly the result of expanding demand for this type of hosiery, but failure to hold their share in world markets for cotton hosiery also accounts for this change. High tariffs erected by Germany in 1879, by France, Austria, Russia, and Spain in 1882, and by America in 1891, affected hosiery manufacturers in all exporting counties, but although the superior quality woollen hosiery of Leicester manufacturers successfully penetrated these barriers, after violent fluctuations exports of cotton hosiery declined.[53] Where Nottingham hosiers failed, the German manufacturers succeeded, for the Germans built up a highly efficient industry producing articles superior in quality and lower in price. A Nottingham hosiery manufacturer noted:

> American buyers used to come over to England and stop a week or ten days at Nottingham and then go to Germany. But now they go to Germany and do not come near Nottingham.[54]

By the close of the century Germany was beginning to monopolize American cotton hosiery imports.[55] Only the success of British exports of woollen hosiery prevented an even greater fall in total hosiery exports than actually occurred during the late nineteenth century. (See Table XIII.) Fierce competition to secure profits in overseas markets was accompanied at home by an equally competitive struggle for larger shares in the domestic market, a situation which developed as a result of the entry of many small firms into the industry who, in the scramble for orders, underbid each other, while trying to keep pace with their competitors who adopted newer machinery.[56] The number of hosiery manufacturers in Nottingham rose from forty-eight in 1854 to sixty-four in 1881, and to eighty in 1891. The depression that occurred in the nineties, however, reduced their number to seventy-three by 1900.[57]

While manufacturers struggled to increase or maintain their profit levels, in many cases by raising productivity, the workers who entered the factories to operate the new machines were quick to benefit. In 1860 male operatives in Nottingham using steam-powered rotaries earned between 20s. and 35s. per week, and women,

TABLE XII: Hosiery Exports (Annual Values) in £'s as published by the Board of Trade, 1853–1900.

Year	Cotton stockings	Other cotton hosiery	Woollen & worsted stockings	Other woollen and worsted hosiery
1853	461,360	238,025		
1854	301,909	189,091		
1855	184,187	211,705		
1856	308,592	325,403		
1857	266,279	382,535		
1858	160,114	269,848		
1859	261,129	328,539		
1860	313,065	344,322		
1861	197,163	353,049		
1862	282,304	173,225*		
1863	284,485	171,400		
1864	247,126	203,183		
1865	240,534	204,341		
1866	405,091	381,976		
1867	387,127	394,791		
1868	364,572	272,989	71,890	147,856
1869	325,316	447,309	71,577	199,015
1870	292,630	507,552	51,824	276,149
1871	291,630	674,259	233,236	468,790
1872	418,839	687,624	319,970	749,685
1873	416,842	659,439	288,821	1,128,609
1874	361,436	625,517	290,531	699,254
1875	378,221	618,290	306,644	474,025
1876	364,054	526,413	278,055	402,334
1877	371,958	462,342	293,611	379,046
1878	389,982	414,578	290,835	392,809
1879	370,805	487,416	288,405	447,288
1880	401,858	541,463	320,026	418,312
1881	489,917	612,863	278,148	423,128
1882	621,913	643,397	382,595	356,859
1883	536,315	634,052	396,909	281,199
1884	569,345	510,684	485,521	302,480
1885	519,346	222,476	301,795	208,068
1886	487,378	376,420	676,363	230,368
1887	443,454	411,309	734,533	210,153
1888	441,974	280,666	757,806	225,641
1889	394,643	339,699	885,602	191,579
1890	355,861	308,131	913,680	199,491
1891	316,729	239,876	821,636	196,270
1892	254,634	238,698	739,640	172,898
1893	205,219	187,480	730,861	168,401
1894	228,708	165,176	670,211	158,544
1895	220,414	195,818	832,877	188,701
1896	230,376	229,918	860,790	232,188
1897	168,562	189,294	826,251	203,146
1898	174,888	159,700	783,572	202,609
1899	175,598	146,833	909,358	213,223
1900	228,814	165,476	898,606	235,505

* From 1862 'small cotton wares' are excluded under the heading 'other cotton hosiery'.

between 12s. and 20s. Steam driven warp frame workers earned up to 35s. Men making hosiery on wide hand frames could earn between 16s. and 30s. (in 1865 the average was 15s.), but men and youths working the narrow hand frames received only between 6s. and 24s. weekly (in 1865 they averaged 10s.). The earnings of auxiliary workers were also affected. In factories their jobs were simplified, facilitating greater speed in their tasks, and whereas their domestic counterparts received a weekly average of 4s., warehouse employees could earn more than twice this amount.[58] The improvement in living standards continued. Giving evidence before the Factory and Workshops Commission in 1876 George Kendall, one of the trade union leaders, said:

> we used to have formerly long periods of depression, but latterly the periods of depression never last so long. People wear better things than they used to generally . . .[59]

In 1890 hosiery workers operating rotary and circular frames earned 33s. per week, while in the production of fashioned hosiery by the use of Cotton's Patent machine 38s. 3d. was an average weekly wage.[60] The need for child labour in the production of hosiery had diminished even before the Factory and Workshops Act of 1867, though in the auxiliary trades children continued to be an important source of labour until 1876, when legislation required all children under the age of fourteen to attend school. Inside the factories children benefited from protection afforded by the Factory Act. Ten years was the minimum age for employment, and women and young persons might work a maximum legal day of ten and one-half hours between 6 a.m. and 6 p.m. in summer, and 7 a.m. and 7 p.m. in the winter; the total working week was not to exceed 56½ hours.

Working conditions at some factories and warehouses were in striking contrast to those of the average domestic workshop. The Nottingham Manufacturing Company, for example, provided several amenities for employees, including a club entirely under the workmen's management, where skittles, draughts, and bagatelle were played. The company also ran a benefit club on generous terms, while annual factory excursions, a brass band, and sports events were other features of the management's welfare policy.[61] However, not all employers were as generous in their dealings with employees as Hine and Mundella, directors of the above company, and conditions of work and wages were influenced by the ability of workers to press their claims when the economic climate was favourable.

The technological and organizational changes in the hosiery trade during the mid-century had important repercussions upon industrial relations. Following the depression in the hosiery industry up to the 1840s, the period of brisk trade beginning in 1849 reflected not only an improvement in general economic activity but also the particular developments in the manufacture of hosiery previously outlined.[62] Framework knitters recognized an opportunity to revive their trade societies and to agitate for higher piece rates. The opening up of a wider market for an increasing variety of hosiery reinforced the bargaining strength of machine operatives and hand frame workers, for both belonged to the same societies. Technical innovation and deterioration in labour relations produced the need for some sort of joint action in an attempt to solve the problems of transition. Changeover to power machinery was gradual, and although there was no widespread technological unemployment as had been feared earlier, certain problems of this kind arose. In the very early stages of mechanization in the fifties there was extra work for the hand framework knitter in adding feet and finishing articles made on the rotary frames, but later, as improved machinery produced better quality hosiery, he found himself in direct competition with the machine.

The traditional importance of the large merchant hosiery producers when making agreements in the trade and maintaining price lists was still apparent in the 1850s, and the largest hosiery union occasionally acknowledged the tendency for these to adhere to agreed price lists when trade was slack. Relations with the leading hosiers were good.[63] Nevertheless, the scattered location of frames resulted in diversity and ignorance of trade practices and piece rates, and it was not until the factory system was adopted that the listing of piece rates could be enforced at all effectively. The cyclical downturn in 1857 seriously affected lace and hosiery merchants. As unemployment increased, the framework knitters' unions experienced a temporary eclipse. In the subsequent economic revival rotary and circular machine-produced hosiery was in greatest demand, and the resultant difference in earnings of factory workers and hand framework knitters led to a series of strikes by the latter, one of which in 1860 lasted eleven weeks. Many of the hosiers were uneasy at the prospect of a general lock-out and three leading manufacturers, Mundella, Lee, and Ashwell were appointed to confer with middlemen and workmen. Mundella remarked that a thousand hosiery workers were unemployed and were receiving support from workmen in every other branch. He, himself, was losing £20 per week by the loss of frame rent as a result of his outdoor hands being on strike. His factory hands, meanwhile, earned between 25s. and 40s. weekly to support them.[64] Mundella and Lee maintained that competition from Germany made it impossible to pay higher wages and

Mundella suggested that a council should be formed to check the practices of 'bad employers and middlemen' and, on behalf of the manufacturers offered to pay the passage of a workmen's delegation to Germany to investigate the extent of German competition. The operatives' delegates expressed the desire for the establishment of a board of trade on which the manufacturers would assist them in maintaining prices. Eventually, it was decided that a Board of Arbitration and Conciliation should be set up to prevent further disputes.[65]

Collaboration between employers and workmen was by no means a new departure for the industry. In the past, the dominant hosiers had periodically met with workmen's committees to discuss revision of the piece rate list which was, in practice, little more than a norm paid by leading hosiers. At these meetings employers and workmen joined in condemning the production of inferior hosiery, employers fearing competition and workmen anticipating wage reductions should inferior hosiery gain a greater share in the general market for hosiery. Occasionally the hosiers had undertaken to support workmen who struck against the smaller firms and the producer of inferior goods who paid less than list prices.[66] Henson had advocated the establishment of trade boards to regulate the industry, and Felkin had urged framework knitters to agitate for trade regulation courts, while in 1845 the biggest hosiery union of cotton stockingers had petitioned Parliament for the establishment of Courts of Conciliation and Arbitration.[67]

The Board's first meeting was held at the Commercial Exchange on December 3rd, 1860, the same year as the establishment of the Nottingham Chamber of Commerce, several of whose members served on the Board. It consisted of nine leading manufacturers and an equal number of workmen, representing various branches of the trade; Mundella was appointed Chairman. Rules were drawn up in which the object of the Board was declared to be conciliation in the event of disputes, and arbitration of any question of wages that might be referred to it. Although called the Board of Arbitration, it is important to recall Mundella's stress on an arrangement for open and friendly bargaining between two sides on equal footing. Decisions were to be reached jointly and were not to be left to an umpire, as the word arbitration implies today. The Board was to meet quarterly for the transaction of normal business, but special meetings could be convened by either side at seven days' notice. In theory the Committee of the Board (the Committee of Enquiry) could not make an award but only use its influence in the settlement of dispute before bringing it before the Board. In practice about three-quarters of the disputes referred to it were settled by the

Committee, and in these cases submission to the full Board became merely a formality.[68]

From the outset the question of wages, the manner in which certain classes of work should be performed, and the rate at which new classes should be paid, provided the Board with abundant mental exercise. With the onset of depression, caused by the American Civil War and the subsequent dislocation of Anglo-American trade, the full Board did not meet for almost three years following March, 1862. Nevertheless, the essential part of the Board, the Committee of Enquiry, continued to function.[69] Since wages were reduced it would appear that the trade unions made little effort to resist, and the full Board meetings were unnecessary so long as the Committee functioned efficiently and effectively. The role of Mundella cannot be overestimated. Originally a framework knitter, he had cultivated good relations between management and men in his own firm. His popularity with trade unions was remarkable, a fact he explained as being the result of the high wages he paid; and indeed this rapport did much to hold together the Board of Arbitration.[70]

The success of the Board in Nottingham promoted two very important ideas. One was that trade unions could be a positive force in helping business, an idea that led to a growing recognition of workers' organizations and a respect for these bodies and their aims to improve working men's standards of living. The second was the acceptance and promotion of discussion between employers and workmen (equally represented) on such basic issues as hours and wage rates.[71] Within a decade Boards existed as vehicles for collective bargaining in the coalfields of Durham, Yorkshire, and Northumberland, and in the Wolverhampton building trades.[72]

In 1865 the Rotary Framework Knitting Society was established in order to be represented officially on the Board which was to meet again in June. The Hosiery Manufacturers' Association was also re-established in 1865. In that year several rates, specifically for power-produced hosiery, were revised upwards, with differentials according to types and combination of materials used. Impressed by these advances, workmen in the villages, who had hitherto held aloof, hastened to declare their allegiance to the Board. At Kegworth and Heanor the two main leaders, Kendall and Saxton, conducted meetings to organize those wishing to affiliate.

After the depression following dislocation in the American trade and the sharp fall in the price of cotton, the hosiery industry recovered quickly. In spite of the failure of financial houses in London in 1866 improvement in trade continued, culminating in the boom of 1872–3. The Board of Arbitration once more swung into operation and, encouraged by the improvement in trade activity and general trade union developments, the several district framework knitters' societies coalesced temporarily into one comprehensive union.[73] In June, 1866, a meeting of hand framework knitters from the three counties met to pass several resolutions, forming themselves into a general amalgamated and consolidated union called 'The United Framework Knitters' Society'.[74] Executive power was vested in an annual conference of delegates from local unions, though special meetings could be convened to deal with problems which might arise. It was the delegate's job to bring disputes to an amicable settlement or, if he failed, to bring the subject to the attention of the Board of Arbitration. The union was organized in the old style with nominal contributions and power to levy in emergency, the various branches maintaining a great measure of autonomy.[75] Since its re-establishment, the Board had acquired considerable prestige. When in August, 1866 the rib top branch, which was not a sufficiently large body to have a representative on the Board,[76] encountered difficulty in securing adequate payment for extra work, it was unanimously resolved that Kendall, the United Framework Knitters' Society Secretary and an important member of the Board, should accompany a deputation to the employers. In the event of this deputation proving unsuccessful it was decided to take the matter before the Board, which, ran the resolution, 'we have no doubt will see justice done.'[77]

The truck system, which was still fairly common in the villages, very soon occupied the attention of the Board. Through an advertisement inserted in the local newspaper, the Board expressed its determination to abolish this pernicious system of payment of wages in kind, by prosecuting offenders and by removing the machinery from any middlemen guilty of such practices. According to Felkin, prosecutions led to substantial abandonment of trucking practices in the area around Nottingham.[78] Another practice attacked by the Board was the custom of paying workmen late on Saturday night or early on Sunday morning when no markets were available, thereby necessitating purchases on credit at high rates of discount. The exertions of the Board in this direction again met with success.

The Board was similarly active in obtaining a reduction in frame rents. Some of the more important hosiers, among them those represented on the Board, had already reduced their rents (those producing hosiery in factories having abolished these charges), and a special effort was made to reach an agreement with the employers in the Sutton and Mansfield districts.[79] Undoubtedly the Board was a great success from the point of view of the majority in the trade. Hosiery workers had benefited as a result of its successful campaign against truck, by the advances they had obtained, and the assimilation of piece rates paid by the several hosiers.[80] Manufacturers had benefited from improved industrial relations, and uniformity of rates as agreed in the statement. Samuel Morley was pleased to be able to lay up stock without fear of being undercut by other employers,[81] while Mundella thought that the plane of competition in the industry had altered; in his words the question was no longer 'who shall screw down wages the most?' but, 'who shall buy material best and produce the best article?'[82] Entrepreneurial attention could now concentrate on the efficient management of resources.

When the Board was formed actual fixing of wage rates was not included among its operations. Nevertheless, its decisions and the success with which they were enforced by mutual agreement had inspired so much general confidence that by 1867 there existed a uniform statement throughout the trade, each branch having a separate price list. The Board found it difficult to enforce the statement, especially in the case of small manufacturers, but recalcitrant offenders were brought before the Committee of Enquiry, and such an interview usually proved an effective disciplinary measure. As a last resort the men would be ordered to refuse to work for less than the piece rates agreed to and set down in a statement or price list.[83]

It is interesting to note that confidence in the Board, while helping to boost union membership, tended to delay further the introduction of the principles and organization of the 'new model' unions. Subscriptions remained low, and the men were content to rely upon levies to meet unexpected contingencies.

'They maintain their union just as well and better with the Board as without it,' remarked Mundella, 'their union now costs them only one shilling per year instead of a shilling per week.'[84]

Thus, having rejected the policy of negotiation from strength (a decision which they were later to regret), the men were completely reliant upon the success and continuation of the Board. The minority, however, which consisted of wrought hose hands, was not entirely satisfied with the Board. Their frequent requests for increases in wages when the factory workers were awarded them were refused, and the Arnold and Lambley knitters spoke in scathing terms of 'the new and wonderful system which kept (their) wages low whilst earnings in other branches increased'.[85] Another source of friction was the discrepancy between Leicester and Nottingham statements which became increasingly apparent. A Board of Arbitration was set up to serve the Leicester hosiery trade in 1866, but the prices paid by Leicester employers for articles similar to those produced in Nottingham were often less than those paid by Nottingham manufacturers.

Under pressure from the unions, the rules of the Board were modified in 1870. Since 1867 the Board had consisted of seven manufacturers and seven operatives, Mundella invariably taking the chair as President. Henceforward equal numbers of employers and operatives were joined by a referee who was to have the casting vote. All future voting was to be by ballot.[86] This provision for an umpire represented a fundamental alteration in the nature of the Board. The Nottingham Hosiery Board at that time was not a model of arbitration (although later the development of arbitration followed Mundella's initial efforts), for prior to 1870 the Nottingham machinery was for collective bargaining; there had been no casting vote, and decisions were reached by what the men called 'a long jaw'.[87]

The first major issue facing the reconstituted Board occurred in 1870, when manufacturers offered a reduction to wide frame hands at Nottingham, Carlton, Hucknall, and to all hand frame workers at Sutton.[88] At Ruddington the framework knitters prepared to resist the reductions on 'Sutton' (hand frame knitted) hose by levying threepence per week. All reductions were opposed by the men's delegates, and the manufacturers on the Board threatened that unless the men accepted a reduction they would resign. Two days later, after negotiations had reached a deadlock, W. G. Ward, a partner in a large lace manufacturing company and noted for his sympathies for working men, accepted the invitation to adjudicate in the dispute.[89] The award, which was a compromise, was unpopular with both sides. There was a move on the part of workmen from Ruddington and Nottingham to strike immediately, but the workmen's Board representatives succeeded in forestalling the plan. Kendall, from Sutton, argued that even if it were desirable to strike it would be tactically foolish. It would be wiser now to concur and to build up funds for the future.[90] The rift between the hand frame workers (represented mainly by the Sutton group) and the Nottingham machine operative branches became an outright split the following year. The latter followed the example of the nine hundred wide frame workers at Arnold and broke away from the United Framework Knitters' Society, attempting to form a separate union based in Nottingham.[91] The Sutton group continued their meetings, still calling themselves the United Framework Knitters' Society.

In addition to the new Society formed in Nottingham, the wide hand frame workers at Arnold formed a society in 1871 based on the traditional pattern of earlier unions. Each locality was to be self-governing; there were no regular levies and no provision was made for a representative on the Board. The Sutton workers' society was completely inactive shortly after the split, while a similar fate befell the Nottingham Shirt, Pants, and Drawers Union, sometimes called the Rotary Hand Framework Knitters' Society. Although these three societies continued to exist, they were more in the nature of benefit clubs than trade unions.

By 1871 the Board's 'honeymoon' was over, and the memory of the bitterness and hardship produced by the free-for-all strike-lock-out arrangements which existed prior to 1860 was dim. The year 1870 ushered in a period of growing disenchantment with the Board, a phase experienced by other trades with similar arbitration machinery.[92] Although the Board of Arbitration continued to meet, hosiery workers were split over sectional interests, and petty jealousies weakened their front at the Board table. Workmen's delegates from the Hand Framework Knitters' Union were at odds with the Circular Union and the Rotary Power Society, with the result that the men were consistently outvoted by employers.[93] Workmen in Leicester held aloof from the former United union and this militated against the continued success of the Board, a situation which was to lead to the latter's downfall as Nottingham manufacturers argued that it was impossible to grant wage increases unless the whole trade adopted them.[94]

The ultimate crisis occurred over the implementation of the Truck Act when the Board declined to act on the specific matter of frame rents. The Commissioners' report concerning trucking had revealed that although there was no truck in Nottingham, a considerable amount still existed in the northern district of the county, especially in Sutton and Kirkby where the trade was still largely in the hands of middlemen owning public houses and provision shops.[95] Anti-truck societies and efforts on the part of employers on the Board of Arbitration had proved ineffective. Employers were unanimous in condemning trucking, but they were still extremely apprehensive concerning the men's demands for the abolition of frame rent which framework knitters insisted was a form of truck. In 1872 hand framework knitters in Nottingham and Arnold threatened to strike unless the manufacturers accepted a revised list of prices, conceding a $7\frac{1}{2}$ per cent. reduction in return for the abolition of frame rent and shop charges. The employers refused, but gave way in the fourth week of the ensuing strike which was backed by the Trades Council and the powerful Lace Makers' Society. Nevertheless, the men met with considerable difficulty in enforcing the decision. The Board of Arbitration suffered another blow when, in the same year, several hundred rotary power workers in Nottingham and Loughborough struck for a rise in wage rates, having seceded from the Board after their claim had been rejected. They seemed willing to cooperate in appointing members for an *ad hoc* board, but resolved to stay on strike until the employers agreed to their wage demands. Thus only the circular hands and the wrought hose hands continued to be represented on the Board.[96] After twelve weeks of the strike, which involved seven hundred rotary workmen in Nottingham, three firms acceded to the demands. The Hosiers' Association, members of which were chiefly larger firms, communicated with the three firms who subsequently reversed their decision. A week later the employers consented to meet the demands more than half way.

The operations of the Board never fully recovered, and henceforward it was only called upon occasionally until its final dissolution sometime in 1884. In 1875 Kendall made an attempt to organize a separate board for the decaying wrought hose branch, but with little success. Despite its early triumphs, the normal trade problems with which the Board dealt had become increasingly complicated by the effect of changing technology, which altered the supply and demand for different skills. This resulted in a dissipation of the workmen's confidence in the various branches. The power operatives considered their interests were neglected at the expense of the hand workers who, though a minority, outnumbered them in representation on the Board. The hand workers, for their part, resented the way in which their representatives mildly accepted the manufacturers' refusals of their requests for advances, though newer machinery driven by steam was able to produce similar goods more cheaply. Meanwhile, the earnings of skilled machine operatives rose steadily.

Many of the chief problems facing the hosiery trade—employers and workmen alike—resulted from the general uncertainty arising from an almost continuous stream of minor mechanical innovation. This made it extremely difficult for the Board of Arbitration to maintain a uniform statement, and finally it was left to employers and men in each town or district to settle their own statement of piece rates. Men working newer machines were compelled to accept reductions in piece rates to offset their increased productivity, but because this increased the general downward pressure on rates, those working less modern machinery expressed dissatisfaction with these arrangements. The problem then arose that men on the old machines were unable to accept any reductions, as their earnings were already barely sufficient for subsistence. It was the resulting friction, precipitated by the manufacturers' attitude towards frame rent, which led to the Board's final disintegration.

Ultimately the failure of the Board was due to inability to work in harmony with market forces. The demand for power operatives, relative to supply, increased their bargaining strength. On the Board they could be outmanoeuvred; on strike they held the upper hand. As for power hosiery employers, so long as the Board failed to limit wage increases then arbitration afforded no great advantage. Hence the Board became increasingly ineffective. Dependent as it was upon voluntary cooperation and adherence to majority decisions for its effectiveness, its existence was precarious so long as power lay in the hands of elements either opposed to, or separated from, the main currents of change in the industry. In the absence of institutional flexibility and adjustment to new conditions the Board finally collapsed.

Throughout the nineteenth century, and especially after the discontinuance of the Board, the strength of the town unions contrasted with the impotence of the trade societies in the villages. This imbalance of power helps to explain the relocation of hosiery production within the region. After the federation of the Circular Union with the Rotary Power Union in 1876 their campaign to obtain complete adherence to an agreed wage list prompted many employers to commence production in the villages. In an attempt to combat this removal of machinery, hosiery workers, thrown out of work because of their refusal to accept less than town rates, received compensation from the Union so long as they remained in the town. In addition, the substitution of youths and women for men was fought vigorously but without much success. The Rotary and Circular Unions attempted to organize workers at Arnold and Ruddington, but deputations which visited the areas were roughly handled and the campaign was abandoned.[97]

Following the economic downturn of 1878–9, when hosiery workers submitted to reductions, efforts to recoup the losses proved ineffective, and between 1879 and 1884 several strikes for higher wages only led to a further exodus of machinery into the villages of Arnold, Sutton-in-Ashfield, Ruddington, Mansfield, Heanor, and Ilkeston, where unions remained weak and wage rates were lower than in the town.[98] The removal of machinery continued, and was encouraged by the attitude of workmen in the villages who, in 1886, agitated for a list of piece rates higher than they were receiving, but actually lower than those paid in the town. Recriminations filled the air. Samuel Bower, Secretary of the Rotary Society, accused local manufacturers of failing to introduce new machinery, thereby allowing Leicester and Hinckley to take the lead. Nottingham employers made the counter-accusation that operatives had refused to accept reductions in rates to compensate for their increased productivity on new machinery.

By 1889, according to union officials and members of the Chamber of Commerce, Nottingham was rapidly becoming merely a sales centre for hosiery manufactured in the country districts, although many manufacturers also owned warehouses in the town. By 1908 barely one-fifth of all hosiery manufacture was carried on in Nottingham or Leicester. The ascendancy of the smaller traditional framework knitting centres was unquestioned.[99] Not only was trade unionism weak, wages lower, and working regulations practically ignored, but the development of coal mining in and around these villages had resulted in an expansion of population which provided the hosiery industry with a plentiful supply of female labour, the demand for which was increasing. Technological developments simplified the operation of hosiery machinery and the unions were gradually persuaded to allow women to work small machines.[100] Between 1876 and 1890 the number of women in hosiery factories rose from 5,098, when they barely exceeded men, to 15,630 in 1890, and to more than 30,000 by 1897, when they formed 75 per cent. of the factory labour force.[101]

Despite the spread of factory production in the villages there remained several thousand hosiery workers operating obsolete hand frames in small workshops and dwelling houses. They refused to submit to the pressure of machine competition. Reconciled to a position of industrial impotence, they discarded the strike weapon. The hand framework knitters' leaders revived the agitation to obtain legislation which would require some mark to distinguish between hand-made and steam-power-produced hosiery, and this marked the beginning of the campaign for the Merchandise Marks Bill upon which the frameworkers pinned their hopes. In order to strengthen their representation before Parliament, in 1889 the Nottinghamshire, Leicester, Derbyshire, and Ilkeston Federation became the United Kingdom Amalgamated Union of Hand Frame Workers. The headquarters were at Sutton-in-Ashfield. Subscriptions, which were to be compulsory, were devoted to the formation of a Parliamentary Committee, whose principal duty was to lobby support for the Merchandise Marks Bill. This they did, but without success for the Bill was not enacted.[102]

The last decade of the nineteenth century saw the three unions to which Nottingham hosiery workers belonged—the Rotary Framework Knitters' Society, the Circular Framework Knitters' Society, and the Hand Framework Knitters' Federation—doing their utmost to enforce uniformity. Without the cooperation of an organized body of manufacturers they met with little success, for the rapid turnover in new types of machinery and the disputes arising out of new work and new ways of making traditional articles complicated the issues of standard rates and piece rates related to weekly earnings. On the initiative of the Rotary Hand Framework Knitters' Society, in 1889 six employers met six rotary men under the chairmanship of Thomas Hill (managing director of I. & R. Morley) to discuss the re-establishment of a Board of Arbitration. The employers' view was that it would be unfair to set up a Board strictly for Nottingham; rather, it should include the three counties, bearing in mind a uniform list for all in the trade. After several attempts over the next twelve months, the manufacturers finally decided that only after the unions had equalized wages in country districts and the town, would they consider reconstituting a Board. After some delay the unions agreed, requesting the Manufacturers' Association to give assistance to this end, but the onus was placed firmly upon the shoulders of the men who were urged to organize the outside districts.[103] The Midland Counties Federation of Power Framework Knitters, formed in 1891, immediately embarked upon a concentrated drive for uniformity based on the 1886 statement. Six of the largest firms in Nottingham promised to agree to the statement. Employers were notified in April, but this precipitated a strike at Hinckley over the men's right to belong to the Federation, a strike in which three hundred men and a thousand youths and females were involved. On the matter of principle the operatives were victorious, but they failed to obtain the statement of 1886.[104] Infused with enthusiasm by the partial success of workers at Hinckley, and sustained by favourable economic conditions, the Federation gained strength. In December, 1891 the Circular Hosiery Society affiliated with the Federation, and in 1894 the Rotary and Circular Societies amalgamated, after which steps were taken once more to form a joint Arbitration Board. The Federation also redoubled efforts to recruit members in the villages.

With only I. & R. Morley and one other firm still adhering to the agreement of 1886, in the nineties the Midland Counties Federation recommenced agitation for the 1886 statement less 10 per cent. The strike was settled by a committee of manufacturers and operatives, with Thomas Hill, the respected head of I. & R. Morley, chairing the meetings. The settlement was marred almost immediately by the Circular Union's abrogation of the agreement, but manufacturers' threats to remove more machinery from the town eventually led to a compromise on rates in the circular branch. Meanwhile, some of the rotary employers, who had refused to accede to the operatives' requests, began once more to remove machinery to outside districts. The Nottingham Manufacturing Company moved more of its machinery to the Loughborough factory. Gamble moved machinery to Arnold; Templeman to Ruddington, Eden & Sons to Mansfield, and others replaced Society men with non-union labour. In 1897 more firms followed, drawing attention to the helplessness of unions and the disorganization of employers.[105]

By the end of the century the hand-knitted hosiery trade was virtually extinct, although pants for the army and a narrow range of the very finest goods, like Morley's silk stockings, for a courtly market, were still made by people working on obsolete hand frames in their own homes.[106] Their small trade societies, though linked by federation, provided no friendly benefit and despite their predicament, badly paid and overworked, they clung to the trade and continued to make strenuous efforts to obtain the Merchandise Marks Bill against which Nottingham manufacturers were so strongly opposed. The Board of Trade insisted that existing legislation concerning frauds was sufficient, thereby dashing the hopes of the hand framework knitters. Their remaining prop, and probably the greatest single factor prolonging the existence of hand work, were the specifications of Government contracts which required the production of hosiery of the highest quality. On the strength of this, and stimulated by the demand for army clothing as a result of the war in South Africa, the handworkers defied extinction and even gained some advance in 1900.[107]

Thus, the last quarter of the century witnessed an expansion of the industry's output, a contraction of the labour force, and the centrifugal dispersion of manufacturing units in the traditional hand framework knitting centres surrounding the town. The importance of hosiery in the local economy had been declining since 1850. According to the census of 1901, only 3 per cent. of the male working population was engaged in its manufacture, though hosiery production occupied a larger percentage of women. Nevertheless, hosiery manufacture was no longer the pivot of economic life it had been a century before.

References

[1] *Report of the Commissioners (Framework Knitters)*, 1845, (609), XV. 1. p. 14.

[2] William Felkin, *History*, p. 496.

[3] *N.R.*, August 27, 1847; *Report of the Select Committee (Stoppage of Wages in Hosiery)*, 1854–55, 421, XIV. 1., p. 410.

[4] F. A. Wells, *op. cit.*, p. 142.

[5] William Felkin, *History*, p. 296.

[6] Gustav Willkomm, *Technology of Framework Knitting*, (1879), II, 141–43.

[7] *N.R.*, October 3, 1851.

[8] William Felkin in G. R. Porter and F. W Hirst, *The Progress of the Nation*, (1912). According to Felkin, in 1844 there were 8,951 wide frames in industry and 34,991 narrow frames in the industry; *Report of the Commissioners (Framework Kniters)*, 1845 (609) XV. 1., p. 14.

[9] F. A. Wells, *op. cit.*, p. 144; William Felkin, *History*, pp. 502–03.

[10] W. H. G. Armytage, 'A. J. Mundella and the Hosiery Industry,' *E.H.R.* (1948), Supplement 8, 95–96.

[11] F. A. Wells, *op. cit.*, p. 145.

[12] *Ibid.*, p. 191.

[13] William Felkin, *History*, p. 472.

[14] *Report of Nottingham Chamber of Commerce*, 1860.

[15] F. A. Wells, *op. cit.*, pp. 154; 191.

[16] W. H. G. Armytage, *art. cit.*, p. 97.

[17] Charlotte Erickson, *British Industrialists: Steel and Hosiery, 1850–1950*, (Cambridge, 1959), p. 87.

[18] *Report of the Commissioners (Framework Knitters)*, 1845 (609) XV. 1. ev. of Thomas Carver, pp. 48–50, 62–63, Nathan Hurst, p. 88, John Rogers, p. 92; *Select Committee (Stoppage of Wages in Hosiery)*, 1854–55, (421) XIV. 1., ev. of James Roger Allen, p. 410.

[19] F. A. Wells, *op. cit.*, p. 154.

[20] *Select Committee (Stoppage of Wages in Hosiery)*, 1854–55, (421) XIV. 1., p. 410.

[21] *Ibid.*, ev. of Allen, p. 412.

[22] *Ibid.*, ev. of Street (Carver's manager), p. 432.

[23] *Ibid.*, *N.R.*, September 15, 1848; *N.R.*, June 15, 1849; *N.R.*, September 7, 1849; *N.R.*, March 29, 1852.

[24] *First Report of Commissioners (Employment of Children in Trades and Manufactures not regulated by Law)*, 1863 (3170) XVIII. 1., p. 281.

[25] F. A. Wells, *op. cit.*, p. 146.

[26] *N.J.*, January 16, 1846; The failure of Goddard's factory enterprise was attributed to the refusal of framework knitters to submit to factory discipline.

[27] F. A. Wells, *op. cit.*, p. 145.

[28] Charlotte Erickson, *op. cit.*, pp. 182–185.

[29] *Ibid.*

[30] *N.R.*, October 3, 1851; *N.R.*, October 25, 1867; William Felkin, *History*, p. 506.

[31] F. A. Wells, *op. cit.*, p. 187.

[32] *Ibid.*, pp. 157–58.

[33] Charlotte Erickson, *op. cit.*, pp. 94–99.

[34] *Hosier and Glover's Gazette*, December 15, 1887, p. 297.

[35] *Ibid.*, June 15, 1892, p. 140.

[36] *Hosiery Review*, January, 1888.

U

282 VICTORIAN NOTTINGHAM

[37] F. A. Wells, *op. cit.*, p. 172.

[38] *Ibid.*, pp. 174–75.

[39] H. A. Silverman, *Studies in Industrial Organization,* (1946), pp. 14–15.

[40] *Hosiery and Lace Trades Review,* May, 1891.

[41] Charlotte Erickson, *op. cit.*, p. 138.

[42] F. M. Thomas, *I. & R. Morley, A Record of a Hundred Years,* (1900), p. 32.

[43] *Report of the Commissioners appointed to inquire into the Truck Acts,* 1871, (327) XXXVI, ev. of Mundella, p. 1121.

[44] F. A. Wells' *op. cit.*, p. 179.

[45] *Minutes of Nottingham Chamber of Commerce,* 1867.

[46] *Hosiery Review,* October, 1887.

[47] G. R. Porter and F. W. Hirst, *The Progress of the Nation,* (1912), p. 393; F. A. Wells, *op. cit.*, pp. 188–189.

[48] William Felkin, *History,* p. 549; G. R. Porter and F. W. Hirst, *op. cit.*, p. 394.

[49] *Op. cit.*, p. 194; D. Smith, 'The Silk Industry of the East Midlands', *The East Midland Geographer,* 1962, 3, 1. Pp. 27–28.

[50] *First Report of the Royal Commission on Depression of Trade and Industry,* 1886, (c. 4621) XXI. 1., p. 234.

[51] G. R. Porter and F. W. Hirst, *op. cit.*, p. 395.

[52] *Hosiery Review,* February, 1890.

[53] *First Report of the Royal Commission on Depression of Trade and Industry,* 1886, [c. 4621] XXI. 1, p. 234; G. R. Porter and F. W. Hirst, *op. cit.*, p. 395.

[54] *Hosiery Review,* December, 1894.

[55] G. R. Porter and F. W. Hirst, *op. cit.*, p. 396.

[56] F. A. Wells, *op. cit.*, p. 170.

[57] *Ibid.*, p. 176, f.n. 2.

[58] See Report of the Nottingham Chamber of Commerce reproduced in William Felkin, *History,* p. 514.

[59] *Report of the Factory and Workshops' Commission,* 1876, XXX. 1, ev. of Kendall, p. 401.

[60] *Wages in Minor Textile Trades,* 1890, LXVIII.

[61] *N.R.,* April 17, 1868.

[62] Supra, pp. 257–58.

[63] *N.R.,* February 9, 1855; It was the practice of the larger houses to deliver a ticket with the work put out to indicate the rate they were paying.

[64] Many were contributing 1s. per week for this purpose; *N.R.,* September 21, 1860.

[65] The following account is based on my article, 'Technological Change and the Hosiery Board of Arbitration,' *The Yorkshire Bulletin of Economic and Social Research,* Vol. 15, No. I, May, 1963.

[66] As for example in the campaign of 1820 when a combined effort was made to enforce the 1819 statement, and again in 1827.

[67] William Felkin, *History,* p. 471; *N.R.,* January 10, 1845.

[68] E. Renals, 'Arbitration in the Hosiery Trades of the Midland Counties', *The Journal of the Royal Statistical Society,* (1867), XXX, 548–66.

[69] *Tenth Report of the Commissioners appointed to inquire into the organization and rules of trades unions and other associations with minutes of evidence and appendices,* 1867–68, [3980–vi] XXIX. 1, ev. of Mundella, p. 77.

[70] W. H. G. Armytage, *art. cit.,* p. 25.

[71] S. and B. Webb, *The History of Trades Unionism* (1935), p. 338.

[72] E. H. Phelps Brown, *The Growth of British Industrial Relations; A Study from the Standpoint of 1906–1914,* (1959), p. 126 *et. seq.*

[73] William Felkin, *History,* p. 448.

[74] *N.R.,* June 15, 1866.

[75] *Ibid.*

[76] It consisted of about 150 men; *Webb Collection,* Section C.

[77] *N.R.,* August 10, 1866.

[78] William Felkin, *History,* p. 485; Truck had returned to the villages a few years later.

[79] *N.R.,* July 27, 1866; *N.R.,* November 16, 1866.

[80] *Tenth Report of the Commissioners (organization and rules of trades unions and other associations),* 1867–68 (3980–v) XXIX. 1.

[81] *Ibid.,* ev. of Samuel Morley, p. 80.

[82] S. and B. Webb quoting Mundella in *Industrial Democracy* (1920) p. 724

[83] E. Renals, *art. cit.,* pp. 548–56.

[84] *N.R.,* March 20, 1868.

[85] *N.R.,* April 1, 1869.

[86] William Felkin, *History,* p. 487; *N.R.,* March 25, 1870.

[87] S. and B. Webb, *Industrial Democracy* (1920), p. 323.

[88] *N.R.,* March 4, 1870.

[89] *N.R.,* April 23, 1870; This was the only occasion when a referee was called upon.

[90] *N.R.,* May 25, 1870.

[91] *Ex.,* January 3, 1871; *Ex.,* January 6, 1871; *Ex.,* May 16, 1871.

[92] E. H. Phelps Brown, *op. cit.,* p. 144.

[93] *Webb Collection,* Section C, Ev. of Samuel Bower, p. 234.

[94] *N.R.,* September 16, 1871.

[95] *Report of the Commissioners appointed to inquire into the Truck Acts, 1871* (327) XXXVI, p. 1085.

[96] *N.J.,* June 30, 1872.

[97] *Webb Collection,* Section A, pp. 250–51; *Webb Collection* Minutes of Circular Framework Knitters' Society, June, 1876, pp. 267–70.

[98] *Ibid.*

[99] F. A. Wells, *op. cit.,* p. 195.

[100] *Webb Collection,* Section A, p. 271.

[101] G. R. Porter and F. W. Hirst, *op. cit.,* p. 393.

[102] *Ex.,* August 23, 1879; *Ex.,* September 4, 1880; *Ex.,* October 15, 1889; *Ex.,* December 24, 1889; *Ex.,* January 28, 1889.

[103] *The Hosiery and Lace Trades Review,* February 20, 1890; *Ex.,* January 28, 1889; *Ex.,* April 24, 1891; *Ex.,* February 17, 1891.

[104] *Ex.,* April 17, 1891; *Ex.,* June 11, 1891.

[105] *Ex.,* December 20, 1895; *Ex.,* January 7, 1896; *Ex.,* January 14, 1896; *Ex.,* January 16, 1896; *Ex.,* January 28, 1896; *The Knitters' Circular,* February, 1896, January, 1897 and February, 1897.

[106] *Webb Collection,* Section A, p. 155.

[107] *Royal Commission on Labour,* Vol. II, 1892, [c. 6795–vi] XXVXI, Part II 441, pp. 77–79; *Webb Collection,* Section A, pp. 117, 187; F. A. Wells, *op. cit.,* p. 186.

CHAPTER XI

THE LACE INDUSTRY: CHANGE AND EXPANSION, AND THE AMALGAMATED SOCIETY OF LACE OPERATIVES

FOLLOWING technical innovations, improvements in communication through the introduction of the Penny Post and the opening of a railway line to London, the lace trade underwent considerable changes in the third quarter of the century. The commercial crises in 1857 and 1866 brought temporary set-backs and caused widespread unemployment, but though recovery was swift and foreign and domestic demand for lace expanded slowly, Hooton Deverill's extremely successful application of the jacquard loom to the leavers machine in 1841 had been immediately adopted by the trade. By 1846 more than four hundred machines had been fitted with his mechanism in order to manufacture patterned laces.[1] Progress made in methods of designing and draughting led to the creation of a profusion of patterns with a wide range of appeal. It was estimated that the number of bobbin net machines increased from 3,200 in 1843 to 3,522 much wider machines in 1865, of which almost half were the Deverill-improved leavers machines making fancy lace.[2] Production in large shops had existed during the early years of the century when machinery was hand operated, but the additional economies to be derived from integration, particularly in the production of plain net, had induced more manufacturers to invest in factory production in the forties and fifties. In 1836 there had been twenty-nine or thirty factories in the trade; by 1865 Felkin counted one hundred and thirty 'larger' factories and no more than ninety hand machines at work all of which were in private houses.[3]

But although in 1866 nine-tenths of lace machinery was steam powered, the spread of steam power production did not entirely destroy the 'perverse and impracticable race' of independent machine holders, for although few owners of large amounts of machinery were characteristic of the plain net branch,[4] through the stall system the small entrepreneur survived the spread of factory production and remained typical of the fancy branch.[5] In 1865, according to Felkin, the owners of most of the fancy machines finished and sold their own goods;[6] but already the re-emergence of a specialist class of lace machinery builders was beginning to reverse this process.[7] With the separation of finishing from lace making and with specialization by commission houses, the fragmentation of the industry went further, as demand for ever-multiplying variety of patterns increased. Even doubling mills increased in number in the area around Nottingham.[8] During the last quarter of the century, however, the structure and organization of the lace trade was subject to little striking change, and the adoption of the company form of organization, which Thomas Adams introduced to the trade in the fifties, was slow to spread.

Competition and expansion were major features of the trade during the second half of the century. The vast expansion in the output of British lace, especially during the last quarter of the century, reflected the rising standard of living and the increasing demand for cheap luxuries by the middle classes. The fashion called 'Victorian Gothic' which dated from the middle years of the century dictated a growing extravagance in the decoration of the heavy material and sombre colours fashionable in women's dress.

'What will characterize the present epoch in the history of fashion', wrote one commentator in 1873, 'is the amount of trimming with which we have found it possible to load every separate article.'

Up to eighty yards of trimming might be employed on one of the huge Victorian skirts alone, and lace became one of the most fashionable of all dress accessories. With some decline in the popularity of the crinoline and the introduction of the bustle, between 1860 and 1880 cascading lace falls were worn over skirts, while lace frills and collars, ruffles and chemisettes continued to form a regular part of women's dress until the end of the century. From the 1840s lace veils had been used to adorn bonnets, and after 1850 the wearing of close fitting lace caps indoors became a popular and established vogue. Lace trimmings of all sorts embellished both apparel and linen, while the use of lace curtains was a popular way to ensure, in an attractive manner, the privacy of the Victorian parlour, a need which was felt especially in the growing numbers of homes whose windows looked directly into the street. Nottingham lace became the fashionable Victorian fabric which found favour with the expanding middle classes in Continental Europe, in the United States, and in the British settlements in Canada and Australasia; in cities as far apart as Paris and Philadelphia, Berlin and Buenos Aires, Manchester and Melbourne, Antwerp and Toronto, manufactured Nottingham lace adorned women of middling fashion.

The vogue for lace furnishings and dress sustained a bouyant demand in the domestic market, and despite the tariffs imposed by most European countries and America during the two decades prior to 1900, exports also grew. At the close of the century approximately 70 per cent. of total lace production was shipped overseas, the American market still being the largest single one, followed by Germany. In aggregate, foreign markets took nearly four times the volume of lace exports purchased by British colonies. Total British exports of lace increased from £1·1m. in the quinquennium 1871–75, to £2·3m. in 1896–1900, though the high levels reached in 1881–85 were not attained again until after 1900.[9] (See Table XIII.) Silk lace exports accounted for only 10 per cent. of the total, and were declining at the turn of the century. Lace imports grew rapidly; from

TABLE XIII: *Lace Exports (Annual Values) in £'s as published by the Board of Trade, 1853–1900.*

Year	Cotton lace & patent net	Silk lace	Year	Cotton lace & patent net	Silk lace
1853	596,554	258,209	1877	1,084,340	125,072
1854	514,413	384,737	1878	1,147,075	91,468
1855	470,538	323,482	1879	1,437,815	78,683
1856	424,778	597,013	1880	1,973,816	109,953
1857	400,336	590,952	1881	2,380,610	279,128
1858	389,438	444,937	1882	2,721,535	293,171
1859	397,333	486,053	1883	2,707,694	193,845
1860	341,229	471,731	1884	2,452,556	171,762
1861	287,398	368,219	1885	2,376,837	120,672
1862	518,750	459,724	1886	2,363,683	166,083
1863	450,192	553,520	1887	2,261,471	185,492
1864	367,239	423,276	1888	1,923,386	223,901
1865	465,611	434,839	1889	1,913,547	231,721
1866	536,967	307,549	1890	2,046,847	211,476
1867	470,420	295,690	1891	1,852,967	238,876
1868	475,466	501,672	1892	2,100,405	338,521
1869	632,213	307,498	1893	2,016,406	190,166
1870	839,048	384,386	1894	1,890,053	163,483
1871	969,559	297,386	1895	1,961,812	140,670
1872	1,024,420	268,372	1896	2,049,109	161,793
1873	1,133,307	231,435	1897	2,292,489	152,008
1874	1,108,066	186,858	1898	2,258,997	126,493
1875	1,133,093	137,516	1899	2,376,200	144,631
1876	1,006,051	196,905	1900	2,671,021	144,142

a value of £0·6m. in 1871–75, imports of lace increased to £2·3m. in 1896–1900. However, by 1896–1901 lace to the value of £0·5m. was re-exported from Britain, a feature of the trade which developed between 1881–85 (when re-exported lace first appeared in the trade figures) and 1910.[10] This reflected the tardiness with which British manufacturers adopted machine embroidery, though at the same time the rise of the re-export trade was an indication of the initiative and success of Nottingham lace merchants in securing the widest possible range of articles for sale to their customers.

Britain's inferior provision for technical education had allowed

Continental producers to dominate markets for products whose design was an important factor influencing their appeal to the public, and consequently their ultimate sale. Recognizing the existence of a potential market for 'foreign' lace re-exports, Swiss and German manufacturers succeeded in developing a trade by importing plain net for use as grounds to be embroidered by the Schiffle machine.[11] When this trade began, the number of plain net machines in the industry increased from 300 to 500.[12] Leavers lace manufacturers were thus exposed to growing competition from imports of machine-embroidered lace, but the entire market for lace was growing sufficiently to enable expansion to proceed in this branch too. Between 1875 and 1885 the number of leavers machines rose from 1,550 to 2,250, although during the ensuing twenty years only 300 were added.[13] The curtain branch expanded as manufacturers continued to develop markets for low and medium quality goods, and in the ten years following 1875 the machines increased from 400 to 520.[14] The number of lace factories almost doubled between 1870 and 1890, when they rose from 224 to 403, and whereas in 1870 they employed 8,370 men and women, in 1890 factory employees had risen to 16,930, indicating little change in the size of production units. In 1870 nearly 75 per cent. of those employed in factories were men; in 1890 the proportion had fallen to about 60 per cent. In 1901 10,462 males and 7,440 females found employment in lace factories, while by 1907 the size of the entire labour force connected with lace manufacture was 25,215.[15] The first Census of Production taken in 1906 showed the value of total lace output in England and Wales as £9,578,000.

During the last quarter of the century conditions of rising output, falling prices, and growing competition, together constituted the framework in which manufacturers sought to prevent their profit margins from continuous decline.[16] Meanwhile, the Lace Makers' Society, growing in numerical and financial strength, endeavoured to raise its members' living standards. The conditions of workers in the industry had been investigated in 1860, when the question of extending the Factory Act to the lace trade was re-opened. The movement in favour of the Act was organized by T. B. Charlton Esq., of Chilwell Hall near Nottingham, and a committee was formed under Thomas West, the General Secretary of the Lace Makers' Society.[17] The opponents of legislation were represented by a committee of employers under the chairmanship of Lewis Heymann, the lace merchant and doctrinaire Liberal. In January, 1860 fourteen thousand persons signed a petition to support extension of the Factory Act to the lace trade; two official investigations followed in 1861 and 1862.

Since the 1842 Commissioners' Report the chief developments in the lace trade affecting the pattern of employment had been the concentration of machines into large steam-powered factories, and the increasing amount of work carried on in large warehouses.[18] Among those who gave evidence there was some disagreement; Tremenheere, the Factory Inspector, asserted that the conditions of auxiliary lace workers were much the same as in 1842, and a pamphleteer stated that he was appalled to observe the 'hardship, misery and toil' of workers in the lace trade.[19] William Felkin claimed to detect a definite amelioration in lace workers' conditions since the 1842 inquiry due, he argued, to the pressure of public sentiment which made itself felt after the Report's publication.[20] Long hours were still the rule, although the pressure of work varied. Children under nine or ten worked only in shops and private houses under mistresses, and women were employed more often at the warehouses and dressing rooms. With an eye to greater secrecy and to save the second-hand mistresses' income, since the Enclosure Act a large proportion of drawing, clipping, scalloping, mending, and similar operations had been taken out of mistresses' shops to be performed in the warehouses. Although many splendid new warehouses had been built in Nottingham, where almost the entire English lace production was finished and sold, most of them were hot and close; the dressing rooms, in particular, required a very high temperature and humid atmosphere.[21] Nevertheless, it was because conditions in workshops compared so unfavourably with those of factories and warehouses that Felkin and others opposed the regulation of warehouses.

Felkin argued that the effect would be to promote the movement of work outside warehouses to avoid the Act and so check the 'voluntary course of improvement' which he insisted was taking place. This was due to 'a sort of public opinion, at least an unwritten code of class regulation . . . which distinguishes between business carried on upon such wise and upright principles, and the reverse'. Felkin was particularly gratified by the 'special influence' brought to bear by employers on the personal character of the employees in a large and increasing number of lace and hosiery establishments. He maintained that, perhaps allowing for minimum safeguards such as the registration of workshops with regard to place, number of hours, and labour (though he acknowledged the difficulty of defining domestic and workshop labour), the proportion of work inside warehouses would continue to increase. Workshop conditions, it was argued, would perforce improve in order to retain labour attracted by the higher wages and comfort of the warehouses.[22] He was also confident that by publicizing evidence, impartial opinions, and advice, the current investigation would prove beneficial to the cause of furthering the improvement in lace workers' conditions. Felkin looked forward to the time when employers would voluntarily discontinue working the factory engine eighteen hours a day, thereby freeing men to work during the day and 'so conduce greatly to the comfort and morality of the workmen and their families.'[23]

To some extent Felkin's defence of the larger employers was justified, and his analysis of the improvement seems reasonable enough. The factory and warehouse system did not become typical of the lace trade until after legislation had affected the major textile industries, by which time public opinion had already been aroused. Many large employers were prominent townsmen holding positions of respect in chapel or town government. In addition a number of the warehouses were of recent construction, and besides the pressure of public opinion, which was acknowledged more than once in the evidence, it was occasionally asserted that the late hours were uneconomic and that it was preferable to increase hands rather than hours.[24] Nevertheless, in time of good trade work was carried on far into the night and sometimes throughout the night. Despite this, however, it was generally agreed among working class females that to obtain a situation at a warehouse was in itself sufficient object for ambition.[25]

The adoption of the factory system destroyed the reasons for continuing the trade's exemption from the Factory Act, but there was still some antagonism amongst employers. The investigation carried out by Tremenheere in 1861 revealed that opposition to the Factory Act came mainly from small manufacturers, a majority of whom were independent machine holders making fancy lace. But strong opposition also came from larger employers, John and Charles Thornton, Hardy, and Hodgson.[26] It was alleged that the Act would check production, restrict profits, and involve too great an expense in the installation of the double sets of bobbins which would become necessary if the Act should pass. A local pamphleteer sought to counter these allegations by pointing out that the check on production would mitigate the curse of overproduction from which the trade recurrently suffered. Discounting the forecast of reductions in profits as ridiculous, he suggested that manufacturers were more concerned with the loss of their superiority in the market for the labour of young persons.[27] W. G. Ward, partner in the firm of Cope & Ward, lace manufacturers in New Basford, opposed extension of the Act. In their large new premises with ninety lace machines employing two hundred and forty men and one hundred women, Cope and Ward were already single-handing their machines, which meant that one set of machines was available for preparation while the other set was being worked. This method of working avoided the need for the long hours against which the Act was aimed, and Ward's objection was purely on the principle of opposition to interference in the trade.[28]

The division of opinion did not present itself simply as a group of welfare restrictionists opposing a phalanx of vicious and unscrupulous anti-restrictionists. On the whole, such eminent employers and public figures as Birkin, Heymann, Felkin, Hill, and Doughty were favourably disposed towards the spirit of the Act, but expressed alarm at its harmful effects unless it was modified to meet the trade's requirements. They were convinced of the necessity for women's and children's labour to be spread over long hours with intervals. It was generally acknowledged that if the Act was passed in its entirety there would be strong inducements to some large employers, and certainly to all the smaller ones who often employed members of their families to thread and wind, to remove the operation of these processes outside the factory into neighbouring houses.[29] Tremenheere was much impressed by the contention that such restriction on the supply of labour would be injurious to the trade. He was also persuaded that the cost of an extra set of bobbins and carriages would be a considerable burden upon manufacturers. On his recommendation, therefore, youths between the ages of sixteen and eighteen were permitted to work any nine hours between 4 a.m. and 10 p.m. To compensate for the expense of the extra installations, the fencing of machinery was not required; the supporters of regulation had gained little.[30]

In 1861 Tremenheere had also drawn attention to the large numbers of women and children (two or three times as many as those actually employed inside the factories) who were employed in dressing and finishing lace. These people often worked very long hours in extremely unhealthy conditions. However, as nearly all such labour was performed in workshops it was considered impossible to control this section of the industry by legislation.[31] In the Lace Works Act of 1861 the dressing and finishing of lace was explicitly exempted, but in 1862 the possibilities of extending the Act to embrace warehouses and workshops was investigated more closely by a Royal Commission on Children's Employment.

One of the largest lace establishments in Nottingham, enjoying great prestige and a fine reputation, was that belonging to Thomas Adams, a prominent Evangelical philanthropist who succeeded in securing the erection of half a dozen churches in Nottingham. In 1858 he employed five hundred in the warehouse and about the same number of outworkers. Renowned for his concern for the welfare and comfort of his workpeople, Adams provided a warehouse chapel, while in a separate building he provided a dining room for the employees, a separate tea room for the men, and adequate washing facilities for all. According to the 1862 Report, conditions at Adams' establishment compared favourably with those in other warehouses, although even here young people of nine, ten, and eleven were employed. The hours of work were nine on weekdays, and eight on Saturdays. Adams was in favour of restricting hours by legislation.[32]

At the warehouse of Messrs. Copestake, Moore & Crampton, where between four and six hundred were employed, instruction and guidance in religion were offered each day at a service which was held in the warehouse chapel before work commenced. In busy seasons the firm gave work to mistresses outside the warehouse, but the manager expressed his preference for work done under his supervision on the premises by people of 'better class'. In the rooms where bonnet fronts were manufactured, and where owing to the liberal use of gas the air was very impure, overtime was forbidden after regular hours (8 a.m. to 7 p.m.), while girls who were younger than fourteen were never kept late under any circumstances. The employers insisted on strict rules of behaviour and only a good character reference could secure any position with the firm. Persons under the age of thirteen were not normally employed.[33] Likewise at Heymann & Alexander's warehouse no persons were allowed to work unless they could read and write. Here, a large kitchen was fitted up for the use of those who did not return home for meals, and employees were well cared for. Heymann's attitude towards state intervention was quite definite; as he explained to the Commissioner, 'all legislation with regard to the employment of labour is, I think, objectionable'. He, like Felkin, preferred to leave progress to the influence of public opinion and the individual consciences of employers. He considered that children should not be employed before they reached the age of eight, but that after ten or twelve they should be allowed to work the usual ten hour day.[34]

J. L. Bottom was the owner of a huge dressing establishment, even larger than the majority of the newly-built warehouses and dressing rooms, and superior because of the roof ventilation which was said to have had a beneficial effect upon the health of his workpeople. There were conveniences for washing as well as a library stocked chiefly with religious books. Lambert, another lace dresser with newly-built premises, employed few children under thirteen and favoured staggered hours. Barnett, of Messrs. Barnett & Maltby, showed concern for his workpeople in the provision of a dining room and washing conveniences in the large new warehouses, while Hartshorn and Thomas Herbert were two more employers who paid attention to the comfort of their workpeople but who nevertheless opposed restrictions on labour.[35]

As a result of the investigation in 1862, the Commissioners recommended the extension of the Factory Acts—with certain modifications—to warehouses, workshops, and private houses in the lace and hosiery trades. The Factory Act was, in fact, applied to warehouses, and the hours of labour of outworkers, as opposed to home workers, were restricted by law under the Workshops' Act of 1864; later another Workshops' Regulation Act in 1867 extended the provision relating to private houses and home workers. On the whole these acts were unsuccessful, for despite the praise which Nottingham Corporation earned in its attempts to enforce the Act it was extremely difficult to detect avoidance of the law especially outside the borough boundaries, while those who removed work beyond the borough boundaries could thereby avoid prosecution.[36] By far the most distressing factor explaining the shortcomings of legislation was that section of the Report which stated,

> it is unhappily to a painful degree apparent through the whole of the evidence that against no persons did the children of both sexes need protection as against their parents.[37]

With an increasing number of lacemakers working in factories, trade unionism in the lace trade took permanent root. Earlier associations of workmen had proved only temporary, and the existence of a large number of independent machine holders had tended to complicate and retard trade union development. Although in 1824 Gravener Henson had affirmed that the bobbin net makers of Nottingham already belonged to a union,[38] during the trough of 1825–26 he was responsible for the formation of a committee of the lace operatives to cooperate with machine holders in imposing a limit on output by restricting hours of work, and to build up a fund to defend wages and relieve unemployed lace makers.[39] Wages did fall, however, by about 25 per cent. between 1825 and 1831,[40] and in that year the men again formed a Lacemakers' Union to enforce by striking, their decision to limit daily hours of work to twelve.[41] Shortly after its formation, the Lacemakers' Union became a member of the Nottingham Union of Trades which affiliated with John Doherty's National Association for the Protection of Labour,[42] but local members withdrew their support when, after having given aid to the striking cotton spinners of Ashton-under-Lyme in 1830–31, Lancashire branches of the N.A.P.L. refused to assist Nottingham hosiery workers in their strike of 1831.[43] Subsequently the Nottingham union of lacemakers enrolled in the 'Secret Order of the Operative Trades Union', which was probably a section of the Yorkshire Trades Union Movement; but again the lace makers failed to perpetuate their association.[44] During the middle thirties, due to competition in a market where supply had outpaced demand, at least five hundred small independent owners of machinery either became journeymen again or left the trade altogether. It was in the face of lockouts and reductions during the depressed trade of 1840 that once more journeymen lace makers met at the Durham Ox to form a union, this time for the purpose of raising wages.[45] Female outworkers also rallied, and in the same year more than four hundred lace runners struck against rapidly declining wages and the subletting system, but after two weeks the strike collapsed. The men's union also disappeared until 1846 when, after an unsuccessful appeal to Parliament, the British Union of Plain Net Makers was formed, a short-lived organization which in all probability disappeared during the depression of 1847–48 but whose constitution sought to combine the roles of trade union and friendly society in the style of other progressive unions.[46] In the spring of 1850, what proved to be a permanent association of lacemakers was established on lines similar to those followed in the formation of the 1846 Plain Net Makers' Union, though the latter had excluded workers in the south-western counties.

The Lace Makers' Society held its first official meeting on March 2, 1850,[47] and a union was formed by warp lace makers from the three midland counties in April.[48] The Warp Lace Union included all warp frame operatives, irrespective of the articles that they produced on the frames. Likewise the Lace Makers' Society united all makers of bobbin net, for not until after the mid-century did the sections of the trade become sufficiently distinct to warrant the structural trinity that was later adopted when, owing to technical changes, it became imperative for negotiations to take place on a sectional basis.[49] Although the curtain trade was recognized as a growing but nevertheless small section of the industry, in 1850 curtains were being produced on bobbin, warp, and tickler machines.[50] The Lace Makers' Society was divided by localities into several branches, and these grew in numbers as membership increased.[51] In the 1850s branch meetings were held at public houses in Lenton, Radford, Beeston, and various districts in Nottingham, the quarterly public meetings taking place at the Durham Ox. The Lace Makers' Society was infused with the new spirit which was reanimating the trade union movement at this time. Entrance fees of 2s. in addition to small regular weekly contributions entitled any paid-up member to compensation in case of sickness or permanent disablement and to strike pay. When men fell behind in their contributions, membership was revoked and they were fined on re-entry to the Society. In the case of the return of a blackleg his entitlement to benefit was also temporarily suspended.[52] The Society employed a General Secretary at a weekly salary of £1, auditors inspected the accounts annually, and from 1855 an attorney was chosen to deal with legal problems.[53] It was the Society's hope that its current income would be adequate to finance normal benefits and to support members who refused to accept work below agreed rates according to the desultory settlements reached by employers and workmen, while unofficial strikers were not entitled to receive support from Society funds.[54]

These were characteristics common to several craft unions at that time, though in addition to lace operatives, for the first few years unskilled winders and warpers were also admitted to the Society. No doubt this was in an attempt to monopolize skilled labour, for auxiliary workers were admitted to the Society only on the understanding that they refused to work with blacklegs. But this was not always possible, for although the formative years were eased by favourable economic conditions there were several attempts on the part of employers to outlaw the Society. In at least one Nottingham factory a 'document', in which the signatory undertook not to belong to any trade union, was presented to all workmen for signature.[55] When the Society committee proved to its own satisfaction that any of its members were being victimized, the injured parties were placed on benefit and received compensation.[56] During the union's early years, negotiations for general wage increases absorbed less of the secretary's energy than that spent in efforts to establish standards of payment for different classes of work, according to the width of machine, and the gauge, style, or quality of work. Unemployment, which accompanied depression in 1854 and again in 1857–8, twice threatened the union's existence, but the expedient of reducing subscriptions seems to have been effective, for in March, 1858, Thomas West, the secretary, reported to members that the storm had been weathered, and normal subscriptions were resumed. In December, 1858 membership stood at thirteen hundred.[57]

For several years following the 1857 upset, trade was unsettled and lace prices were depressed by the actions of leading houses unloading large lots very cheaply. Furthermore, political upheavals in America were blamed for the severe depression that occurred in the winter of 1860–61. In an attempt to sap the growing strength of the Lace Makers' Society and to provide room to manoeuvre an adjustment of wages during the depression of prices, three large manufacturers, Tidmas, Berrey, and Burton locked out some three hundred men.[58] Following the example of hosiery workers, the lace makers' union offered to co-operate in the formation of a board of arbitration to settle the dispute, but the employers refused to negotiate. They declined to recognize the union and intimated that they would only receive communications from former employees. The lock-out caused a damaging drain on union funds, and income barely covered expenditure.[59] In November, 1860 the Nottingham branch of the Amalgamated Society of Engineers petitioned London headquarters for an advance of £200 to be extended on loan to the lace makers. Other local societies were equally prompt to contribute financial aid.[60]

In contrast with the conciliatory attitude of employers and workmen current in the hosiery trade, lace disputes generated much ill-feeling. Blacklegs (locally known as black sheep) were jeered and pelted with stones. An effigy of Tidmas was burnt in the street and three men were gaoled for intimidation. Tidmas applied to the workhouse for labour and secured the discharge of several non-union lace workers by offering them work—which the Poor Law authorities obliged them to accept. Their sympathies lay with the lace makers, however, and they appealed to the union Committee for help. It was decided to support them from Society funds and to issue a public appeal for support. The lockout terminated finally after four months when employers and workmen concluded a compromise agreement. Normal subscriptions were resumed in March, 1861.[61] There was even more animosity during the strike which took place at Butler's factory at Radford in 1865, when police protection had saved blacklegs from serious physical harm, though several pickets were prosecuted for violent and intimidating behaviour. The dispute was settled by an improvised board of arbitration when three employers and three workmen met to discuss grievances under the chairmanship of an independent referee, T. B. Charlton, Esq., from Chilwell Hall. The interested parties were not present at the settlement.[62]

In all these disputes the Lace Makers' Society was on the offensive. Funds mounted while the Committee assumed greater confidence as membership grew, and in the context of fluctuating lace prices and bouts of unemployment the union was successful in insisting on high wages for its members. The average weekly wage of 18s., as estimated by Felkin in 1844, increased rapidly during the two ensuing decades. By 1865, 3,500 first class leavers operatives were earning 35s. or more, 2,500 received at least 25s., and 1,800 16s. per week. And despite the absence of organization in the ancillary trades, wages were correspondingly high; male dressers of lace could earn up to 30s., bobbin and carriage makers 33s., and moulders and machine founders 35s.; in the warehouses weekly average earnings were between 8s. and 12s., and 4,200 boys engaged in clearing, winding, and threading bobbins received some 5s. per week.[63]

The success of the *ad hoc* arbitration procedure in 1865, the first essay in arbitration in the lace trade, was reassuring. Mundella cultivated this favourable climate, and at a meeting of the Chamber of Commerce in 1867, after criticizing both employers and workmen for bad relations in the lace industry, he advocated the formation of a board of arbitration similar to that which already existed in the hosiery trade.[64] The union showed its willingness to co-operate in the experiment, and Mundella was asked to arrange a meeting with lace manufacturers to initiate discussion of the proposal for the establishment of an arbitration board. But negotiations were jeopardized by dissension among union members. This arose because of the system whereby members of the committee were elected irrespective of whether they were engaged in the leavers, plain net, or curtain branches, and some of the leavers men accused the plain net workers of attempting to obtain a majority of representatives on the committee in order to increase the amount of funds being spent in connection with a strike in the plain net branch.[65] Edward Smith, leader of the leavers rebels, offered to act as secretary (without remuneration) to a splinter society which seceded from the main body in March, 1867.[66] West, secretary of the 'Old Society', referred to the rebels as 'a lot of discontented men who complained that they didn't get their share of the benefits of the Society and left it.'[67] He gathered up the remaining members, including some leavers men, and continued to negotiate for a board. This was established in 1868 when eight employers and eight union officials met to discuss rules which, in their final form, were very similar to those of the Hosiery Board.[68] Its avowed object was 'to arbitrate upon any question that may be referred to it, from time to time, by the joint consent of conciliatory means'.

For the purposes of negotiation and the achievement of uniformity of contract, practice, and piece rates in the trade, in 1869 the employers joined together in the Lace Manufacturers' Association.[69] Like the revised Hosiery Board, the Lace Board did not provide the chairman with a casting vote, but it did make provision for the appointment of a referee, though during the first nine years, in which the number of representatives on the Board increased from eight to twelve, a referee was called upon only twice.[70] The Board was responsible for the enforcement of statement prices as agreed by its members, and because of the frequent introduction of new fashions and technical improvements the task proved enormously

HOLLOWST

HE LACE MARKET, NOTTINGHAM.

F. C. Tighe, Nottingham Public Library

THE LACE MARKET, STONEY STREET: c.1900
GIRLS LEAVING WAREHOUSES

WILLIAM FELKIN, 1795–1874

difficult. Employers complained constantly that a too rigid adherence to existing lists tended to harm the trade and presented an obstacle to improvement. Consequently the readjustment of price lists and piece rates was an extremely important sphere of the Board's activity, in addition to the settlement of disputes arising out of the payment of existing lists.

Throughout its early years the Board worked efficiently and satisfactorily; indeed, more friction occurred over inter-union disputes than between employers and operatives. The Leavers Lace Trade Association, which had 275 members shortly after secession, claimed to have twice that number two years later, while its financial reserves stood at £1,000.[71] The old Nottingham United Friendly Society of Operative Lacemakers also flourished, and out-of-work pay and strike pay was increased—presumably with the intention of attracting members from the splinter society. A sixth branch was opened in Lenton in 1871, when total membership of the old Society was estimated at 1,300, and its bank deposits amounted to £2,150.[72]

Attitudes towards arbitration were basically similar, but whereas the old Society invited the Leavers Association to be represented on the Board, the latter wanted to see a separate board to serve its own branch, and refused to recognize the existing Board.[73] This situation continued until 1875. In 1873 the Leavers Association struck over payment for day work for which there existed no recognized procedure.[74] The employers retaliated by locking out over a thousand leavers lace makers, affecting also between two and three thousand more operatives. Having previously brought the question of day work before the Board in 1870, the Operative Lace Makers' Society sympathized with the splinter group's action. As members of the Board, however, they were bound by its rules concerning strikes. Members of the old Society urged the leavers group to submit its demands to the Board of Arbitration; they also appealed to the Mayor to act as intermediary between employers and workmen. On his part, Mayor William Foster suggested that the Board be reconstituted, to which in principle both operatives and manufacturers agreed. When the latter insisted on a return to work as a precondition for arbitration, however, the operatives refused.[57] The old Society now rallied to the leavers' defence, criticized the employers' intransigence, and voted £100 per week to support the Association. At the same time it continued to submit its own demands to the Board. The men asked for 5s. per day for alterations; Vickers, the lace merchant who acted as referee, made an award of 3s. 4d. per day for the first two days and 4s. 6d. for each subsequent day. The official union view was that acceptance

V

was obligatory, but individually the men resented the award. This attitude was manifested in a mounting sympathy for the spirited Association out on strike.[76] The two bodies were drawn closer together in their dissatisfaction with the attitude of employers, and both began to realize the extent of their weakness through division.[77] In January, 1874, the Association agreed to a compromise with the employers and its members returned to work after an absence of twenty-two weeks.[78]

In July of the same year, the Committees of both the Society and the Association met to formulate rules for the Amalgamated Society of Operative Lacemakers, which, shortly after its formation, became the second strongest textile union in the country.[79] Each of the three branches—leavers, curtain, and plain net—had its own branch committee which was responsible to the Executive Council. This consisted of nine members, three from each of the three branches. Problems arising in any branch were first investigated by the relevant branch committee, and in the event of difficulty or complications passed on to the Executive Council. Meetings were held in public houses as before, though quarterly meetings were held at the Mechanics Institute. In 1877 the Society purchased premises in Pembridge Place which were converted into offices, and all future meetings were held there with the intention of 'getting clear of the influence of public houses.'[80]

At the request of the now Amalgamated Society, the rules of the Board of Arbitration were altered. The number of representatives from each side was increased to twelve, and a referee was elected annually until 1879. Previous arbitration methods had encouraged the technically unofficial settlement of sectional problems by meetings between branch committees and employers related to the appropriate branch, a similar procedure to that adopted by the Hosiery Board. Under the revised rules this practice was formalized, and the committee was actually given power to settle disputes without any reference to the entire Board. Later, in 1889, sectional committees of employers and union men were officially established as the tribunals to deal with branch questions.[81]

The reconstituted board did not prevent the occurrence of a number of disputes in 1875,[82] a year of indifferent trade for the lace industry, for the new union was strong and its members eager to employ its strength. One dispute in particular witnessed a recurrence of street fighting, molestation, and victimization. Two firms were involved in the dispute which centred upon the employment of apprentices. The Society required all members of the trade to serve a period of apprenticeship lasting seven years, during which time they received special low rates of pay. Each apprentice was attached to a journeyman lace maker for his instruction, and the number of apprentices which any employer was permitted to hire depended upon the number of lace makers in his employment.[83] In this manner the Society placed a strict control upon the rate of expansion of the labour force in order to raise the incomes of its members. This curtailment on the supply of skilled labour lay at the root of the disputes with the two Lenton firms of Bridgett and Sylvester, as indeed during the next twenty years it was the source of many more, when employers moved out of Nottingham in search of more and cheaper labour and to avoid the rules concerning apprenticeship. Sylvester and Bridgett had offended the Society by employing a larger number of apprentices than their quotas allowed. Workmen were ordered to strike, but sixty men who did not belong to the union were obtained to replace the strikers, while Sylvester took the precaution of ensuring police protection for his blacklegs. On one occasion, brass bands accompanied the strikers in a protest march which ended with a demonstration. Twenty union men were charged under the Criminal Law Amendment Act, and three were convicted of intimidation, each receiving sentences of three months imprisonment.[84] The aggressive enthusiasm shown by the rank and file of the Society alarmed its executive committee which criticized the irresponsible element whose actions had injured the Society's reputation. The president of the Society observed that the judge had been more considerate than the offenders had deserved.[85]

When in the next year, partly due to overstocking in the American market and partly to change in fashion at home, the lace trade underwent a sharp recession, there was a considerable amount of unemployment. Out-of-work benefits paid in that year amounted to nearly £3,000, and in the following year a slightly larger sum was distributed to about one thousand of the Society's members—almost one-half of the entire membership.[86] The failures of Messrs. S. G. Packer & Co. and Henry Minnitt caused uneasy feelings in the Lace Market, and the sale of bankrupts' stock once more produced complaints of low profits from manufacturers and especially from the independent makers.[87] The curtain section, hitherto considered a stable section of the trade, was also hit. Employers in this branch pressed for a wage reduction, but the Board, which failed to reach a decision, referred the question to the referee, Crompton, Q.C., who awarded a 10 per cent. reduction to apply for twelve months. By this time trade had improved and unemployment had fallen, and in defiance of the Society's executive council, men in the curtain branch rejected the award, subsequently withdrawing from the Board altogether.[88]

The Board did not reform until 1880 when, at the union's request, the word 'conciliation' was deliberately substituted for 'arbitration'. The rules of the new Board were that there should be thirteen representatives on either side (six leavers, four curtain, and three plain net), there was to be no referee, and the decision of the Board was binding. A committee of inquiry consisting of eight members was the actual working nucleus of the Board; but although it was encouraged to influence decisions, it lacked powers to make awards. In cases of disagreement the Board was instructed to elect one 'expert' from each side; the matter in dispute was then to be laid before them, and their decision upon it was to be final and binding.[89] One of the first tasks of the reformed Board was to investigate complaints made by manufacturers concerning competition from Scotland, and in 1880 a delegation visited Morton's factory, where since 1876 the number of machines had increased from two to twenty-two.[90] Complaints were also made that local manufacturers were suffering from competition from firms in the neighbouring districts of Long Eaton, Ilkeston, and Melbourne in Derbyshire, where several manufacturers had moved to escape the power of the union and to take advantage of cheap labour.[91] F. P. Norris, for example, who owned nine lace machines standing in Oldknow & Hartshorn's factory, after entering a wages dispute with the Society in 1877, hired union men who travelled each day from Long Eaton to Nottingham at his expense. The following year Norris moved his machinery to Long Eaton, where he paid less rent for standings and lower wages.[92]

In order to reduce friction at the factory level, in 1883 the Board adopted a Society proposal that committees should be set up in every factory to check the behaviour of employers. The union's grip on the trade tightened as its membership grew and as it accumulated numerical, financial, and psychological strength with each success. Its exclusive nature is illustrated by the level of its re-entrance fees (which varied from £5 to £15), and from 1879 a member could receive payment for refusing to accept 'inferior situations',[93] i.e. employment at less than union rates. Between June, 1879 and 1881, the membership of the Society increased from twenty-four hundred to thirty-six hundred.[94] From such a position of strength, and with the realization that the cheap labour sources posed a threat to its members, the Society resolved to crusade for the opening of a lodge at Long Eaton. The first lodge which opened there in 1874 had not been well supported,[95] and in 1878 renewed efforts were made to increase membership by temporarily allowing lower entrance fees and contributions. But the attempt failed, for many of the lace workers at Long Eaton were rehabilitated hand frame workers suspicious of the new model unions, reluctant to join them for fear of victimization, and in any case content to earn between 12s. and 22s. per week.[96] In 1883 the Society could claim that Nottingham was 'unionist to a man', its membership was over four thousand, and it possessed a capital of £30,000, but at Long Eaton, where there were between six and seven hundred lace-makers, only one hundred and fifty belonged to the Society. In the same year the Long Eaton members were locked out.[97]

The town Society dug in its heels and refused to allow members to follow machinery which had been removed to the districts unless their employers offered them exactly the same as the union was successfully insisting upon in Nottingham; those who did were struck off the Society's books.[98] But the attempt to obtain Nottingham pay and conditions in the surrounding districts failed, and the exodus of machinery continued unchecked. Between 1883 and 1886 Springthorpe and Bates took their machines to Melbourne; Towle, Hitchen, Sisling, and Fletcher moved theirs to Long Eaton; Attenborough, Trumans, Tattersall, Howard, Mariott, Launts, Jones, and Skevington removed to Ilkeston, and Gregory moved to Southwell.[99] Moreover, several employers joined the core of manufacturers who had orginally discharged members of the Society.

In trying to combat the employers after the boom of the early eighties had ended, and when heavy unemployment affected the lace industry, the Society was forced to draw heavily upon its reserves. In 1884 £9,500 was granted in out-of-work benefit payments; in 1885 about 2,500 recipients were given a further £10,537,[100] while during the twelve months ending in December, 1885 £5,200 were withdrawn from the bank, the weekly excess expenditure having averaged £100. The Society was not only giving trade grants to members who had been dismissed by employers because of their Society membership, but also to men who had refused offers of the resulting free situations. Furthermore, even minors were allowed 15s. per week if they refused to blackleg, for 'minor' labour was at a premium among anti-union employers.[101] The Long Eaton lock-out was partially terminated in March, 1885, when the Society conceded the claim of employers to employ non-union men and declared all Long Eaton shops 'open', where the employers did not victimize its members. Despite this gesture to open shops, Long Eaton employers showed reluctance to employ Society men at Nottingham rates. They realized that the Society was on the defensive and that bad trade conditions had forced concessions in the hope that some of the men out of work might find employment, thereby relieving the pressure on Society finances. In August, 1886 it was stated that the amount of readily available cash was just less than £3,000, that the weekly income was £200, and expenditure £350. It was decided that out-of-work pay must be reduced from 7s. to 5s., and sick pay and trade grants from 15s. to 12s. Union officials received cuts in their salaries.[102] In 1886 the Chamber of Commerce showed signs of mounting desperation, and in view of the serious loss to the town through the extensive removal of lace and hosiery machinery outside Nottingham the Chamber urged the Mayor to call a public meeting to consider what action might be taken to arrest the movement.[103]

The disparity between Long Eaton and Nottingham wage rates amounted to 25 per cent., and both manufacturers and the union agreed that this affected the leavers branch more than others, though curtain manufacturers complained of similar conditions. After protracted negotiation, in December, 1886 Nottingham employers in both sections were successful in forcing what amounted to about a 15 per cent. reduction in payment for leavers and curtain goods. The Society was in no position to offer strong resistance, though the original proposal had been for a reduction of 33⅓ per cent., but this had been modified by the Board. Many manufacturers resented this compromise and some continued to move machinery, while others threatened their workmen with dismissal in order to obtain wage reductions. Men who accepted such abatements privately were ignored by the Society when disputes arose, and when good trade returned they were obliged to fend for themselves. Faced with the difficulties of private agreements and the persistent removal of machinery, the Board of Conciliation broke up when leavers and curtain branches refused to elect representatives for the Society in 1887.[104] In 1889 conditions deteriorated further, although already in October, 1888 no fewer than two thousand lace workers were unemployed. In the absence of a Board, agreement on wages reverted to private contracts. During this time the union theoretically claimed to be withdrawing labour from employers whom they knew to be paying reduced prices. In practice, under pressure of the depression, union rates were insisted upon and maintained only in large unionist factories, and many members applied to the society for grants towards the cost of emigration to Canada, America, and Australia.[105]

Early in 1889 the Lace Manufacturers' Association again requested a revision of the Board's constitution, but leavers and curtain branches once more refused to elect representatives. Later in the year the manufacturers gave notice of a 40 per cent. reduction on curtain goods, 25 per cent. on leavers goods, and 15 per cent. off all other cards of prices. As the operatives still refused to elect representatives, employers suggested that an independent arbitrator should be agreed upon, but this proposal was rejected. Some of the manufacturers outside the Association stated their position unequivocally, and Fletcher threatened the men working his leavers

machines that unless they accepted a 25 per cent. reduction forth-
with, he would remove his machines to Long Eaton—which he did.
This brought the total number of lace machines at Long Eaton to
two hundred and seven, although here there were only sixty paying
members of the Society. At Ilkeston there were one hundred and
twenty machines and eighty paying members.[106]

When the Manufacturers' Association presented the proposed new
list of rates to the Lacemakers' Secretary, the latter called a meeting
to take place at the Mechanics Hall which more than two thousand
men attended. A strike was called for July, 1889, when eighteen
hundred leavers and seven hundred lace operatives took part. Three
thousand warehouse workers were also affected.[107] There were, however, about twenty larger manufacturers who had not given notice
of the reduction, the largest of which was the Midland Lace Company. According to W. H. Farmer, the Company's director, the
group remained aloof from the Manufacturers' Association, of
which sixty of the sixty-six members had given their men dismissal
notices, because they considered that there were too few members
and because no provision was made to penalize offending member
firms which did not adhere to agreements. On agreement between
both sides, Alderman Renals acted as mediator to end the strike.
It was agreed that the new card would be suspended, while the men
would resume work pending the formation of a new Board of Conciliation. After protracted negotiations the lock-out strike, which
cost the Society over £1,200 weekly, terminated at the beginning of
September.[108]

The rules of the new Board differed from previous Boards in that
in the event of the experts themselves failing to agree, experts
chosen by either side could each select an assessor. Equally important was the rule which provided for penalties and punishments for
employers and workmen who, being members of the Board, did
not comply with its decisions. When it was found necessary in
future to strike against an offending employer, the Lace Manufacturers' Association undertook to defray half the cost. The new
list, which allowed for an average reduction of $12\frac{1}{2}$ per cent. in
both branches, came into operation on November, 11th 1889, and
this card ruled the trade until the close of the century.[109] Nevertheless, although the new Board met with considerable success a trickle
of machinery into the villages persisted. Thirty-eight machines were
taken to Sandiacre, Ilkeston, and Long Eaton in 1889, while Elsey,
one of the largest curtain manufacturers in Nottingham, began to
transfer his seventy machines to the factory of Messrs. T. Hooley
at Sandiacre.[110] (See Table XIV).

TABLE XIV: *Distribution of the Lace Trade of Nottingham and District in 1887.*

	Leavers	Curtain	Plain Net	Warp	Swiss	Total
Nottingham	878	263	400	134	80	1,755
Radford	326	83	60	11	12	492
Lenton	132	58	2	10	11	213
Basford	241	134	—	—	2	377
Hyson Green	26	12	—	2	—	40
Sherwood	—	—	70	—	—	70
Beeston	98	31	—	12	—	141
Long Eaton	512	20	—	15	—	549
Ilkeston	83	—	—	62	—	145
Derby	80	—	200	—	—	280
Daybrook	—	16	—	—	—	16
Stapleford	—	—	—	75	—	75
Breaston	—	—	—	40	—	40

Source: *Daily Express Reprint* (1905), p. 7.

The Nottingham Society received a severe shock in 1889 when, with the sanction and approval of Long Eaton employers to whom the rules had been submitted previously, the Long Eaton and District Association of Operative Lacemakers was formed. This union froze Long Eaton prices slightly below the Nottingham level.[111] Reconciled to retreat, in 1890 the Nottingham Society declared all shops in the outlying districts unconditionally open to trade, thereby giving official sanction to the discrepancy of wage rates. Factories within the Nottingham district (including Bulwell and Southwell) were opened on condition that the Board of Conciliation agreed list of prices should be obtained.[112] This retreat was the cause of much bitterness among Nottingham lace manufacturers. As a result of this concession by the union, and on the grounds that town manufacturers were thereby placed at a disadvantage, in 1896 twenty-two large firms joined the Nottingham Lace Manufacturers' Association in anticipation of a confrontation with the Society. In face of a revival in trade, however, the employers revised their plans and decided not to act.[113] Again in 1899 the Association tried to persuade the Board of Conciliation to tackle the problem of wage differentials, but the Board was in a weak position, and until the union succeeded in gaining control over the workers in outside districts the issues remained unresolved.

Although the lace makers' society failed to settle the problem of differential piece rates in the localities, and despite the lower level of rates paid outside the town and the reductions in union rates accepted in 1886 and 1889, most of the union's members enjoyed a rising standard of living throughout much of the second half of the century. In 1865, according to Felkin's estimates, about half the machine operatives earned a weekly average wage of 25s., while another one-third earned 35s.[114] An official investigation carried out in 1906 concluded that an average weekly wage for lace makers was 39s. 2d. These figures are approximations and are therefore of limited value, but they suggest an upward movement of money wages in the lace industry.[115] Furthermore, during the intervening period separating these two years, retail prices fell by about 15 per cent. between 1880 and 1900, rising slightly thereafter, while it has been calculated that between 1860 and 1900 average real wages in England and Wales rose by up to 100 per cent.[116] That lace operatives shared this increase is indicated by a comparison of the overall average industrial weekly wage, which in 1906 was 30s. 6d., with the Nottingham lace maker's average weekly income of 39s. 2d. Equally interesting is the figure quoted for the Nottinghamshire and Derbyshire districts where lace operatives were earning 44s. 8d. The higher productivity of labour operating modern machinery in the villages, it would appear, was more effective in raising wages than the efforts of the trade union in the town.[117]

The period of the so-called 'great depression' witnessed a shift in the location of manufacturing units in the midland lace industry which was to the town's disadvantage. Nevertheless, in spite of gloomy prognostications to the contrary, dressing and finishing processes and merchanting continued to be carried out in Nottingham, for transport to Long Eaton, the chief rival in the district, was good and frequent. In fact, although the movement of the machinery into outlying districts had been dramatic in periodic intensity, the volume of machinery operated in these areas was fairly small compared with that owned by Nottingham manufacturers who held on firmly to the quality trade.[118]

Although the Society's policy must bear the major responsibility for these changes, it has already been pointed out that Long Eaton, which by the end of the century was fast earning recognition as a major centre of the leavers lace making trade, had been a potential lace manufacturing district since the advent of the Midland Railway in 1839 had linked it with Nottingham.[119] With the strengthening of trade unionism after the sixties, it was an ideal situation for employers who wished to move beyond the reach of the Nottingham Society and yet still maintain close contact with the Lace Market. Moreover, Long Eaton became a haven for non-union men since it was sufficiently close for its employers to share Nottingham's labour supply. The success of Long Eaton manufacturers in their competition against employers in Nottingham can be attributed to a variety of factors. The lace factories newly-erected at Long Eaton were generally long, one-storeyed, airy, and well-lit buildings, immensely superior to the tall, narrow, Nottingham factories, and much less liable to risk of fire. Furthermore, the best modern machinery, which could not be accommodated in many of the Nottingham factories because of its weight and width, was installed here without difficulty.[120]

Despite Nottingham manufacturers' lead in skill and quality of design, at the end of the century they were compared unfavourably with the enterprising Long Eaton employers. Jardine, the leading lace machine builder was one harsh critic, who stated:

> We have been making bobbin pressing machines which work with a tenth of the labour and a quarter of the time occupied by the old method. We have put in these machines at Nottingham free of charge and at the end of three months remove them if unwanted . . . We have succeeded in placing two in Nottingham . . .[121]

Several years earlier Lowenz and Farmer had complained of the same conservatism among Nottingham manufacturers, particularly over their reluctance to adopt the Schiffle machine for embroidering lace;[122] as a result the leavers embroidered lace trade suffered.[123] Conservatism in the face of foreign competition appears to have been one of the main reasons for the difficulties of Nottingham lace manufacturers in the last quarter of the century, though competition behind rising tariffs in Europe and America made the selling of laces both at home and overseas more difficult.[124] Another aggravating element was the organization of industry whereby entry was made easy, both by the stall system and by the practice of machine builders who let out machines on hire. This led to the proliferation of an already large body of independent lace makers and increased the danger of overproduction which was the cause of frequent complaints at this time. So intense was competition that in the early years of the twentieth century restrictive organizations reappeared, as they had during the industry's infancy.[125] Until that time the lace trade remained unstable, and the town was fortunate in so far as other industries had developed since 1850 diversifying the local economic structure.

References

1 William Felkin, *History*, p. 396.

2 *Ibid.*, pp. 396–7.

3 William Felkin, *History*, pp. 398, 340–41.

4 *Report to the Home Secretary upon the Expediency of subjecting Lace Manufacture to Regulation of Factory Acts*; *with Evidence*, 1861, (2797) XXII, 461, ev. of Cox, p. 39.

5 'The Lace Trade and the Factory Act,' reprinted from the *New Quarterly Review*, (1860).

6 William Felkin, *History*, p. 552.

7 *Ibid.*, p. 509; *Report to Home Secretary upon the Expediency of subjecting Lace Manufacture to the Factory Acts 1861*, (2797) XXII, 461, p. 55.

8 William Felkin, *History*, p. 551.

9 For statistics of the British lace trade see G. R. Porter and F. W. Hirst, *op. cit.*, pp. 397–399.

10 *Ibid.*

11 G. R. Porter and F. W. Hirst, *op. cit.*, pp. 398–399.

12 *First Report of the Royal Commission on the Depression of Trade and Industry* 1886. (c. 4621) XXI, ev. of Brooksbank, President of the Nottingham Lace Manufacturer's Association, p. 239.

13 *Ibid.*

14 *Ibid.*, ev. of Carver, p. 236; ev. of Birkin, pp. 237–243.

15 G. W. Porter and F. W. Hirst, *op. cit.*, pp. 393–394.

16 *Nottingham Chamber of Commerce* Annual Reports, published: *Ex.*, January 30, 1890; December 30, 1893; December 30, 1895; December 31, 1897; December 31, 1899.

17 'The Lace Trade and the Factory Act,' reprinted from *The New Quarterly Review*, (1860).

18 *First Report of the Childrens' Employment Commission* 1863, XVIII. 1. ev. of William Felkin, pp. 235–236.

19 'The Lace Trade and Factory Act,' reprinted from the *New Quarterly Review*, (1860).

20 *First Report of the Children's Employment Commission*, 1863, XVIII. 1. ev. of William Felkin, p. 237.

21 *Ibid.*, pp. 182–86.

22 *Ibid.*, ev. of Felkin, p. 237.

23 William Felkin, *History*, p. 399.

24 *First Report of the Children's Employment Commission*, 1863, XVIII. 1, ev. of Cresswell, p. 213.

25 *Ibid.*, ev. of Clayton, p. 211.

26 *Report to Home Secretary upon the Expediency of subjecting Lace Manufacture to the Factory Acts*, 1861, (2797) XXII, 461.

27 'The Lace Trade and the Factory Act,' reprinted from the *New Quarterly Review*, (1860).

28 *Report to the Home Secretary upon the Expediency of subjecting Lace Manufacture to the Factory Acts* 1861, (2797) XXII, 461, p. 709.

29 'The Lace Trade and the Factory Act,' reprinted from the *New Quarterly Review*, (1860).

30 *Report to Home Secretary upon the Expediency of subjecting Lace Manufacture to the Factory Acts*, 1861, (2797) XXII, 461, pp. 17–18.

31 *Ibid.*, pp. 27, 60.

32 *First Report of the Children's Employment Commission*, 1863, XVIII, 1., p. 196.

[33] *Ibid.,* p. 210.

[34] *Ibid.,* p. 212.

[35] *Ibid.,* pp. 189, 192, 197, 215.

[36] *Minutes of Nottingham Chamber of Commerce,* January 9, 1871; In the beginning there was some difficulty over the problem of definition of outwork and homework which was not classified until the Consolidation Act of 1878. Forster's Education Act of 1870 helped to reduce the child labour supply.

[37] *Fifth Report of the Children's Employment Commission,* 1866, XXIV, 1.

[38] *Fourth Report of the Select Commitee on the Export of Machinery,* 1824. (51) V, 281.

[39] *Supra,* p. 94.

[40] William Felkin, *History,* p. 340.

[41] *Ibid.,* p. 343.

[42] *N.R.,* September 15, 1830; *N.R.,* September 28, 1830.

[43] S. and B. Webb, *The History of Trades Unionism,* (1912), pp. 122–23.

[44] *N.R.,* October 25, 1833.

[45] *N.R.,* August 14, 1840; *N.R.,* August 21, 1840.

[46] *N.R.,* March 27, 1846; William Felkin, *History,* p. 378.

[47] *N.R.,* May 2, 1851. On its 1st anniversary the Lace Makers' Union had 1,600 members.

[48] *N.R.,* February 1, 1850; N.R., April 5, 1850.

[49] In his *History of the Lace Makers' Society,* (Nottingham, 1960), Dr. Cuthbert maintains that from the beginning there were three separate and autonomous unions which served artisans in the plain net, leavers, and curtain sections of the trade; unfortunately, the documents upon which this conclusion is based have disappeared. My own conclusions are based on the accounts of the quarterly public meetings which were reported in the *Nottingham Review* between 1850 and 1869, and on the first *United Kingdom Directory of All Trade Unions* published in 1861. The view that until the reforms of 1874 there was only one union (except for the leavers splinter society formed in 1867, *infra,* p. 296) has been corroborated by Mr. D. E. Varley, whose research into the history of the Midland Counties Manufacturers' Association led him independently to this conclusion.

[50] *N.R.,* August 23, 1850.

[51] *N.R.,* June 20, 1856; For a complete list in 1861 see *U.K. First Annual Trades Directory,* 1861, pp. 74–75.

[52] *Lace Makers' Union Branch Contributions Minute Book* 1853–59; *N.R.,* December 17, 1858.

[53] *N.R.,* February 14, 1855.

[54] *N.R.,* July 4, 1855; *Lace Makers' Union Branch Contributions Minute Book,* 1853–59.

[55] *N.R.,* May 12, 1854.

[56] *Lace Makers' Union Branch Contributions Minute Book,* 1853–59.

[57] *N.R.,* March 5, 1858; *N.R.,* December 17, 1858.

[58] *N.R.,* August 10, 1860.

[59] *N.R.,* September 14, 1860.

[60] *N.R.,* September 14, 1860; *N.R.,* November 2, 1860.

[61] *N.R.,* November 2, 1860; *N.R.,* March 15, 1861.

[62] *N.R.,* March 24, 1865; *Minutes of the Nottingham Chamber of Commerce,* January 14, 1867.

[63] William Felkin, *History,* pp. 397–98.

[64] *Minutes of the Nottingham Chamber of Commerce,* January 14, 1867.

[65] *Webb Collection,* Section B, ev. of Leatherland (secretary of the Lace Operatives' Society 1870–75), pp. 332–33.

[66] *N.R.,* April 2, 1859.

[67] *Ex.,* March 6, 1871.

[68] *Webb Collection,* Section B, p. 388; *Minutes of the Lace Board of Arbitration.*

[69] *Webb Collection,* Section B, Rules of the Lace Manufacturers' Association.

[70] *Webb Collection,* Section B, p. 388.

[71] *N.R.,* April 2, 1869.

[72] *N.R.,* March 18, 1870; *Ex.,* March 6, 1871; *Ex.,* March 13, 1871.

[73] *Ex.,* December 31, 1870; *Ex.,* March 6, 1871.

[74] Day work consisted of changing patterns and making adjustments to the machine during which time no racks of lace were made.

[75] *N.J.,* September 19, 1873; *N.J.,* October 31, 1873; *Ex.,* November 22, 1873; *Ex.,* December 12, 1873.

[76] *N.J.,* December 15, 1873; *N.J.,* December 19, 1873.

[77] *Webb Collection,* Section A, p. 388.

[78] *Ex.,* January 10, 1874.

[79] S. and B. Webb, *The History of Trades Unionism,* p. 435.

[80] *A.S.L.O. Council Minutes,* August 11, 1874; *A.S.L.O. Contributions Book,* 1874–1914; *A.S.L.O. Sick Book.*

[81] *Webb Collection,* Section A, p. 338.

[82] *Ibid.*

[83] N. Cuthbert, *op. cit.,* p. 53.

[84] *N.J.,* October 9, 1875; *N.J.,* September 18, 1875: *Ex.,* August 28, 1875; *N.J.,* April 1, 1876.

[85] *N.J.,* April 8, 1875.

[86] *Accounts and Papers, 1889,* LVI, p. 329.

[87] *Ex.,* November 18, 1877, April 21, 1877; June 30, 1877.

[88] *Ex.,* June 12, 1877; *Ex.,* July 31, 1877; *Webb Collection* Section A, p. 389.

[89] *A.S.L.O. Council Minutes* August 11, 1879; January 17, 1880; January 6, 1880 (Rules).

[90] *Board of Conciliation Minutes* April 26, 1880.

[91] *Ibid.,* December 19, 1883.

[92] *Ex.,* October 16, 1886.

[93] *Board of Conciliation Minutes,* December 19, 1883.

[94] *A.S.L.O. Council Minutes,* June 25, 1881.

[95] *Ibid.,* February 17, 1876.

[96] *Ibid.,* March 23, 1878; September 14, 1878.

[97] *Ibid.,* January 20, 1880; September 22, 1883; September 18, 1883; March 8, 1884.

[98] *Ibid.,* August 25, 1883; June 29, 1883; August 4, 1883; September 26, 1885.

[99] *Ibid.,* April 3, 1886; April 24, 1886; April 3, 1886; November 2, 1886; November 27, 1886.

[100] *Accounts and Papers,* 1886, LVI, p. 329.

[101] *Ibid.,* October 16, 1883; December 29, 1885; October 18, 1884; October 16, 1883; November 24, 1883.

[102] *Ibid.,* October 18, 1884; December 20, 1884; September 26, 1886.

[103] *Ibid.,* quarterly meetings January 3, 1885; September 15, 1886.

[104] *Ibid.*, January 29, 1887; May 14, 1887; July 14, 1888; November 27, 1888, April 20, 1889.

[105] *Ibid.*, November 22, 1887; December 12, 1887; May 14, 1887.

[106] *Ibid.*, May 14, 1889; June 1, 1889; June 4, 1889; June 7, 1889.

[107] *Ibid.*, July 9, 1889; *Ex.*, July 29, 1889.

[108] *Ex.*, July 25, 1889; *Ex.*, July 27, 1889; *Ex.*, August 3, 1889; *Ex.*, August 6, 1889; *Ex.*, August 17, 1889; *Ex.*, August 20, 1889; *Ex.*, September 10, 1889.

[109] 'The Lace Trade in Nottingham and District,' (1905), *Express reprint*, p. 5.

[110] *Webb Collection*, Section A, p. 337; 'The Lace Trade in Nottingham and District,' (1905), *Express reprint*.

[111] *Ex.*, July 9, 1889.

[112] *A.S.L.O. Council Minutes* September 6, 1889; *Ex.*, July 9, 1889; 'The Lace Trade in Nottingham and District,' (1905), *Express reprint*, p. 4.

[113] *Ibid.*, p. 13.

[114] William Felkin, 'The Lace and Hosiery Trades of Nottingham'. Notices and Abstracts of *B.A.A.S.* 1866–7, p. 129.

[115] *Report of an Enquiry into Earnings and Hours*, 1906 (c. 1545), p. xvii.

[116] W. Ashworth, *An Economic History of England*, (1960), pp. 200–201.

[117] *Infra*, p. 306.

[118] 'The Lace Trade in Nottingham and District,' (1905), *Express reprint*, p. 7; *Ex.*, October 2, 1886.

[119] D. E. Varley, *op. cit.*, pp. 11–12.

[120] 'The Lace Trade in Nottingham and District,' (1905), *Express reprint*, p. 9.

[121] *Ibid.*, quoting Jardine, pp. 52–56.

[122] *First Report of the Royal Commission* (*Depression of Trade and Industry*) 1886 (c. 4621) XXI, ev. of Lowenz.

[123] *Ibid.*, ev. of Fox, p. 234.

[124] *Ibid.*, pp. 236–44; *The Hosiery and Lace Trades Review*, November 20, 1890.

[125] See D. E. Varley, *op. cit.*, Chapter V.

CHAPTER XII

VICTORIANS AND ECONOMIC SOCIETY

IN the early years of the nineteenth century the tradition of paternalism weakened as the ideas of individualism, with their emphasis upon self-reliance and the harmony of self and public interest, gained acceptance. Although the ideas of individualism were not considered to be inconsistent with state action in promoting the greatest happiness of the greatest number, not until the third quarter of the century did the general presumption against state intervention begin to diminish. Henceforward, greater stress was placed upon the collectivist elements contained in Benthamite thought, while the state came to play an increasingly important role as an instrument for the achievement of minimum standards of justice, education, and health for all.[1] Benthamite Utilitarianism was one major force to which the growth of collectivism was indebted; the other great force in the spiritual and intellectual life of this period was that of Evangelical Christianity. Together these powerful influences affected the shifting balance of emphasis upon the responsibilities of the state and of other bodies, while in Nottingham, as in other towns, Evangelicalism emerged as a major common denominator among those who, through voluntary effort, sought to cope with some of the social problems presented by the new industrial society.

Ignorance and poverty were not, by any means, features new to English urban society in the nineteenth century, but the greater concentration of people in towns tended to worsen the evils and in Nottingham, where the livelihood of the majority of the population had depended upon the state of two industries, both of which were sensitive to fluctuations in overseas trade and the vagaries of of fashion, the scale of the slumps in the early decades of the century had been unprecedented in the town's history.[2] Except for traditional forms of relief through the several charitable endowments such as the Lambley, Plumptre, Collins', and Willoughby's Hospitals, which catered mainly for a small number of widows, widowers, and out-pensioners; and by the numerous bequests distributed in the form of bread, coal, or cash to the poor,[3] the response of the townspeople at first took the form of *ad hoc* arrangements.[4] Due to their frequent necessity, however, the public relief subscriptions soon became an all too regular feature of the local scene. Where the local response was on more than a merely *ad hoc* basis voluntary effort was forthcoming, for the most part, from a small number of middle class professional and business-men who, especially from the thirties, when local social conditions deteriorated, devoted considerable energy to the needs of the working classes and to the improvement of public health. This was the period of which William Booth (later to become General Booth, founder of the Salvation Army), son of a speculative builder who lived in Sneinton, later wrote,

> the degradation and helpless misery of the poor stockingers of my native town wandering gaunt and hunger stricken through the streets, droning out their melancholy ditties, crowding the Union or toiling like galley slaves on relief works for a bare subsistence kindled in my heart yearnings to help the poor which have continued to this day and which have had a powerful influence on my whole life.[5]

With good reason Booth's first mission was to the ragged children of Nottingham.

Earlier modest contributions to public welfare had been made by a handful of professional men, most of whom we have previously encountered. In 1800, with the hope of reducing the danger of smallpox, Dr. John Attenburrow, a surgeon at Nottingham General Hospital, inaugurated a free vaccination service for the poor. His example was followed by other doctors, and in 1805 in order to extend the service a public subscription was opened for the purpose of hiring a surgeon; from 1813 St. Mary's Workhouse made use of this service.[6] Beginning in 1829, twice weekly at the dispensary John Calthrop Williams offered the local working classes free treatment for eye complaints, and in the forties he was a member of the committee which undertook a private investigation into the town's sanitary condition.[7] The state of Nottingham's public health at that time was bad enough, but undoubtedly it would have been much worse without the previous improvements, described earlier, carried out by Thomas Hawkesley, who introduced to Nottingham what has been described as 'one of the greatest civic innovations of the age'[8]: filtered water, supplied under pressure, for the use of the working population. As we have also noted, Hawksley had been a persistent advocate of the enclosure of Nottingham's common land.

Until the middle decades of the century the Corporation, as a body, eschewed radical reform, remaining deaf to ideas for municipal progress. But among its ranks, and outside it, a number of Radicals and Independents revealed their support for progressive ideas on political and social matters. In an especially strategic posi-

F. C. Tighe, Nottingham Public Library

SLUM DWELLINGS IN LEWIS SQUARE, SUSSEX STREET

F. C. Tighe, Nottingham Public Library

NOTTINGHAM MARKET PLACE, C.1900

tion for exerting influence in the cause of popular interests were the Suttons, an Evangelical family with, as we have seen, Radical political views, who, after Charles Sutton had worked as a printer on his own account for fifteen years, in 1808 established the *Nottingham Review*.[9] In an age when the communication of news, information, and ideas was effected either orally or by print, the newspapers—especially through their editorials—were potentially powerful instruments for moulding public opinion. The policies advocated in the columns of the *Nottingham Review* were similar to those canvassed in other middle class provincial newspapers, especially, for example, in the columns of the *Sheffield Independent*,[10] but although the newspaper drew its main support from middle class dissenting Radicals, there was a conscious attempt to appeal to the poorer sections of the community. The *Review* editorials reflected the Suttons' views on national and local issues but their public activities were largely confined to chapel administration, Sunday school teaching, and lay preaching.[11]

By contrast, Thomas Wakefield, who came from a wealthy Unitarian family and who was the town's leading Radical during the early years of the century, not only spoke frequently in the Radical cause but belonged to many charitable and educational societies, and was described by the Town Clerk in 1833 as 'the kind friend of the distressed on all occasions'.[12] He was founder member of the Nottingham Literary and Scientific Society and a moving spirit in the promotion of the Nottingham Artisan's Library, the Lancasterian School, and the Mechanics Institute.[13] It was also through charitable works and the promotion of educational associations that Samuel Fox, the Quaker grocer, sought to benefit the local population.[14] Fox was a member of the first local Benevolent Society which had been founded by Bott, another Quaker, in 1776.[15] Its aim was the provision of relief for those which the poor laws neglected, and its methods included the distribution of necessities and the granting of medical aid, both of which were administered at the discretion of appointed visitors. The Benevolent Society served as a model for others which proliferated in the first three decades of the century at churches, chapels, and public houses.

Co-founder of the celebrated Nottingham Adult School in 1798 and of the Boys and Girls Lancasterian Schools, Fox was also among the promoters of the Nottingham Mechanics Institute formed in 1837, and which stood for the diffusion of knowledge among all classes.[16] Besides Samuel Fox, honorary officials included a number of businessmen: William Vickers, lace merchant and the Institute's first president, John Wright, High Churchman and banker whose gift of land made the venture possible, Thomas Wakefield, the

w

Unitarian merchant, and hosiers John Rogers and Richard Morley, Evangelical dissenters. In addition to the Reverends Carpenter and Gilbert and surgeon Dr. J. C. Williams, hosiers and lace manufacturers John Heard, Thomas Herbert, Sneath, Bottom and Myers were also among the life members pledged to support the Institute. Richard Enfield was another leading Evangelical member of the Mechanics Committee, as well as being a committee member of other philanthropic bodies—the General Hospital, the Eye Infirmary, the Midland Institute for the Blind—while playing an important role in the town's educational movement.[17]

The Mechanics Society aimed at widening the horizons of its members who, it was hoped, would be mainly artisans. From the beginning all political controversy was explicitly avoided and the curriculum during the first years included free lectures on physiology, astronomy, music, poetry, silk manufacture, railways, printing, botany, and science; classes in the latter being conducted by Thomas Hawksley.[18] In 1838 the Mechanics Committee introduced classes in English, French, mathematics, and art. Fulfilling the role of an adult school, which despite the founders' intention appealed to a largely middle class audience, the Institute became a centre of culture. In 1845 Milton Street was the site for new premises which consisted of lecture hall, library, reading room, classroom, and museum. Despite these attractions the Institute for many years lacked support and funds, though Wright, Herbert, Fox, and Richard Enfield were liberal donors.[19] Nevertheless, it survived the century and remains today an active monument to the generosity and concern of a handful of philanthropic townsmen.

In 1846 George Gill, a Unitarian who frequently attended the Friends' Meeting House, donated £1,000 to open a subscription for the founding of the Nottingham People's College; based on the model of the Sheffield institution formed in 1842, the Nottingham College offered day schooling for boys and girls and evening classes for adults.[20] Its aims were to provide education at low cost to the working classes, to enable them to grasp opportunities, and to raise their economic, social, and political status. This was also the purpose of the People's Hall in Beck Lane, which likewise was the result of Gill's initiative and generosity. It was intended that the Hall should become a social centre for the working classes, where money clubs, sick and friendly societies, and similar bodies could hold their meetings. The Hall incorporated a library, reading room, lecture hall, and refreshment rooms, and Gill and the founders expressed the hope that 'intellectual pursuits and mental improvements' might be substituted for the 'attractions of the Tavern.'[21] When Hugo Reid, master of The People's College, retired in 1851 he put forward a proposal for establishing a University College in Nottingham, a project which was supported by two Evangelicals, Richard Enfield and Lewis Heymann, the lace manufacturer, both of whom were instrumental in bringing the project to fruition some twenty years later.[22]

While voluntary efforts were made to foster adult education, the number of libraries in the town also increased. The Subscription Library at Bromley House dated from 1816 and catered for a predominantly middle class readership, but in 1824 the Artizans' Library was established on Smithy Row, with Thomas Wakefield as president.[23] During the thirties and forties several libraries for working men and women were opened at public houses. In 1835 and 1836 one was formed at the Rancliffe Arms, another at the King George on Horseback, and a third at the Pheasant. Each possessed more than a thousand volumes, and the entrance fee of 2s. 6d. was supplemented by weekly subscriptions of a penny. Between 1841 and 1844 three more were formed at the Queen Adelaide in Sneinton, the Cricket Players in Hyson Green, and the White Swan at Radford. The Englishman's Library was opened at the *Nottingham Journal's* offices in 1841, and the Protestant Association Library in St. Paul's vestry opened in 1844. Several dissenting chapels provided libraries for their congregations and many local booksellers ran small libraries.[24]

The increase in the number of libraries, inspired not only by philanthropic effort but also by the profit motive, suggests that the population of Nottingham was becoming more literate. To some extent this was true, but the proliferation of libraries and the provision of institutes, like the Mechanics Institute and the People's College, could make only a marginal contribution towards the crusade for enlightenment. In the context of widespread apathy on the subject of education, however, the achievements of the Evangelicals in Nottingham deserve recognition.[25] In 1833, by which date aproximately one-half of the population worshipped regularly, no fewer than ten of the existing thirty-three places of worship had been built since 1800, and eight of these were nonconformist: four Independent, two Methodist, and two Baptist.[26] According to the national census of religious worship taken in 1851, although the index of attendance for all towns of more than 10,000 population was 49·7, that of Nottingham was 57·7, and among larger industrial towns or those of comparable size Nottingham ranked second only to Leicester.[27] A drive to improve education grew out of the Evangelicals' search for edification, though the underlying aim of the Nottingham school movement, in common with that of the movement elsewhere, was to 'improve' the behaviour of the working classes, helping thereby to reduce crime and general restlessness among that section of the population.

At the turn of the century so vigorous had been the movement since the establishment of the first general town Sunday school in 1786 that, assuming one-quarter of the town's population (of 1801) was between the ages of five and fifteen, 26 per cent. of that age group were attending a Sunday school: i.e. nine hundred the Methodist, four hundred the Established Church, two hundred and seventy-five the General Baptist, one hundred and fifty the Independent, and one hundred and thirty-eight the Particular Baptist Sunday school.[28] The Sunday school movement received further impetus when, in 1810, the Sunday School Union was formed, its primary aim being to open Sunday schools in areas hitherto neglected, especially in those districts having large numbers of poor children. The founders of the Union sought to ameliorate the conditions of the poor:

> to dispel ignorance, instruct the offspring of the poor in the first principles of religion, to habituate them to the observance of the Lord's Day, to attend the means of grace, to be dutiful to parents and superiors and to do to all men as they would that they should do to them.[29]

By 1833 more than 60 per cent. of the town's children between the ages of five and fifteen were enrolled at one of the town's twenty-seven Sunday schools.[30] In 1865 slightly more than eighteen thousand pupils attended Church Sunday schools, and over twenty-three thousand went to non-conformist schools.[31]

Education of a more general material application was given to equip the children for reading and writing from the Bible, and, though religious education was the prime object of these schools, arithmetic and sewing were also taught. After the decision of the Methodist New Connexion and the Castle Gate Sunday school governors that arithmetic should not be taught on Sundays, during the second decade weekday evening classes were offered. Even so, while it became possible for a Sunday school scholar to spend fifteen hours in class in a week, it was exceptional if pupils devoted half that time to education.[32] The Evangelical mission not only established Sunday schools all over the town and in the new suburbs, but was also responsible for bringing about an expansion of day school places. Of the total number of children attending public day schools in Nottingham in 1834 (about 22 per cent. of the age group between five and fifteen years), approximately 96 per cent. were taught in schools established since 1810,[33] a situation which reveals the extent to which the Evangelicals had succeeded in influencing the Corporation which, prior to 1800, had been dominated by a group of wealthy and influential Presbyterians.

The appearance of this new religious force in municipal politics had been followed by immediate action and, with the cooperation of the older nonconformist section, in 1810, the town's first Lancasterian school was opened. In 1815 the Corporation body presented the site for a new school building, although when the Girls' Lancasterian School was opened five years later no school building was provided and instruction took place in a room in Houndsgate.[34] The establishment of the Lancasterian schools marked an important step forward in the education movement, but little could be expected of institutions which children attended for an average of only twelve months. In a society where the earnings of a whole family were very often necessary for subsistence, and where child labour was important for lace and hosiery production, lengthy schooling received little encouragement from parents. The products of these schools at this time were, for the most part, barely literate when they commenced work, and a similar condition was to be found at the National School which had been opened by members of the Established Church in 1811. This was the first local response to the nonconformist challenge in this sphere, and pointed the way for continued inter-denominational rivalry during the succeeding decades which produced a commendable increase in school building and an increase in the number of places.[35] Private academies also contributed to the expansion of the town's educational facilities. In 1834 the progressive Standard Hill Academy and seventy other private institutions catering predominantly for children of the middle classes supplemented the denominational day schools; thirty of the academies had been opened since 1815. In the third decade of the century it has been estimated that approximately 80 per cent. of children belonging to the age group three to thirteen were associated with educational establishments of some kind, a situation comparable with that in Manchester and Birmingham, but a considerably higher proportion than that at Sheffield.[36]

In 1868 a group of leading figures from church and chapel, including A. J. Mundella, W. B. Rothera, Richard Enfield, J. B. Paton, and W. B. Windley, met to form a local branch of the Birmingham Education League which aimed to promote free and compulsory non-sectarian education for children up to the age of fourteen. It aimed to support the establishment of School Boards where necessary, to provide and maintain schools by local rates, and to have them supplemented by government grants.[37] When the Nottingham School Board was formed in 1870, research by its statistical committee confirmed the view that the major problem in local education was not a shortage of places but the apathy which families showed towards existing institutions.[38] There was a deficiency of barely eleven hundred places, and although twelve thousand school places were available, less than two-thirds of them were filled; only the Free Grammar and the High Pavement Schools had waiting lists. These statistics provided the basis for the conclusion that day schools, Sunday schools, and the private academies had together succeeded in keeping pace with the growing demand for education in the middle and, to a smaller extent, the working classes. However, schools in the Leen side and Broad Marsh districts were still few, and this has been interpreted as evidence of declining vigour in local Evangelicalism, the strength of which had earlier inspired the crusade for the education of the working classes. A recent argument points out that although the rising social status of its members enabled Evangelicals to wield greater influence in the corporate leadership of the town, it was accompanied by diminishing sensitivity to the needs of the working classes. In effect, while Evangelicalism had become respectable, respectability had stifled initiative, sapping much of the spontaneous energy so characteristic of the early converts.[39] Nevertheless, the shortcomings of the Evangelicals should not be allowed to obscure their successes, for in early and mid-Victorian Nottingham the conscience, spirit, determination, and energy of such people acted as a leaven in the comunity.

The successful establishment of the Cooperative Movement in the district was also due to the efforts of Nonconformists. Benjamin Walker, lace manufacturer, and Thomas Bayley, leather manufacturer, were responsible for the formation of a local movement twenty-three years after a group of working men had failed to establish their own society.[40] The opening of a grocery store in Lenton on cooperative lines followed the Industrial and Provident Societies Act of 1863, which had conferred legal status upon Cooperative Societies. During the next few years grocery stores, a boot and shoe store, a bakery, and flour mill were opened, and by 1873 the local movement had gained such recognition that the original Lenton Cooperative Society became the Lenton and Nottingham Cooperative Society, with Nottingham as its official centre.[41] Here a building costing over £9,000 which housed grocery, boot and shoe, tailoring, bakery, and butchering departments also contained a hall to seat six hundred.[42] There was also some experiment among local lace makers and mechanics with cooperative production, but without conspicuous success.[43]

Having drawn together various elements of philanthropic activity until the middle decades of the century,[44] it is time to direct attention to the changing attitudes towards the relationship between the individual, the state, and social welfare, attitudes which inevitably affected the nature and scope of voluntary effort. The decline in the paternalistic tradition of action by the early years of the century was succeeded by a different type of philanthropy which, while deriving much of its strength from religious zeal, had its roots in *laissez-faire*. After the middle decades less emphasis came to be placed on the responsibility of the individual in the struggle for improvement, and collective action for welfare assumed greater prominence in discussions of social policy.[45]

These changes in thought can be seen in the attitudes and activities of three local men of distinction, each of whom left his imprint on life and labour in Nottingham in the nineteenth century: John Gravener Henson (1785–1852), William Felkin (1795–1874), and Anthony John Mundella (1825–1897). In some respects the differences in outlook of these three men symbolize the general development of thought concerning life and labour during this period. Felkin and Mundella shared similar religious and educational backgrounds and their humble beginnings were followed by successful business careers which propelled both into the comfortable orbit of the solid middle classes; Gravener Henson, however, remained essentially an artisan, and for this reason leaves less scope for direct comparison with Felkin and Mundella. But Henson's activities, while indicating the existence of a gulf in the early years of the century between the urban proletariat and the employers, also show his struggle to come to terms with a changing society. Both Felkin and Mundella too were disturbed by the lack of social harmony in contemporary society; and while Felkin directed some of his energy towards improving the abilities of the individual to cope with the demands which the new industrial society was making, Mundella sought to redress the balance of social forces with the aid of state intervention.

At the turn of the century a state of war and the related industrial fluctuations, food shortages, famine prices, and apprehension of revolutionary movements created conditions which were not conducive to a growing understanding between an expanding urban proletariat and the manufacturers, on whom an increasing number of the working classes depended for their livelihood. The riotous decade prior to 1800 and the sixteen years which followed were periods of acute social tension.[46] Although a handful of professional men employed talent and time in the service of the poorer section of the community during these early years, and while assistance from the relief committees and the early benevolent societies helped to mitigate their condition, restrictive government regulation impeded the efforts of the working classes to grapple with the problems that arose in an urban industrial society.

Within this context Gravener Henson, who was said to have been acquainted with every trade combination in the three midland counties between 1800 and 1840,[47] earned a reputation as the outstanding leader among the local working classes. A historian of working class movements has recently stated that he, with John Gast and John Doherty, was one of the three truly impressive leaders to emerge during this period.[48] A literate and thoughtful man, he was first an apprentice stocking maker and subsequently became a maker of point net. Such was his success that at one time he employed eleven journeymen, but with the decline of the point net trade during the second decade of the century Henson became a bobbin net maker. In the forties, one trade directory listed him as an author, while in the directory which was published shortly after his death he was described as an accountant, but he died in humble circumstances at the age of sixty-seven.[49]

Henson first became involved in the labour movement at the request of his fellow workmen in 1808.[50] Henceforward his knowledge of industrial and trade union law together with his self-assurance, wit, and energy were brought to bear upon problems affecting workmen in the hosiery and lace trades. Henson's letters to his colleagues show a forceful character and remarks contained in them, as well as comments made elsewhere, reveal an attitude towards the framework knitters which consisted of sympathy as well as impatience.

'Damn the trade,' he wrote in 1812, 'they seem determined on their own destruction; they are the most backward dilatory, *unwilling to do good race of Men on Earth.*'[51]

In 1848, after Henson had retired from the leadership in trade union affairs, he observed that had the framework knitters shown devotion and energy in the formation of combinations in the early years of the century much of their suffering could have been avoided.[52] However, Henson recognized that ignorance explained much of their behaviour. This was the reason, according to Henson, why 'a few artful men (were) able to mislead them at times.'[53]

He might well have been thinking of the way in which his own lawful agitation for the redress of the framework knitters' grievances had given way to violence, intimidation, and the destruction of private property. Henson, who appears to have disapproved of the Luddite tactics, said that the members of the branch responsible for the machine wrecking did not belong to a formal combination, as did the silk framework knitters, and that they took that course of action because they conceived that policy to be the only means of bringing pressure to bear upon the hosiers' combinations.[54] From the beginning, Henson endeavoured to restrain the frame breakers while championing their cause through constitutional processes, urging the stockingers to form clubs and trade associations.[55] Shortly after the hosiers' resolution to reduce wages had appeared in the newspapers a suspicious notice was inserted in the *Nottingham Review* which referred to the ownership of frames. Henson, fearing that the Luddites were about to recommence their violent methods, tried to bring legal action against the hosiers under the Combination Act, but his attempt failed owing to the refusal of the magistrates to cooperate.[56] Early in 1816 he succeeded in organizing the prosecution of two 'respectable' employers under the Truck Acts, and Henson attributed his own arrest later that year to the animosity which he thereby incurred.[57] The actual reason for his detention was that one of the convicted Luddites had implicated Henson (although no specific evidence was produced). Nevertheless, Nottingham magistrates informed Lord Sidmouth of this, and the suspension of *habeas corpus* at the time enabled the police to arrest Henson on his arrival in London where he was to present a petition for mercy on behalf of the condemned Luddites.[58] Immediately on his return to Nottingham after his stay in prison between April, 1816, and November, 1817, he helped to organize a strike of framework knitters in the three midland counties, and in 1821 he was instrumental in securing the annulment of the conviction of members of the Framework Knitters' Committee under the Combination Act.[59] He then determined to secure the repeal of this Act.

In 1823 he was joint author of a pamphlet on the laws which affected industrial relations, in which the case was argued for the replacement of existing legislation by an entirely new set of laws which would place workmen's combinations on an equal footing before the law with employers' associations.[60] It was urged that greater importance should be attached to written contracts which should include a clear statement of terms of employment, and that these contracts should be legally binding on both sides. Besides the abolition of truck and the limitation of overtime, the other main proposal was for the establishment of arbitration machinery in which it would be the responsibility of the magistrates to enforce the decision by the imposition of stiff penalties.[61]

The contents of this pamphlet formed the basis of a Bill drawn up by Henson and introduced to Parliament in 1824 by Peter Moore, the Radical M.P. for Coventry.[62] Commenting on the Bill and its two architects, Henson and White, Francis Place wrote that it was

> 'a beautiful scheme of legislation, as complicated and absurd as two such ill-constructed men could well contrive. They meant well but did not understand the means necessary to do

well', but he conceded they were both 'active and indefatigable'.[63]

How and why Place succeeded in manoeuvring to prevent the enactment of the Bill while securing the repeal of the Combination Acts himself is well known.[64] Their motives for securing the repeal differed, for whereas Place was intent on legalizing trade unions he was also opposed to further interference in the relations between employers and their workpeople. Henson, by contrast, saw the repeal as a beginning, and had hoped to secure legislation to erect an elaborate structure which would regulate industrial relations. The difference between the views of Place and Henson reflected the wider debate which was taking place at this time between the advocates of *laissez-faire* principles, as propounded by the political economists, and the supporters of the conventional wisdom which opposed the reduction in state control and regulation in economic affairs.[65] Indeed, many of Henson's views were close to those which Adam Smith had attacked in *The Wealth of Nations*. In 1812 he had been one of the principal members of the Framework Knitters' Committee which petitioned for legislation to regulate the quality of production,[66] while an earlier attempt to revive the powers of the Framework Knitters' Company had also received Henson's approval.[67] However erroneous was his interpretation of the effects of the trade companies, this provided the basis for his attack on a *laissez-faire* economic society which destroyed 'certainty and stability . . . moderate wages and regular employment', the principal advantages which, according to Henson, the operative had received under the trade companies.[68] The system of apprenticeship, he said, tended to reduce crime owing to the careful tutelage of youths during the 'thoughtless period' between the ages of fourteen and twenty-one, while the journeyman was accorded 'a degree of consequence' as a skilled craftsman.[69] He maintained that without such regulations on the conduct of trade and where, as a result, the motive of self interest was afforded every encouragement, a vicious and unstable society would develop founded on a fundamentally anti-social ethic. An industrial system based on *laissez-faire,* he wrote,

> placed every man's hand against his fellow . . . Make them selfish—destroy every restriction, set them one upon the other and then see the result . . .[70]

After the repeal of the Combination laws and the rejection of Henson's Bill, he turned away from his function as strike organizer for the framework knitters, though he continued to act as mediator between framework knitters and hosiers when disputes arose.[71] Regularly for several years he discussed trade matters with the manufacturers, and it is likely that the achievement of uniformity of wage rates was often the main subject for consideration. Henson was convinced that one of the major reasons for wage differences in the trade was a widespread ignorance of rates paid in the villages surrounding Nottingham.[72] The circulation of information as to wages paid in the locality (and indeed in foreign countries), and the prices of articles on foreign markets would, he thought, destroy much of the suspicion which exacerbated relations between hosiers and workmen. More knowledge, he maintained, would be accompanied by a greater appreciation of the true character of the competitive situation, and negotiation could then take place with factual information as a frame of reference.

'I consider', he said, 'that if the masters and men can be brought together there will be very little combination, it is only when they have kept asunder that they have disagreed.'[73]

Thus, by middle age Henson appears to have eschewed forceful industrial action, while he criticized the general trades unions which sprang up in the thirties for the victimization which they had encouraged, and which he took action to check.[74]

As a bobbin net maker it is not surprising that after 1820 Henson should spend less time among the framework knitters than among the bobbin net journeymen. Moreover, many years of largely fruitless industrial action had failed to check the decline of rates and earnings in the hosiery trade, and the futility of trying to use the workers' own power to improve their condition had become evident. In the machine made lace industry wages rose without powerful trade union pressure, and while there was a decline in the level of earnings for some fifteen years after the boom of 1825, the condition of lace makers was generally superior to that of framework knitters.[75] The principal factor accounting for this difference was the stream of technical invention which revolutionized the manufacture of lace and which led to trade expansion and a growing demand for labour.

However, Henson was dissatisfied with the law as it affected invention on two counts; one was unfair treatment of the inventor, while the other was the inhibiting effect which, he claimed, the law had upon technical progress.[76] In 1825 he tried, unsuccessfully, to enlist the support of Francis Place in pressing for the reform of the Patent Laws. In a lengthy letter he outlined the history of patent legislation from the Tudors, followed by a detailed analysis of the procedure for obtaining patent rights and its effects.[77] Referring to Heathcoat's monopoly of the bobbin net machine, which had combined the ideas of four other mechanics, Henson argued that the effect of the law was to deter 'the man of real genius or the real inventor', pointing out that by the purchase of patent rights a rich man could obtain the benefits of others' skills. He criticized the administration of the law which was under the control of the Attorney General and the Lord Chancellor acting on the Crown's behalf. These men, who knew little of invention and technical matters, possessed sole powers of conferring patent rights, and he cited an example of their incompetence in issuing two separate patents for the same machine. He urged that a more public procedure for patent grants be introduced as a safeguard against the abuse of the law which penalized the inventor of humble means.[78] Henson was still concerned with this problem in 1837 when he stressed the importance of a free circulation of technical information for the mutual benefit of all people in the trade.[79]

As Chairman of the Nottingham Society of Inventors and as the author of a series of weekly articles on trade and technology published in the *Nottingham Journal* between 1834 and 1850, Henson hoped to improve the performance of the Nottingham trades.[80] Two major themes which he pursued throughout these years was the need for experiment and investment in new methods of making lace and hosiery, and the importance of producing new articles which would find favour with the public. He urged the gentry and nobility to encourage fashions which would benefit the Nottingham trades and declared that,

> every operative ought to make up his mind resolutely to endeavour to oblige his master to the utmost of ability and energy in making any new articles.[81]

He urged experiments to produce fabric on bobbin net machines which, hitherto, had been made exclusively on looms. If Nottingham men succeeded in this, he argued, the faster rate of production of their machines would enable them to supersede the weavers.[82]

While the encouragement of technical experiment and improvement in design were two of Henson's ideas to counter competition from producers on the Continent, Henson sought for many years to attack the problem of foreign competition at its source. In 1814 and again in 1834 Henson belonged to local committees which were set up to prevent the illegal export of lace machinery, and in 1835 Henson defended his own case when proceedings were taken against him for the illegal seizure of a machine which its owner had planned to ship overseas.[83] When a Select Committee inquired into the question of the export of machinery in 1824, Henson gave evidence in favour of the retention of the laws which made removal illegal, and urged their more effective administration. He pointed out that machinery was smuggled out of the country and that in 1823 between fifty and sixty bobbin net machines were discovered in Calais alone, most of which were operated and maintained by English workmen with whom he had been acquainted during their earlier life spent in Nottingham.[84]

> 'Never did nation or people', he wrote, 'commit so great a political error . . . as when the Bill was passed which allowed foreigners to seduce English artisans to emigrate.'[85]

He attacked the 'poverty mongers of the political economical school' and their free trade policies which, he forecast, would reduce the English workman to a level of life in which his diet would consist of 'black bread and soup *maigre,* instead of roast beef, plum pudding, and good ale'.[86] In 1837 he noted that Calais was rising on the ruins of Nottingham.[87] Free trade, he argued, especially that in machinery, was the fundamental reason why English manufacturers, and their workmen, were struggling to compete with French producers, but Henson acknowledged that other important factors gave French manufacturers certain advantages. He singled out for praise their Conseils de Prud-hommes, and their Tribunaux du Commerce and which were not 'complete mockeries', as he described the English chambers.[88] Their schools of design also received Henson's attention and he advocated the establishment of similar institutions in England,[89] but he repeatedly stressed the importance of the protection of their markets against English producers as a major factor accounting for many of the difficulties in which local manufacturers found themselves. In 1834 he was a member of the local deputation that submitted a petition to Parliament requesting that a ban should be imposed upon the importation of foreign lace.[90] To combat foreign competition Henson urged the formation of two chambers to represent the trade, one consisting of artisans, the other to include employers. In order to preserve the trade, he argued that it was important that 'good' masters and men should join forces to oppose 'bad' masters and men.[91]

When the Artisans' Chamber of Commerce met in 1838 it consisted of ninety-four members representing lace makers and framework knitters from Nottingham and district.[92] The functions listed in the rules of the Chamber bore Henson's stamp. The Chamber was to handle inventions, communicate with official bodies, consider technical education, enforce commercial law and diffuse information.[93] However, two months later, when the committee reported its findings as to the cause of the current depression, the Chartist delegates took the stage and persuaded the assembly to pass a resolution which stated that the absence of political representation was the primary cause of distress.[94] Henson remained aloof from Chartism, mainly it seems because he distrusted the motives of the leaders. While sharing with Chartists an abhorrence of the new poor law and the test system, he argued that it did not distinguish between the really needy who were unwillingly unemployed and the spongers and imposters. Henson accused the Chartists of reckless-ness and argued that the national strike, planned to take place in 1842, would merely overwhelm the working classes with misery: 'The Charter, the Charter, they cry, but they do not describe what laws and regulations we are to have from the Charter'.[95] Thus Henson remained outside the political arena moreover, he differed from other working class leaders in so far as he looked beyond the use of the power of combinations to raise the living standards of his fellow workmen. Recognizing that if local trades flourished workmen as well as manufacturers benefited, Henson saw that there were two ways in which the problem of poverty might be approached most effectively, though they were not mutually exclusive. National wealth could be redistributed, or the level of national wealth itself could be raised. As Assistant Secretary to a Society for the Amelioration of the Condition of the Working Classes in 1837, Henson asserted that one of his chief aims was to '. . . improve the wages of the working classes and everything con-nected with their benefit'.[96] Especially after 1824 it was mainly by proposing measures which would affect the level of economic acti-vity rather than alter the distribution of income that Henson sought to achieve this end.

This latter ultimate aim, and to a certain extent the methods he advocated—although with important differences—were shared by William Felkin, who, indeed, worked with Henson on the trade restriction committees and on the committees set up to prevent the export of lace machinery. Like Henson, Felkin was apprenticed to a stocking maker but later became connected with the lace industry; both were predominantly self-taught, both were authors who wrote industrial history, and both sought to advance the interests of the working classes. In this last sphere the differences in their philos-ophies becomes apparent. William Felkin, born in 1795 at Ilkeston in Derbyshire, was the son of a Baptist minister who in 1800 moved to Kegworth. Here, at a school run as a part-time venture by a self-taught stonemason, Felkin received his only full-time education, even though his father by then had opened his own school while struggling to support a large family.[97] Owing to these poor circum-stances Felkin was obliged to leave school at the age of twelve and was apprenticed to a baker where, he later maintained, through extremely long hours of work without respite, he learned self-reliance and self-discipline. In 1808 he was apprenticed to his grand-father at Bramcote as a framework knitter, and under his tutelage Felkin quickly acquired skill in his work, at the same time, judging from his own views in manhood, absorbing some of his grand-father's philosophy:

> let each man by his economy, sobriety, and industry so provide as that it should never be worth his while to accept of un-reasonably reduced wages.[98]

A year later he left for Nottingham to become apprenticed to Heard, Son & Hurst the leading hosiers, and here he came under the influence of Nathan Hurst, whose practice it was to encourage in-tellectual discussion at literary seminars arranged for the appren-tices, a stimulus which sharpened Felkin's appetite for learning. After a spell at the firm's warehouse in London until his apprentice-ship was completed in 1814, Felkin entered business on his own account as agent selling hosiery in London; then some six years later he began his connection with John Heathcoat, moving from Tiverton back to Nottingham in 1826 as Heathcoat's agent. Six years later, still maintaining his connection with Heathcoat, Felkin partnered Vickers in a commission agency, and by the late thirties their partnership was manufacturing as well as selling lace. During the next decade Felkin became a manufacturer on his own account with a factory in the Lace Market and another at Beeston, where in the middle fifties he manufactured hosiery using steam powered circular frames.[99] By 1864 he was in dire financial difficulties for reasons which are open to speculation, but to forestall legal pro-ceedings his friends settled outstanding debts and purchased an annuity.[100] In recognition of his customary concern for their wel-fare his employees presented him with a timepiece.

Like his father, William Felkin was an Evangelical Baptist, and on his return to Nottingham in 1826 he became a teacher at the George Street Chapel Sunday School and later taught at the Work-house School. As an Evangelical with a great personal interest in learning he played a role in the campaign for popular education in the town. In 1826 Felkin tried to start an Education Society on interdominational lines after the style of the London Society, but his scheme to analyse through this body the types of education needed in society and to disseminate information concerning the appropriate education required for different sections of society was frustrated.[101] This abortive project illustrates two related features of Felkin's approach to the solution of social problems. One is the crucial role which he assigned to education; the other was his use of the scientific method in the field of social problems. In moral education he saw the key to social harmony and improvement, technical education he saw as the remedy for the problem of unem-ployment caused by foreign competition. Aware of the indifference of artisans to the educational needs of their offspring, in 1836 he advocated that the state should fulfil the educational responsibilities to those children whose parents made no provision for them, and that only properly qualified teachers should be employed; but this idea was not repeated and found no place in the concept of a *laissez-faire* society which Felkin came to embrace.

In the thirties, Felkin, like some middle class leaders in other industrial towns, become engrossed in the statistical analysis of various facets of social life. In 1837 and 1839 the results of Felkin's research into the condition of the labouring classes in Nottingham and into the origins of local poverty were accompanied by public lectures on the subject of self-help, in which he urged the use of friendly societies, benefit clubs, and the Nottingham Savings Bank, institutions which, his survey revealed, were almost entirely ignored by the working classes.[102] Before his investigations in the early thirties there is no record of Felkin's donating to charitable subscriptions, but in 1837 and 1839, having become aware of the practical limitations of working class self-improvement, he became a member of Public Relief Committees, and in 1837 was an energetic worker for the Nottingham and District Provident Society which sought to assist the working classes by encouraging self-help.[103] These activities were consistent with his general social philosophy which sanctioned *ad hoc* charity and discriminating benevolence for relief in the short run in order to avoid irrevocable pauperism. But he believed that permanent relief could only be expected from improved trade dependent upon free private enterprise and free trade (with some exceptions), upon the provision for technical education, confidence in credit institutions, and lighter financial pressures on the middle classes.[104]

Thus Felkin was close to the views of the Philosophical Radicals in his economic liberalism and in his acceptance of the implications of a *laissez-faire* economy—and in direct opposition to Henson's fundamental standpoint. Looking back on his own part in the marts and restriction committees of the twenties. Felkin later commented that there could be no justification for departure from the laws of supply and demand.[105] But between 1833 and 1835 he was chairman of the Nottingham Committee which had been set up to prevent the export of lace machinery, and as late as 1841 pressed the government to exempt lace machinery from any legislation that would abolish duties on exported machinery.[106] During the forties Felkin also campaigned to establish a school of design in Nottingham, a movement which led to the establishment of the government-subsidised Nottingham School of Design in 1843. By the end of the decade trade was expanding, and Felkin, affected no doubt by the general euphoria which accompanied the Exhibition in 1851 and ignoring his earlier pleas for the retention of machinery export duties, wrote:

> Surely the value of that competition which produces excellence in the place of mediocrity, and places the means of enjoyment in the highest perfection within the reach of mankind will not be questioned . . .[107]

Felkin conceded, however, that whatever 'beneficial proceeds' resulted from competition, the principles which determined their distribution might be disputed with regard to equity.[108] Admitting this, he still considered that long run changes instrumental in making for a better society should be left to the interaction of individuals pursuing their enlightened self-interest.

> The highest patriotism and philanthropy consist not so much in altering laws and modifying institutions, as in helping and stimulating men to elevate and improve themselves by their own free and independent action:[109]

this quotation from Samuel Smiles' 'Self Help', first published in 1859, comes close to the spirit of Felkin's views on this subject. In 1837 he had written that a workman

> who practices economy and foresight will ordinarily obtain what neither acts of parliament nor any foreign aid can secure— a healthy body, an independent mind, domestic happiness and general esteem. He will be an ornament to the class to which he belongs, and be serviceable in no small degree, to the community at large.

So it was that during his lifetime the Liberal and nonconformist ethics of self-reliance, sobriety, and industry not only sustained his own character, but also provided a text which Felkin expounded to others with enthusiasm and conviction.

A fluent speaker and forceful personality, Felkin had succeeded in becoming a leading Whig member of the Town Council by the fifties. An advocate of enclosure and a member of the Association for the Improvement of the Town of Nottingham, he was caught up in the public health movement, and after taking part in an investigation into the sanitary condition of Nottingham became leader of the town's Sanitary Committee formed in 1848;[110] he was elected Mayor in 1850 and 1851. Thus, although Felkin's philosophy prevented him from advocating a massive and fundamental transformation of society, piecemeal remedial reform in the sphere of public health, while it did not offend his basic precepts, allowed him scope for pursuing his main purpose. This he defined in 1837 when, referring to the working classes, he wrote,

> I have sprung from that class and am mainly dependent upon it and have devoted that portion of time and talent I could

command beyond the requisite attention to my private business, to the improvement of their physical and moral condition and the promotion of their real happiness.[111]

In connection with this, and in his capacity as an expert witness before parliamentary inquiries into the lace and hosiery trades, Felkin spent much time in investigating the condition of the working classes and in examining the causes of poverty. His researches also led him on to an analysis of the condition, size, distribution, and history of Nottingham's staple trades and much of the information he gathered is included in *A History of the Machine Wrought Hosiery and Lace Manufacture* which was published in 1867 and which was (until recently) the standard work on both industries.

The knowledge of industry that he accumulated in the course of his research and his contacts with labour and management in his various capacities as workman, agent, entrepreneur, and commentator on trade affairs led Felkin to conclude that industrial peace could best be promoted through the setting-up of machinery for arbitration. Giving evidence before the Select Committee on Masters and Operatives in 1856 Felkin declared himself in favour of arbitration, and although he advocated the establishment of a national industrial court after the model of the Conseils de Prud-hommes, he did not envisage intervention in disputes over wages.[112] These he considered to be the proper concern solely of the employer and workman; in effect, Felkin saw the wage contract as a purely personal agreement between each workman and his employer. His conception of an industrial tribunal was one whose functions it would be to collect and publish information and statistics relevant to the various disputes submitted to it. The role of this clearing-house for data was to be completely passive, but it was to provide the foundations for the settlement of industrial disputes. Public opinion, Felkin assumed, would exert pressure for negotiations, and swift and reasonable settlements would be facilitated by a government-appointed judge who must be an expert in the appropriate trade.[113] Ignorance, he stressed, lay at the root of bad industrial relations, and he repeatedly emphasized the importance of 'airing a problem' in full view of the public, in order that the parties involved and others might possess all the facts so as to enable them to form balanced opinions. Implicit in this was Felkin's wish to cultivate a 'trade conscience' through which he hoped employers and workmen would recognize their mutual interests and their respective responsibilities. He anticipated beneficial influence from enlightened employers who (assuming a high demand for labour), by virtue of the advantages they offered employees, would be in a strong position to compete for labour.[114] Felkin saw this need to improve conditions of employment as a spur to voluntary reform in the factories.

Although in 1833 Felkin professed to have been disturbed by conditions in factories, he opposed legislation which would limit the hours of work.[115] He argued then, and again in 1842, that if the introduction of steam-powered machinery into factories was speeded up, employees would benefit because more would then work in factories where conditions were superior to those in domestic workshops. Legislation reducing the hours of work in factories, he thought, would retard the spread of steam power and for this reason would be undesirable. By 1862, when the greater proportion of work was carried out in factories, Felkin had accordingly modified his views. Asserting sympathy with the principle of protecting child and female labour he contended that given 'minimum safeguards', the proportion of work carried on inside factories and warehouses would continue to increase due to the attraction of higher wages and better conditions. Workshop conditions must also be expected to improve if shop employers were to retain labour. As a postscript to his evidence, Felkin recorded his belief that the mere publication of the Report on conditions in factories would have influence. Evidence, impartial opinions, and advice, he thought, would help to crystallize public opinion which, because it would be well-informed, could exert pressure in the appropriate places.[116]

One local figure who propagated the philosophy of social harmony through enlightened government intervention was the man who, when William Felkin became an alderman, succeeded him on the Council—Anthony John Mundella. Although separated by a generation, the lives of the two men show some similarities which, together with their coincident interests, make their contrasting approaches to the same general problems rewarding to consider.[117] Both grew up in humble circumstances and both were nonconformists. Mundella attended for a short time a school supported by voluntary subscriptions which provided education for the working classes. At the age of eleven he was apprenticed to a framework knitter at Leicester, where he came under the influence of the leading Chartist, Thomas Cooper.[118] His flirtation with Chartism, which occurred in his youth, developed in early manhood into Liberalism and in 1848, by this time an overseer of two large hosiery warehouses in Leicester, Mundella spoke from the same platform as the Chartists, advocating an alliance between the two groups in the movement for parliamentary reform and universal suffrage.[119] Felkin was never such a democrat and mistrusted the Chartists.[120]

At the age of twenty-three Mundella moved to Nottingham where he entered a partnership with Benjamin Hine to manufacture hosiery. Soon the firm of Hine & Mundella became renowned for its pioneering innovations in the mechanized production of hosiery, while it also acquired a reputation for sound labour relations, a notable achievement in an industry with a poor record in this field. Shortly after the opening of a splendid new factory, in 1851 the workmen gave a party to honour the heads of the firm and on this occasion one of the men made the following speech:

> You have already laid before us those rules which you thought necessary to regulate this establishment and we cannot help noticing the good feeling that is manifested in them towards us, raising as it does a corresponding one in our minds towards you. We hope to convince you that it will not stop here, that exertions will show you that we are resolved to carry out our wise endeavours to make this house one noted for punctuality and correctness, which we all know tend to mutual satisfaction and prosperity.[121]

A good spirit existed in this progressive firm where efficient organization reduced delays between processes and where men worked a nine hour day. Mundella held no illusions concerning his own popularity:

> Why do all the Trade Unions stand by me so firmly? Because I have helped to double and quadruple their wages. I don't want to dwell upon this, but since I became an employer I have carried my feeling for the workpeople to the verge of Quixotism. Had I been less considerate for the good of others I should now have been a very rich man.[122]

Herein lies another contrast between Felkin and Mundella. Both were generous employers, but whereas Felkin mistrusted the trade union movement (even though on occasion the framework knitters had sought his advice on strike action),[123] Mundella recognized the the necessity for workmens' organizations to counterbalance the employers. Mundella's popularity with trade unions was quite remarkable and this rapport was a crucial factor which did much to hold together the Hosiery Board of Arbitration which he created almost single-handed. His prestige, popularity, and tact won him immense respect, not only in the midlands but in the country at large where the demand for his services as industrial peacemaker grew rapidly after his initial success in the hosiery industry; indeed, Mundella has been called the father of arbitration.[124]

Peace in industry was one of the necessary elements of his formula for social harmony; the other important ingredient was education. He was confident that compulsory elementary education would provide a panacea for crime, immorality, and industrial malaise, and for many years he drew attention to the appalling lack of technical education in this country, maintaining that this was one of the reasons for the difficulties of the hosiery industry in the face of foreign competition.[125] As a member of the Board of Nottingham's People's College and Superintendent of a Sunday school, a leading member of the Chamber of Commerce and the Board of Arbitration, and vice-chairman of the local Liberal Party, Mundella became a prominent and popular public figure. On his return from Sheffield, where he had achieved victory in the parliamentary elections of 1868, he was greeted in Nottingham by a crowd whose number was estimated at around twenty thousand people. To the accompaniment of a sax-tuba band they sang his praise.

> His interest is the poor man's cause,
> And all their right he will maintain;
> His aim will be to make good laws,
> Success and honour to his name.[126]

It was appropriate that Mundella should have taken Felkin's seat on the Council, for in some respects the change serves to symbolize the development of social philosophy during the middle years of the century; although the attitudes of both Mundella and Felkin received support concurrently for many years, the views of the latter are more readily identified with early and mid-Victorian ideas while those of Mundella anticipate twentieth century society. Although both men believed in progress through reciprocal understanding in industry and improvements in education, the essential difference between the two figures lies in the shift of emphasis from the almost complete responsibility of the individual for his own well-being, so crucial to Felkin's philosphy, towards Mundella's position. He would have agreed that the unity of society was desirable, but he recognized that it was, as yet, no more than an ideal, a goal which was impossible to attain without collective effort and increasing state intervention to redress the balance of social injustice and improve the quality of life in industrial society. The contrasting views represent a distinction between individualism—the social philosophy of an orthodox Liberal—and a form of Benthamism modified by the influence of Mill and Chadwick: an eclectic philosophy of legislative reform and social service organization which can be identified as a premature Fabianism. After Bentham, collective action for social welfare gradually increased. In the sphere of social policy the scope of local and central government expanded, the sequel being the emergence of modern bureaucracy.

References

[1] W. H. B. Court, *A Concise Economic History of Britain from 1750 to Recent Times* (1958), pp. 252–253.

[2] *Supra*, Chaps. II and IV.

[3] *Evidence before the Commissioners appointed to inquire into Municipal Corporations printed verbatim for the Nottingham Constitutional Club* (Nottingham 1833), p. 13; W. Dearden, *op. cit.*, pp. 60–62.

[4] *Supra*, p. 106.

[5] William Booth, *In Darkest England and the Way Out* (1890) preface.

[6] J. D. Chambers, 'Population Change in a Provincial Town, Nottingham 1700–1800,' *Studies in the Industrial Revolution, Essays presented to T. S. Ashton*, ed. L. S. Pressnell, p. 118.

[7] S. D. Chapman, *'William Felkin 1795–1874'* (unpublished M.A. thesis, University of Nottingham, 1960), p. 77.

[8] J. D. Chambers, 'Population Change in a Provincial Town, Nottingham 1700–1800,' *Studies in the Industrial Revolution,* ed. L. S. Pressnell, p. 118; For Thomas Hawkesley see D.N.B.

[9] W. Dearden, *op. cit.*, p. 68; W. H. Wylie, *op. cit.*, pp. 232, 353.

[10] See Donald Read's pioneering study of three provincial newspapers in *Press and People* 1790–1850 (1961).

[11] J. C. Weller, *'The Evangelical Revival in Nottingham'* (unpublished B.D. thesis, University of Nottingham, 1957), pp. 94–96; S. D. Chapman, *'William Felkin 1795–1874,'* (Unpublished M.A. thesis University of Nottingham, 1960), p. 76.

[12] *Evidence before the Commissioners appointed to inquire into Municipal Corporations printed verbatim for the Nottingham Constitutional Club* (Nottingham 1833), ev. of Henry Enfield, p. 123.

[13] S. D. Chapman, *'William Felkin 1795–1874,'* (Unpublished M.A. thesis, University of Nottingham, 1960), pp. 68–69.

[14] J. Lomax, *History of Quakers in Nottingham 1648–1948* (Nottingham 1948) R. Mellors, *Men of Nottingham and Nottinghamshire,* (Nottingham, 1924), p. 215.

[15] S. D. Chapman, *'William Felkin 1795–1874,'* (unpublished M.A. thesis, University of Nottingham, 1960), p. 98.

[16] See J. H. Green, *The History of Nottingham Mechanics Institution 1837–1887,* (Nottingham, 1887).

[17] R. Mellors, *Men of Nottingham and Nottinghamshire* (Nottingham, 1924), pp. 306–307.

[18] J. H. Green, *op. cit.*, pp. 4–8.

[19] *Ibid.*, pp. 16–17.

[20] W. W. Fyffe, *op. cit.*, p. 16; S. Pollard, *A History of Labour in Sheffield,* (1959), p. 36.

[21] W. W. Fyffe, *op. cit.*, p. 17.

[22] A. C. Wood, *A History of the University College, Nottingham* (Oxford, 1953), p. 7 f.n. 1.

[23] W. Dearden, *op. cit.*, pp. 56–66.

[24] F. and J. White, *op. cit.*, p. 169.

[25] See J. C. Weller, *'The Evangelical Revival in Nottingham'* (unpublished B.D. thesis, University of Nottingham, 1957), p. 39.

[26] See the Nottingham Church Census of Richard Hopper whose figures are reproduced in S. D. Chapman, 'The Evangelical Revival and Education in Nottingham,' *Transactions of the Thoroton Society,* LXVI, (1962), pp. 40–41.

[27] *Ibid.*, p. 36.

[28] *Ibid.*, p. 38.

[29] Quoted in J. C. Weller, *'The Evangelical Revival in Nottingham'* (unpublished B.D. thesis, University of Nottingham, 1957), p. 39.

[30] S. D. Chapman, 'The Evangelical Revival and Education in Nottingham,' *Transactions of the Thoroton Society*, LXVI, (1962), p. 44.

[31] Edith M. Becket, *'The Development of Education in Nottingham in the Nineteenth and early Twentieth Centuries'* (unpublished M.A. thesis University of London, 1922), p. 92.

[32] S. D. Chapman, 'The Evangelical Revival and Education in Nottingham,' *Transactions of the Thoroton Society*, LXVI (1962), p. 45.

[33] This excludes dame schools. See the table in S. D. Chapman *'The Evangelical Revival and Education in Nottingham,'* *Transactions of the Thoroton Society*, LXVI (1962), pp. 48–49.

[34] Edith M. Becket, *'The Development of Education in Nottingham in the Nineteenth and early Twentieth Centuries,'* (unpublished M.A. thesis, University of London, 1922), p. 51; See also S. D. Chapman, 'The Evangelical Revival and Education in Nottingham,' *Transactions of the Thoroton Society*, LXVI (1962) pp. 53–54.

[35] N. Haycocks, 'Nottingham as a Centre of Education,' in J. D. Chambers *et al. A Century of Nottingham History* (Nottingham, 1951), p. 43.

[36] S. Pollard, *op. cit.*, p. 112; A. Briggs, *History of Birmingham*, (1954), p. 106.

[37] Edith M. Becket, *'The Development of Education in Nottingham in the Nineteenth and early Twentieth Centuries,'* (unpublished M.A. thesis, University of London, 1922), pp. 101–04.

[38] S. D. Chapman, 'The Evangelical Revival and Education in Nottingham,' *Transactions of the Thoroton Society*, LXVI, (1962), p. 66.

[39] *Ibid.*

[40] See F. W. Leeman, *The History of the Nottingham Cooperative Society Ltd.*, 1863–1944 (Nottingham, 1944), pp. 4–11.

[41] F. W. Leeman, *op. cit.*, pp. 15–21.

[42] *Ibid.*, pp. 21–24.

[43] *N.J.*, January 15, 1872; *N.J.*, November 7, 1873; *Ex.*, August 7, 1857; *Ex.*, January 30, 1888.

[44] For the activities of other Evangelicals—Orange, Barnett, Roworth, Heymann see *Supra*, Chap. V.

[45] J. B. Brebner, 'Laissez Faire and State Intervention in the Nineteenth Century,' *J.E.H.* (1948) Supp. 8, p. 70.

[46] J. D. Chambers, 'Population Change in a Provincial Town, Nottingham 1700–1800,' *Studies in the Industrial Revolution, Essays presented to T. S. Ashton*, ed. L. S. Pressnell, p. 117; There were bread riots in 1795, meat riots in 1792 and 1795, and political riots in 1793, 1794, and 1795.

[47] William Felkin, *History*, p. 240; Since the completion of this book the life and thought of Gravener Henson have been examined in greater detail in a forthcoming article by Roy Church and S. D. Chapman, 'Gravener Henson and the Making of the English Working Class', in *Land, Labour, and Population; Essays in honour of J. D. Chambers*, ed. G. Mingay and E. Jones (1966).

[48] E. P. Thompson, *The Making of the English Working Class* (1963), p. 774.

[49] William Felkin, *History,* p. 240. *Report from the Select Commitee on Postage,* 1837–8, XX, II, ev. of Henson, pp. 209, 213; See the Nottingham trade directories of Pigot (1829), and of F. and J. White (1832, 1844, and 1853). William Wylie, *Old and New Nottingham* (1853), p. 234.

[50] *Report from the Select Committee (Postage)* 1837–8. XX, II, ev. of Henson, p. 209.

[51] Henson to Roper quoted in *B.R.,* VIII, 147, 1812.

[52] *N.J.,* August 25, 1848.

[53] *Report from the Select Committee (Postage),* 1837–8, XX, II, ev. of Henson, p. 214.

[54] *Fourth Report from the Select Committee (Emigration, Combinations and Machinery),* 1824 (51) V. 183, ev. of Henson, p. 281.

[55] *Ibid.,* p. 282.

[56] *Ibid.,* p. 280.

[57] J. L. and B. Hammond, *The Skilled Labourer,* (1919), p. 236.

[58] *Ibid.,* p. 241.

[59] *Fourth Report from the Select Committee (Emigration, Combinations, and the Export of Machinery)* 1824, (51) V. 183, ev. of Henson, p. 281.

[60] Gravener Henson and George White, *A Few Remarks on the State of the Laws at present in existence for regulating Masters and Workpeople* (1823), pp. 15–17.

[61] *Ibid.,* pp. 129–132.

[62] G. Wallas, *Life of Francis Place* (1898), pp. 207–210; E. P. Thompson *op. cit.,* p. 518.

[63] *Place Papers,* 27, 798. Proceedings for the Repeal of the Combination Laws, 1823.

[64] Wallas, *op. cit.,* chapter VIII; S. and B. Webb, *History of Trade Unionism* (1894, revised 1920), chapter II.

[65] See E. P. Thompson, *op. cit.,* pp. 543–550.

[66] *Supra,* p. 44.

[67] Henson's view on the relative merits of a regulated economy with those of an economic system based on laissez-faire principles are to be found scattered throughout his book, 'The Civil, Political, and Mechanical History of the Framework Knitters in Europe and America.' Vol. I, (only one volume published), Nottingham, 1831.

[68] *Ibid.,* p. 232.

[69] *Ibid.,* p. 233.

[70] Henson and White, *op. cit.,* pp. 138, 140.

[71] *Report from the Select Committee (Postage),* 1837–8. XX, II, ev. of Henson, p. 221.

[72] *Ibid.,* p. 214.

[73] *Ibid.,* pp. 211, 221.

[74] *Ibid.*

[75] *Supra,* pp. 121–22.

[76] *Report from the Select Committee (Postage),* 1837–8, XX, II, ev. of Henson, p. 214.

[77] Henson to Place; *Place Papers,* 27, 807.

[78] *Ibid.*

[79] *Report from the Select Committee (Postage),* 1837–8, XX, II, p. 219.

[80] *Ibid.,* p. 219.

[81] e.g., *N.J.,* March 23, 1835; *N.J.,* June 29, 1838; *N.J.,* November 20, 1840.

[82] *N.J.,* March 23, 1835.

[83] *Fourth Report from the Select Committee (Emigration, Combinations, and the Export of Machinery)* 1824 (51)V. 183, ev. of Henson, p. 275; William Felkin, *History*, p. 354.

[84] *Ibid.*, pp. 274, 276; *Report from the Select Committee (Postage)*, 1837-8, XX, II, ev. of Henson, p. 217.

[85] *N.J.*, January 16, 1835.

[86] *N.J.*, December 12, 1834.

[87] *Report from the Select Committee (Postage)*, 1837-8, XX, II, ev. of Henson, p. 217.

[88] *N.J.*, January 16, 1835.

[89] *Report from the Select Committee (Postage)* 1837-8, XX, II, ev. of Henson, p. 219.

[90] *N.R.*, August 1, 1834.

[91] *N.J.*, April 6, 1838; *Report from the Select Committee (Postage)* 1837-8, XX, II, ev. of Henson, p. 221.

[92] *N.R.*, April, 16, 1838.

[93] *N.R.*, April 16, 1838.

[94] *N.R.*, June 22, 1838.

[95] *N.J.*, November 25, 1842; *N.J.*, September 2, 1842.

[96] *Report from the Select Committee (Postage)*, 1837-8, XX, II, ev. of Henson, pp. 207-8.

[97] For an excellent biography of this Evangelical Radical see S. D. Chapman, '*William Felkin 1795-1874*,' (unpublished M.A. thesis, University of Nottingham, 1960).

[98] *Ibid.*, quoted, p. 22.

[99] *Ibid.*, pp. 11-56; *Report from the Select Committee appointed to inquire into the expediency of establishing equitable tribunals for the amicable adjustment of differences between masters and operatives with Proceedings, Minutes of Evidence, Appendix, etc.* 1856 (343) XIII. 1., p. 47; R. Mellors, *Men of Nottingham and Nottinghamshire*, p. 71.

[100] S. D. Chapman, '*William Felkin 1795-1874*,' (unpublished M.A. thesis, University of Nottingham, 1960), p. 57.

[101] *Ibid.*, pp. 117-19.

[102] See William Felkin, *Remarks upon the Importance of an Inquiry into the Amount and Appropriation of Wages by the Working Classes in 1837* (1837), p. 16. William Felkin, 'Statistics of the Labouring Classes and Paupers of Nottingham,' *Journal of Statistical Society* II (1839), 457-59.

[103] S. D. Chapman, '*William Felkin 1795-1874*,' (unpublished M.A. thesis, University of Nottingham, 1960), pp. 102-05.

[104] *Ibid.*, p. 111; William Felkin, *The Exhibition in 1851 of the Progress and Industry of all Nations its Probable Effect upon Labour and Commerce* (1851), p. 30.

[105] William Felkin, 'The History and Present State of the Machine-Wrought Lace Trade,' *Journal of the Society of Arts*, IV (1856), 482.

[106] First Report of the Select Committee on the Laws affecting the Exportation of Machinery, 1841 (201) VII. 1. p. 175.

[107] William Felkin, *The Exhibition in 1851 of the Progress and Industry of all Nations its Probable Effects upon labour and Commerce*, p. 13.

[108] *Ibid.*

[109] Samuel Smiles, *Self Help*, (1876), p. 3.

[110] *Supra*, pp. 195-97.

[111] William Felkin, *Remarks upon the Importance of an Inquiry into the Amount and Appropriation of Wages by the Working Classes in 1837*.

[112] *Report from the Select Committee* (*equitable tribunals for differences between masters and operatives*) 1856 (343) XIII. 1. ev. of Felkin, pp. 83–86; William Felkin, *History,* ch. XXIX; As the Webbs point out, the Conseils de Prud hommes only provided for the settlement of disputes arising out of existing contracts or, in some cases, the application of the law. They did not provide for the fixing of wages for future engagements. They were 'merely cheap and convenient legal tribunals.' S. and B. Webb, *Industrial Democracy,* (1920), p. 226.

[113] *Report from the Select Committee* (*equitable tribunals for differences between masters and operatives*) 1856 (343) XIII. 1. ev. of Felkin, pp. 85–86.

[114] *Ibid.*

[115] *First Report of the Children's Employment Commission, 1833,* (450) XX. 1. ev. of Felkin, p. 520.

[116] *First Report of the Children's Employment Commission,* 1863, (3170), XVIII. 1. ev. of Felkin, p. 237.

[117] The existence of W. H. Armytage's biography *A. J. Mundella 1825–1897, the Liberal background to the Labour Movement* (1951), explains the very brief treatment here.

[118] *Ibid.,* pp. 15–18.

[119] *Ibid.,* p. 20.

[120] S. D. Chapman, '*William Felkin 1795–1874,*' (unpublished M.A. thesis, University of Nottingham, 1960).

[121] Quoted in W.H.G. Armytage, *A. J. Mundella 1825–1897, the Liberal Background to the Labour Movement,* p. 25.

[122] *Ibid.*

[123] S. D. Chapman, '*William Felkin 1795–1874,*' (unpublished M.A. thesis, University of Nottingham, 1960); *Report from the Select Committee* (*equitable tribunals for differences between masters and operatives*) 1856 (343) XIII. 1., ev. of Felkin.

[124] J. R. Hicks, 'The Early History of Industrial Conciliation in England', *Economica,* X (1930), p. 27.

[125] W. H. G. Armytage, *A. J. Mundella 1825–1897, the Liberal Background to the Labour Movement,* (1951) p. 59.

[126] *Ex.,* November 20, 1868.

CHAPTER XIII

THE EMERGENCE OF A MODERN MUNICIPALITY

THE middle decades of the nineteenth century marked the great era of permissive legislation.[1] Thereafter, national legislation and administrative pressure from the central government became increasingly important in a wider range of matters which, hitherto, had been the responsibility of local authorities. Municipal corporations could not avoid the increasing intervention of the central government, but it frequently caused resentment. In 1872 the Nottingham Town Council decided not to apply for a government grant to meet half the cost of employing two officers, because the latter were to be ruled from London.[2] However, in the year following the Public Health Act of 1872, the following year the Town Council, as the Urban Sanitary Authority, was obliged to appoint its first Medical Officer of Health. Later the same year, Edward Seaton, in cooperation with Tarbottom, submitted to the Council a Report on the Sanitary Condition of the Town.[3] The Report, which was the result of the combined research of Seaton and Tarbotton, emphasized the insanitary condition of houses in the Meadows, and others in the lower parts of the town. Nottingham's eight thousand back-to-back houses were the object of fierce criticism, while the continued erection of insanitary dwellings likewise drew condemnation from the town's officers. Ashpits for houses in the Meadows were situated at the rear, several feet below street level and considerably lower than the Trent flood level in that area. The result was that when the river rose each season, water was carried into the yards and sewage poured into the houses.[4] During the serious flooding in 1875 three thousand dwellings were affected and many families were rendered homeless. However, in 1874 the annual danger arising from liquid sewage in the Meadows was reduced when the Council acted upon Seaton's recommendation that the official flood level of the Trent should be raised, and that no part of any building should be permitted below that level. These provisions were included in the Nottingham Improvement Act of that year.[5]

Under the Improvement Act of 1878 Seaton sought to reduce the danger of epidemic, which was closely connected with the existence of insanitary property. For this reason, Nottingham became the first town to adopt a Local Act for the notification of infectious diseases.

Seaton's decision which led to its adoption encountered hostile criticism from a large number of the town's doctors, who maintained that the danger of infection was greater inside the hospitals than in people's homes. Seaton defended his action and, while admitting the possibility of infection in hospitals, urged the building of separate isolation hospitals to avoid that danger. The doctors' attack continued, but the Council supported Seaton in requiring the notification of small pox, typhoid, typhus, and scarlet fevers, cholera being added to this list in 1885.[6] Bagthorpe isolation hospital was opened in 1890.[7] After eleven years of service Seaton resigned in 1884 to take up a similar post in Chelsea, while the same year brought the death of William Richards, who had been Nottingham's chief Inspector of Nuisances since 1847. Seaton's final annual report, presented in 1883, had drawn attention to the activities of the Health Committee during the previous ten years.[8] The Report also drew attention to the importance of water in promoting public health, and commented upon the achievement of Thomas Hawksley fifty years before in connection with a constant service providing for running water.

The town's water supply was a subject which had long absorbed the Council's attention. Since 1845, when the Nottingham Old Waterworks Company and the Trent Waterworks Company had amalgamated, the town had depended for its water supply upon the Nottingham Waterworks Company which owned all the existing local works.[9] Shortly after the formation of this monopoly, the Council, as a substantial consumer of water and impressed with a Sanitary Committee report which touched on the connection between water and public health, requested the Waterworks Company to reduce its charges. The Company's refusal was followed by a ratepayers' meeting which ended with a resolution urging the Council to purchase the Company or, failing this, to set up a municipal enterprise in competition.[10]

By this time more than a dozen municipalities already controlled their water supplies, and in the fifties the Nottingham Town Council was one of several to consider a similar policy.[11] The Nottingham Committee, set up by the Council to investigate the proposal of the ratepayers, reported in favour of acquiring the waterworks, expressing the same view which Chamberlain was later to use when he decided that Birmingham should control its own water supply.[12] The Committee considered that it was

> highly objectionable that the supply of water—so essential for the daily use and health of all classes and for all sanitary purposes, and which costs only the expense of collection and distribution should be made the source of large profits to capitalists.[13]

Twice the Committee put forward a recommendation for outright purchase, but the motion was defeated in Council on financial grounds, the rock on which the mooted takeover in Birmingham also foundered in the fifties.[14] However, the Nottingham Council requested from the Company the power to buy unlimited shares at market price, a vote to be attached to each block of ten shares.[15] The Company refused, and the matter was allowed to drop until 1871, two years after the Royal Commission on Sanitary Reform had recommended that the country's water supplies should be taken out of private hands.[16] Negotiations for the purchase of the Waterworks commenced in 1870, and an offer similar to that successfully made to the Gas Company was presented to the Waterworks Company in 1873. After the Company had refused, the Council moved to obtain compulsory powers for its purchase, but once more without success. Finally, under the Nottingham Improvement Act passed in 1879, the Council reached an agreement with the Company after the Council undertook to pay perpetual annuities to shareholders of 7 per cent. on the par value of their holdings (the Council had previously offered to pay up to 6 per cent.), in addition to a lump sum of £10,000. New works were begun almost immediately with the building of a new reservoir and waterworks on Mapperley Plains and Papplewick, and in twelve years profits from the waterworks relieved the rates by an amount equal to the lump sum payment. In 1899 the Nottingham authorities joined with those at Derby, Leicester, Sheffield, and Derby County in a project which involved the utilization of the waters of the Derwent Valley.[17]

Compared with the acquisition of the water supply, the transfer of the town's gas supply from private to municipal ownership presented few difficulties. When the 1854 Committee had considered the desirability of taking over the Gas Light and Coke Company (at the same time as the Waterworks Company had been under scrutiny), it had concluded that acquisition of the gas undertaking would involve the Council in unwarranted risk.[18] By 1874 more than fifty municipalities in England and Wales were manufacturing their own gas,[19] and the success of these undertakings suggests that the Nottingham Councillors had been unnecessarily timid in the matter of municipal enterprise. The Nottingham Corporation (Gas) Act of 1874 gave the required powers to the Council to purchase the Company. Under the terms of the transaction, shareholders received perpetual annuities at the rate of 6 per cent. on the par value of their holdings, while the Council reserved the right to extinguish annuities whenever it chose to do so.[20] The subsequent history of the gas enterprise to the close of the century is similar to that in other towns where a municipal monopoly sold gas in a rapidly expanding market, and where the threat of competition from electricity was slow to develop. From the beginning, under the able chairmanship of Alderman John Barber, the Nottingham Gas Committee presented annual accounts which showed successively larger profits. A substantial part of these were placed in reserve in a sinking fund, but during the first seven years of municipal ownership, the price of gas was reduced four times by 2d. per thousand cubic feet—not always without opposition.[21] Birmingham Gas Committee brought about a reduction of 9d. in the price of gas over the same period.[22] At last, municipal corporations found themselves governing to promote the common good while running an immensely profitable enterprise, which made possible lower prices, further amenities, and helped to slow down the rise in rates.

The motive for acquiring the town's gas supply was profitable gain for the community; the acquisition of the Waterworks Company was in the interest of public health, and considerations of public health explain the beginnings of municipal housing enterprise in Nottingham during the last quarter of the century. The annual report of the Medical Officer of Health in 1873 had drawn attention to the existence of much insanitary housing, both in the centre of the town and in the suburbs, and it had stated that it was impossible in the short run to relieve the serious shortage of healthy dwellings for the working classes. In theory, laws relating to nuisances which arose from overcrowding might have been used to reduce the high population density in some areas, but it was stated that

> the Inspectors of Nuisances are obliged not to see overcrowding which exists in many parts . . . The manufactories of the town require the services of workmen who must live within a certain radius of the factory or workshop and the effect of strictly enforcing the sanitary laws with respect to overcrowding would be to cripple to a great extent the commercial interests of the town . . . Some thousands of workpeople are now driven to the outskirts of the town and have to come to and from long distances . . . Until something is done . . . it is clearly impossible for the Council to carry forward any measures for street improvements or for opening closed courts and for providing better ventilation for alleys, where such alterations demand the removal of the dwellings of the working classes.[23]

The Improvement Committee argued that the regulations laid down in the Enclosure Act prevented the erection of workmen's cottages in those areas of the town where building land was available, although during the fifties stipulations as to the type of dwellings to be built on enclosed land had, in many instances, been disregarded.

Thus, housing conditions were far from satisfactory, and a comparison of the death rates of 20·9 in the recently built suburbs, with 31·2 in the old town, indicates the gravity of the situation for those dwelling within the old borough boundaries.[24]

Nevertheless, beginning with the development of the suburban villages in the third decade of the century and the increase in building which took place within the old borough boundaries after the Enclosure Act of 1845, housing for the working classes had improved. Thereafter, fewer three-roomed back-to-back houses were built which, by the end of the century, were reckoned to be inferior to the typical working class dwellings.[25] After enclosure the erection of dwellings for the lowest income groups had proceeded slowly. Most were plain fronted, red brick, terraced houses which contained three rooms; each terrace consisted of about eight houses built on either side of a paved courtyard which led from the main street, though some houses possessed small front gardens and a main street entrance; behind the buildings was a yard, which was either divided between tenants or used in common. The newer buildings in the suburbs tended to be larger, while the three-roomed terraces were largely occupied by labourers, colliers, and railway employees.

It was to the four and especially five-roomed terraced houses, almost invariably built straight from the pavement line, that, from the second quarter of the century, the town's artisans were attracted. Both types of houses had front and back entrances, but only the five-roomed dwellings sometimes contained a workshop or attic. In the five-roomed houses, which in 1905 was the predominant type of working class dwelling in which 71·7 per cent. of the town's population lived, the street door opened directly into the parlour, twelve feet by nine feet. Behind the parlour was a kitchen and a scullery; the water closet, and sometimes the coal cellar, were in the yard, though occasionally the cellar was inside the house with access between kitchen and parlour. Of more recent construction, some of the five-roomed houses included a third bedroom built over the scullery at the rear and in 1905 these were still the homes of the higher wage-earning artisans. Six-roomed dwellings were normally occupied by white collar workers and their families, by foremen, insurance agents, clerks, and people of similar occupations. The major distinguishing feature of the six-roomed house was the layout of the ground floor whose front door, instead of opening into the parlour, opened into a passage with direct access to the kitchen or scullery. Apart from this feature, there were two main types of houses of this size; one consisting of three storeys which contained two rooms on each floor, and the other containing two parlours and a kitchen (but no scullery) on the ground floor, and three bedrooms on the first floor, corresponding in position to the rooms below. Some of the three storey buildings also included bathrooms built over the scullery.[26]

Although the types of working class dwellings erected had thus improved in the course of the century, until the seventies the rate of population growth and the need for workmen to live within easy reach of their places of employment had totally defeated the aims of the Council to rid the town of insanitary housing. While the Liverpool Town Council had secured its pioneer Sanitary Amendment Act of 1864,[27] the Nottingham Council allowed itself to be completely overawed by the vast amount of insanitary property in existence until after the Nottingham Improvement Act of 1874. This included among its provisions powers to enforce building regulations and to build artisans' dwellings, thereby anticipating by one year national legislation in the form of the Artisans' Dwellings Improvement Act,[28] a measure which was designed to assist and encourage local authorities to attack the problem of slum clearance by areas. The Nottingham Improvement Act also preceeded the Public Health Act of 1875 which, while granting to local authorities some of the powers for which the Council had applied in their own private Act, also created a national sanitary administration under the supervision of a central Local Government Board.[29]

In 1875 the Industrial Dwellings Committee reported in favour of erecting dwellings for Corporation employees, and building began on Bath Street. These buildings, known as the Victoria Dwellings, were completed in 1877 at a cost of £11,000. Built in the form of flats, they were intended for the poorest inhabitants and let below rents which could be obtained for similar property on the open market.[30] After the Artisans' and Labourers' Dwellings Improvement Act of 1875, which enabled local authorities to prepare reconstruction schemes for areas of insanitary property, Seaton immediately designated Broad Marsh as an unhealthy area, and on the recommendation of the Health Committee the Council approved the compulsory purchase of the site, the demolition of old buildings, and the letting or sale of land for commercial buildings. The Committee also recommended the erection of artisans' dwellings between Ortzen Street and Forest Road to provide compensatory living accommodation.[31] Another unhealthy area selected for development was that bordering St. Ann's Street near Glasshouse and Charlotte Streets. This included two yards in which thirty-two houses were deemed to be unfit for human habitation, and their demolition was ordered in 1876.[32] The third and largest area to receive attention was that between Long Row and Upper Parliament Street; plans for its redevelopment in 1881 affected about one thousand houses.[33] This area became the site for Queen Street and King Street, where the new Post Office and the Prudential Assurance buildings were completed in 1897. In this project Nottingham became one of the three urban sanitary districts which in that decade acted under the Artisans' Dwellings Act, though Birmingham, Leeds, and Bradford had proceeded under local acts.[34] The Council also adopted a scheme to rehouse those affected by the demolition of the Long Row and Parliament Street dwellings on the outskirts of the town, and in connection with this project building began on land near Hunger Hills Road in 1883.[35]

While the Council was unwilling to subsidize, most commercial builders were reluctant to invest in improved working class accommodation which could only be offered for sale at modest prices.[36] New homes were erected in the nineties, after the Great Central and Great Northern Railway Companies purchased the slum property then standing on the site of Victoria Station in 1896. After the demolition of similar property in the St. Ann's Well Road area, in 1899 the Council erected working class dwellings on Coppice Road and found it impossible to discover persons willing to take the remaining land on lease for the erection of other dwellings.[37] In 1900 Seaton's successor as Medical Officer of Health, Phillip Boobyer, admitted that the Coppice rehousing scheme had proved useless as a means of providing houses for the very poor. Rents were at least twice that which slum tenants could afford to pay.[38] In the same Report he expressed the Health Committee's reluctance to construct tenements for the working classes, and notwithstanding the failure of the Coppice rehousing scheme the Committee hoped to solve the problem by building small cottages on the town's periphery which would be linked to the town centre by transport.

Overcrowding was seen as one important source of disease as well as discomfort, mainly because overcrowding tended to occur inside inferior insanitary dwellings. As early as 1854 the Nottingham Sanitary Committee had stressed the superiority of water closets and had urged the substitution of these for existing methods of domestic sewage disposal.[39] In 1894 Phillip Boobyer once more drew the Council's attention to the inadequacy of the pail closet system with its difficulties of disposal, especially during winter, wet, and frosty weather. He argued that when new buildings were erected the Council should display its wisdom by insisting that all must contain superior sanitation systems. In 1895 a Joint Committee recommended that all newly-built houses and buildings with an annual rental of £18 and above should be equipped with a water closet, and that no tub closets or middens should be installed in new houses. The first resolution was adopted in 1895, the others being deferred

Y

for consideration until the Stoke Farm Committee had submitted its comprehensive report upon sewage disposal for the entire borough.[40]

Some indication of the progress of the Sanitary and Health Committees is given in the movement of the mortality rate in the town. The death rate for Nottingham for the five years beginning in 1856 had been 27·2, compared with 22·2 for England and Wales, and 26·1 for eight large towns for the decade 1851–1861. By 1865–1870 the Nottingham death rate had fallen to 23·8, which was still slightly higher than the figure for England and Wales but three points lower than the figure for eight large towns between 1861 and 1871. During the following five years the Nottingham figure rose to 24·9.[41] Thereafter, the improved climate of opinion which surrounded the general problem of public health, the implementation of the greater powers in the hands of the Council, and the efforts of its permanent officials, brought about a sustained decline in the death rate. Similar factors exerted influence in other towns and the national average death rate fell from 22·0 in 1871–5 to 17·7 in 1896–1901. During the same period the Nottingham death rate dropped from 24·9 to 18·5. Although this fall in the mortality rate could be partly attributed to the work of the Sanitary, Highway, and Health Committees, the town's reputation as one of the healthiest cities in England was largely due to the town's relatively late industrial development when municipalities were already fortified with rudimentary compulsory powers. The availability of building land after enclosure also had important effects upon local population density, for although during the boom which occurred in the early seventies Seaton had been concerned about the amount of overcrowding in the district, the Census of 1891 showed that with its average house population of less than five, Nottingham, with Leicester and Derby, was one of the most comfortable urban areas in Great Britain.

However, Nottingham's reputation as one of the country's most comfortable and healthy towns was marred by an unusually high rate of infant mortality, a depressing feature of life in many textile towns. The annual report of the Medical Officer of Health in 1883 revealed that of 4,571 deaths in 1882, more than a quarter of these were of infants, and of a thousand born in that year 188 had died before reaching the age of one.[43] The Borough Coroner voiced suspicions concerning the high number of post mortems, which suggested that some irregularity was connected with infant deaths. A report in 1883 stated that although the majority of infant deaths were certified as due to 'natural causes', in fact starvation or some other form of neglect were nearly always '... virtually the causes of death'.[44] The improper use of drugs, administered by mothers to quieten the infants, offered more evidence to suggest that working mothers, of whom there were large numbers in the lace and hosiery trades, were often unsuccessful in performing two roles simultaneously; unhappily, the financial difficulties of many poor families made it necessary for the whole family to work.[45]

Hitherto separated from the industrial villages by the unenclosed lands which surrounded the borough, during the late sixties and seventies the Council began to consider the integration of the whole area for purposes of drainage and other public health matters, gas and water supplies, police, and transport. A Royal Commission, which had visited the town in 1868, stressed the need for administrative changes in general by enlarging local authority areas, and this prompted the Council to draft a Bill which would unite the Leen Valley and Sneinton with Nottingham.[46] However, fierce opposition on the part of the local authorities whose powers would be affected led to the Bill's withdrawal. Progress made with the formation of the Nottingham and Leen District Sewerage Board was followed in 1876 by further negotiations for an extension of the borough boundaries.

Objections to the Bill were overcome by compromise. Trustees of the Gregory Estate were persuaded to accept the Bill after the promise of a new road, Gregory Boulevard, which would link the Mansfield Road with Alfreton Road. Owners and occupiers of property in Standard Hill and the limits of the Castle, who were concerned about preserving privacy as well as the maintenance of the roads, received a rate concession, while the Council also agreed to the request of the Duke of Newcastle's Trustees to allow the Park to continue as an unrestricted area responsible for its own roads and buildings. Two more concessions were those which acceded to the demands from Clifton parish that the River Trent where it faced Wilford and Lenton should stay outside the Council's control, and that the boundary there should be the north bank of the river. As compensation for loss of revenue by the county magistrates the borough agreed to pay £15,000; the Police Stations and part of the police force were also taken over. One point which arose during discussions on the new large borough was made by the Radford Local Board, whose insistence that unfair advantage should not be secured by any district was welcomed by the Nottingham representatives, enabling them to demonstrate their intention of behaving with complete impartiality in their dealings with all parties. The Borough Extension Act became law in 1877, bringing within the new borough limits the parishes of Sneinton, Lenton, Radford, Basford and Bulwell, Standard Hill, the limits of the Castle, Brewhouse Yard, Wilford north of the Trent, and the portion of the parish of Gedling which contained part of the Asylum. Thus the area encompassed by the enlarged boundaries increased from 1,996 acres to 10,935 acres, while its population rose from roughly 86,000 to 157,000.[47]

The comparatively small amount of reform of the Council's organization that was found necessary after this extension is indicative of the wisdom of those members who had undertaken its revision in 1859. Amalgamation took place between the Chamber and Bridge Estates Committees; the Public Walks, Burial Grounds, and Commons Committees joined together; the University College Management Committee and the Free Libraries Committee were united; and the Watch Committee took over the duties of the Lighting Committee.[48] Hence the number of separate committees was reduced, and in 1879 the enlarged Council, which now consisted of forty-eight councillors and sixteen aldermen compared with forty-two and fourteen in the old body, insisted that the committees were subordinate to it and that all expenditure must receive preliminary Council sanction.[49] This change was significant inasmuch that the composition of the Council altered during the seventies. Partly due to retirement or death, a number of senior men who had long been members of the Council disappeared from that body, while the revision of town wards and their increase in numbers also encouraged the entrance of new men into the Council ranks, many of them members of the Conservative Party. The scale of municipal expenditures was also growing rapidly during this decade, and the Council reaction against the powers of the committees was a sign that rising expenditure would not be allowed to continue unquestioned; hence the ensuing friction during the next few years.

One drain on Council revenues was the annual payment of burgess parts, whose increase after 1845 caused serious concern which led to a final solution of the whole problem associated with the rights and status of the freemen of Nottingham. The Enclosure Act of 1845 had given as compensation to the freemen a landed estate and a share in the Bridge Estate. The Council had continued to be responsible for keeping the register of freemen, and for distributing the allotment of burgess parts from the Bridge Estate. The practice of allotting portions of land, however, had been replaced by annual payments in money. Meanwhile, the number of burgess parts increased, while income from the Freemen's Estate rose with the upward movement of land values. Writing on the Council's behalf, in 1877 the town clerk queried the right of the Freemen's Committee to add to the numbers of burgess parts, and although the clerk to the Estate defended the freemen's position, negotiations began to transfer the Estate to the Council, to terminate the privileges of free-men, and to limit the enrolment of burgess-born freemen to children living when the Act became operative. These clauses, together with the financial terms of the agreement, were included in the Notting-ham Corporation Act of 1882, while administration of the new order became the responsibility of a joint committee of Council members and freemen. The financial agreement required the Council to underwrite any deficit in income from the freemen's former estate in order to pay all burgess parts in full; through application to the Court of Chancery, the Council was permitted to retain any sur-pluses from the estate. Thus, the allotment of burgess parts was to end, the drain on Council revenues in this connection was to cease, and freeman status was also to disappear.[50]

At the same time that the Council was seeking to discontinue payment to the freemen, it was rapidly increasing its expenditure on town improvement. After the political and administrative integra-tion of Nottingham and district had been effected, the Council had set about the task of improving communications in the area. Aris-ing out of the agreement with the trustees of the Gregory Estate, by 1880 Gregory Boulevard was well under construction, and in the same year the Improvement Committee agreed upon the formation of a similar low level road which would connect Nottingham centre with Old and New Lenton and Old Radford. By providing an alter-native route for traffic leaving Midland Station bound for Lenton or Radford, the steep gradients encountered on Ilkeston Road and Derby Road would be avoided; Castle Boulevard was opened in 1884. In Basford, Vernon Road had been opened in 1882, while Radford Boulevard first came into use in 1887.[51] Later, Highbury Road, leading to Bulwell Market Place, was constructed. The first four highways together cost £111,000, and improvements carried out in St. Peter's Gate during the same decade cost another £149,000.[52] Other improvements included the widening of Stoney Street, Pilcher Gate, Fletcher Gate, Warser Gate, Upper Parliament Street, Greyfriar Gate, and Bulwell Lane.[53]

In 1897 the Council took further steps towards improving the town's internal communications when it acquired control of the Nottingham tramway system. Private companies had built tramways in other towns before 1870, and in 1874 the Nottingham Tramway Company had obtained Council permission to operate horse tram-ways from St. Peter's Gate to the east end of Station Street, and from the junction of Station Street and Carrington Street, along Arkwright Street to London Road.[54] Routes were extended so as to connect with Carrington and Hyson Green. In 1882 the Company proposed to use steam-propelled trams on the Basford and Carrington Routes, but the Council laid down unrealistic conditions concerning smoke, steam, and noise, and promptly met to consider taking over the enterprise.[55] However, under the Tramways Act of 1870 the private companies could retain ownership for twenty-one years after which local authorities were given the option of compulsory purchase.[56] Thus not until 1897 was the transaction effected, when the Council purchased at par eight thousand £10 shares. The Tramways Committee issued a report in the following year in which plans for expansion and re-equipment were set out,[57] while the Committee also recommended that the entire system should be equipped for electric overhead traction. Extensions were begun in the following year, the market place becoming the centre of Nottingham's electric tramways system.[58]

The use of electricity in Nottingham was of very recent origin. Although in 1882 the Electric Lighting Act had given local authorities power to permit private companies to install electric systems, retaining, as in the case of tramways, the option of purchase after twenty-one years, until 1898 the Council refused all applications. This was the result of recommendations made by the Gas Committee that the Council should apply to the Board of Trade for a provisional order to supply their own electricity, while the Committee also urged opposition to any measures calculated to reduce the Council's independence in this matter.[59] Having obtained the Provisional Order the year before, in 1891 the Electric Light Committee advised that the Council should undertake electric lighting 'in a tentative way, and in a form which will entail the least possible expenditure.'

In 1895 Market Place was illuminated by eight 4000 candle-power lamps, marking the opening of the Nottingham Electric Lighting Station, and one year later the Electric Light Committee pronounced the £45,000 project a success. Already, however, demand necessitated an immediate enlargement of the generating station, and although additions costing £40,000 were begun in 1896, a continued electricity shortage encouraged a private company to seek powers to supply electric power to those parts of the town which the municipal system had excluded, and, moreover, at lower rates. The Council rose to the challenge of competition by undertaking to supply the town at rates comparable with those quoted by the General Power Distributing Company. These pledges were made in the Council's opposition to the Bill, indeed additional works costing £150,000 were already in progress even as the Bill lay before Parliament, thereby anticipating the Company's defeat in the House later in 1899.[60] Thus electricity was tardily introduced to the town. The initial recommendation made by the Gas Committee was doubtless influenced by its own success in managing a municipal enterprise, but it is also probable that this success persuaded many Councillors that the establishment of another competitive municipal undertaking would be superfluous. The Electric Lighting Committee's cautious approach did not encourage quick action, while its recommendations were postponed for consideration so often that twelve years passed between the Gas Committee's approval of the provision of electricity by the Council and the opening of the generating station in 1895.

Acquisition of the town's four public utilities, construction of the new roads, street improvements, and measures connected with public health, in addition to the erection of new Council Offices, land purchase for recreation, and the provision of schools and cultural amenities which are yet to be considered, made large demands upon the financial resources of the new enlarged borough. The increasing complexity of detailed accounts had led to the reorganization of the accounts department in 1872 (when the double entry system was adopted), and after the Extension Act of 1877 the Finance Committee recommended the discontinuance of the Council's usual practice of mortgaging town property to finance large scale expenditures.[61] Under powers granted by the Nottingham Corporation Loans Act of 1880, the alternative adopted was the issuance of consolidated stock, and in this, Nottingham shared with Liverpool Corporation the distinction of pioneering in the field of municipal finance.[62] The Act enabled the Council to create £2,000,000 capital stock with $3\frac{1}{2}$ per cent. dividend; the actual issue of this was to be at the discretion of the Finance Committee while current loans were converted into consolidated stock. Since the time of completion and payment for the new Trent Bridge, after accepting obligations for maintenance and repair the general borough funds had been swelled by income from the Bridge Estate; but this sum was small compared with the Council's rapidly growing expenditures.[63] Rates in the new borough rose from 1s. 8d. in the pound in 1878 to 3s. $11\frac{1}{2}$d. in 1884, to 4s. 6d. in 1890, and reached 5s. 6d. in 1896.[64] This escalation was similar to that which occurred in other large towns, while the acrimonious debates which accompanied the annual rate-fixing were also familiar occurrences in council chambers throughout the country.[65]

Objections to rate increases became especially marked during times of depressed trade. In 1878, for example, the Finance Committee reduced the estimates submitted to it by the standing committees, and imposed a rate of only 1s. 8d. in the pound compared with 3s. $6\frac{1}{2}$d. in 1881. Rates continued to rise, but owing to a recession in the economy in 1887 estimates of the various committees were cut, and although a rate of 4s. 3d. was requested it remained at the previous level of 4s..[66] In the same year, a resolution passed requiring a second assent from the Council for any scheme of public improvement or works involving a loan of more than £500; this second sanction was to be received after at least one month following the scheme's adoption.[67] A proposal, introduced the next year, to cut the rate by reducing the salaries of Council officers was rejected. In 1892, after the Council had ordered the rate to be scaled down from the level recommended by the Finance Committee, the latter's Chairman, Edward Goldschmidt, resigned together with three other members.[68] Two years later, after the Finance Committee had once more received instructions to revise estimates and lower rates, the Committee reported that it had obeyed the Council's directive but only by postponing necessary public works; a rate of 5s. was adopted.[69]

One partial casualty in the rates battle was the scheme to build a new Guildhall. Under the Borough Extension Act the size of the Council had increased from fifty-six to sixty-four members, with the result that the accommodation available at the Council Chamber in Weekday Cross became inadequate. During one year of meetings held in the lecture hall of the Mechanics Institute, the Exchange Hall was converted into a Council Chamber,[70] but as the Council's permanent duties grew the need for more office accommodation became evident. Four years prior to the Extension Act a committee had been set up to investigate the possibliity of providing new municipal offices[71], but its recommendations were not taken up as they were overshadowed by the negotiations to form the larger borough. Recommendations included new buildings for Quarter Sessions and Police Courts, Public Library, University College, and Town Hall; but only the building of a new Court house had received the Council's approval.[72] Another report, issued in 1882, indicated the urgency of the Council's need for public offices, and the new Guildhall was begun in 1885. However, on the grounds that the cost of carrying forward the entire plan would involve higher rates, in 1884 the new municipal offices were abandoned; on their completion in 1888 the new Guildhall buildings in Burton Street housed the Police Courts, the Central Police Station, and the Fire Service.[73]

Before the rates began their rapid rise during the early eighties, the Council's acceptance of two conditional offers cast the Nottingham Town Council in the unusual roles of patron of the arts and of higher learning. In view of the Council's tardy adoption of the Free Libraries and Museums Act, it would be difficult to underestimate the contribution to the cultural life of the community by the individuals who made these offers, and the enthusiasm of a small number of councillors who espoused them almost as personal crusades. The first proposal came early in 1872 from the Director of South Kensington Museum, Henry Cole, whose contact with the Nottingham School of Art prompted his suggestion that a Museum of Science and Art might be established in the town. Cole envisaged an institution which would give prominence to illustrating the town's staple trades, and offered to make annual loans of material from the South Kensington Museum as a nucleus for the early exhibitions.[74] The Council accepted the offer immediately; it was agreed to use the Exchange Hall as the museum's temporary premises, its management to be entrusted to a committee which consisted of Council members and an equal number of representatives from the Committee of the Nottingham Government School of Art. During its first year the museum attracted one hundred and thirty-two thousand visitors, an attendance which encouraged the Committee to press immediately for permanent and more spacious facilities.[75]

Meanwhile, the Council had become the custodian for a natural history collection. This followed the burning down of the Mechanics Institute in 1867; the specimens in its museum had been saved from the conflagration, but lacked accommodation. The Naturalists Society then offered to add the Institute's collection to its own, which was then housed in rented premises in Wheeler Gate. The Institute's conditions for approval was that within two years the Society should secure more permanent premises for both collections. The Council's adoption of the Free Libraries and Museums Act, however, later led the Naturalists Society to propose the handing over of its library and its collection of specimens to the town, as the basis for a public natural history museum. The Council agreed, and in 1872 the Wheeler Gate free museum was opened to the public.[76] Between 1872 and 1874 the Museum Site Committee sought accommodation for natural history exhibits as well as fine art and some industrial artefacts. It was agreed that the natural history collection should have space in the new library building, but for the display of fine art the Committee favoured the Nottingham Castle, which was in the hands of the Trustees of the late Duke of Newcastle.

Led by W. G. Ward, the chief architect of the Council's scheme, the Committee succeeded in obtaining a lease of five hundred years, the rent for the first and second years set at £40 and fixed thereafter at £200 annually. Conditions in the lease required the Castle to be used solely for the promotion of general education and cultural recreation, for which the building must be altered to render it more suitable to perform its new function; for this purpose the lease stipulated a minimum of £15,000 expenditure.[77] These clauses were included in the Nottingham Improvement Act of 1874. So favourable was public response to a Council appeal for financial support that £9,000 was soon forthcoming, while the Council borrowed the remaining £6,000. From its opening in 1878 payment was required on admission, except upon one day each week; in 1888 free admission was allowed on two days, and in 1890 on four days each week. The character of the exhibitions held at the Castle were influenced more by the stipulations of the Trustees and the interests of the Committee, than the recommendations made by Cole in 1872, and initially stimulated interest in the scheme.[78] Thus the Castle Museum did not become a showcase for local artefacts and industrial technology for from its inception exhibitions of fine art were the Committee's main preoccupation. The enthusiasm of the Committee, and especially of W. G. Ward,[79] the response shown by the public, and the enlightened terms laid down by the Duke's Trustees, together produced a successful municipal venture to which the Prince of Wales at the ceremonial opening referred with great approval. He congratulated the town of Nottingham on taking the lead in such a worthwhile project, describing it as '. . . an example which I trust will speedily be followed by other municipal bodies in the United Kingdom'.[80]

A pioneer in the provision of a permanent municipal museum and art gallery, nevertheless the Council had lagged behind other provincial towns in providing a public library. Manchester Corporation had allowed only one year to pass before it adopted the Free Libraries Act of 1850,[81] and other towns had soon followed this example. In Nottingham, initiative in this matter was prompted by an offer of the financially embarassed Artisans' Library.[82] The latter offered its collection to the Council to form the basis for a free library on the condition that the library's debts of about £100 would be met by the Council. The result was that in 1867 the Council set up a Free Library Committee to investigate the operation of the Act and to compare library facilities in other towns with those of Nottingham. The Committee reached the conclusion that although a number of subscription libraries existed, the principal ones being the Nottingham Subscription Library, the Library of the Mechanics Institute and the Artisans' Library, their number was disproportionately small, and that therefore the town's library facilities should be increased.[83] The statutory meeting of ratepayers endorsed the Council's recommendation that Ewart's Act should be adopted, and in the same year the Thurland Street premises of the Artisans' Library became the home of the Nottingham Public

Library. The first Library Committee included Richard Birkin, A. J. Mundella, Lewis Heymann, and W. B. Rothera. During the first six months of the Library's existence in 1868, more than eleven thousand books were available to the 3,823 borrowers who enrolled, and the average daily issue stood at 422. By the end of the third year, in point of issues the Nottingham Public Library held fifth place in the whole country, the first four towns possessing much larger populations than Nottingham.[84]

Up to this time the largest of the town's libraries had been that at the Mechanics Institute, which also housed the beginnings of a museum and art gallery. Indeed, while the Mechanics Institute was the principal cultural centre in the district, its facilities for the further education of adults and young persons above school age also justify its claim to be the forerunner of the town's civic university, though instruction was well below that of university level.[58]

Support for the establishment of a local university dated from 1851 when Hugo Reid, a leading educationalist, had lectured at the Institute and had urged the establishment of a 'collegiate institution' in Nottingham where young men and women might receive instruction up to the age of twenty-one and twenty-two. Two people who supported him on the platform were Alderman Lewis Heymann, the lace manufacturer, and Richard Enfield, a member of the prominent local family of solicitors. The project had been welcomed by the *Nottingham Journal,* but it came to nothing for more than twenty years.[86] When the Council began to discuss the establishment of a university it was in response to initiative taken independently but which nevertheless involved the Council in the crucial decision. Twice in its recent history the Council had been placed in positions which were similar in principle to that in which it was to find itself in 1874. In the former instances the Council's actions had resulted in its committment to the maintenance of a library and a museum. The course adopted in the seventies in connection with the proposed university involved more than the employment of statutory powers; it required initiative, enterprise, and considerably greater financial resources than was needed to provide the community with a library and a museum and art gallery.

Prior to the Council's debate on the possibility of founding a municipal university, it had already become responsible for elementary education in the town, for by Forster's Education Act of 1870 local authorities had been drawn into the new national educational system. This Act sought to provide compulsory elementary instruction for all children, and was a logical sequel to the electoral increase which resulted from the household franchise act of 1867.

Before the Education Act the chapels and churches had been pace-

makers in the field of education, though considerable energy had
been absorbed in sectarian disputes.[87] Nevertheless, in 1868 leading
local churchmen and non-conformists met with the Mayor to discuss the advancement of elementary education in Nottingham.[88]
Four of these men later figured prominently in the establishment of
the university.[89] Two were members of the clergy, the Reverend John
Brown Paton, first principal of the Congregational College and a
supporter of the Mechanics Institute, and the Reverend Francis
Morse, vicar of St. Mary's Church. The other two were Richard
Enfield and George B. Rothera. Rothera was a lawyer who, during his term as a Councillor, had been connected with the establishment of the Nottingham Public Library. Richard Enfield was
one of the town's most distinguished figures and was involved in the
Sunday School Movement, the People's College, and the Mechanics'
Institute. The meeting was also attended by A. J. Mundella, leading educational campaigner and advocate of free education, and
the Reverend Stephenson, a Baptist minister. As a result of their
discussion, the following year saw the formation of a local branch
of the National Education League.[90]

In 1870 the Council applied for permission to establish a School
Board for the town in pursuance of the Education Act of that
year.[91] Under this Act, a voluntary system aided and supervised by
the state was left to compete with a state system working through
School Boards as local instruments. The Act did not destroy any
schools, provided that the inspectors judged them efficient, while it
sought to fill any existing gaps. For the first few years School Board
elections were closely contested by the supporters of denominational
schools, whose views were opposed by those who argued that the
appropriation of public funds to finance denominational instruction
in school was an abuse of public money. At the first election, which
took place in 1870, the Church or sectarian party succeeded in
securing only six of the thirteen places on the Board, but three years
later the sectarians resigned *en bloc* after one of the opposing faction had been returned at a bye election. One of the first tasks performed by the Board was to conduct a survey of education in Nottingham. The information collected showed that the town's shortage
of only several hundred school places to meet the requirements of
the Education Act was small, compared with deficiencies of between
eight and eleven thousand in Sheffield. However, in view of the
rising population the Nottingham Board resolved to apply for
Board Schools to accommodate two thousand children, adopting at
the same time the payment of fees and the principle of compulsion.
The School Board faced difficulties from two directions: parental
apathy, which in some cases was connected with the reluctance to

forgo the children's income from employment; and opposition by the Council to financing the School Board activities. In 1872 and again the following year the School Board threatened the Council with legal action unless their expenses were met. Despite initial Council hostility on account of the expenditure involved, the School Board made progress. In 1872 the British Schools in Duke's Place, which were connected with Stoney Street Chapel, transferred to the School Board, and in 1874 the first Board Schools which opened in Bath Street offered places for three hundred boys, three hundred girls, and two hundred and fifty infants.

In 1879 the People's College School, which had been previously conducted as a voluntary school with quite an advanced curriculum, was transferred to the School Board and recognized as a Higher Grade School. Attendance gradually increased, as in other towns, although irregularity and short periods of attendance were common. The new curriculum emphasized science and technical subjects, despite the fact that the three local schools already offered science and another art.[92] The Nottingham School Board acted with speed and enthusiasm, and by the middle eighties places provided by the Board Schools outnumbered those in voluntary schools. Between 1883 and 1886 places in voluntary schools increased by two hundred, from 16,166 to 16,366, while Board School places during the same period rose from 15,883 to 19,947. Expenditure increased to £21,000 in 1884 and to £31,000 in 1888, and when in 1897 £50,000 were spent, the Council began to levy a special town rate which in that year amounted to 1s. 3½d. in the pound.[94] By 1903 the Nottingham School Board had erected thirty-six new blocks of school buildings, equivalent to the growth of the child population.[95] In Nottingham, as in Sheffield schools, due to the vigilance of visitors and to the strict implementation of bye laws with respect to school attendance, attendance improved markedly during the eighties. In 1891 Nottingham raised its exemption from compulsory education from grade V to grade VI, abolishing all fees except at the four High Grade Schools, the predecessors of the modern grammar schools.[96]

After the initial friction that marred relations between the Council and the School Board, an uneasy relationship ensued. The Council proceeded to increase its newly-won stature in the sphere of education, achieving recognition in 1899 as local authority for the promotion of education. This followed the taking over by the Council of the Government School of Art and Design in 1888; this step was taken in order to save the school from closure through lack of finance. The Council had also been responsible for erecting a technical school facing Bilbie Street.[97] This development, which followed the Technical Instruction Act of 1889, was indicative of the general concern which was beginning to find expression over technical education, for it occurred after the local branch of the Committee of the National Association for the promotion of Technical Education had petitioned the Council to this effect. Thomas Hill, managing director of I.& R. Morley, pledged on the firm's behalf an annual subscription to support a local technical school; the Drapers' Company offered to donate £3,000 while the Plumbers' Company indicated its willingness to help to furnish such a school. The Council accepted these offers, and, after raising a loan of £6,000 to meet the major cost of finance, the schools were opened in 1893.[98] These activities tended to enhance the Council's reputation as an education authority, and the Council then attempted to destroy the power of the School Board and to assume the right to govern the town's elementary as well as its secondary education.

With these aims in view, in 1900 the Council resolved to promote an appropriate Bill to submit to Parliament. However, the Education Act of 1902 endowed all local authorities with the powers which the Council was seeking, and with the dissolution of the School Board the Council became the sole education authority for Nottingham.[99] The 1902 Education Act was important, too, inasmuch that it provided for a considerable improvement in secondary education, and this helped to remedy the situation whereby, owing to curtailment of instruction at the age of fourteen, young men and women from the working classes were ill-equipped for higher academic training at their own civic college. From its opening in 1881, however, provision had been made for the complete remission of fees to a number of meritorious students who must be resident in Nottingham.[100]

The history of Nottingham University College[101] brings us back to the role of the Council in the life of the town during the last quarter of the century, and in particular to the widening of its responsibilities to the community. It also recalls the important contributions made by a handful of enlightened middle class philanthropists and men of public spirit towards social organization in Nottingham,[102] for in the founding of the University College the two elements fused. It is important, therefore, that in the final chapter we should consider the development of the University College and the quality of civic leaders before ending with a brief survey of life in the Victorian City of Nottingham.

References

1 W. Ashworth, *The Genesis of Modern Town Planning*, (1954), p. 64.
2 D. Gray, *Nottingham Through Five Hundred Years*, (Nottingham, 1960), p. 207.
3 Edward Seaton, *The Sanitary Condition of Nottingham*, (Report of M.O.H., 1873).
4 D. Gray, *Nottingham Through Five Hundred Years*, (Nottingham, 1960), p. 212.
5 *Ibid.*
6 D. Gray, *Nottingham Through Five Hundred Years*, (Nottingham, 1960), p. 213; *B.R.*, IX, 312, November 17, 1884.
7 *B.R.*, IX, 345, May 5, 1890.
8 *B.R.*, IX, 305, November 12, 1883.
9 *B.R.*, IX., 287, July 11, 1881.
10 *B.R.*, IX, 95, November 15, 1852; 98, November 7, 1853.
11 H. Finer, *Municipal Trading*, (1941), p. 41.
12 Asa Briggs, *Victorian Cities*, (1963), p. 227.
13 *B.R.*, IX, 101, January 30, 1854.
14 Asa Briggs, *Victorian Cities*, (1963), p. 226.
15 *B.R.*, IX, 101, February 6, 1854.
16 Asa Briggs, *Victorian Cities*, (1963), p. 227.
17 D. Gray, *Nottingham Through Five Hundred Years*, (Nottingham, 1960), pp. 227–8.
18 *B.R.*, IX, 101, January 30, 1854.
19 H. Finer, *loc. cit.*
20 D. Gray, *loc. cit.*
21 *B.R.*, IX, 246, October 18, 1875; 250, September 11, 1876; 258, September 24, 1877; 265, August 12, 1878.
22 H. Finer, *Municipal Trading*, (1941), p. 49.
23 *B.R.*, IX, 231, October 24, 1873.
24 *Ibid.*
25 See *Report of an Enquiry by the Board of Trade into Working Class Rents, Housing, and Retail Prices*, 1908, (cd. 3864)) pp. 352–3.
26 *Ibid.*
27 B. D. White, *A History of the Corporation of Liverpool 1835–1914*, (Liverpool, 1951), p. 63.
28 *B.R.*, 232, November 12, 1873.
29 W. Ashworth, *The Genesis of Modern Town Planning*, (1954), p. 73.
30 *B.R.*, IX, 243, October 24, 1873.
31 *B.R.*, IX, 246, October 21, 1876.
32 *B.R.*, IX, 252, January 8, 1877.
33 *B.R.*, IX, 289, October 25, 1881.
34 Liverpool and Huddersfield were the other towns; *Accounts and Papers* (*Local Government*), 1889, p. 2.
35 *B.R.*, IX, 289, October 25, 1881; 303, July 2, 1883.
36 *Annual Report of M.O.H.*, to the Council, (Nottingham, 1900).
37 *B.R.*, IX, 396, July 4, 1898.
38 *Annual Report of M.O.H.*, to the Council, (Nottingham, 1900).
39 *B.R.*, IX, 105, November 27, 1854.
40 *B.R.*, IX, 375, April 1, 1895.
41 The mortality rates for Nottingham are to be found in the annual reports of the M.O.H., to the Council, 1873–1900.

[42] J. H. Clapham, *An Economic History of Modern Britain*, Vol. III, (1938), p. 460.

[43] *B.R.*, IX, 305, November 12, 1883. Between 1884 and 1900, Infant mortality rates in Nottingham varied between 10 and 25 per cent. above that of the national average figure. M.O.H. reports to 1900.

[44] *B.R.*, IX, 280, February 7, 1881.

[45] George Newman, *Infant Mortality, a Social Problem*, (1906), p. 103; Margaret Hewitt, *Wives and Mothers in Victorian Industry*, (1958) p. 148.

[46] D. Gray, *Nottingham Settlement to City*, (Nottingham, 1953), p. 78.

[47] D. Gray, *Nottingham Through Five Hundred Years*, (Nottingham, 1960), pp. 204–5.

[48] *Ibid.*, pp. 208–209.

[49] *Ibid.*, p. 208.

[50] *Ibid.*, p. 205–206.

[51] *Ibid.*, p. 215; *B.R.*, IX., 260, December 13, 1877; 255, February 19, 1877; 277, July 5, 1880, 276, June 7, 1880; 294, April 3, 1882.

[52] *B.R.*, IX, 326, July 1, 1886.

[53] D. Gray, *Nottingham Through Five Hundred Years*, (Nottingham, 1960), p. 215.

[54] *B.R.*, IX, 233, February 2, 1874.

[55] D. Gray, *Nottingham Through Five Hundred Years*, (Nottingham, 1960), p. 226.

[56] A. Briggs, *Victorian Cities*, (1963), p. 15.

[57] *B.R.*, IX, 394, April 4, 1898.

[58] D. Gray, *Nottingham Through Five Hundred Years*, (Nottingham, 1960), pp. 226–7.

[59] *Ibid.*

[60] *Ibid.*

[61] *Ibid.*, p. 211.

[62] Asa Briggs, *Victorian Cities*, (1963), p. 39.

[63] D. Gray, *Nottingham Through Five Hundred Years*, (Nottingham, 1960), p. 210.

[64] *Ibid.*, p. 211.

[65] Asa Briggs, *Victorian Cities*, (Nottingham, 1960), pp. 38–39.

[66] *B.R.*, IX, 266, December 12, 1878; 284, June 23, 1881; 331, June 13, 1887.

[67] *B.R.*, IX, June 29, 1887.

[68] *B.R.*, IX, 359, September 5, 1892.

[69] *B.R.*, IX, 369, May 28, 1894.

[70] D. Gray, *Nottingham Through Five Hundred Years*, (Nottingham, 1960), p. 205.

[71] *Ibid.*, p. 209.

[72] *Ibid.*

[73] *Ibid.*, p. 210.

[74] *Ibid.*, p. 220.

[75] *Ibid.*, p. 221.

[76] *Ibid.*, p. 222; A. C. Wood, *A History of the University College, Nottingham, 1881–1948*, (1953), p. 8.

[77] D. Gray, *Nottingham Through Five Hundred Years*, (Nottingham, 1960), p. 221.

[78] *Ibid.*

[79] R. Mellors, *Men of Nottingham and Nottinghamshire* (Nottingham, 1924), p. 226.

[80] *Ex.,* November 11, 1878.
[81] Asa Briggs, *Victorian Cities,* (1963), p. 133.
[82] D. Gray, *Nottingham Through Five Hundred Years,* (Nottingham, 1960), p. 221.
[83] *B.R.,* IX, pp. 184–187, May 16, 1867.
[84] *B.R.,* IX, 201, January 4, 1869.
[85] A. C. Wood, *A History of University College, Nottingham, 1881–1948,* (1953), p. 13.
[86] *Ibid.,* p. 7, f.n. 1.
[87] E. M. Becket, *The History of Education in Nottingham,* (unpublished Ph.D.thesis, University of London, 1933), pp. 92–98.
[88] *Ibid.,* p. 101.
[89] *Infra.* Chap. XIV.
[90] E. M. Becket, *op. cit.,* 104.
[91] The following account of educational developments in Nottingham is based on the thesis of E. M. Becket, *The History of Education in Nottingham,* (unpublished Ph.d. thesis, University of London, 1933), and N. Haycocks 'Nottingham as a centre of Education' in *A Century of Nottingham History, 1851–1951,* (Nottingham, 1951).
[92] N. Haycocks, 'Nottingham as a centre of Education,' *A Century of Nottingham History 1851–1951,* (1951), p. 49.
[93] *Ibid.,* p. 51.
[94] D. Gray, *Nottingham Through Five Hundred Years,* (Nottingham, 1960), p. 219.
[95] *Ibid.,* p. 49.
[96] *Ibid.*
[97] D. Gray, *Nottingham Through Five Hundred Years,* (Nottingham, 1960), p. 219.
[98] *B.R.,* IX, 344, January 6, 1890; *B.R.,* IX, 345, March 3, 1890.
[99] D. Gray, *Nottingham Through Five Hundred Years,* (Nottingham, 1960), p. 219.
[100] A. C. Wood, *A History of the University College Nottingham, 1881–1948,* (1953), p. 22.
[101] The following account is based on A. C. Wood, *A History of the University College, Nottingham, 1881–1948,* (1953), Chapters I–II.
[102] *Supra,* pp. 311–19.

CHAPTER XIV

VICTORIAN CITY: THE UNIVERSITY COLLEGE AND SOCIAL DEVELOPMENT

THE late sixties had seen the beginnings of university extension lectures when James Stuart, a recent graduate of Trinity College, Cambridge, lectured in towns such as Liverpool and Manchester, Sheffield and Leeds.[1] Stuart's campaign was warmly received in several of these places, and nowhere was stronger support forthcoming than from Nottingham, where a number of men, who were already campaigning for an improvement in elementary education, formed the nucleus of a crusade for higher education. Richard Enfield, the Reverend J. B. Paton, George B. Rothera, and the Reverend Francis Morse were joined in this crusade by Dr. W. H. Ransom, an eminent local medical practitioner who had supported the agitation for a free public library and who was an important figure in the Mechanics' Institute, and Louis Heymann, the leading lace curtain manufacturer who had been the town's first foreign-born Mayor and who, in 1844, had been instrumental in establishing the Nottingham School of Design, the fore-runner of the College of Art; Heymann was also a vice-president of the Mechanics' Institute. Another Nottingham Jew who played an important part in the development of higher education was an influential silk merchant, who was also a brewer, Edward Goldschmidt, although his support of the college plan—important owing to his influential position as chairman of the Council Finance Committee—occurred at a later stage of its early history.

In 1871 the need for higher education among working men was supplied chiefly by the Mechanics Institute, where the quality of instruction tended to be superficial. In that year a meeting of between fifty and sixty workmen carried a resolution, which had been proposed by Richard Enfield, indicating their support for the establishment of classes for instruction in 'those subjects most important to them as workmen, as fathers of families, and as sharers in the political power of the country'. To ensure that these classes would be of appreciably higher quality than the normal standard of lectures at the Institute, Enfield and Paton secured backing from trade unions, the Trades Council, and the Chamber of Commerce, and they persuaded Leicester and Derby to cooperate in forming a small lecture

362

circuit. In 1873 the Cambridge syndicate, which organized local lectures, consented to provide lecturing staff to conduct extension courses on this circuit, and although many of the working men found themselves out of their depth in the academic waters of Cambridge erudition, the lectures proved to be an encouraging success. Enfield, however, contended that the extension system must eventually lead to the establishment of local colleges. Indeed, this became Enfield's goal for Nottingham, and it is unlikely that mere chance prompted a friend to inform Enfield of his willingness to donate £10,000 towards the provision of a permanent centre where the extension lectures could be held. The donor, who remained anonymous but who is now thought to have been William, the son of Lewis Heymann, subsequently acted on the suggestion made by the extension lecturer in political economy that by a shrewd offer the Town Council might be persuaded to render assistance. The result was Enfield's letter to the town clerk delivered in January, 1875, in which the formal offer was made as follows:

If the Corporation will within a reasonable time (say twelve months from this date) erect buildings for the accommodation of the university lecturers to the satisfaction of the lecturers of the University of Cambridge, and on a site to be approved by the intending donor, and dedicate them to the use of such lecturers rent free, so long as the lecturers authorized by the syndicate . . . shall be conducting regular courses of instruction in Nottingham, then a friend of mine is prepared to place £10,000 in the hands of trustees . . . in support of such lectures . . .

By attaching conditions to his endowment for extension lectureships, the anonymous intending donor thus attempted to obtain from the Council a committment to build permanent accommodation for the extension classes.

The situation which caused the donor to be optimistic as to the success of this particular offer was the Council's current preoccupation with the erection of a building to house the new public library and the natural history museum. The combination of all three in one building was likely to appeal to the Council on grounds of economy, while from the students' standpoint it is difficult to imagine a more convenient arrangement. In 1875 the Council agreed to the scheme, and after some discussion the 'educational buildings' were erected in Shakespeare Street on Horse Fair Close, an area of land not far from the market place. On behalf of the donor, Richard Enfield became life member of a committee formed to manage the university extension building; the remainder of the Committee consisted of thirteen members of the Town

Council who were elected annually by the Council; five persons outside the Council, who were either resident in the town or within a five mile radius but who were elected each year by the Council; and up to four people selected yearly by large subscribers to the lecture fund. Building began in 1877, and the elaborate Gothic edifice was completed in 1881. Owing to revised estimates the Council had increased its contribution during these four years from the original sum of £37,000 to £61,000, a step which, after acrimonious debate, was sanctioned by a majority of fourteen votes out of fifty-seven. Taking into account land prices, on its completion the whole scheme cost nearly £100,000. The scheme drew comment from the national newspapers, and the *Times* leading article looked forward to the future development of the extension college into a new University of Nottingham. Excluding Oxford, Cambridge, London, and Durham, in 1877 the new institution in Nottingham was one of six provincial bodies which offered training at university level. Apart from Owens College, Manchester, founded in 1851; the College of Medicine at Newcastle, which grew out of the University of Durham in 1852, Queen's College, Birmingham, another College of medicine which opened in 1843 and which was followed by Mason College begun in 1875, Nottingham was one of four new institutions of higher learning set up during the seventies at Leeds, Bristol, and Liverpool.

During its earliest years the extension buildings became known as the University College, though this was not its official title (which remained unstated), and the principal part of the programme there consisted of technical instruction in the form of classes transferred from the Mechanics Institute. Anxious to promote technical education, in 1882 the Drapers' Company appealed to the Council for a grant in aid of forming classes in mechanical engineering, and for five years the City and Guilds Institute made an annual grant for this purpose. Another grant of £200 helped to finance the purchase of equipment, while further sums of money were donated by lace manufacturer, Councillor J. H. Jacoby, and hosiery manufacturer, F. C. Cooper. The new school of mechanical engineering accepted its first students in 1883. This development reinforced the vocational emphasis of the early curriculum at the University College and, apart from the extension lectures given by Cambridge teachers, the slender basis for continuous academic study at the College consisted in the preparation of students for three years, in order to enable them to qualify for two years further study towards a degree at Oxford or Cambridge (an exemption privilege which Nottingham was the first provincial college to obtain). In the eighties this was a minor function of the College, but its important influence upon the future development of the university was increased by the growing success of London's system of external degrees, which gradually led to a closer relationship between the Nottingham College and London.

The unique feature in the history of the College's foundation was the role of the Town Council. All other provincial universities had been launched by individual wealthy benefactors or by public subscription. At the time of the establishment of Nottingham University College, Jesse Boot was little more than a retailing chemist, and only in 1883 did he register his drug-manufacturing enterprise as a limited company.[2] Boot was busy laying the foundations of a fortune from which, in the twenties, the College was to benefit magnificently in the form of land, buildings, endowments, and money, amounting in total to something in the region of three-quarters to one million pounds. After initial outlay on buildings and equipment the annual current cost of operating the combined college, free library, and museum was reckoned at £6,500. More than £6,000 of this was met from municipal revenues, though in 1889 the College received a Treasury grant of £1,200 a year, which was raised to £1,500 seven years later. This followed the Treasury Inspector's favourable report on the operation of the new institution. The report commented that for the first time in the history of English education the governing body of an English town had assumed responsibility for the provision, organization, and maintenance of the higher and technical education of a community:

> That a municipal corporation should recognize the needs of higher education and that it should have the support of the community is a very remarkable thing . . . The College being thus supported mainly by the rates, may be said to be the most democratic institution of the kind which we have seen . . .[3]

Given the differing interests of the College staff and the Council, it would have been equally remarkable had this alliance between College and municipality been a completely harmonious one. Although, in theory, the thirteen municipal members of the committee of management shared their powers with up to fourteen persons unconnected with the Council, from the beginning the Council completely controlled the committee. For while the four committee members appointed by Oxford and Cambridge rarely attended, the Council occasionally failed to appoint the other five non-Council members: the right of certain large subscribers to elect up to four representatives also quickly disappeared. The management of the College was thus completely under the direction of the Council, while the Principal, who was one of the professors elected annually by the Council, lacked real powers. The handful of professors who taught at the College found themselves in an equally unsatisfactory relationship with their employer, and economy in staffing the college resulted in a wide range of subjects being taught by each man. In 1887 the College staff was affected by the Council's general economy drive, and Professor Blake, who held the chair of natural sciences and taught geology, biology, botany, geography, and physiology, and who had already been involved in a battle over salary with the Council, was asked to resign. Geography and physiology were, henceforward, excluded from the teaching programme, and not until 1893 was a new professor appointed. The teaching of classics also suffered from the cuts.

These measures might have indicated a lack of interest by the Council as to the content of the courses given by its professors, but the management committee became concerned when some of its members learned that Professor John Symes, who lectured on political economy, was using the socialist Henry George's *Progress and Poverty* as one of his texts. In 1887 Symes became the whipping boy for the Unionist press who accused him of propaganda in support of Irish home rule. Two years later Symes presided at a meeting of the Nottingham Social Democratic Federation at which William Morris spoke. Symes was immediately pilloried by the ratepayers who were aghast to see one of their professors flirting with the socialists, even though Morris's address, which he entitled 'Art and the Working Classes', was manifestly innocuous. Thus, between its foundation in 1881 and the end of the century, friction was characteristic of the relations between the College, and the Council and the general public. In terms of academic education, the development of the College was not greatly encouraged by municipal control, and as one historian has remarked,

> Disinterested and generous in spirit and purse though it had been, and remained to the end, it was incompatible with the freedom and responsibilities of a more adult status.

It was to be several decades, however, before the College achieved university status.

The establishment of Nottingham University College represented the culmination of several trends which underlined the character of English Victorian cities during the last quarter of the nineteenth century, for it was only through the exertions of philanthropic individuals (Paton, Enfield, and Heymann were also nonconformists) coupled with the acceptance of responsibility and the active participation of the Corporation, that the ideal was transformed into practical success. It reflected the greater assumption of responsibilities based on a wider conception of civic duty which flowered during these years. In other spheres humanitarian feeling became vigorously and more widely expressed. This was due in no small measure to the effects of unemployment in the eighties, which, by drawing attention to working class conditions, supplied proof that supplementary voluntary effort had failed to solve the problems of suffering, poverty, and ignorance. The feeling grew that such problems must be tackled with the aid of more legislation, increased state interference, and greater activity on the part of municipalities. Although, for the most part, reform had its roots in religion and philanthropy, the slumps of the late seventies and eighties sparked off a more radical current of opinion which stressed the removal of causes—hence the emergence of the Fabians and Socialism.

These developments in thought were reflected in municipal activities in Nottingham. The first Council flats were erected, while that body also formulated more stringent regulations with regard to the sanitation of new houses; the University College was founded, and the new technical school and Board Schools succeeded in improving the facilities for elementary and secondary education. The building of the boulevards and other main roads revealed that there was some conception of planning for the future, while profits from the gas and water undertakings were employed for the benefit of the community. Compared with local government in Leeds and Sheffield,[4] and despite the annual battles over the rates, the petty squabbles concerning the College, and the slow progress made in the sphere of public health and housing during the last quarter of the century, this was a period of significant municipal achievement in Nottingham.

The widening range of activities in which the Council became involved mirrored the interests and energies of the councillors, while the efficiency with which the Council operated depended on the quality of its growing staff of permanent officers. Between 1815 and 1870 the Enfield family had supplied the town with able town clerks, and on the resignation of William Enfield in 1870 the Council had made him an alderman in recognition of his services.[5] His successor, Samuel George Johnson, was not a local man and, unlike his predecessor, he was a full-time officer, continuing to hold his position for thirty-eight years until his death a year later.[6] Johnson was a firm opponent of the trend towards the centralization of control over local government affairs, and he supported Council policies consistent with this view. For example, in 1875, when reporting to the Council on the recent Public Health Act by which government grants could be obtained to contribute towards the salaries of a Medical Officer of Health and Inspector of

Nuisances, Johnson drew attention to the conditional clauses in the Act. If the grants were accepted, the appointment of the two officers concerned would be subject to regulations laid down by the Local Board of Health.

'Can local government, properly so called, be said to exist' Johnson demanded, 'while the actual power is centralized in the the Local Government Board?'[7]

The Council drew the appropriate conclusion to Johnson's rhetorical question and declined to accept the grant, preferring instead to preserve the Council's independence. Again, when he expressed his opinion concerning the move to centralize police superannuation funds he drew an analogy with the Greek horse which had brought about Troy's downfall.[8]

Johnson was a shrewd man, who, like Sir Joseph Heron, Manchester's outstanding town clerk,[9] was much more than a legal adviser, and influenced the Council's policies. For this he needed not only the Council members' respect for the abilities he showed in his official capacity as town clerk, but also tact and a strong personality. During one Council debate, an angry member accused him of being two-faced; Johnson replied: 'Nay, I am sixty-faced,' a reference to the sixty-four Councillors whose differing views Johnson sought to reconcile in order to carry all sections of the Council in a final decision. His success in negotiation was also manifest in his handling of the borough extension in the seventies.[10] A powerful figure in local government, Johnson held firm opinions concerning the role of municipal bodies and their responsibility to the community. Though a lawyer, he was prepared to act unlawfully if he thought that such an action would benefit the public interest. Before the town had appointed a Health Officer, a smallpox epidemic had occurred in 1871. With Johnson's sanction the Sanitary Committee had appointed Dr. Truman as public vaccinator under the title of temporary Medical Officer of Health, and, without legal authority, four thousand people were vaccinated. The legal responsibility for taking measures to check the epidemic lay with the Board of Guardians, but Johnson later explained, 'we could not wait while the people were dying for the Board of Guardians to act.'[11] The Council again acted illegally in 1874 when the Great Northern Canal Company was paid to flush out the Nottingham Canal whose dangerously insanitary condition was caused by sewage which flowed in from the Leen. A similar threat to public health from insanitary wells caused the Council to force their closure, leaving the owners to bring action if they wished. Because the poor would not buy disinfectant, it was also the Council's practice to distribute it to families who lived in the lower parts of the town. Johnson admitted that some of the Council's actions were illegal, but he declared that a town would be worthless if it lacked spirit to act in the public interest.[12] After a lifetime of valuable service, Johnson retired through ill health in 1908; his outstanding career having earned for him the honour of a knighthood in 1893, a secure post on his resignation, and the honorary freedom of the city whose history he did so much to shape.[13]

Two other permanent officials contributed much to municipal progress in Nottingham after 1860. One of these was Marriott Ogle Tarbotton who, in 1859, was appointed as the first full-time surveyor-engineer to the borough estates and to the Local Board of Health. As the Council's activities grew, Tarbotton was also given the management of the gas and water undertakings and of the sewage works, though his burden was lightened somewhat in 1880 when his assistant, Arthur Brown, took over the post of Borough Surveyor and Engineer. Tarbotton retained the combined appointment until his death in 1887, after which three separate posts were created.[14] The progress made in the town's drainage system was largely the result of Tarbotton's repeated exhortations to the Council, while the regional sewage system, begun in the seventies, was a tribute to Tarbotton's vision and ability as a professional engineer. Dr. Edward Seaton, who was appointed Medical Officer of Health for Nottingham in 1873, was the other salaried official whose efforts to promote town improvement contributed towards municipal progress. His firm opposition against a majority of the town's doctors on the issue of compulsory notification of infectious diseases showed Seaton's conviction that it was the responsibility of local authorities to take the initiative in matters which affected public health. He had argued that without notification,

'the town is practically at the mercy of some medical man to whom all considerations of public health are subordinate to the private interests of those who employ him'. He had continued: 'Many persons may find it difficult now to meet the expense of medical attendance, but we should hardly expect to lessen that difficulty by allowing disease to go spreading unchecked'.[15]

Seaton resigned from his post at Nottingham in 1884, after the Council had refused to accept the recommendation made by the Health Committee that his salary should be increased by one-third. The Committee had proposed that the Council should accept grant aid to pay one-half of his increased salary under the Public Health Act of 1875, but the Council adhered to the principles expounded by its eloquent town clerk, and in so doing lost an able and energetic health officer.[16] His successor, Dr. Whitelegge, stayed for only four years, but Phillip Boobyer, hitherto the health officer of the Basford

Union, was appointed to Whitelegge's post in 1899, and remained in that office until after 1900.

To the extent that there was truth in one conclusion drawn by a contemporary student of local administration, namely that the excellence of municipal government bore a direct relationship to the influence of the permanent officials,[17] much credit is due to Nottingham's own salaried administrators who, during the final three decades of the century, were instrumental in shaping the town's development. The rate of progress that could be achieved by the officials who constituted the administrative sub-structure of municipal government, depended upon the pace set—or allowed—by the local governing body which employed them. Thus the involvement and calibre of members of the Council was still of paramount importance in determining the course of town development. When a contemporary included Nottingham among other medium-sized parliamentary towns, like Derby, where the councils consisted, according to him, not of

> persons of influence or position in the town . . . but of persons in the lower ranks of life, who have accumulated a little property, and who wish to obtain a position in the town,[18]

he showed an extremely superficial knowledge of the social composition of the Nottingham Town Council. Writing in 1875, G. C. Broderick remarked that the wealthiest capitalists in manufacturing centres failed to find gratification in the government of towns, implying that municipal government could not provide problems of management and administration comparable with those encountered in industry and trade, and that the social rewards to be expected were inadequate to overcome the sense of self-importance of the richest businessmen. These were the reasons he offered to explain why the town councils remained outside the orbit of many of the country's ablest practical men of affairs.[19] It is likely that Broderick might have excluded Nottingham from this generalization on the grounds that the character of local industry was such that, compared with the cotton lords of Manchester or the merchants of Liverpool, very few of Nottingham's capitalists could claim to be included among the nations's wealthiest business magnates, and their horizons, therefore, were more restricted.

It is not true, however, that the town's richest capitalists shunned municipal office. At the time when Broderick was writing, the Nottingham Town Council included a number of leading local manufacturers whose participation in the government of the town during the middle decades of the century was coming to an end.[20] The most influential men in local government, the aldermen, still included among their number William Vickers, the eminent lace manufacturer who had been elected mayor in 1843; Thomas Cullen, also a former lace manufacturer, but described in the directories as 'gentleman', and who was twice mayor of Nottingham (in 1852 and 1860); J. L. Thackeray, mayor in 1854 and 1866, a cotton doubler; and lace manufacturer J. Reckless, who filled the mayoral office in 1853. The leading hosiery manufacturer, A. J. Mundella, was completing almost twenty years of Council membership. Sir James Oldknow, mayor in 1869 and 1878, was another alderman lace manufacturer, while W. Lambert, principal of the firm of lace dressers, bleachers, and dyers was mayor in 1875.

Lambert, who was elected mayor a second time in 1855, also held a directorship on the board of the Nottingham & Nottinghamshire Banking Company and was chairman of the Nottingham Real Estate Investment Company.[21] From the 1870's his most enduring achievements were those made in his capacity as chairman of the Public Parks and Recreation Committee, for during his years in office he secured no fewer than four public parks; he was also instrumental in the formation of the Victoria Embankment Park scheme begun in 1898. After acting as a member of the Improvement Committee during the years when the borough extension was planned and negotiated, lace manufacturer W. G. Ward, mayor of Nottingham in 1871 and 1878, was remembered as the prime mover in the Council scheme to establish the municipal Castle Art Gallery and Museum.[22]

Two outstanding entrepreneurs who joined the Council in the early seventies were Edward Goldschmidt and John Turney, but already in 1874 they had become members of the powerful Finance Committee. The former eventually resigned through ill health in 1895, Turney retiring after forty-six years of valuable service with the Council. Goldschmidt had emigrated to England and settled in Nottingham in 1851, setting up as a wholesale stationer two years later. By 1861 he had become an importer of silk and a silk throwster, and became chairman of the Nottingham Brewing Company in 1870. Goldschmidt was chairman of the Finance Committee for twelve years, and was instrumental in piloting the University College scheme through the Council.[23] Turney began as a leather manufacturer, but acquired directorships of numerous companies in the course of his career. In 1900 he was chairman of the Raleigh Cycle Company, Clifton Colliery Company, Hall's Glue and Bone Works Ltd., Murray Bros. & Co., and the Masonic Hall Co. He was an alderman for twenty-three years, and during that time acted as chairman of the important General Works and Highways Committee and the Electric Lighting Committee.[24] Goldschmidt was twice elected mayor, in 1881 and again in 1889; Turney also filled this office twice (in 1886 and 1887), after which, in recognition of his services to municipal government, Turney received a knighthood.[25] Edward Gripper, a Londoner who moved to Nottingham in 1855 to establish the huge Builders' Brick Company at Mapperley, also joined the Council in the seventies becoming mayor in 1880, and in later life spent up to six hours daily on public affairs.[26] Besides acting as chairman of the School Board for thirteen years, for some time he was chairman of the successfully managed municipal water supply. An equally able local figure, John Barber, a member of the old-established Nottingham family of grocers, was responsible for the negotiations which resulted in municipal ownership of the gas supply. Barber, who was a member of the Council for fifty-four years, was largely responsible for the early financial success of the gas undertaking.[27] Anderson Brownsword, who served on the Council from 1886 and became mayor in 1892, was a silk merchant. He was also chairman of three companies, City Tramways, Thomas Bayley & Co., and B. Walker & Co.[28] E. H. Fraser, mayor of Nottingham for three consecutive terms beginning in 1896 following twenty years of Council activities, was a solicitor by profession, but he held directorships in three large companies and was chairman of the Nottingham Permanent Building Society.[29]

During the last quarter of the century local industry provided the Council with several more aldermen, albeit somewhat smaller in public stature than those already listed. These included J. P. Ford, box manufacturer, Robert Dennett, building contractor; T. R. Starey, coach builder; F. J. Perry, lace manufacturer, and H. S. Cropper, principal of a large engineering works. The occupations of the other aldermen ranged from solicitor, like Frederick Acton who was an alderman for eleven years, and Joseph Bright, elected mayor in 1894 and 1895, to grocer, like John Manning who was also a bank director, and who was elected in 1870, 1875, and 1883, and John Bowers, who filled that office in 1876. During the last twenty years Nottingham's mayors also included a director of the *Nottingham Daily Express,* a bank director, a pharmaceutical chemist, and a draper.[30]

One must conclude that perhaps because few of the town's industrialists could claim to rival the industrialists whose businesses were conducted on a very large scale, a national reputation in public life lay beyond their grasp; A. J. Mundella was the only exception, for Samuel Morley, principal of the important Nottingham hosiery firm, who also became a member of parliament for Nottingham as did his son Arnold, was born in London and managed the company from the London warehouse. The conclusion emerges that a number of local manufacturers showed a willingness to belong to an urban aristocracy which fulfilled its social obligations by serving the community as Council members. Furthermore, the introduction of municipal trading and the growing scale of finance involved in local government and town improvement increased the value and importance of bringing business perspective to bear upon many problems. At the municipal elections in 1877 the editor of the *Nottingham and Midland Counties Daily Express* argued that the quality of the municipal body depended upon the balance of brain and business capacity which its members possessed.[31]

Aldermen, among whose numbers many of the urban aristocracy were to be found, accounted for only one-quarter of the total Council membership, furthermore there is evidence to suggest that the power of the aldermen declined somewhat after 1879. The Council had long been liberal in the extent to which it had delegated power to standing committees whose chairmen together constituted the Finance Committee. But by this time, rapidly rising expenditure caused the reformulation of the Council-committee relationship after the Standing Orders Committee's report had recommended that the Council should possess complete control of finance. Henceforward, all committee expenditures were administered by the Council, and any innovations which entailed new expenditures first required its sanction.[32] From 1879, therefore, councillors, as distinct from aldermen, increased their powers, and this helps to explain the fierce disputes that took place between the committees and the general Council, where during the last quarter of the century the proportion of 'persons in the lower ranks of life,' the small property owners and tradesmen, was increasing.[33] Nevertheless, the last two decades of the century—but especially the eighties, when Turney and Goldschmidt four times filled the mayoral office—were years of municipal progress. Taken together, these facts tend to support the contention that the calibre of municipal leadership was a more important influence upon the quality of local government than the biasses of councils' social composition.[34] Although the Trades Council had formed a Labour Representation Committee in 1885 in order to secure the candidature of a trade unionist,[35] the Council had refused to hold evening meetings. This meant that even if working class candidates were to be elected they would be unable to attend meetings,[36] though in 1890 two Liberals were returned as 'direct labour representatives.' As for the general political composition of the Council, the Liberals were still in control, though the party itself was a somewhat more democratic body than when the Whig-Liberal caucus had dominated its activities until the reforms of the sixties. The number of Conservative representatives, however, increased during the last quarter of the century, and by 1900 there were twenty-two Conservative Councillors and twenty-six Liberals.[37] The movement towards political parity also helps to explain an increase in the intensity of Council disputes during the last two decades of the century, for the Conservatives tended to become identified as the party which opposed the rapid rise in municipal expenditure, a key issue in municipal affairs.

In 1897 Council members of both parties rejoiced to become governors of a city, the title which, in the year of Queen Victoria's Diamond Jubilee, Her Majesty had granted to Nottingham, an acknowledgement of the many important changes that had taken place in the town since the Enclosure Act of 1845. By the closing years of the century the old town was rapidly becoming a service centre for factories which, as a result of late enclosure, were concentrated in the suburbs at Radford, Lenton and Basford, and for the industrial villages beyond, especially Long Eaton. The warehouses and offices of lace and hosiery manufacturers were located mainly in the vicinity of the Lace Market where the narrow streets and steep gradients still evoke some of the atmosphere of mid-Victorian Notingham, while Market Place and the streets surrounding it continued to be the chief retailing and commercial centre. To the west, around the site of the Castle, were situated more commercial premises, offices, and residential streets which reached the large villas and spacious gardens of the exclusive Park Estate. South of the market place, and beyond the limits of the old borough in the Meadows area, tall factories and working class housing indicated the geographical segregation of major social groups within the old town.

The advent of tram and bicycle had encouraged the outward drift of population which, owing to the tardy enclosure of the town's immediate environs, the dispersion of industry had encouraged. Enclosure and novel forms of transport had also affected the manner in which people spent their leisure hours. Building development that had taken place since 1845 meant that open spaces which might have been used for recreational purposes were gradually swallowed up. However, the Council Public Parks and Burial Grounds Committee, for many years under the chairmanship of W. Lambert, had recognized that the Arboretum and the walks formed in 1845 would be inadequate to meet the needs of the rising urban population, and under the Improvement Act of 1879 the Committee had negotiated for the acquisition of Bulwell Forest, fifty acres of which were to be used as parkland.[33] Four years later St. George's Close, near Queen's Walk, was set aside for recreation, and in 1888 the Gregory Trustees allotted land at Lenton, just off Derby Road, as another public park.[39] The Society of Friends made its contribution in 1886 when two burial grounds, known as the Walnut Tree and Mount Street Burial Grounds, were formed into public recreation grounds.[40] Thus by the close of the century Nottingham possessed considerable areas of parkland, which the trend towards reduced working hours offered greater opportunities to enjoy.

After about 1860, changes in the timetables of factories and warehouses and greater control over the hours of work in workshops and private homes made possible more frequent trips away from the growing town, and at the same time encouraged the formation of sports clubs which were able to meet regularly. In 1861 many hosiery manufacturers in Nottingham had replaced holidays taken at the time of the races, the fair, and on other special occasions, with a regular half-holiday on Saturdays.[41] However, long hours of work continued to absorb most weekday evenings, while the majority of hosiery workers remained outside the factories until the last quarter of the century. Intermittent agitation to obtain the Saturday half-holiday in warehouses had begun in 1856, but although some employers were beginning to comply with this demand by 1870, it was not until after pressures from employees in the early seventies that the timetables of lace warehouses became similar to those in hosiery establishments. This renewed agitation for shorter working hours was inspired by the successful introduction into the town in 1871 of the nine hours movement, when one short strike by the engineers had been followed by a general agreement in 1872.[42] While other sections of the population were enjoying reduced working hours—and in the eighties were pressing for an eight hour day—the shop assistants waited until 1880 before mounting a determined campaign to secure the weekly half-holiday. This object was achieved by many assistants shortly afterwards, and in 1883 the Nottingham Thursday Half-Holiday Association held its first annual excursion.[43]

Shorter working hours, improved communications, and a rising standard of living for most people during the last quarter of the century, made it possible to escape temporarily from the growing conurbation. For those people for whom a stroll in a park was a poor substitute for a tramp through meadow and coppice, developments during this period were of especial importance, for as Nottingham became linked by rail with nearby towns and villages the railway companies developed excursions to attract the rambler and the cyclist. In the nineties the Midland Railway Company drew up a list of twenty-seven stations around Nottingham to which a passenger might book a ticket, make his own way to another, returning thence to Nottingham.[44] One major innovation which altered the pattern of recreation during the last quarter of the century was the cycle, and although until the introduction in 1879 of the first chain-

driven safety model, cycling was a sport of athletes, in 1882 a
reporter for the *Nottingham Daily Express* declared,

> tricycles, which are very fashionable in London, appear to be
> rather more popular in Nottingham and it is nothing unusual to
> see them carrying a lady along the country roads.[45]

Half-holidays attracted Nottingham cyclists to Wollaton, Stapleford, and Bramcote, although the sports enthusiasts, like the members of the Nottingham Cycling Club founded in 1876 and which
was the second oldest in Britain, held races at Trent Bridge.

Trent Bridge was also a centre for amateur athletics where
after 1868 regular meetings were held, the events including shot
putting, pole jumping, and throwing the cricket ball, besides the
usual foot races; the Nottinghamshire Lawn Tennis Association,
established in 1886, also held annual tournaments here.[46] But the
Trent Bridge continued to be the shrine of Nottinghamshire cricket.
The County Championship Competition was introduced in 1860,
but not until 1873, when they tied with Gloucestershire, did the
Nottinghamshire team achieve premier honours. Nottinghamshire
were sole champions in 1875, and they shared the honour with
Lancashire four years later, as they did again in 1882. But in 1880,
and from 1883 to 1886 inclusive, Nottinghamshire won the competition. Their win in 1889, when Lancashire and Surrey were also
co-champions, was the last of this impressive series of victories until
1907,[47] and this must be partly attributed to the retirement of
Nottinghamshire's outstanding all-England cricketer, William Gunn.

Gunn, who opened a sports outfitting store in Nottingham, also
represented his country playing association football,[48] a sport which
aroused increasing enthusiasm in the hearts of the town's menfolk.
Indeed, although a Sheffield Club, which was formed in 1857, is the
oldest club in existence, the Nottinghamshire County Football
Club, established in 1862, remains the oldest existing club in the
Football League.[49] In 1865, two years after the Football Association
was founded, Nottingham Forest Football Club was formed. The
League Championships eluded both clubs until the end of the cen-
tury, but Notts. Forest reached the semi-final of the F.A. Cup in
1878–9, while Notts. County played in the 1891 Cup Final. Three
years later, local football supporters cheered a victorious Notts.
County whose win against Bolton brought the cup to Nottingham.
In 1898 the cup returned to Nottingham when Forest defeated
Derby County.[50]

Another sport whose popularity dates from about the same time
is rowing, and following the formation of the Nottingham Trent
Aquatic Club in 1845, Regattas began to take place on the river. In
1862 the Nottingham Rowing Club was formed, and this was

followed by the appearance of the Nottingham Britannia Rowing
Club in 1869, the Nottingham Union Rowing Club in 1871, and the
Nottingham Boat Club in 1894. Sailing enthusiasts formed the Trent
Valley Sailing Club in 1887.[51] Swimming in the Trent had long been
a popular pastime and in 1857 the Council had provided changing
rooms and the services of a paid attendant for the benefit of bathers
in the Trent Bridge area; subsequently bathing accommodation was
extended.[52] During the last quarter of the century the Council opened
several baths in various parts of the enlarged borough, including
the Victoria Baths which were built on the site of the Gedling Street
Baths in 1896.[53] The Nottingham Swimming Club was formed in
1880. While the Council was thus providing facilities for the town's
swimmers it also sought to protect public rights of fishing, though a
Fishing Rights Bill, drawn up in 1887, was eventually dropped.[54] In
1899 the Nottingham Anglers' Protection Association urged the
Council to allow it to take over the fishing in the River Trent on land
acquired by the Council where it bordered the river.[55] Angling clubs
grew in number during the late nineteenth century, the Nottingham
Piscatorial Society, founded in 1891, being one of the many bands
of fishermen who journeyed to Shardlow, Clifton, Colwick, Burton
Joyce, Hoveringham, and Hazelford to enjoy their sport. These were
also popular destinations for the Nottingham Society of Artists
whose members travelled by train to sketch and paint in the country-
side.[56]

Horse racing was on the decline in Nottingham, nevertheless the
Duke of Portland was still one of the foremost patrons of the turf
and in 1879 nine horses from his stables between them won thirty-
four races, bringing the Duke's total prize-winnings for that year to
£74,000.[57] But by the closing decades higher prizes offered at the
Derby and Leicester courses succeeded in attracting more competitors to those towns, to the detriment of the Nottingham meetings;
though it was the Council's reluctance to continue to play the role
of racing impresario which resulted in the final discontinuance of the
Forest meetings from 1891.[58] The town was not deprived of horse
racing, however, for another course was acquired by the Colwick
Racing and Sporting Company at Colwick on the banks of the
Trent.[59]

The second half of the century saw the growth of commercial
entertainment in Nottingham. The town's numerous musical
societies, to which had been added the Mechanics Operatic
Society, catered largely for performers and audiences with refined
tastes in music. By 1867 Nottingham already possessed two music
halls and the Old Malt Cross Music Hall opened in 1877. A typical
Victorian Music Hall, the Old Malt Cross was a licensed house

AA

which also served grills; at week-ends a number of popular musical attractions were presented to increase custom, when 'order and decorum (were) most rigidly enforced.' The town's chief successful Music Hall, however, was 'The Talbot Palace of Varieties' which opened in Market Street in 1876.[60] The Talbot had formerly housed the Alexandra Skating Rink, but it continued successfully as a palace of varieties until 1887, when it became the Temperance Theatre of Varieties. By 1900 bolder spirits had prevailed, and the Gaiety Palace of Varieties opened its doors to the public. In 1898 the Nottingham Empire Music Hall opened, while public dancing at the Victorian Halls was another popular attraction.[61] Thus Nottingham at the turn of the century was a thriving centre of popular entertainment.

Entertainment which might also be described as popular, but of a less innocent character, could be found in Parliament Street and in the lesser lanes of that vicinity where, in order to avoid police supervision, the proprietors of notorious establishments similar to 'Prew's Rooms' in Kingston Arms Yard disguised prostitution behind the facade of Working Men's Clubs.[62] Inflamed by excessive consumption of beers and spirits, uncontrolled passions sometimes turned the streets in the centre of Nottingham into a minor battleground and, according to one observer in 1879, Long Row was often the scene of fights and brawls, where by eleven each night 'the fun was fast and furious with Bacchus, monarch of the Row.'[63]

Although the temperance movement had been alive in Nottingham for many years, it was during the seventies that protests against the growing prevalence of drunkenness and immorality gathered strength. Thus 1878 saw the establishment of the Nottingham Temperance Mission and the formation of a local branch of the Church of England Temperance Society. The Nottingham Town and County Social Guild was also much concerned with the problems of drunkenness and immorality, and in 1879 the Guild appointed a committee to investigate the particular effects of Goose Fair in this connection. Several medical men expressed the view that it promoted seduction and venereal diseases; members of the ministry were of the opinion that the Fair encouraged intemperance and moral laxity, it was the time 'when Templars break their pledges most often' and, according to Reverend Samuel Cox, the Fair effected more harm in a week than we preachers can do in a year.'[64]

Safer from such temptations of the flesh were the growing numbers of men who belonged to Nottingham's clubs which catered for the town's businessmen and men from the professions. The Nottingham County Club, which was run in a similar manner to the gentlemen's clubs in London, opened in Victoria Street in 1864 and quickly enrolled two hundred and sixty members. The Town Club was established in 1873 and the Nottingham Liberal Club opened in the same year. It was followed in 1879 by the opening of the Nottingham Conservative Club.[65]

Three years before the century closed, a new society was established whose members' common interest was the county's own history. The Thoroton Society of Nottinghamshire, founded in 1897, was, and continues to be, an acknowledgement of the interest and affection which the city and the region could arouse in its people. The achievement of city status in the same year emphasized the changes that had taken place, while the formal manifestation of a desire to learn more of the city's history chimed happily with this historic event. Greater Nottingham had forfeited much of the intimacy and colour of the compact mid-Victorian town, for the closely-knit community was being gradually replaced by a sprawling conurbation. But the city constituted a community nonetheless, and in some ways it contrasted favourably with the more intimate urban society which had existed fifty years before. Industrial progress, to which the external benefits from urbanization were contributory factors, had improved living standards; the growth of new industries and their effects upon occupational distribution in the town had greatly reduced the threat of local depression comparable in extent with those of the first half of the century, even though in the nineties both lace and hosiery manufacturers had found it increasingly difficult to hold markets against foreign competitors.

Through the rates and taxes which they paid and the services they received, in their daily lives the people of Nottingham were affected by public bodies to an extent which would have seemed almost inconceivable in 1851, the year when, in characteristic mid-Victorian fashion, Mayor William Felkin had reaffirmed his faith in individualism and progress. Since that time the franchise had twice been extended, while there had arisen greater concern for the social costs which had accompanied the growth and localization of industry. Furthermore, armed with powers conferred by central authority, municipal bodies had begun to accept wider responsibilities for the health, education, and cultural environment of its people. Nottingham in 1900 was an administrative, commercial, and service centre for its region; it was also the focus of political and social activities, a centre in which increasingly democratic institutions supplemented voluntary effort in meeting the cultural needs of a city population numbering nearly a quarter of a million people.

Nottingham stands with other Victorian cities whose ancient past had long since placed them in the forefront of national affairs. During the industrial revolution the advance of the great new urban

AA*

centres of Manchester and Birmingham, and indeed many other northern industrial towns, outstripped the development of most historic centres. Early in the nineteenth century Nottingham had been one of several old towns whose urban vigour depended on the prosperity of their staple trades. In Nottingham, as in some other towns, the staple industry stagnated; but whereas in Bristol and Coventry, for example, the transformation of the local economy awaited the second half of the century, the readjustment in Nottingham began much earlier. For much of the nineteenth century the city's fortunes depended largely upon the growing but fluctuating demands of Victorians at home and abroad for articles made of lace. Furthermore, the development of new industries, producing goods which were as characteristic of twentieth century habit and taste as was Nottingham lace of the middle and late Victorian decades, formed an economic foundation for urban progress. The history of Nottingham shows the advantages and disadvantages of its position as an old provincial centre during a period of rapid economic and social change. In an established community where tradition and entrenched interests were powerful there were strong impediments to change, and the transformation of existing institutions, rather than the creation of new ones, exercized the minds of the city fathers. Nevertheless, while the postponement of enclosure retarded development until the second half of the century, the existence of a provincial culture in which a tradition of civic pride was an important part provided the basis for continuing vitality in urban life. Sensible of their city's historic past, two of Nottingham's Victorian historians writing in 1893 acknowledged their awareness of continuity through change:

> Amid the unresting roll of our modern machinery and the din of today's business we may hear, if we only listen, the voices of a venerable past.[66]

Achievements in the Victorian age had enabled the city's progress to continue; the Victorians, these men seemed to imply, would not be judged as failures by succeeding generations.

References

[1] The following account is based on A. C. Wood, *A History of the University College, Nottingham,* 1881–1948, (1953), Chapters I–II.

[2] *Supra,* p. 241.

[3] Quoted, *B.R.,* IX, p. 391, October 4, 1897.

[4] Asa Briggs, *Victorian Cities,* (1963), p. 239.

[5] D. Gray, *Nottingham Through Five Hundred Years,* (Nottingham, 1960), p. 205.

[6] *B.R.,* IX, 208, July 25, 1870.

[7] Quoted by D. Gray, *Nottingham Through Five Hundred Years,* (Nottingham, 1960), p. 207.

[8] *Ibid.,* p. 208.

[9] Asa Briggs, *Victorian Cities,* (1963), p. 241.

[10] R. Mellors, *Men of Nottingham and Nottinghamshire,* (Nottingham, 1924), p. 260.

[11] *Report from the Select Committee on Municipal Boroughs* (1874) ev. of Samuel Johnson, p. 8.

[12] *Ibid.*

[13] D. Gray, *Nottingham Through Five Hundred Years,* (Nottingham, 1960), p. 236.

[14] *Ibid.,* p. 228.

[15] *B.R.,* IX, 297, July 13, 1882.

[16] D. Gray, *Nottingham Through Five Hundred Years,* (Nottingham, 1960), pp. 207–8.

[17] A. L. Lowell, *The Government of England, II,* (1908), p. 179.

[18] G. C. Broderick quoted by Asa Briggs, *Victorian Cities,* (1963), p. 237.

[19] *Ibid.*

[20] The personnel of Nottingham Town Council is given in Wright's directories, See *Wright's Nottingham Directory, 1874–1900.*

[21] J. Potter Briscoe, *Nottinghamshire and Derbyshire at the Opening of the Twentieth Century,* (Nottingham, 1901), p. 188.

[22] R. Mellors, *Men of Nottingham and Nottinghamshire,* (Nottingham, 1924), p. 226.

[23] J. Potter Briscoe, *Nottinghamshire and Derbyshire at the Opening of the Twentieth Century,* (Nottingham, 1901), p. 182.

[24] *Ibid.,* p. 197.

[25] *B.R.,* IX, 337, January 7, 1889.

[26] R. Mellors, *Men of Nottingham and Nottinghamshire,* (Nottingham, 1924), p. 232.

[27] *Ibid.*

[28] J. Potter Briscoe, *Nottinghamshire and Derbyshire at the Opening of the Twentieth Century,* (Nottingham, 1901), p. 175.

[29] *Ibid.,* p. 136.

[30] Brief sketches of the town's leading citizens are to be found in R. Mellors, *Men of Nottingham and Nottinghamshire,* (Nottingham, 1924), and J. Potter Briscoe, *Nottinghamshire and Derbyshire at the Opening of the Twentieth Century,* (Nottingham, 1901).

[31] *Ex.,* November 2, 1877.

[32] *Supra,* p. 348.

[33] The Trade directories allow identification of each Council member by occupation.

[34] Asa Briggs, *Victorian Cities,* (1963), p. 238.

[35] *Minutes of the Joint Committee of the United Trades Council,* April 15, 1885.
[36] *B.R.,* IX, 329, March 7, 1887.
[37] Results of the annual November municipal elections were published in the local newspapers.
[38] D. Gray, *Nottingham Through Five Hundred Years,* (Nottingham, 1960), p. 223.
[39] *Ibid.*
[40] *B.R.,* IX, 326, July 1, 1886.
[41] *Children's Employment Commission, First Report,* 1863, (3170), XVIII, p. 267, ev. of J. and H. Hadden, ev. of Thomas Ashwell.
[42] *Ex.,* December 16, 1871; *Ex.,* November 21, 1871; *Ex.,* November 29, 1871.
[43] *N.J.,* February 25, 1880; *N.J.,* July 5, 1889.
[44] *City Sketches,* (Nottingham, 1898–9).
[45] *Ex.,* July 8, 1872.
[46] *V.C.H., Notts.,* II, p. 419.
[47] F. S. Ashley-Cooper, *Nottinghamshire Cricket and Cricketers,* (Nottingham, 1923), p. 393.
[48] R. Mellors, *Men of Nottingham and Nottinghamshire,* (Nottingham, 1924), p. 107.
[49] A. H. Fabian and G. Green (ed.), *Association Football,* (1960), p. 21.
[50] *Ibid.*
[51] *V.C.H. Notts.,* II, pp. 413–418.
[52] *B.R.,* IX, 124, June 12, 1857.
[53] *B.R.,* IX, 391, October 4, 1891.
[54] *B.R.,* IX, 330, June 6, 1887; 337, November 12, 1888.
[55] *B.R.,* IX, 400, May 1, 1899.
[56] *City Sketches,* (Nottingham, 1898–9).
[57] *V.C.H. Notts.,* II; p. 393, 396.
[58] *B.R.,* IX, March 2, 1891.
[59] *V.C.H. Notts.,* II, p. 396.
[60] H. L. Featherstone and N. Summers, 'The Old Malt Cross Music Hall,' *Transactions of the Thoroton Society,* LXVII, 1962, pp. 97–8.
[61] Information on the Theatres and Music Halls in Nottingham has been supplied by Mr. F. C. Tighe, the Librarian of Nottingham Public Library.
[62] *B.R.,* IX, 252, February 5, 1877.
[63] See *The Midland Jackdaw,* May 9, 1879, quoted by J. D. Chambers, 'Victorian Nottingham,' *Transactions of the Thoroton Society,* LXIII, 1959, p. 14.
[64] *Report of the Goose Fair Enquiry Committee,* (1878), pp. 7–12.
[65] C. N. Wright, *Wright's Nottingham Directories.*
[66] W. H. Wylie and J. P. Briscoe, *History of Nottingham,* (Nottingham, 1893), quoted in Asa Briggs, *Victorian Cities* (1963), p. 381.

INDEX

Acland, James, 219.
Acton & Co., 6.
Acton, Frederick, 372.
Adams, Thomas (& Co.), 228, 231, 285, 290–1.
Albert Street, 179, 198, 199.
Alexander, 76, 77.
Allen, James Roger, 35, 38, 181, 259, 260; family 168.
Alliott, 175; see also Manlove and Alliott.
Alliott, Rev. Richard, 49.
Allotment schemes, 107, 109–111, 144, 149–50.
Ambergate . . . Railway Cos., 174, 175.
Amberley, Lord, 220.
America: civil war effects, 155, 231, 271, 294;
  cycle trade, 244;
  exports to, 28, 285–6;
  market, 26, 50, 114, 262;
  market for lace and hosiery, 13, 100;
  market for lace machinery, 246;
  rotary frame, 257, 258;
  tariffs, 266, 285–6, 306.
Angois, Paul, 243, 244.
Anti-Corn Law Association, 137, 138.
Anti-Corn League, 137, 219.
Apprentices: avoidance of regulations, 3, 39, 45;
  became freemen with vote, 123, 140, 163–4;
  colting, 45;
  dispute, 298–9;
  premiums, 67;
  training, 39–40, 322.
Arbitration: Felkin and, 330;
  Henson and, 321;
  lace, 295(2), 296.
  See mainly under Hosiery Board of Arbritration.
Arboretum, 184, 210, 213, 374.
Army: and Chartists, 105, 130, 132, 133, 134, 135–6, 140, 143, 146;
  bread riots, 146;
  commander, 129–30, 147–8;
  fired on, 135, 136;
  reason for presence, 136.
Arnold: allotments scheme, 110, 111;
  bag hosiers in, 33, 35;
  brickmaking, 229;
  corn prices, 35;
  Moore brothers' firm, 263;

parish contribution to union, 49;
ratepayers' support for strikers, 152;
steam-powered frames, 52;
unemployment, 155;
wrought hose discontent, 273, 275.
See also under Industrial Villages.
Art—see Design.
Art Gallery—see Museum.
Artists, Society of, 377.
Artisans and Labourers Friend Society, 109–111.
Ashwell, John, 190 n 26.
Ashwell, Thomas, 181, 269, 382 n 41.
Associations for the Prosecution of Felons, 10.
Association of Organized Trades, 249, 256 nn 125, 126.
Astill, William, 84, 104 n 81.
Attenborough (firm), 75, 301.
Attenburrow, Dr. John, 312.
Aulton, George, 100.

Babbington Colliery, 230.
Bagley, John, 62–3, 73.
Bailey, 74.
Bailey & Hollingsworth, 75.
Bailey, Philip, 215.
Bailey & Shaw, 229.
Bailey, Thomas (wine merchant), 24 nn 55, 81.
Bailey, Thomas (newspaper proprietor), 217.
Bailey, William, 212.
Ball, John, 101 n 56.
Banking, 14, 77, 328;
  bankers on Council, 182, 371;
  crises, 93, 145–6, 150, 154, 230;
  currency reform, 146, 150;
  industrial capital, 70, 91, 263;
  joint stock, 231;
  law, 248;
  local, 2, 70, 80 n 67;
  railway promotion, 171;
  Savings Bank, 107–8, 109, 328.
Banks, Gould & Banks, 93.
Baptists, 326, 327, 356;
  number of chapels, 315;
  on unreformed Corporation, 168;
  Sunday schools, 316;
  see also Nonconformists.
Barber, John H., 182, 190 n 26, 342, 372; family, 168.
Barber, Jonathan, 40, 128, 132, 150–1.

383